AN EXAMINATION OF
THE TRIALS FOR SEDITION
IN SCOTLAND

AN EXAMINATION

OF THE

TRIALS FOR SEDITION

WHICH HAVE HITHERTO OCCURRED

IN SCOTLAND

BY

LORD COCKBURN

TWO VOLUMES IN ONE

[1888]

AUGUSTUS M. KELLEY · PUBLISHERS

NEW YORK 1970

First Edition 1888

(Edinburgh: David Douglas, 1888)

Reprinted 1970 by

AUGUSTUS M. KELLEY · PUBLISHERS

REPRINTS OF ECONOMIC CLASSICS

New York   New York   10001

. . . .

S B N   678 00586 9

L C N   73 100122

. . . .

PRINTED IN THE UNITED STATES OF AMERICA
by SENTRY PRESS, NEW YORK, N. Y. 10019

AN EXAMINATION

OF THE

TRIALS FOR SEDITION

WHICH HAVE HITHERTO OCCURRED

IN SCOTLAND

BY THE LATE

LORD COCKBURN

ONE OF THE JUDGES OF THE COURT OF SESSION

"When our ashes shall be scattered by the winds of heaven, the impartial voice of future times will rejudge your verdict."
MUIR's *Speech to his Jury.*

VOLUME FIRST

EDINBURGH: DAVID DOUGLAS

MDCCCLXXXVIII

PREFATORY NOTE.

ON now revising the following pages, I am still of opinion that, from the interest of the subject, and the duty of never letting Braxfield and the years 1793 and 1794 be forgotten, they are not unworthy of publication. Indeed, if William and John Murray, the sons of Lord Henderland, and Lord Dunfermline, the nephew of Lord Abercromby, and George Swinton, the son of Lord Swinton, did not survive (and long may they do so), I rather think that I would publish it myself. My friend Swinton is of far less consequence than the other three, because his long residence in India has withdrawn him from the knowledge of these things. But, on the whole, it is better to wait.

H. COCKBURN.

17th August 1853.

CONTENTS OF VOL. I.

CONTENTS OF VOL. II.

INTRODUCTION.

BARON HUME says, in his Commentaries, that there was no trial for sedition in Scotland between the years 1703 and 1793. This is true; but the statement might have been carried much further; because, so far as I (who, however, am no antiquary) can discover, there was never *any* trial for pure sedition in Scotland till 1793. The acts in which sedition would now be held to exist had no doubt occurred with great frequency, and been punished with bloody severity. But I do not see that they had ever been prosecuted merely *as seditious*. They had been dealt with as offences of a different character—chiefly as leasing-making and as treason— and were tried on different principles and with a view to a different result from what proper sedition would have been. Trials for sedition are the remedies of a somewhat orderly age. They can scarcely occur in times so rude or so tyrannical as to exclude the idea that political intemperance may be a mere excess in the exercise of constitutional liberty. In the summary reasoning of barbarous power, every opposition to existing authority is high treason. It may be doubted whether even the word Sedition was known anciently as a legal term in our

law, at least in its present sense.[1] But carrying
the absence of trials for sedition no further back
than 1703, then the fact is that during the ninety
years between that period and 1793, our law of
sedition had not been ripened by a single judicial
case.

In 1793 the memorable cases which arose out
of the French Revolution began. These continued,
but at considerable intervals, till 1802, and all the
important ones were over in 1794. After 1802 there
was a pause till 1817, when there were two trials
more. These were followed by one in 1819, and
by the case of Macleod in 1820 ; and then by that
of Grant and others in 1848, since which time the
sword has slept in its scabbard. The result is, that
between 1703 and 1848,[2] a period of 145 years, we
have only had 23 charges of sedition, including all
the outlawries and the affair of Captain Johnstone,
which, though connected with sedition, was a matter
of contempt.

This handful of examples, most of them disposed of during seasons singularly unfavourable for
the calm exercise of judicial reason, constitute the
whole body of our sedition law, in so far as it depends on native precedent ; and none even of these

---

[1] I only see two examples of it—both noticed by Pitcairn in his
Criminal Trials, vol. i. p. 204, A.D. 1537, and vol. i. p. 330, A.D. 1543.
But though the word be employed there, the thing is not our modern
sedition. One of the charges is for exciting " *Sedition and insurrection
between the neighbourhood and the inhabitants of the burgh of Air.*" The
other is a complication of stabbing in court, invading magistrates, and
convocation of the lieges. Mackenzie's Title on Sedition implies that his
mind had not conceived our modern meaning of this term.

[2] This, though written years ago, was revised in 1848.

cases existed when the first trials began in 1793. So that, though diffidence certainly does not seem to have weakened the judges of those days, *they had actually no precedent whatever to guide them.* They were the makers of the law. Indeed, so entirely were they its very creators, that the whole law since *evolved by their successors* amounts to nothing beyond a general adoption of what was said and done by the judges of 1793 and 1794.

It is very important to examine the spirit in which the law was thus made. There are no judicial proceedings in which the public has a greater interest than in those touching sedition. Its law is intertwined with the exercise of public rights; it is very liable to be abused ; and public excitement, which chiefly generates the offence, tends to involve numbers in its consequences.

Now, *What is Sedition?* considered, I mean, as a *public crime,* distinct from what the law of England treats as libels upon individuals.[1] It is only the offence as *against the public,* though this offence may be committed by libelling individual public officers *as such,* that is dealt with as sedition by the law of Scotland. To denote this public crime, our

---

[1] And what a mercy it is to keep out of the English law of personal libel ! It has got some common sense put into it of late. But still its rules about the admissibility and the rejection of truth, as a defence or as a palliation ;—about the different effects of different forms of proceeding, as by *ex officio* information, criminal information, or action of damages ;— about the principle of provocation to break the peace ;—and about various other matters,—make it so peculiar a mass that it can be used by no other legal system except as a beacon. See *Edinburgh Review,* No. 53, Art. 6 (which I have no doubt was written by Brougham), for an exposition of it.

law generally employs, and always should employ, the simple term Sedition. The law of England (as I understand) does not use this word as a *nomen iuris* by itself, but considers seditiousness as only a quality of some other offence. But this difference of expression makes no substantial difference on the thing itself. In one form or other, the law of both countries recognises seditiousness as criminal.

WHAT IS IT?

Few have handled this matter without lamenting their incapacity to answer this question with much precision. Nor have they merely thought themselves baffled in trying to give a logical definition of it—that is, a definition which, while it comprehends all that ought to be included, excludes all that ought to be omitted ; but they seem in general to have been oppressed by their inability to furnish such an *explanation* as may suffice for the practical guidance of the lieges.

It does not seem to me that they have been so unsuccessful as they suppose. But, apparently, they have mistaken the *rule* for its *exemplifications* and its *application*. They have, in fact, given the rule, or at least its principles, accurately enough ; but they have very often confused it by bad illustrations. And people view special cases of sedition in such opposite lights, that wherever the example is incorporated with the definition as a part of it, the chance is that the definition will not be universally assented to.

Lord Brougham says, in his evidence before the Commons Committee in 1834 : "I have never yet seen, nor have I been able myself to hit upon anything like a definition of libel, or even of sedition, which possessed the qualities of a definition; and I cannot help thinking that the difficulty is not accidental, but essentially inherent in the nature of the subject." He adds that the absence of definition creates no practical inconvenience. "People talk as if libel were the only thing not defined. But I should like to know what definition could be given of assault, or cheating, or conspiracy, that is not vague."

Certainly, they are all vague; that is, not *absolutely* exact. Few definitions of moral things are. But, for practical purposes, and discarding mere logical nicety, there is a difference both in the degree and in the nature of the vagueness, in the descriptions of sedition, and in the descriptions of most other crimes, that is real and important.

The inquiry in ordinary trials is over as soon as two things are ascertained: *First,* Was the act charged done?—was a person killed? *Secondly,* If done, was it done criminally? that is, was the act justified, or palliated, by any of the fixed legal defences or mitigations? This last consideration may seem to throw everything as loose as in a trial for sedition, where the question always is, Was the deed done criminally? But there is this essential difference, that the rules furnished by the law for fixing its true character on the act of killing, are infinitely clearer than those applicable to sedition, and there is little or nothing to warp people's minds in applying them. There is no question of *expediency* in the trial of other offences ; nor is their investigation much perplexed by doubts about *intention*. Considerations of expediency are excluded by the law ; of intention by the facts. The law does not announce that fabricating another man's signature, or abstracting his purse, are criminal or innocent *according to their tendency*. Holding its own opinion of their tendency, and not leaving this to be speculated about, it condemns the acts absolutely. And since the act is positively prohibited, and obedience to the law is an obligation, the guiltiness of the motive, that is, of the intention to break the law, is generally involved in the existence of the fact charged. No prisoner, charged with robbery or perjury, dreams of defending himself on the plea that he did not know that the acts constituting these offences were criminal, or that he had any discretion as to performing them.

If the people had no political rights, the law of sedition would be capable of being equally clearly applied. But they have rights ; the exercise of which, and the excess called sedition, are extremely apt to run into each other. These rights are chiefly, (1) That free political criticism is the privilege of every subject of this realm. Every person may not only form, but he may express, his honest opinion of every public principle, every supposed defect, every measure, and every public man as such ; (2) That in order to give effect to his opinion, he may not only petition Parliament, or any of its branches, freely, but, under certain restrictions, may try to bring the public to his way of thinking. Mr. Justice Allybone, to be sure, simplified the law, on the trial of the bishops, by laying it down that "no private man can take upon him to write against the *actual exercise* of the Government, unless he have the leave of the Government, but he makes a libel, *be what he writes true or false.* No private man can justify taking upon himself to write *concerning* the Government. For what has a private man to do with Government unless his interest be shaken?" (*State Trials,* vol. xii. p. 427.) Phillipps thinks that this opinion "was the last, probably, of the kind delivered from the English bench." (Phillipps's *Collection of State Trials,* vol. ii. p. 319.) But Mackintosh says (*Reign of James II.,* p. 267, 4to) that "*it has often been repeated in better times, though in milder terms, and with some reservations.*" Whether it was repeated or not, on the Scotch bench, in equally positive terms, and with no qualification whatever, the following trials will enable any one to determine.

Now this privilege of free discussion entitles every man, on trial for sedition, to plead that the tendency of the act imputed to him was not politically hurtful; and that the act being innocent, his intention in performing it cannot be considered bad. The relevancy of this defence introduces the legitimate consideration of political topics and occurrences. There is thus always a debateable space between the accused and the State, which is the natural field of sedition. It is a field, on the opposite sides of which the State and the people are very apt to try to encroach ; and it requires a long practice of good government to regulate the competition properly. The first point is, to tell the people, as distinctly as possible, what it is that they may, and what it is that they may not, lawfully do. Every holder of a privilege so liable to be exceeded is well entitled to require the law to solve, for his guidance, the problem of what amount of liberty remains to him after exhausting the legal restraint.

Speaking generally, it seems to me that there are three qualities that enter into, and complete, the composition of sedition :—

1. There must be a *publication of sentiment*. Most other crimes are committed by *acts* alone. It is only by the illegal expression of thought that sedition can be perpetrated. This is usually done by spoken, or by written, or printed words; but it may be by banners, pictures, effigies, signs, gestures, inarticulate sounds, such as hissing or groaning, or by any other expression of opinion or feeling. And it is immaterial in what style or form the feeling is evinced—statement, denunciation, invective, irony, allegory, ridicule, prose or verse—anything will do that conveys the criminal thought.

2. The guilt, when analysed, resolves into *disrespect towards the authority of the State ;* meaning by *disrespect* all criminal obloquy or ridicule, or defiance ; and by the *State*, not merely the supreme

power, but all the high political bodies and officers that represent it. The quality indicated by the term political (or by some equivalent term) is essential; because there are many merely *public* officers or bodies, who, as they represent none of the power of the State, can scarcely be the objects of seditious attack. I do not see how the East India Company or the Bank of England could, as such, be libelled seditiously. To give the attack the quality of seditiousness, it must be capable of being justly viewed as a contempt of public authority. Hence the usual objects of the offence are, the sovereign, the Houses of Parliament, the administrators of justice, public officers and departments wielding and representing the State's power or dignity. It is the public majesty that must be assailed, and that must be required to be protected. Sedition is the same thing, in principle, against the State, with the misconduct of the member of the private society, who, because he dislikes something that is done, insults the president and defies the majority. The guilt of sedition is often described as consisting of its tendency to produce *public mischief*—and so it is. But it is not every sort of mischief that will exhaust the description of the offence. It must be that sort of mischief that consists in, and arises out of directly and materially obstructing public *authority*. There may be much mischief in the success or failure of a public measure ; which, however, it may not be seditious to promote, or to resist. And it

is an abuse of the law of sedition to stretch it so as
to make it apply to distant evils. The present
generation cannot be gagged for the comfort of the
next. The crime is not committed by what merely
excites the dread of remote, and still less of unknown, consequences. It has often been said of
incipient sedition, "There is no harm yet; but if
this be allowed to go on, *no man can tell what may
happen!*" If no man can tell what may happen, it
is not actual sedition. The evil must not merely
be visible, but palpable. It must be immediate,
or nearly so—well-founded alarm, however, of near
danger, being a present evil.

3. Besides being actual, the mischief must be
done, or attempted, *malo animo.*

The guilt of sedition is not contracted by the
mere publication of language calculated to excite
disaffection or disorder: for this may be done by a
lunatic, or a clerk of court reading an indictment, or
the speaking machine. There must be a *criminal
mind.* This state of mind is usually described by
saying that the mischief for which the publication
was calculated, must have been *intended;* because
such an intention is usually the fact. But it is not
meant by this, and it is certainly not necessary, that
the accomplishment of that particular mischief should
form the exact motive. A criminal indulgence in
even a good motive will do; as if a person should
inflame the rabble from love of power, or of applause.
And there may be a *culpable indifference of consequences;* in which absence of motive there may be

as much wickedness as in the operation of the worst motive. All these, and many other, mental conditions are states of *malus animus.* The great error to be avoided is the error of supposing that sedition can ever consist in *the mere use of the language, abstracted from every other consideration.* Such a principle would be inconsistent with the right of public discussion. Not that the *malus animus,* that is, the wickedness, must always be established *as a substantive fact by separate evidence.* It may be inferred from the whole circumstances, and especially from the words, or the act or acts, charged. It is a fair presumption that people mean what they say, and intend what they do. But it is competent to the prisoner to exclude the application of this presumption. And consequently, since it is a matter of evidence, it is for the jury to decide it. Of course, no prisoner can claim an exemption from obedience to the law, or can succeed before a sensible jury in showing that he had no *malus animus* in wilfully violating it. His peculiar view of the impropriety of the law, and his consequent notion of duty in disregarding it, is no more a defence to him than fanaticism is to the religious lunatic, whom it impels to murder a person whom he thinks a heretic. But, short of this attempt to make the court itself an instrument for the violation of the law, a prisoner charged with sedition is always entitled to extinguish, or to palliate, his guilt by proving the absence of *malus animus;* and among other ways of doing this, by showing the purity of his motives.

He is entitled to oppose his accuser ; and since the accuser may prove bad intention, the accused may meet this by proving good intention.

The only *apparent* symptom that I have met with of an inclination to deny this, is in Holt's book on *Libel* (p. 114), and in Archbold's *Criminal Practice* (p. 881), where Lord Ellenborough is referred to as saying that " Whether the defendant *really intended* by his publication to alienate the affections of the people from the Government or not *is not material*. If the publication be *calculated* to have this effect, it is a seditious libel." The cases referred to for this doctrine (being those of Cobbett, *State Trials*, vol. xxix. p. 1; Harvey in Barnewall and Cresswell, ii. 257; and Burdett in Barnewall and Alderson, iv. p. 95) do not seem to warrant the statement that Ellenborough ever delivered it. He may have said that a direct intention to alienate the popular affection was not *necessary*, because there may be other wickedness ; but that he ever said it was not *material* may be doubted, because the materiality of this, or of any other, mitigating circumstance, is indisputable. The other part of the statement, that whatever is calculated to excite disaffection is, *by the force of this single circumstance*, seditious, *so that a court could hold a verdict which found nothing else*, to be a conviction of sedition, is inconsistent with the law laid down by subsequent judges. *Chief-Justice Best*, a man very intolerant of sedition, goes only this length (Burdett's case), that it is *competent* to infer bad intention from the language alone. " It is enough if its existence (that is, the intention) be highly probable, particularly if the opposite party *has it in his power to rebut it by evidence, yet offers none.*" Justice Bayley (a very high authority) says : " I take the law to be, that where a particular consequence *necessarily* results from any act, the party doing the act is to be held, *prima facie,* as intending the necessary consequence of that act." This is the clear principle. Not that evil design, or any other form of *malus animus,* is ever immaterial ; or that the use of dangerous language is *of itself,* and independently of all *animus,* sedition ; but that the tendency of the language is *presumptive evidence* of *malus animus,* but evidence that may be met, and that, consequently, it is for the jury to determine the whole matter.

The necessity of *malus animus* is best established by the fact that all indictments, I believe, in England, and certainly all in Scotland, require it to be set forth that what is charged was done *wickedly,* or *feloniously,* or *seditiously,* or from *bad intention,* or in some such way. A charge asserting nothing beyond the abstract fact of the use of dangerous words would be insufficient.

These three things seem to be the essence of sedition. It is usual to describe the crime by saying that it is that which tends to expose the sovereign, or the law, to contempt—to sow disaffection—to introduce troubles, etc. This is true ; but *why* do these and such things constitute sedition ? on what principle ? Because—as I view

the matter—they imply defiance of public authority.
These are not *the crime*. They are its *fruits*. The
guilt that produces them is the guilt of obstructing
or weakening the majesty of the State.

My notion of sedition then is, that it is the
publication of any sentiment intended and calculated materially and speedily to obstruct or weaken
the legal authority of the State. This description
may appear to include many things not seditious—
such as mobbing, which is a defiance of the public
power, but which does not operate by the publication
of criminal thoughts.

This explanation is not substantially different
from those commonly given. And they do not leave
the law more vague than it ever must be, when it is
stated by reference to other general terms, each of
which terms admits of an infinity of particular
examples. The law which prohibits blasphemy,
gross immorality, neglect of public duty, etc., is
clear enough; but the acts that may be held to
fall within this law admit of no precise enumeration.
The looseness complained of in the definitions of
sedition is in the examples, and not in the definition. And since the fact of each given example
falling within or without the rule, must depend
partly on the political opinions of those to whose
decision each case is submitted, the examples can
never be made precise. It is easy to say that
Sedition consists of a certain proceeding calculated
and intended to produce a certain political result.
But what does this imply ? It implies, that in

trying a case of sedition it is not enough, as in most other cases, merely to ascertain whether certain facts occurred. Their *tendency* and their *design* must be got at. Were the words *calculated* to bring Parliament into contempt? Does the sermon libel the constitution? Were the resolutions passed at the meeting likely to bring trouble and dissension into the realm? And was all this *meant*? Now these are matters on which no two men may agree. A similar difference may occur in other cases; but to a far less extent. No prisoner meets a charge of murder, after the killing is proved, by professing not to have known that shooting through the head tended to produce death; or that though it did, death was not his object; or that though it was, killing does no harm. But what may a person charged with sedition not plausibly, or at least relevantly, profess, as to the political tendencies and motives of his actions? The whole complication of politics may be brought into discussion; and jurymen can scarcely be expected to condemn in a prisoner what they themselves approve of. A trial for heresy would be something like a trial for sedition, if it were left to a jury composed of men of different creeds to determine what was religious truth, or a trial for nuisance from smell, by twelve jurors each of whose noses likes an opposite odour.

These remarks may be illustrated by the citation of a few of the recognised accounts that have been given of the offence. I refer to these chiefly for

the sake of showing three things—1st, that the
general rule is satisfactory enough ; 2d, that many
of the applications are questionable ; 3d, that the
judicial discretion of the jury is the only guiding
star.

Starkie [1] lays it down in his work on Libel, that
anything is indictable as a libel on *Religion* which
tends and is meant " to *weaken those religious and
moral restraints* without the aid of which mere
legislative prohibitions would often prove ineffectual." (p. 485, edition 1813.) This is plainly
far too loose. A jest could scarcely escape the
minute and flexible meshes of such a net. Accordingly, after citing various authorities in illustration
of his rule, he introduces exceptions which just
undo it, unless perhaps in the case of coarse and
offensive blasphemy. He explains that " it never
was a crime, in the contemplation of the law,
seriously and conscientiously to discuss theological
and religious topics, though in the course of such
discussions doubts may have been both *created and
expressed* on doctrinal points, and the force of a
particular piece of Scripture evidence *casually*
weakened." He adds that " it is notorious to all
literary men that not only particular and subordinate matters of belief have been canvassed and
discussed, but that even *the authority of particular
miracles has been questioned, and the authority of*

[1] Almost any other English law work would do as well ; for they all
state the law in nearly the same words. But I prefer Starkie because
he is more explanatory, and seems to have more sense than most of his
institutional brethren.

most important texts disputed; yet these discussions have never been considered as libellous, *though frequently tending to weaken particular evidences.*" This does not appear very reconcilable with the general principle he sets out with. And his result is this : " Upon the whole, it may not be going too far to infer from these principles and decisions, that no author or preacher who *fairly and conscientiously promulgates the opinions with whose truth he is impressed,* for the benefit of others, is, for so doing, amenable as a criminal." (p. 496.) A just and sensible principle. But it plainly leaves every man to his own discretion in the first instance ; without any better protection than the discretion of his jury, if he should be accused of going wrong, in the last.

The *constitution* is said to be criminally libelled by whatever tends, and is designed, "to excite popular tumult, sedition, or rebellion, by engendering distrust or dissatisfaction in the minds of the subjects," founded on "alleged defects in, or misrepresentations of, the constitution or form of government." (p. 505.) A plausible rule ; but, in applying it, some people might think the defect real, and consequently the dissatisfaction expedient. Accordingly, he admits that " *speculative* remarks about the constitution *cannot be reduced to any determined scale by which their intrinsic legality, that is, their tendency, can be ascertained.*" (p. 509.) They may extend, he says, from a useful hint to high treason. What rules then is a reformer, conscious of ardour, but anxious to be correct, to walk by ?

By this one—which is the summation of the practical
directions. " The intrinsic essence of a libel consists
in its *tendency to do mischief.* The question, therefore, as far as concerns its libellous quality, is,
whether from its terms it is *calculated* to alienate
the mind of the person who reads it, from the
government under which he lives, and to *inflame him
to acts of violence and sedition;* or merely to instil
those *wholesome and salutary* principles which *may
be applied to public advantage,* and *soberly* and
rationally to point out those *partial* defects, under
some of which the most perfect system of government *must* labour; not for the purpose of exciting
unthinking men to seek a *violent* remedy, in attempting which the political constitution *may* perish
altogether; but for the more wise and benevolent
design of pointing out to those *who have political
power,* how it may be best exerted for the benefit
of the State." (p. 509.) *Alienation, inflammation,
wholesome, salutary, soberly, rationally, unthinking*
men, *violent* remedy—who is to judge of all this ?
Only the tryers, according to whatever wholesome-
ness suits their political temperament. As all
power is vested ultimately in the nation, the last
part of the rule concedes most of the licence that
libellers could wish to enjoy—the first part only
concedes what few enemies of public discussion
would care to withhold.

The *king* is libelled indictably by " maliciously
asserting anything concerning him which tends to
lessen him in the esteem of his subjects, or raise

jealousies between him and his people." (p.513.) This seems a plain and just rule ; and the case it regulates is so simple, that even its application can create little doubt. There is no matter proper for discussion, that may not be discussed without laying a profane hand upon majesty, and it is necessary for monarchy that the sovereign should be protected by almost unapproachable awe.[1]

The author sees the difficulty which an honest

[1] The case of Perry (*State Trials*, vol. xxxi. p. 335) shows the dangers that may lurk under general descriptions of discretionary crimes, when these come to be subjected to particular constructions. The defendant was a gentleman, held in the highest esteem, and by high people, but he was the proprietor of the *Morning Chronicle*, the best Whig paper of the day. These words appeared in it : " What a crowd of blessings rush upon one's mind that might be bestowed upon the country, in the event of a total change of system. Of all monarchs, indeed, since the Revolution, the successor of George the Third will have the finest opportunity of becoming nobly popular." *For these words*—for these *alone as they stand*—explained by no innuendo, and aggravated by no relative passage, or act, or spoken syllable—*for these words*, he was prosecuted on an *ex officio* information by Sir Vicary Gibbs, who might have been Attorney-General to Henry the Eighth, and who had forty such informations for libel on the file in one year. He maintained that these words implied that blessings were kept from the country by George the Third, and that this lowered his Majesty in the esteem of his people. And so it did, which only shows the precariousness of this as an invariable criterion of libel. Even Ellenborough was in favour of the acquittal that took place. But the prosecution shows what Attorneys-General may do.

And Bishop Fleetwood's case shows what the House of Commons may do. That House voted that the preface to his sermons was " a malicious and factious libel, highly reflecting on the present administration of public affairs under her Majesty, and tending to create discord and sedition among her Majesty's subjects ; " after which the House, as usual in those days, called in the aid of a fire and the hangman, to promote the sale of the book. And what were the peccant words ? These : the bishop lamented that " God, for our sins, permitted the spirit of discord to go forth, and sorely to trouble the camp, the city, and the country, and to spoil, for a time, the beautiful and pleasing prospect which the nation had enjoyed." (*Tindal*, vol. xix. p. 537.) But he was a Whig and a Low Churchman ; and hazarded these words in the Tory part of Queen Anne's days.

and temperate citizen must often experience in trying to combine the exercise of political privilege
with that abstinence from exciting discontent which
he is told is his legal duty.　He sees that the two
may sometimes be irreconcilable ; because the most
effective, the best, and the most necessary, mode of
obtaining the removal of a real grievance, is by making people discontented with what exists; and after
avoiding the difficulty in the established way, by
saying that every man may complain, but that this
must be done *properly*, he at last settles into a test.
"The test of intrinsic illegality must, in this as in
other cases, be decided by the answer to the question—Has the communication a plain *tendency* to
produce public *mischief*, by perverting the mind of
the subject, and creating a general dissatisfaction
with the Government?　This tendency must be
ascertained by a number of circumstances capable
of infinite variety.　It is evidenced by the wilful
misrepresentation, or exaggerated account of facts
which do exist, or the assertion of those which do
not ; mingled with inflammatory comments, addressed to the passions of men, and not to their
reason, tending to seduce the minds of the multitude,
and irritate and inflame them.　It may be said,
Where is the line to be drawn?　Discontent may
be produced by a fair statement of facts, inasmuch
as it is very possible for an imbecile or corrupt man
to be employed in the administration of public
affairs.　To this it may be answered that, to render
the author criminal, his publication *must have pro-*

ceeded from a malicious mind; bent, not upon
making a fair communication, for the purpose of
exposing bad measures, but for the sake of exciting
tumult and dissatisfaction." (p. 525.) This, as a
general description, is perhaps as satisfactory as the
subject admits of. But still, though the finger-post
be exhibited, it gives opposite directions on its
opposite sides.

The *administration of justice* is libelled by whatever is calculated and meant "to bring it into
hatred and contempt," or even to "*infuse sus-
picions* against it." This is true, but only under
the general caution, that judges and courts require,
and usually deserve, all reverence. But these
" Lions under the Throne " also deserve and require
the protection of free discussion ; only their disparagement must not be the object.[1]

There is no use in referring to more English
institutional authority ; but the following description is too curious to be omitted :—" Every English-

[1] Starkie refers to the case of *Hurry* v. *Watson*, which certainly
deserves the serious attention of all those who may be inclined to murmur
against courts of law. Paley's moral rule is, that every man is bound to
obey the law, but no man to approve of it. I had a notion that it was
perfectly lawful for people to proclaim their belief of a convicted friend's
innocence. But, according to the violent old notions, this is a mistake.
For Watson sued Hurry for payment of eleven shillings, and afterwards
indicted him for perjury, from which charge Hurry was acquitted.
Hurry then sued Watson for malicious prosecution, and got a verdict for
£3000 of damages. The majority of a corporation to which Watson belonged, paid these damages, and resolved that " Mr. Watson *had been
actuated by motives of public justice.*" For this resolution an information
was granted, on the ground that if the resolvers were right, the Court
must have been wrong, and that thus blame was imputed to the Court
by implication, and for this constructive insult they were sentenced to
three years' imprisonment !

man has a clear right to discuss public affairs *freely*, inasmuch as, from the renewable nature of the popular part of our constitution, and the privilege of choosing his representatives, he has a particular, as well as a general, interest in them. He has a right to point out *error and abuse* in the *conduct* of affairs of State, and *freely* and *temperately* to canvass every question *connected* with the public policy of the country. But if, instead of the *sober* and *honest* discussion of a man *prudent* and *attentive to his own interests*, his purpose be to *misrepresent*, and find a handle for faction; if, instead of the *respectful* language of *complaint* and *decorous remonstrance*, he assumes a *tone* and *a deportment which can belong to no individual in civil society*; and if, forgetting the *wholesome* respect which is due to authority, and to the maintenance of every system, he proposes to reform the evils of the State by lessening the reverence of the laws; if he *indiscriminately* assign bad motives to *imagined* errors and abuses;—if, in short, he use the liberty of the press to cloak a malicious intention, to the end of *injuring private feelings*, and disturbing the peace, *economy*, and order of the State, the law, under such circumstances, considers him as abusing, for the purposes of anarchy, what it has given him for the purpose of defence." (Holt's *Law of Libel*, p. 103.) Is this accumulation of discretionary negatives, positives, and postulates all that a considerate and institutional expounder of the law can give to a well-disposed man for his guidance?

The reports by the Commissioners on the Criminal Law of England demonstrate the fitness of these reformers for the task they undertook. Their views and proposals evince knowledge, candour, and judgment, particularly in their efforts towards realising the great object of not only making the law right, but of letting the people know what it is. Yet their success in making sedition depend more upon fixed rule, and less on judicial pleasure, is not greater than that of others.

Agreeably to their good practice, they first explain their principles, and then reduce these to a code. In treating of offences against the State, inferior to treason, they give their account of sedition in the following words :—" Although there is no offence, or class of offences, recognised by the law of England under the title of sedition, there are several which are punished by reason of their seditious tendency, viz., seditious assemblies, seditious libels, and seditious conspiracies. Such offences, though inferior to that of treason, are so far similar, that they tend to injure and endanger the political constitution, by engendering public dissensions, tumults, and conflicts ; by exciting discontents in men's minds against the constitution and laws, or against the manner of their administration ; or by exposing the Sovereign or public functionaries to hatred and contempt ; and thus exciting the people to effect sudden political changes by unlawful means. Such offences, therefore, may be regarded in the light of assaults on the Constitution, which, though they do not aim at its destruction, ought, for the sake of its safety and security, to be prohibited under proportionate penalties. A third and numerous class includes all cases which *tend, more remotely and indirectly,* to *impair the administration of the political system,* particularly by any contumelious expressions derogatory of the dignity of the Sovereign, by *calumniating* either the Constitution itself, or the manner in which public authority is administered, or by exposing either to hatred or *ridicule,* or by personal attacks on those intrusted with the administration of justice, or *any other branch of the Executive power.* Such practices, *though they do not amount to direct attempts to injure or impair the Constitution, or to endanger its safety, tend indirectly* to effect these mischiefs. Neither the system itself, *nor the manner in which its affairs are administered,* can be rendered odious or *contemptible* without producing *a sense of grievance* and injury, and exciting and encouraging an *improvident* desire of sudden and violent change."

Besides the looseness of this exposition, it is surely questionable in point of soundness. The law, as laid down here, seems to me to amount to a condemnation of all censure and all ridicule of authority, and of all attempts at public change even by moral efforts. It may be true that sedition is generally, and may always be, committed by means of one or more of these things; but it does not follow that one or more of them cannot be committed without sedition, and what could an

absolute monarch desire beyond a law which entitled him to punish whatever *tended indirectly to
impair* the existing Constitution? There was sedition, according to this, in the effort of many of our
best patriots to emancipate the Catholics, or to
reform the House of Commons. No minister of any
tyrant could frame a rule fitter for his or his master's purposes, than one which made it criminal
indirectly to *impair* the *administration* of the political system, or to expose to *ridicule* any person
intrusted with the *administration* of any branch of
the *Executive* power. What the learned Reporters
really mean is perhaps clear enough; but their expressions and illustrations are not happy.

Yet this fatal doctrine certainly has the sanction
of the great name of Holt, which shows how long
a period of the regular practice of constitutional
freedom it requires to enable even the most liberal
intellect to throw off the maxims and the feelings of
unsettled times, if it has been trained under them.
He lays it down, in Tutchin's case (*State Trials*,
vol. xiv. p. 1128), that "To say that corrupt officers
are appointed to *administer* affairs, is certainly a
reflection on the Government. If people should not
be called to account for possessing the people with
an ill opinion of the Government, no government
can subsist. For it is very necessary for all governments that the people should have a good opinion
of it. And nothing can be worse to any government
than to endeavour to procure animosities as to the
management of it; this has always been looked

upon as a crime, and no government can be safe without it be punished."

It is plain that by *government* he means *ministry*, or *administration;* and if it be so, the doctrine is, that all popular opposition is criminal—unless it operates by not blaming the party in power, which is impossible.

"It appears," says Hallam (*Const. Hist.*, vol. ii. p. 330, 8vo edition, chap. xv.), "to have been the received doctrine in Westminster Hall, *before the Revolution*, that no man might publish a writing reflecting on the Government, nor upon the character, or even capacity and fitness, of any one employed in it. Nothing having passed to change the law, the law remained as before. Hence in the case of Tutchin, it is laid down by Holt, that to possess the people with an ill opinion of the Government, that is, of the Ministry, is a libel. The Attorney-General, in his speech for the prosecution, urges that there can be no reflection on those that are in office under Her Majesty, but it must cast some reflection on the queen who employs them." This, which seems to concur in substance with the view taken by the Law Commissioners, was the doctrine *before* the Revolution. But Hallam adds : "It is manifest that such a doctrine was irreconcilable with the interests of any party out of power, whose best hope to regain it is commonly by prepossessing the nation with a bad opinion of their adversaries. Nor would it have been possible for any ministry to stop the torrent of a free press, under the secret guidance of a powerful faction, by a few indictments for libel. They found it generally more expedient and more agreeable to borrow weapons from the same armoury, and retaliate with unsparing invective and calumny." "And both parties soon went such lengths in this warfare, that it became tacitly understood that the public characters of statesmen and the measures of administration, are the fair topics of pretty severe attack." "The just limit between political and private censure has been far better drawn in these later times, licentious as we still may justly deem the press, than in an age when courts of justice had not deigned to acknowledge, as they do at present, its theoretical liberty." Since these are the principles which the Revolution has ripened, the Law Commissioners, if literally construed, must have reported before it.

On the doctrine of Holt, that it is criminal to possess the people with an ill opinion of the Government, Lord Campbell expresses " our *surprise and mortification,*" and calls it, in another passage, " Law which, if acted upon, would be fatal to the press, and indeed to public liberty." (*Lives,* vol. iv. p. 445, also *Lives of Chief Justices,* vol. ii. p. 147.)

The practice of these jurists seems better than their philosophy ; for the law of their code is better than the law of their reasoning. It greatly narrows the range of discretion. Their code gives three rules, as applicable to the three most common cases of sedition, each rule proceeding on the same principle, and expressed in nearly the same words ;

1. A libel against the *State* is committed by every person "who shall *maliciously* compose,[1] print, or publish, any seditious libel expressing or signifying any matter or meaning tending to bring into hatred or contempt the person of her Majesty, or her government, or the constitution of the United Kingdom as by law established, or both houses, or either house of Parliament; or to excite her Majesty's subjects to attempt the alteration of any matter in church or state as by law established, *otherwise than by lawful means.*" 2. Any *assembly* is seditious by which "three or more persons shall unlawfully assemble, etc., *with intent*, by public speaking, exhibiting of flags, inscriptions, etc., to excite in the minds of the subjects of the realm hatred and contempt of her Majesty," etc., repeating the foregoing words. 3. A seditious *conspiracy* is committed "if two or more persons shall conspire to excite"—repeating the same words.

These descriptions are not perfect, in point either of fulness or of precision. But they are the best that I have seen. They all resolve into the word "*maliciously.*" The worst, as applied to a detached point, is contained in Lord Ellenborough's charge in the case of Cobbett. (*State Tr.*, vol. xxix. p. 1.) The libel consisted solely of a publication which sneered and laughed at certain public officers—particularly the Lord Lieutenant of Ireland—as to whom the great, and almost the only, sting of the thing was,

---

[1] Whether the mere composition, without publication, will do, is still an open question. I say No.

that his wooden head resembled the Trojan horse, which was full of peril to the country. The defendant was convicted ; as, according to the judge's charge, he might have been for far less. That charge instructed the jury that, "By the law of England there is no impunity to any person publishing anything that is injurious *to the feelings and happiness of an individual,* or *prejudicial to the general interests* of the State. It is illegal if it tends to the *prejudice of any individual.*" "Can there be any other meaning in this (the comparison to the wooden horse) than to impress the people of Ireland with *a contemptible opinion of the abilities* of Lord Hardwicke ?" "It has been observed that it is the right of the British subject to exhibit the *folly or imbecility* of the members of the Government. But, gentlemen, we must confine ourselves within limits. If, in so doing, *individual feelings are violated,* there the line of interdiction begins, and the offence becomes the subject of penal visitation." (p. 53.) If the charge be correctly reported, it seems to be a very extravagant one. The prejudicing an individual, or hurting his feelings, is no criterion of liability, even in a civil action. As applied to discussing the qualifications of a public officer, and to a penal prosecution, it is outrageous.

Our Scotch descriptions of this offence are, in substance, the same with the English ones.

It is needless to notice Mackenzie's few sentences about what he calls sedition, because it is plain that in using this term, he does not refer to the thing which the term is now understood to denote. (Criminals, Title 7.) It is evident from his utter silence about it, or rather from his total unconsciousness of it, that the modern offence of sedition was not known to his mind. He says, " Sedition is a *commotion of the people without authority;* and if it be such as tends to the disturbing of the government, *ad exitium principis, vel senatorium ejus,* and *mutationem reipublicæ,* it is treason ; but if it only be raised on any private account, it is not properly called treason, but it is with us called a convocation of the lieges. These *publick* seditions are called *seditio regni vel exercitus,* and this species of sedition is punishable as treason." " This crime of simple convocation is ordinarily pursued before the council, and is seldom punished either by the council or justice court, *tanquam crimen per se,* but as the aggreging quality of a riot or other crime." The whole ancient history of Scotland attests that what we now call sedition—that is, whatever *tended to disturb* the government — was deemed treason, and that there was then no other sedition.

Baron Hume's exposition is summed up in the following passage:—" I shall not attempt any further to describe it (sedition), being of so various and comprehensive a nature, than by saying that it reaches all those practices, whether by deed, word, or writing, of whatsoever kind, which are *suited and intended to disturb the tranquillity of the State,* FOR THE PURPOSE *of producing public trouble or commotion, and moving his Majesty's subjects to the dislike, resistance, or subversion of the established government and laws, or settled frame and order of things.*" This abstract rule is distinct enough. But, if it were to be taken as the *whole* rule, it would be rather favourable to the seditious, because it would require a great deal to bring them within the legal interdiction. But then come the illustrations. " Under this description would fall a work, such as it has been reserved for the wickedness of the present age to produce, which should teach that *all monarchy and hereditary rank, or all clerical dignities and establishments of religion,* are an abuse and *usurpation, and unfit to be any longer suffered;* or, though the *piece* should not set out on so broad a principle as this, if it *argue,* like many compositions which have lately been pressed upon the world, that the power of the king is overgrown, and ought, *at any hazard,* to be retrenched ; or that the House of Commons are a mere nominal and pretended representation of the people, and *entitled to no manner of regard,* and that the whole state is full of corruption, and the people ought to take the office of reforming it on themselves." He afterwards adds—" The same judgment ought to be given with respect to him who, in a pamphlet, sermon, or other advised discourse, shall exhort the dissenters to refuse payment of taxes till the repeal of the Test Act ; or shall *question the lawfulness of septennial parliaments, and advise the people to meet at the end of three years,* and *choose another parliament for themselves.*" (vol. i. p. 544.)

What is *meant* by this crowd of cases, and qualifications, and conditions may, perhaps, be made out. But, as the words stand, they are surely very obscure. And their darkness is deepened by its not being explained whether certain passages are to be read conjunctively or disjunctively. For instance, is it meant to be said that it is seditious to question the lawfulness of septennial parliaments,—which has been done by loyal subjects ever since the date of the Septennial Act,—or only that it is so *when combined* with advice to the people to set up a rival parliament of their own triennially? Is it sedition to assert that the crown's power has become overgrown? or only when, in consequence of this supposed fact, the people are recommended to retrench it "*at any hazard*"? Every passage suggests the doubt whether its parts are to be united, or to be separated. If they are always to be united, and the crime is not to be deemed committed unless all the qualifications concur, the learned commentator narrows the range of sedition more than he probably means. If they must be all separated, he exceeds by widening it. For instance, it might surely have been maintained, even in Hume's illiberal days, without sedition, that clerical dignities and religious establishments are inexpedient, and consequently ought no longer to be suffered. This might have been maintained, without legal criminality, at any period of our modern history removed from the impression of the murder of

Louis XVI., even of monarchy and hereditary rank. There is ground for suspecting, however, that the author uses some important terms in a peculiar sense. By the people he probably means, not the nation but the mob,—a confusion very common when he wrote; and an institution "unfit to be any longer suffered," may be intended to denote an institution proper to be instantly destroyed by popular force. But all this is left unexplained. And, throughout, there is too sparing a recurrence to the necessary quality of evil intention.

All that Alison makes of the matter is this:— "It is extremely difficult to define with precision *in what sedition consists*"—(he plainly means the *acts* by which it may be committed, for the sentence goes on),—"because it is evident that the same language or publications which are calculated at one period to stir up immediate dissension, may be diffused at another without the slightest danger; and the language which in one age is stigmatised as highly inflammatory, is to be found in another, in every newspaper or pamphlet of the day." (*Princ. of Crim. Law*, p. 580.) This is true of the proceedings in which the crime may be embodied. These are infinite. But whatever the variable body may be, the difficulty is, and the institutional object ought to be, to discover its universal spirit.

Kenyon makes a very gallant dash at this spirit in his charge to the jury in the case of Cuthell (*State Trials*, vol. xxvii. p. 675):—"After all, the truth of the matter is very simple, when stripped of all the ornaments of speech, and a man of plain common sense may easily understand it. It is neither more nor less than this, that a man *may publish anything which twelve of his countrymen think is not blameable, but that he ought to be punished if he publishes that which is blameable.*" In so far as he means to say that, *in point of fact*, every charge of sedition depends for its result on the discretion of the jury, he is right. But if he means to say that even an honest and intelligent jury can never err, by acquitting a person really guilty of sedition, or by condemning one really innocent, so that the verdict always expresses *the law* of the case, he is clearly wrong. Bentham improves on this description, by saying that a libel is "*anything which anybody, at any time, may be pleased to dislike for any reason.*" But neither the Chief Justice nor the legal reformer is quite correct. It does not, except in its result, depend on the mere *pleasure* of twelve men, or of any men. What is sedition, or what is a libel, depends on the application of facts to a rule ; and though a jury may decide on the facts, they cannot alter the law. Moreover, "*any*" men won't do. They must be *right* men. Lord Campbell mentions a definition which completes Kenyon's, if indeed Lord Campbell's be not merely a different edition of the same definition. "We have now the best definition of a libel,—a publication which, in the opinion of twelve *honest, independent,* and *intelligent* men is mischie-

vous, and ought to be punished." (*Lives*, v. 350—
Life of Camden.)

I suppose that it was this idea that Lord
Camden had in view when he said in the debate in
the Lords on the Libel Bill (*Par. History*, vol. xxix.
p. 731), "I have long endeavoured to define what
is a seditious libel, and have not been able to find
any definition which meets either the approbation
of my own mind, or ought to be satisfactory to
others. Some judges have laid it down that any
censure of the Government is a libel. Others say
that it is only groundless calumnies on Government
that are to be considered libels. But is the judge
to decide, as matter of law, whether the accusation
be well founded, or ill founded? You must place
the press under the power of judges or juries ; and
I think your Lordships will have no doubt which to
prefer."

The true spirit of sedition, according to Selden,
resolves into mere Discord. "*Seditio*," as an
approved author says, "imports *Discordiam*, viz.,
when the members of one body fight against
another." Sedition is nothing but *Division*.[1] (*State
Trials*, vol. iii. p. 254.)

And, in some senses, neither it is—particularly
when it sins, not so much against Power, as against
Custom. It is the sin of non-acquiescence in what
society is pleased with, or submits to. A contented
community, whether the content be that of reason

---

[1] This is said in Selden's own case. None of the arguments were
delivered by himself, but it is stated, biographically, that he prepared
them all.

or of stupidity, hates to be disturbed by the novelties, however wise, of solitary independence. Its pride is offended by the imputation that its system is not perfect, and it dislikes the trouble of defending itself. In tribes far back in the theory and practice of freedom, this feeling amounts to an absolute prohibition of all independent opinion. Any head that thinks for itself is cut off. And even after civilisation has introduced rival factions, it is amazing how long and how eagerly they all act on the instinct of intolerance. Each revels in its own law of sedition. Every non-conformist is a monster. These bigotries do not always spring from active hostility or ambition. One powerful cause of them is the passive aversion to be disturbed. A zealous man, even of their own community, is odious, just because of his zeal. He may be right ; but the society is satisfied, and therefore it is sufficient to make him unpopular, that he is restless. Hence with sensible reformers nothing is more anxiously shunned than that unnecessary offensiveness which, on its own account, is the delight of the conceited reformer. They are rather inclined to respect that desire of repose, which though it may often render society impervious to what they may think truth, they regard as a natural sedative of what to others may be teasing effervescence. They recognise the *vis iners* of public contentment as the best check to the over-action of the *vis medicatrix* of re-form.

There are chiefly three forms in which sedition

displays itself—that of insult, of resistance, and of doctrine.

By the sedition of *Insult*, I mean that sedition which consists in libelling public political bodies, or public political officers, as such.

The necessity of considering such libels as public crimes, is involved in the obvious necessity of covering authority with at least external respect. No government could subsist—it would not be government—under a legal licence of political *defamation*. It may often be a question of prudence whether contempt or patience would not be wiser than prosecution; and whether the trial be not worse than the sedition. But whatever the *administration* of the law may be, the necessity of having a law against the political insult of authority is certain. There cannot be government without general obedience; there can be no general obedience where every one may with impunity abuse. Government could no more be exercised without protection from *calumny*, than police would be exercised without its officers being protected from blows. Individual propriety of feeling would be but a partial and a feeble shield; especially in those seasons of excitement when protection is most necessary. Those whose intemperance baffles moral restraint, would riot in an atrocity of abuse fatal to that very freedom of discussion which is sometimes set up as its defence, an atrocity which would corrupt greater numbers than it would disgust, and would extinguish those decorous habits of official deference, which are so

natural and so useful. He who fancies that un-
bridled vituperation implies freedom of speech
should subject himself to an Irish discussion, and be
wiser. It is in countries truly free that a law for
abating intemperance of language, and thereby mitigating one of the excitements of intemperate sentiment, is chiefly valuable. Under any judicious
administration of a right law of sedition, enough of
freedom will remain to satisfy all the claims of
argumentative exposure, of ridicule, or scorn, or fair
excitement.

This sedition of defamation is the meanest of all
seditions. It is the offence of the vulgar, the awkward, and the intemperate, and discredits every
respectable cause. It has no dignity; and, except
for the temporary and lower purposes of faction, no
public importance. And it is not calculated to be
dangerous by much following. Every libel is attrac-
tive to the person who gratifies his passion by composing it, and to the idle who read it; but few of the
entertained adhere to their amuser in the day of his
calamity. And no man's character or position is
improved by a conviction for libel. He may flatter
himself by the idea of his ability and boldness, and
partisans may applaud him; but he and they are
always depressed by the humiliation of detection
and punishment. It no doubt sometimes happens
for a little that even a just conviction, instead of
repressing, for a season disseminates and gives
importance to the calumny, and makes a greater
man of the libeller than he was before. But this

result is very seldom produced among the better class of observers; the partial sympathy dies away; and if the trial and the punishment be right, the person convicted generally wishes, before it be all over, that he had been more moderate, or at least more dexterous; and his admirers are thankful that they have escaped.[1]

Defiance of the law is the object of the sedition of *resistance*. It displays itself by printed and spoken denunciation, public meetings, pretended petitions, bannered processions, delegates and committees, the mysteriousness and self-importance of which last are so dear to the domineering leaders. But these things may exist without guilt. They are the ordinary, and the necessary, implements even of innocent men, when they are obliged to confederate for a lawful end. It has, in many instances, been by such organisation, far more than by the quiet wisdom either of government or of individual reformers, that practical improvements have been secured. The leaders of these movements, seen outwardly, may appear to be defying the law, when they are honestly trying to improve it, and are only warning power, and guiding opinion. The guilt is not in the machinery, but in its uses and its motive. The essence of its criminality consists

[1] Deducting the insane blackguardism of Ireland, the most effective modern specimen of this sort of sedition was given by Hone about 1820, in his savage abuse of the Prince Regent and most of his ministers. The Regent's character made it generally unsafe to try to defend it; and Hone had been long defiled by his own libellous matter; so he was never prosecuted for these eloquent atrocities.

in the operation of an intention to set the law at defiance, either as an instrument, or as an ultimate end; and whether it be the innocent case, or the guilty, must be determined by circumstances. Where guilt predominates, its usual course is, that a grievance is exaggerated, and redress peremptorily demanded; and if this, however difficult or impossible, be not yielded to as soon as those who require it think reasonable, the fire of general discontent and abuse is blown up by agitators, who teach their dupes to expect nothing from time or justice, but to be confident of everything from menace. All the apparatus of meetings, and inflammatory harangues, and wild resolutions, and public demonstrations, is got up; and the general result transpires, if indeed it be not avowed, that if the law be not altered, it is to be trampled upon. In promoting, as in resisting the cause, follies are generally committed on both sides, which, when the calm comes, and they recover their senses, make all parties stare. Government may discover that its alarm was the result of blindness, selfishness, and obstinacy; and that good order, and even its own strength, have been promoted by the change it so long withstood. The people, after obtaining what they wanted, may find that it has not removed all the evils of their situation, and that they were misled by crazy speculators, by hypocritical meddlers, eager only for pay, no matter from whom, and especially by the presumptuous leader, gifted with the fatal, and tempting, quality of bad eloquence. This, in a greater or a lesser degree, is the natural history of an improper struggle between a place and its local rulers, and between the people and the State. Similar passions and proceedings may occur even where the conflict is for the most momentous objects, and is conducted on the purest principles; but in such civil campaigns, though the combatants on the right side may be equally tumultuous, they will generally have higher leaders, and a victory with better fruit.

The criminal battle sometimes arises from no cause except that the popular mind has got into a seditious state; in which condition anything excites it. But, though it certainly does sometimes occur, this atmospherical predisposition is very rare. The sedition of resistance can generally be traced to popular *distress, wildness,* or *wrong.*

There is little reasoning with hunger, and great excuse for its desperation; and with our population, our system of pauperism, and the masses of workmen who are apt to be thrown idle by lulls of trade, want is a cause of discontent of which we can never be free. When it occurs, it is the great preparer of victims for the mob orator, who tells them that their sufferings are neither caused by nature, nor by their own folly, but by the cruelty of those above them. This conviction poisons their minds, and excites them to seditious hostility against all authority.

By *wildness,* I mean those fits of extravagance, which sometimes seize on the whole people, or on

large portions of them ; for example, the Popish plot ;
the intemperance prevalent both in the upper and
in the lower classes, though in opposite directions,
during a certain period of the first French Revolution ; the popular outbreaks against machinery ;
and the craziness of Ireland under O'Connell.
These epidemical attacks do not disturb despotisms ;
but they are indigenous in countries where freedom
is combined with bad popular education. They
may be excited by anything ; but their common
causes are priestcraft, political claims, and public
delusions. And it is not always among the uneducated alone that the frenzy prevails. Faction
may inflame even knowledge ; and when it is united
with religious intolerance, these two seem to mislead nobody more effectually than the best educated
classes. While these fevers operate, the infected
respect no authority but their own, and sedition
rages.

But of all the causes of this sedition of resistance,
none is so powerful as the feeling of public *wrong;*
especially when the wrong consists in injustice,
severe exaction, or provoking resistance to some
just and long demanded claim. Even when the
feeling is unreasonable, it engenders seditious discontent, which a wise government will rather try
to alleviate by explanation, than to aggravate by
contemptuous force. When the grievance is real,
or is generally thought so, its sedition is always
formidable ; especially as its contagion is sure to
operate in the jury box. And even when it is

a grievance which only affects a particular class, others are apt to adopt the complaint of that class, and to be drawn into a criminal sympathy with its excesses. When the complaint is general and well founded, what in law is sedition is sure to prevail; however it may be condemned, it commonly triumphs even over the law. It is true that public policy ought never to be changed hastily, even when it is foreseen that a change is due, and must in time take place. To a certain extent, the very difficulty of useful change is useful. At least it is better than the insecurity of easy, and consequently of perpetual alteration. But however effectual this truth may be in averting sedition, it is feeble in putting it down if sedition breaks out. Although, therefore, slowness of improvement contributes towards that staid solidity which is the best bulwark against the levity of constant vicissitude, the principle must not be intolerably prolonged. If it be, the removal of the evil will not at once remove the discontent. The recollection of past injuries, too long clung to, effaces the impression of present justice, and tends to maintain a chronic spirit of discontent. Where, however, the sedition of the wildness is not supported by actual or recent wrong, and is a mere outbreak of destitution or delusion, its trial can seldom present much difficulty to a good court.

By the sedition of *doctrine* I mean that sedition which consists in the propagation of what are supposed to be dangerous opinions. This, in a pure

State, is the least common, and the most important, of all sorts of sedition.

Different schemes have been adopted by different legal systems for regulating freedom of thought, and the freedom of its publication. It has sometimes been recommended that there should be an absolute exemption of all control over either ; and the opposite scheme of an absolute control over both, has also been defended, and has been far oftener enforced. The discovery of a good principle, between these extremes, has at last been elaborated, as well as perhaps it practically can be, by the British Constitution.

According to this Constitution, *thought* is free absolutely. There is no crime in our thinking what we please. There are occasions on which, *if we claim certain things*, our opinions are liable to be tested. But where we are not claimants, we may lock our thoughts up, and no Star Chamber can scrutinise our creed. No heretic, civil or ecclesiastic, can be troubled, as a criminal, for any heresy which he keeps to himself. Unimportant, from our familiarity with it, as this independence of private judgment may now seem, its establishment is a great and difficult advance in the progress of reason. Very few nations have made it ; and even in Britain it was only secured by the Revolution.

But the *publication* of thought affects others, and therefore it is subject to regulation. But it is another great principle, now thoroughly settled, that criminal law takes no cognisance of any expression of opinion, *in reference merely to the soundness or unsoundness, that is, to the truth or falsehood, of the opinion.* Error of doctrine is no longer punishable *on account of its mere error.* It was a long time before this principle was fixed. That curious and melancholy repertory of judicial folly and iniquity, the *State Trials,* is full of examples of fallible men punishing mere deviation from supposed truth ; and there are very few religious sects, if any, which would not still persecute on this ground, if they could. Tyranny, in its natural course, first claims the privilege of detecting what lurks in the breast ; and after being excluded from this sanctuary, it clings as long as it can to the kindred right of punishing error that is disclosed. The extinction of this Inquisition against the progress of reason, is another of the thousand blessings that followed in the train of the Revolution. Penal law now charges itself with the peace of society, not with the formation of opinion. The suppression of an opinion may be, and often is, the real object of a prosecution, but it cannot be reached directly and criminally, on the ground of its erroneousness. An indictment setting nothing forth except its unsoundness, would be laughed at. It must be charged as *intended and calculated to produce a certain description of public mischief,* and therefore as seditious. On a trial under such an accusation, the abstract truth or falsehood of the opinion will always be incidentally talked about ; but it cannot be regularly ascertained as, *of itself, the substantive object of examination.*

But parties are often tempted to go into it *as evidence* of the properly substantive matter. Because (as is argued) the truth of a doctrine is conclusive against its publication being pernicious ; and the existence of evil design is less probable where what is propagated is true than if it be false. The truth or falsehood, therefore, may plausibly be made to affect the questions of tendency and of intention. Accordingly the prosecutors of the civil tendency of doctrine rarely fail to declaim against the doctrine as false ; and the accused invariably finds the best theme for his eloquence in its truth. An accuser would be in an awkward position if his indictment contained an admission that the opinion which he wished to put down was sound ; and an accused, if his defence admitted that it was unsound. Where this question happens to be open, the discussion, resolving into a mere matter of opinion, is always unsatisfactory.

It is therefore comfortable to courts that in many instances it is not open. The law has often settled it, and in this situation there can be no evidence, and ought to be no discussion, against the law's decision. This rule, for example, makes it the duty of courts to assume the truth of all the principles of the Constitution, and to reject all evidence or argument against them. It may be a fair question what these principles are ; and each party invariably struggles to bring his view within them. But assuming the principle to be certain, a court must adopt it. No judge can sit and hear it discussed whether monarchy be, or ought to be, a part of the British political system. In the same way, a court would violate its duty, if it admitted evidence or argument against the truth of Christianity ; and this, not because, in the opinion of the court, Christianity is true, but because the law has declared it to be so. A judge who disbelieved this religion would be bound to support the law. There is no reason to doubt that Sacheverell believed that the doctrine of passive obedience, which he preached, and of the guilt of the Revolution and of all those who had promoted it was well founded. But these matters being all settled the other way, the prosecutors produced no evidence, and wasted no direct argument, to establish their erroneousness ; but held their case to be complete when they showed that the sermon did impeach the principles on which the Revolution had proceeded. And the accused, though he endeavoured incidentally to shelter himself behind analogous writers, yet knowing the hopelessness, or rather the absurdity, of maintaining that to be true which a great parliamentary arrangement had declared to be false, made his main defence consist in an attempt to put an innocent construction on the language he had used. This rule clears the way in many trials for the publication of seditious doctrine. For as such doctrine is from necessity generally pointed against some part of the existing system, the law furnishes the standard by which the truth must be determined.

Where no such standard exists, its absence

necessarily reduces the dispute to a mere competition of opinion. Each party, there being no direct
adjudication by the law, appeals to its analogies and
supposed implications. The aid of authors and of
important speakers is called in ; and of these there
is seldom much paucity either way. Partisan is
made to contradict partisan, philosopher to refute
philosopher ; the talent and eloquence of the scene
is displayed in such demonstrations as declamation
can convey that the true principle is all on the side
of the orator who is speaking ; the hall resounds
with the sacred names of Justice and Liberty ; opposite views of expediency are asserted with equal
confidence ; the prevailing feelings and opinions of
the age are brought into operation ; one of those
judicial spectacles which, though they may introduce many loose and irrelevant topics, dignify courts,
and mark the proceedings of a free people, is exhibited ; and at last the verdict expresses little else
than the jurymen's previous creed.

The extent to which falsehood, or what at the
time shall be thought falsehood, is to be deemed
evidence of guilty design, depends chiefly, if not
entirely, on the nature of the falsehood. It may be
so nearly allied to mere error, and so plausible, that
it evinces little moral blame, and may be practically
harmless. But it may be so detestable, and so need-
lessly abhorrent to the feelings of the community,
as to make it impossible to ascribe its publication
to anything but wickedness, or to anticipate any
result from its publication except mischief. It is

sometimes very difficult to determine the deference due to the sensations of the public, for the public is sometimes too easily shocked. Party spirit is apt to excite or to weaken its nerves. Mere novelty is sure to offend intolerance. Yet the novelty, though founded in error, and dangerous, may express the genuine belief of a conscientious and benevolent man. Error alone, therefore, so far from being conclusive of guilty intention, is scarcely even an element in the evidence of it. Besides logical, there must be moral, falsehood,—not a mere failure to discover the truth, but the guilt of endangering society by the dissemination of opinions believed to be false. When Paine, at a period of great excitement, did not merely advise the people to seek the redress of certain grievances, but exerted the force of his very popular style of writing to convince them of the absurdity and the groundlessness of the most essential principles of the Constitution, the effect of which, if they believed him, was to induce them to consider the whole political system as a fraud upon their natural rights, he could expect no credit either for his motives, or for the tendencies of his recommendations. But others, who, acknowledging allegiance to the Constitution, merely urged the expediency of certain reforms, such as those of annual parliaments and universal suffrage, did nothing that any public censor, not within the influence of temporary faction, could recognise as evidence of criminal design.

No doubt it has sometimes been laid down, and

from seats of authority, that it is criminal to publish even truth, though with the best intentions, provided the known condition of people's minds at the
time makes this dangerous. This principle is a
necessary part of every despotism; but it is the
most alarming of all the limitations that can be
imposed on the right of free public discussion. It
virtually destroys it.

Of course it must be assumed that the danger is
not admitted by the person who propagates the
doctrine; because without this it would be unreasonable to give him credit for good intention. But
assuming his good intention, and the truth of what
he publishes, I conceive it not to be the law that his
conduct must be deemed criminal as soon as a jury
shall be satisfied of the danger. A special verdict
finding that a principle maintained in a book was
sound, and that the author was actuated by no bad
intention in proclaiming the principle, but that, in
point of fact, its annunciation was calculated to
produce immediate public mischief, would not (as
I conceive) warrant a conviction of sedition, or of
any other offence. For example, a pamphlet appears
containing nothing but what is true, such as a correct
exposition of the popular elements of the Constitution
by a whig, or of the prerogative of the Crown, and
the privileges of the peers, by a tory. But the
people happen to be in a state which makes it probable or certain that they will be excited into a
misapplication of either view, and that public commotion will follow, though this be not the author's

object. The question is not whether morally a well-disposed man would discharge such a shot into such materials, but is he *criminal* in doing so? It is assumed throughout many of the following trials that he is. The judges often condemn the conduct of the prisoner on the ground that, admitting his opinions to be correct, *this was not the time to publish them.*

But if a well-intentioned man cannot proclaim truth because of its dangerousness, men of superior virtue and intellect, instead of leading their age, which morally is their duty, their right, and their destination, may be compelled by law to let it walk in its errors, and to follow it. No publicly offensive truth can be announced. Protestantism could not be openly preached in Catholic Ireland; nor, until lately, could toleration to Catholics be recommended to Protestant Britain. Personal violence, pillage, and the conflagration of chapels, was the almost certain consequence of either. Within a much shorter period, a public outbreak would have followed any strong speech against the slave-trade in the ports stained with that traffic. A public defence of the Union drives many parts of Ireland into rebellion at this moment. To be freely proclaimed is the prerogative of public truth. He who undertakes to enlighten his age, of course incurs all the danger of addressing a generation that differs from him as to what truth is; and the noble army of martyrs shows the extent of this danger. But when he and his age happen to agree, there is no authority in our or in any good system of law for holding that the publication of truth must be abstained from, because it would be inconvenient. Such a principle would enable, or rather compel, ignorance to cling to the errors it is so attached to as to be ready to rise into violence in their defence, for ever. Neither ignorance nor tyranny could desire a law better suited for their purposes than one that would entitle them to suppress whatever opposition elevated the hopes, by dispelling the darkness, of their slaves. The privilege of sending all well-intentioned public truth abroad may certainly often lead to present troubles. But freedom of thought and of communication on public interests, to which we owe everything good that we possess, including the correction of freedom's own incidental inconveniences, could not be impaired on account of these accidents without inconveniences of a far worse kind. The right of free discussion, certainly

> " May, in time,
> Win upon power, and throw forth great themes
> For insurrections arguing."

But great themes could not be thrown out otherwise, for society's adopting. A sage is not to waste himself upon the wilderness, because he is too wise for a generation that either will not receive or will abuse his instruction. No; instead of hiding his light, he scatters it abroad, though at first it may dazzle their eyes, and makes his memory immortal by anticipating the wisdom of a better age. This is the course of most of the triumphs of principle. If Milton and Locke had been tried under the Stewarts for sedition they would probably have been convicted, because their doctrines were calculated and *intended* to excite the notion against established power. But if this plea had failed, they could not have been convicted *legally* on the ground that, though their principles were innocent and well meant, they *tended* to produce the Revolution. According to the usual course of dealing with premature reformers, Wickliffe ought to have been burned, because very few in his day believed in the soundness of either his views or his designs ; but if they had, the *tendency* of his doctrines to produce the Reformation would have supplied no legal justification, according to our present notions, of his condemnation.

Even Kenyon, with all his narrowness of mind, admitted this. In charging the jury in the case of John Reeves, accused of libelling the Constitution, he said (*State Trials*, vol. xxvi. p. 591): "The power of free discussion is certainly the right of all the subjects of the country. We owe more to it than to almost any other right which the citizens of this country have exerted. I believe it is not laying too much claim on the behalf of free and temperate discussion to say that we owe to it the Reformation, and that we owed to it afterwards the Revolution. The discussion which was made by Luther, Melanchthon, and the other persons who preceded the Reformation, opened the eyes of the public; and they got rid of the delusions which had been spread by the Pope of Rome, and emancipated mankind from the spiritual tyranny they were under, and brought about the establishment of that religion which we now enjoy in this country." This could not have been said if the mere tendency of well meant truth to produce incidentally what at the time may be thought mischief, implied legal criminality. No stronger cases can be conceived than the overthrow of the established religion, and the overthrow of the established Government, by the Reformation and the Revolution. If it was not sedition to promote these changes by the well-designed promulgation of truth, how can such promulgation be ever deemed criminal ?

Erskine, while speaking as a counsel, often on these matters of political law dignifies and perpetuates his eloquence by enriching it with the wisdom of a philosopher. We have an example of this in his defence of Paine, where he says (18th December 1792): " The proposition which I mean to maintain as the basis of the liberty of the press, and without which it is an empty sound, is this :— that every man, not intending to mislead, but seeking to enlighten others with what his own reason and conscience, however erroneously, have dictated to him as truth, may address himself to the universal reason of a whole nation, either upon the subject of governments in general, or upon that of our own particular country ;—that he may analyse the principles of its constitution,—point out its errors and defects,—examine and publish its corruptions, warn his fellow-citizens against their ruinous consequences,—and exert his whole faculties in pointing out the most advantageous changes in establishments which he considers to be radically defective, or sliding from their object by abuse. All this every subject of this country has a right to do, if he contemplates only what he thinks would be for its advantage, and but seeks to change the public mind by the conviction which flows from reasonings dictated by conscience. If, indeed, he writes what he does not think,—if, contemplating the misery of others, he *wickedly* condemns what his own understanding approves,—or even admitting his real disgust against the government or its corruptions, if he *calumniates* living magistrates, or holds out to individuals that they have a right to run before the public mind *in their conduct*—that they may oppose *by contumacy or force* what private reason only disapproves,—that they may *disobey the law* because their judgment condemns it,—or *resist* the public will, because they honestly wish to change it,—he is then a criminal upon every principle of English justice, because such a person seeks *to disunite individuals from their duty to the whole*, and excites to *overt acts of misconduct* in a part of the community, instead of endeavouring to change, by the impulse of reason, that universal assent which, in this and in every country, constitutes the law for all." I agree with Lord Campbell in holding this to be " *admirable discrimination*." (*Lives*, vol. vi. p. 457.)

Where this species of sedition (that of doctrine) is not combined with others—where it is not meant to insult, or to incite to direct resistance—but consists purely in the enunciation or maintenance of opinions, its prosecution can rarely do any good in a free country. It may extinguish an obnoxious man ; but within the sphere of a free press, no principle, or its discussion, was ever suppressed by prosecution. A taste for indicting doctrines, therefore, is generally useless—if putting down the doctrine be the object. And it can only cease to be dangerous, when it shall be settled what old opinions are sound, and whose infallibility is to judge of the new ones. A person anxious for principle alone, therefore, will always attest his sincerity by avoiding whatever may justify the suspicion that he is impelled by other motives, and has lower ends in view. The philosophical patriot, though elevated to a purer region, is sometimes tempted to stoop to alliances with faction, and its acts ; and thus gets into connections which appear to arraign truth, or its discussion, before a criminal bar ; while, in reality, they only arraign the unworthy aids by which truth has been attempted to be advanced.

Though it be useful, logically, to discriminate these three sorts of sedition, it is scarcely necessary to say that practically they seldom occur separately. He who is in a seditious mood generally *abuses* as an instrument of *resistance*, and is anxious to dignify his resistance by some pure *doctrinal* object. But the one or the other predominates according to public or personal circumstances.

The *causes* of sedition are as numerous as the causes of public discontent. Folly, poverty, faction, bigotry, intemperance of thought or speech, the love of power, and unredressed grievance—are the most common of them. Its most ordinary *defence, or apology*, is the provocation of public wrong, and excusable excess in the exercise of the constitutional privilege of complaining.

Strictly speaking, wrong, or grievance, can never amount to an absolute justification of *admitted* sedition. While the law's supremacy subsists, crime cannot be a legitimate mode of obtaining redress.

But in ascertaining *whether* the crime of sedition has been committed, the existence of wrong, or of grievance, may be material. And even where these do not avoid the offence, genuine, or even honestly believed injury, is always a palliation,—not a palliation that prosecutors can almost ever admit, because they cannot be expected to concede that the Government which they serve has done wrong; but it is one that all other people, and particularly jurymen, will generally recognise.

The supposed exercise of privilege is a much more common apology. And it is the strongest that exists; and is often very difficult to be dealt with. In a country like Russia where no one is safe in

saying anything against the Government, or like
America where every one seems to be safe in saying
anything he pleases, obedience to the law is easy.
But in countries like ours, where the law wishes to
combine criminal responsibility for excess, with a
real and spirited exercise of the right of public
censure and suggestion, the best-disposed man is
frequently the most perplexed how to act. Prosecutors think that they remove all doubt by saying
that the safe middle path is marked by law. And,
no doubt, it is marked, and as distinctly as anything can be marked by vague general words
resolving the whole matter into each individual's discretion. A well-meaning man enters upon this path
perfectly cool. But he cannot advance two steps
in it without feeling that coolness is a temperature
inconsistent with the earnest use of his privilege.
Sincerity, instead of being a protection, is the very
thing that, by its warmth, effaces the legal line. A
quiet, honest man may no sooner be committed by
his oration or his pamphlet, especially if these have
been made worse by modesty and want of practice,
than he may discover that he is in jeopardy from
mere awkwardness of words, or from unconscious
ardour of feeling. This risk has the unfortunate
effect of keeping back the judicious and the sensi-
tive, and makes leaders of the skilful and the
audacious, who alone think that they can steer between the opposite legal repulsions. And as privilege must be lost if only exercised with a paltry
timidity, contempt of prosecution is the tone natural

to the strenuous, and this again leads people of this temperament into greater excesses than their quiet judgments approve of. This not unnatural connection of the exercise of privilege with its abuse, even in the hands of good men, ought to make conviction little grudged where the privilege has plainly been made a mere pretence by a false, impudent, and voluble fellow.

Those who wish to be seditious cunningly, put themselves into the form of constitutional discussion or petitioning, and think that they are safe, under this shelter, in violating the very law that protects them. This is the seditious city of refuge. It is the favourite sanctuary of the criminal orator, whose cowardly audacity of harangue is inspired by his shield. With him, sedition and privilege play into each other's hands.

It is sometimes exceedingly difficult to distinguish these two cases in actual practice. Many men, especially in former times, who, because they were honestly meaning to do no more than to exercise their right, ought to have been acquitted, have been condemned ; and some, especially in modern times, who have professed vast indignation at what they declaimed against as tyrannical interferences with their pretended right, have had this profession too gently disregarded. Law can easily give the tests ; but, as usual, the administration of practical justice depends less on the rule than on the sagacity and candour with which it is applied. (1) Privilege is no defence, where it was made a mere pretence of. It is of no use as a cover. (2) Even though there was no pretence originally, privilege is no defence for sedition, or for any other crime, committed in the course of its being exercised. Criminal outrageousness or irrelevancy may be engrafted on what, if not abused, might have been the correct exercise of privilege. A speech in praise of rebellion may be delivered at a meeting for loyally addressing the sovereign. The lawfulness of the occasion, and of the general object, will not justify all incidental guilt,—a principle which the promoters of legal meetings are too apt to forget. (3) Wherever the fact of pretence, or of excusable excess, is doubtful, the construction ought to be in favour of the accused ; and this not merely because innocence is always to be presumed till guilt be proved, but because the exercise of the constitutional right is never to be unnecessarily restricted. Even though the legal presumption was in favour of guilt, the fact that the abuse of the privilege is uncertain ought to be sufficient *as evidence*, and *as of itself a circumstance,* to bind a court to conclude that, in truth, it was genuinely exercised.

In judging of all this, and indeed in reference both to the essence and the proof of the crime, it is very important to mark what was the general tone and air of the accused on the occasion for which he is brought into legal trouble. There is such a thing as a seditious *manner.* It requires a good eye to detect it, and a good head to apply it to its consequences ; and as manner may be assumed, and may be accidental, it is never a criterion to be absolutely relied upon. But it is often disclosed sincerely, and often produces a strong and just impression. No wise jury can view in the same light the rash speech of the man of peaceable character but of utter inexperience, and the loud, lying impudence of the practised talker; or the exaggerations of the pamphleteer, who, like Swift or Cobbett, amidst all their sedition, have generally a lawful object in view, and the purposed atrocity of Paine and Carlisle, whose exaggerations are plainly resorted to merely to mislead and to inflame. The manner of a man *upon his trial*, though very apt to be acted upon by courts, if at all relevant for consideration, can very seldom, if ever, be of importance in reference to his extra-judicial conduct. It depends much upon temperament; upon mistaken views of what is expedient for the defence; and upon the behaviour of the court itself. But the manner of the speech or of the pamphlet are the man's own, and generally reflect his mind.

Since sedition consists in the wickedly intended production of a certain species of immediate, or nearly immediate, political mischief,—and what is to be deemed mischief is sometimes a mere matter of opinion,—it is very difficult, and would sometimes be improper, to exclude the operation of the political prepossessions of the jury. But a distinction must be noticed, which prejudiced or dishonest jurymen are too apt to disregard.

There are institutions and principles which the law has taken specifically under its charge, and which, though it never saves them from discussion, it protects by positive prohibition from insult or resistance. In these cases a right-minded juryman will feel that though he may happen to differ from the law as to the expediency of shielding these things, he is bound to respect it; and, consequently, that his duty is confined to putting a right construction on the facts. If a prisoner be on his trial for attempting to bring the monarchy into contempt, the juror who acquits upon the ground that he himself prefers a republic is guilty of as clear perjury as if he were to acquit a prisoner of murder because he disapproves of the mode in which murder is punished, or thinks that, as the deceased was a bad man, it was meritorious to kill him. A dissenter, who condemns all religious establishments, or a Quaker who condemns war, may be on juries for the trial of a seditious libel on the church or the army, every syllable of which they may approve of. Nevertheless, they woefully deceive themselves if they fancy that though, being in the box, they have the power, they have also the right to acquit merely because they dislike the law. They are perjured jurymen if they act on this ground. It is through the operation of such misplaced feelings that the greater number of unjust verdicts in cases of sedition have been pronounced. A man who honestly endeavoured to exercise a constitutional privilege, and neither meant harm, nor had any idea that he was in the course of doing any, is accused of sedition, and the jury are all satisfied of these facts. But they are tories of the old school, and detest all popular privileges, and therefore they convict. Who can doubt that this is perjury? And thus, if jurors do not resolutely steer by the law, but act each on his own political opinion, many political trials should end as soon as the jury is balloted.

But there are other cases where the rule furnished by the law is not so clear and conclusive as to supersede all individual discretion. It forbids *intended mischief,* but it leaves the truth of the intention and of the mischief to be inferred from the acts. In these cases the jury may, and must, be swayed, to a certain extent, by their own convictions of the nature and the beneficial or hurtful tendency of what was said or done. This applies chiefly to seditious doctrines. There is nothing criminal in maintaining the preferableness of a republic to a monarchy,—or of excluding the Lords spiritual from parliament,—or of dissolving the Irish Union,—or of any given reform of parliament,—or of almost any given public opinion. But under the charge of wickedly intended mischief the *tendency* of the opinion is a fair and important circumstance for consideration. It is receivable, on strict legal grounds, *as evidence.* And in appreciating this evidence the jury are not only entitled, but, indeed, they are obliged, to act in some degree on their own general prepossessions. They cannot be expected, nor are they fitted, to try the case, if they were to take their seats, like images, in a state of pure abstraction from all political knowledge, or creed, or feeling. They are warranted and bound to take into the box the ordinary information, and the established constitutional principles, of men of sense and of practical life,—certainly not the prejudices of partisans, or that wickedness which has often made jurymen value their position as affording them an authoritative opportunity of promoting the principles of their faction. Indirectly, this is perjury also. But where the case is of that nature that the general rule of the law can only be applied by the exercise of a certain portion of discretion, the personal convictions of the jurors as to what is publicly useful or pernicious, must come into operation. A good juryman will lean as much as he can upon the law, and will be jealous of his own partiality. A bad one will encourage his prejudices, and be proud of despising the law.

But, practically, most cases, in passing through the juryman, will have their colour tinged by the colour of his mind. This may lead to occasional error or unfairness ; but, if not abused, it may, upon the whole, be sometimes a useful corrective of stretches of the law either way, where the public has the *intelligence, independence, and candour which constitute the proper jury mind.* No better way of determining a charge of sedition could be desired than by reference, under good judicial guidance, to such a jury. A tribunal erected out of such a public, while it will have a salutary distaste of violence, will be jealous of undue interference with constitutional privilege, and will, above all feelings, have a genuine reverence for the great principle of mutual toleration. Such a tribunal suits all times. For it reflects on every case the light of prevailing opinions, and of whatever liberality the age may possess. It encourages the patriot not to be timid, provided he be pure. By enabling reformers, in whose sight, as in that of the bigoted enemies of reform, prudence is so often contemptible, to see the exact measure of their danger, and of their power of doing good, it abates the too common ambition of the inflamed zealot, the detestable demagogue, and even the philosophical innovator, to signalise themselves by startling prevailing habits of thinking. It may be by those they startle that they may be judged. Mackintosh says that Wakefield's libel was so bad that he would have been convicted though Somers had been Attorney-General, and Locke one of the jury. These names indicate the spirit in which a political prosecution ought to be resolved upon and tried. Neither a reasonable prosecutor, nor a reasonable public, nor a reasonable prisoner, could desire to be better protected. With a fair accuser, a fair court, and a fair jury, there is little danger in the vagueness of the words of the law.

But there is the utmost possible danger in it where the public reason is unsound. What is the value of trial by jury, where jurors carry their party passions into court, and have them inflamed there, rather than subdued, by men who are judges only in their robes and their position. How precarious is the best law of sedition then! What an instrument may it be in the hands of one party against another! Every extravagance on the side of existing power, or against it, may be safe; while every imprudence on the opposite side may be magnified into serious guilt. An innovation of system, or of opinion, for which the author may confidently anticipate the applause of history, is shuddered at, and its promoter tried, by present ignorance. A patriot, superior to the errors of his age, is subjected to the disposal of those who, because they hate, or do not understand, his suggestions, deny his purity, and are burning for a sacrifice. And on the other hand, a person clearly guilty of gross sedition may be acquitted by the sympathy of jurymen who approve of his opinions, and are eager to promote them. A fair trial for sedition is one of the rarest and most honourable of the triumphs of justice.

There is one blunder, or artifice, by which this triumph has been often obstructed. It consists in misrepresenting the true character of the crime. It is natural for a prisoner, however clear and gross his guilt, to make privilege and the liberty of the press, a cover for the violation of both. A prisoner has nothing but his own safety to care for. But the opposite exaggerations of judges and prosecutors have been less excusable, and more successful, when they have told juries that because sedition tends to disturb public tranquillity, it involves the very being of society, and that, consequently, he who commits sedition is guilty of all the crimes which the dissolution of society implies. This sentiment has been frequently stated not only in Scotland, but in England, and in modern times. " As by the dissolution of the social compact," says a Scotch judge —Swinton—(*State Trials*, vol. xxiii. p. 233), " it (sedition) made way for, so *it might be said to include every sort of crime — murder, robbery, rapine, fire-raising—in short, every species of wrong, public and private.*" And in summing up against Sidney, Chief-Justice Jefferies instructed the jury that the unpublished writing found in the prisoner's desk, which, at the worst, was only treasonable, " contains all the malice, and revenge, and treason, *that mankind can be guilty of.* It fixes the sole power in the parliament and in the people." (*State Trials*, vol. ix. p. 893.)

There is no form or degree of sedition, or even of high treason, as to which these principles are either legally or morally true. They might just as well be employed against a thief. Society could not exist without private property, and therefore he who steals does an act which ought to have all the guilt ascribed to it that the dissolution of society involves. Fraud, forgery, conjugal infidelity, or almost any other violation of the criminal or the moral law, might be viewed in the same light. So far are these representations from being true, that it is certain that the worst political offence may be committed by a person who would be guilty of

no other crime. It may be expedient to prosecute
political delinquency, even to the death, but certainly not necessarily on account of the moral
iniquity of the accused. Amidst conflicts of opinion,
each half of the community is seditious in the sight
of the other. When governments are unsettled, it
has often been doubtful, with the purest characters,
whether treason itself was not a duty. The English
revolution made traitors *in law* of men of the highest
personal honour ; nor was it till things got solid, by
the subsidence of the loose matter connected with
that event, that personal integrity and political
innocence became the same. To see no difference
between political and other offences is the sure mark
of an excited or of a stupid head. " Some acts, it
was said, which fell under the definition of treason
are such that a good man may, in troubled times,
be led into them even by his virtues. It may be
necessary for the protection of society to punish
such a man. But even in punishing him we consider him as legally rather than morally guilty,
and hope that his honest error, though it cannot be
pardoned here, will not be counted to him for sin
hereafter." (Macaulay's *Essays*, vol. iii. p. 296.)

It is only when the prosecutions are judicious,
and the trials correct, that the public sympathy can
be secured for the court and the accuser. It is
rare to hear the common course of criminal justice
exclaimed against ; so far from it, that even the
acquitted (in Scotland at least) are very seldom
viewed except as lucky. It is not always so in

political trials. The difference proceeds chiefly from two causes : *first*, because there is generally a party that espouses the object in the promotion of which the prisoner has fallen ; and, *secondly*, a political delinquent need not necessarily be a bad man in other respects. But it sometimes arises also from a cause for the avoidance of which no fair sacrifice ought ever to be grudged—namely, the impression that the prosecution was not dictated by a pure sense of justice, but was a party step. No just, and, if possible, no plausible ground should ever be given for this suspicion. It is difficult to read the *State Trials* without feeling that if it had not been for the purpose of getting rid of a political adversary, or to promote a party object, scarcely one out of ten of the political accusations with which that record is loaded would have been preferred. The only way to prevent this sympathy with crime is to be sure that it is guilt, and for its own sake, that is prosecuted, and that it is properly tried. And it is not enough that the guilt be real. It ought also to be great. Even a conviction, in a weak case, does no good. The confines of sedition are so easily and so unconsciously got into, that a good deal of the crime must be winked at. And an act ought to be very atrocious before it be indicted, if it be a single one ; though in computing whether it be single or not, the acts of others with which it is connected must be taken into view. It is when sedition, by the open repetition of the crime, plainly means to throw down the gauntlet to the law, that

the guilty should never get the encouragement of
a triumph, by the law being compelled to decline
the challenge.

A calm man, who has often seen how party
passions are roused, and how they evaporate, and
how unnecessary were the clamour and the severity
that were resorted to in order to compose them,
will have some patience for even a little perseverance in sedition, so long as it merely effervesces in
the course of otherwise innocent party contention.
Its black aspect is, when it takes advantage of a
morbid condition of the popular mind to produce
sheer ruinous mischief. There are three circumstances on which it delights to operate, but can
never do so without great guilt—religious discord,
prevailing wildness about political theories and
pretensions, and popular distress. These are the
troubled waters which sedition rejoices to trouble
more. When the people are excited by political
mania, he who, instead of soothing them, or letting
them alone, rouses them into higher insanity, and
thus brings them within the wrath of the law, and
exposes rational reformers to discredit—and all
from such wretched motives as revenge or contemptible popularity, is entitled to no portion of the
apology due to error, or to the extravagance of
honest zeal. The disturber of society by purposely
inflaming that religious hatred which, for its own
objects, he despises, but uses as an instrument of
social violence, is yet a greater criminal. The
passions he evokes are more horrid, and less con-

trollable. The evil spirit that works in the lower and darker region of popular destitution and ignorance is the worst of all. Yet every crisis of popular misery supplies demons who take advantage of it for pure mischief. Indeed it is melancholy to see how rarely even parties, otherwise respectable, have virtue to abstain from acquiring a little dangerous and momentary power by encouraging the criminal follies of this sad class,—a class which knows property only by seeing it in other hands, and the law by feeling its restraint. How deep is the guilt that is contracted by talent or influence when they are employed to aggravate and mislead the useless discontent of the uneducated and the unfed !

Sparing or smiting such criminals is always a question of mere policy. But, even in these cases, a public accuser is sure to bring himself into just trouble, if, in selecting cases for trial, he compares the conduct of the proposed prisoner with the words, rather than with the spirit of the law. He must never forget that a tendency towards what, strictly speaking, is sedition, is almost a natural offset of British freedom. Sedition can rarely disturb the stateliness of an aristocracy—which implies the suppression of the people. It is too insignificant to be noticed amidst the turbulence of a republic. And it cannot be recognised in a despotism, where the thought of independence is treason. But our mixed Government is a soil prepared for it. The weed springs with the constitutional plant. Rever-

ence for royalty, rank, property, and law is wrought
into the fabric of the public mind ; but it is combined with tolerance of all religious sects ; with
popular privileges, which those only whose blood is
frozen can exercise quite coolly ; and with the constant practice of earnest public animadversion. The
promotion, and the resistance, of change is the
occupation and the glory of hostile factions, whose
existence is indispensable for the conduct of our
public affairs. In the course of the incessant
struggle between what is, and what it is said ought
to be, attacks are made, and principles asserted,
and authority incidentally dared, with such unthinking boldness, by our greatest men, that moral
sedition may almost be said to be the field in which
their lives are passed, and their laurels earned.
They are only kept out of the legal offence by the
purity of their intentions ; not by their conformity
to legal moderation.   Hence they are all frequently
exposed to be confounded in the same condemnation.   But, in practice, it is found expedient to let
penal law glean only the bad cases.   The impression
on all sides, that it is difficult to engage in political
warfare without encroaching on the neutral legal
ground, makes all the law's injudicious captures
useless.

All wise parties, accordingly, aware how easily
accusation may be retaliated, are so shy of enforcing the letter of the law, that frequent prosecutions
for sedition always imply the confident predominance of a single party.   And then it is exactly

under such predominance that the true spirit of the law is apt to be forgotten. Amidst mutual arraignment and vituperation the law's liberality is disregarded by one party from insolence and security, and its power by the other from provocation and despair. In scenes of such excitement —especially if it be a conflict of principle—the language of sedition, or of what is flavoured by it, is apt to become the eloquence of party men. Thus it is sometimes difficult to say whether we would be worst off with no law of sedition at all, or with a good law ill applied. In the one case, the violent, free from legal control, would make public discussion too coarse for the moderate, and too calumnious for the decent, and would secure it all for themselves. In the other case, if everything that in strict law is sedition had, since the Revolution, been excluded from British discussion, by being prosecuted with the indiscriminating accuracy that is applied to ordinary crimes, what would now have been the state and character of the country?

Trials for this offence, therefore, are the touchstones of courts. " The integrity of judges is put to the proof as much by prosecutions for seditious writings as by charges of treason." (Hallam, *Const. Hist.* chap. v.) Except where the guilt is too gross to admit of doubt, or to require the exercise of any discretion, a trial for sedition slides more easily into party feelings, and the sacrifice or defence of party victims, than a trial for treason, where the law is far more precise and palpable. Where factions are unequally balanced, and the times violent, there is no department of criminal justice where such extensive unfairness may be plausibly practised under the forms of law.

Hence the painful interest that will ever attach to almost all the trials for sedition that have hitherto taken place in Scotland, particularly those that occurred under the influence of the first revolution in France. These cases deserve to be more accurately known, and more constantly remembered than any judicial proceedings in Scotland since the expulsion of the Stewarts. If there be any man who believes that the impartiality of courts, the superintendence of parliament, or the humanity of the age, are adequate securities for the purity of justice during the ferocity of party spirit, let him study these trials.

I was too young then to understand fully what was passing. But I lived in the midst of the local ministerial managers, some of the principal of whom were my relations, and all of them in almost daily intercourse with my father and his family ; and I was old enough to hear, to observe, and to remember. In a very few years afterwards, while events and impressions were still fresh, I had occasion, like other students of law, to examine the proceedings, and I have watched their descent into history ever since. And now, having a deep conviction of their true character, I think it a duty to point out circumstances which cannot be safely forgotten, and thus to explain the grounds of that nearly unanimous verdict of condemnation which posterity has passed upon the manner in which these trials were conducted, and the sentences with which they were closed.

If there was no future interest at stake, the credit of individuals and of the country would require the whole proceedings to be cast into perpetual oblivion. But subsequent judges have made this impossible. With one exception, the whole modern court has applauded what their predecessors did, and has professed to be ambitious of the honour of copying it.[1] Since Scotland is exposed to the danger of having these trials transmitted authoritatively, as models for imitation, it is proper that their true nature should be understood.

In examining the cases I proceed upon the authority, whenever it exists, of Howell's *State Trials*. The editor came to Edinburgh for the purpose of seeing the original records, and of correcting the ordinary reports by personal information ; and, with this view, he put himself into direct communication with the surviving counsel. The dispassionate statements of this very intelligent stranger may be more safely relied upon than accounts given by friends, or by enemies, during the intemperance of the period in which they wrote. But, indeed, the whole reports substantially agree. The original ones were prepared and published chiefly by Mr. Creech, bookseller, whose devotion to the party in

---

[1] See the case of *Gilbert Macleod*.

power was afterwards rewarded by his elevation to our civic chair; and his reports and Howell's are very nearly the same.

It is impossible for any one who has been born in a happier age to conceive these trials without carrying the fact along with him that when they took place Scotland was at nearly the lowest point of political degradation.[1] It was almost totally devoid of the constitutional checks by which public or private liberty can be protected. The party in power, therefore, was left to the freedom of its own will; and it does not need to be stated how absolute power is exercised in a small and poor country. Moral influence, too, was very strongly on the side of intolerance, which was armed with the terrors of the first French revolution. The profession of a desire to prevent the atrocities of that revolution being introduced into this country made nearly the whole upper ranks the willing tools of existing authority; and any one, of whatever rank, who dared to speak, or affected the slightest independence, was a proscribed man. Is any one disposed to doubt this, or to wonder at it? Let him recollect that we had then no popular representation, no reformed burghs, no effective rival of the Established Church, no free press, no public meetings, no trial by jury at all in civil actions, and no other trial by jury in criminal cases than what was consistent with every juryman being named by the presiding judge. Against this crushing load of the

[1] See some particulars in the *Life of Lord Jeffrey*.

hardest and most absolute toryism there was literally nothing except the steadiness of a small whig
party, composed chiefly of lawyers, without whose
resolution and intelligence Scotland, politically,
would have been nearly as prostrate as if it had
been a province of Austria or Russia.

The whigs, both here and in England, had
espoused the great question of parliamentary reform,
which indeed was their watchword and their leading
object. Their scheme, as expounded in parliament,
was exceedingly, indeed contemptibly, moderate.
But, like other moderate parties, they were afflicted
by adherents ambitious of signalising themselves by
extravagance; and nothing short of universal suffrage and annual parliaments would satisfy these
zealots. The cause was brought into great discredit
by this folly. Though distinctly disclaimed by the
higher and wiser men who had been associated in
England for the purpose of conducting the case,
annual parliaments and universal suffrage were
pertinaciously represented by Government and its
friends as the essence of the only reform truly
aimed at; and therefore reform and anarchy were
dealt with as identical.

The discredit which the Scotch propounders of
universal suffrage and annual parliaments brought
upon themselves was greatly increased by their
setting up what was called the British Convention.
This was a political association, which met, but
only for a few days, in Edinburgh, with affiliated
branches, and all the usual apparatus of such bodies.

Its real object was the reform of the representation. And if it had adhered to this object simply, and had promoted it in the way in which political measures are usually struggled for in this country, even the extravagance of its aim would not have so shocked the imagination of the age. But on the idea of giving themselves importance, and of casting a formidable air over their meetings, they chose to mimic the outside of the French National Convention, by copying its forms and phrases. This confirmed people's terrors, and would have ruined any of the associations even of charity or piety.

But notwithstanding this culpable folly, and deducting any incidental guilt that may have attached collaterally to individuals, there was no ground on which it ought to have been held that sedition adhered necessarily to all those who maintained this measure of reform ; or even to those who, in addition to this, used the British Convention as an engine for advancing it. It has been said, first, that maintaining universal suffrage and annual parliaments implies sedition ; secondly, that this and all other reforms were mere pretexts ; and that over and above the ultimate extinction of the Constitution, which must be the consequence of these, its immediate overthrow was the real design. This was easily said and credited at that time. But I do not believe that anything that history or justice can recognise as evidence of any such purpose ever existed, and certainly no sufficient evidence of it was produced at these trials. Unquestionably the imputation is not warranted by the belief or the impression at the time, and still less, on reflection, of those of a higher class who knew the principal actors, and strongly disapproved of their proceedings.

Many of the most peaceable and enlightened men in Britain had hailed what had at first appeared to be the dawning of liberty in France. But the splendid delusion soon vanished, and there was no party, and no individual worth then noticing, or capable of being now named, who showed a disposition so late as 1794 to imitate any part of the French proceedings, *for their own sake*, in this country. Accordingly, if the British Convention had merely abstained from advocating a measure of reform which, besides being hopeless, was absurd, and from the horror, ridicule, and odium of aping French terms, it would not have been disowned by the otherwise kindred society of the Friends of the People, which could boast of some of the greatest and purest names in the empire.

That in the furtherance of their views many, or all, of the leading members of the Convention were guilty of sedition may be assumed, without any knowledge of the real fact. This offence may be committed in the prosecution of an innocent, and even of a loyal object. Whether the accused were proved *by legal evidence* to have been guilty *of the exact sedition laid to their charge* is a very different question. Since they chose to incur the peril of having their conduct construed by terrified and hostile juries, their conviction, if the proceedings had been correct, would have been a result which few would have grudged them. But they should never have been allowed to have the advantage of being able to say, even plausibly, that they had been violently tried, or cruelly punished.

Hallam observes, with his usual sense, that "as men who are accused of a conspiracy against a government are generally such as are beyond question disaffected to it, the indiscriminating temper of the prejudging people from whom juries must be taken, is as much to be apprehended when it happens to be favourable to authority as that of the government itself, and requires as much the best securities, imperfect as the best are, which prudence and patriotism can furnish to innocence." (vol. ii. p. 327, 8vo edit., chap. xv.) At the period of these trials the law of Scotland afforded no such securities whatever.

The jurymen were filtered into the box by a process which made them very much the creatures of the court. When a trial was to be in *Edinburgh*, each of the sheriffs of the three Lothians sent a list of forty-five names to the Justiciary office. The names put upon these lists depended entirely upon the sheriffs' discretion. Out of these three lists the Justiciary-clerk selected in certain fixed proportions from each county forty-five, who alone were ordered to attend on the day of trial. The clerk, though not removable, was appointed by the Lord Justice-Clerk, who was under no open control in

his selection. The only difference for *Circuit* trials
was that the Sheriff-clerk of each county in the
district sent its list of forty-five names to Edinburgh,
and out of these either the Justiciary-clerk, or the
clerk who was to be upon the circuit, selected the
forty-five who were to be summoned to try the case.
In reducing these three lists of forty-five to one list
of forty-five, the clerk not only might, but frequently
did, consult the judge who was to go that circuit,
and from this fact it has been inferred that the
judge was consulted also for trials in Edinburgh ;
but whether this inference be correct or not I cannot say. It is immaterial. When the forty-five
appeared in court, and the trial was about to begin,
the presiding judge proceeded to *pick* (as Erskine
calls it) the fifteen who were to try. This he did
by looking at the list and calling out any fifteen
names he chose. The selection proceeded at his
absolute, unexplained, unchecked, unquestioned,
unquestionable, mysterious, pleasure. And after he
named his men, there was no peremptory challenge
whatever ; and Hume explains that the challenges
for cause could only be grounded on a conviction
inferring infamy, on special malice, insanity, deaf-
ness, dumbness, and minority ; or in other words,
that such challenges were useless and nearly unknown. The most gross and notorious political
intemperance, or even hostility, could not be
relevantly stated.

It is impossible to aggravate or to palliate the
mischiefs of this system. In a political case, most

men's politics, in a small community, being known, it very nearly gave the judge the power of returning the verdict. In such cases, accordingly, the jury was no sooner named than the faces of the spectators showed that the result was clear, in their opinion. The tendency of the system to confer irresponsible power on the court could scarcely have been better proved than by the eagerness with which it was clung to and defended by all the judges, except the solitary whig then on the criminal bench, when the odious privilege was abolished in a better age. One of its many evils was, not that it produced bad verdicts, but that it encouraged factious trials. There were so few calm jurymen to be got, that the verdicts most probably would have been the same, though they had been chosen by ballot. But whatever the result might have been, nobody would have blamed the ballot-box. But while it was the judge's duty to select, he was bound to select right men; and he could scarcely be expected to think those right whose public opinions, on the very matter of the trial, he held to be dangerously wrong; and thus every trial began by a pre-established harmony between the picker and the picked. This was bad for both, and impaired public confidence. The presence of a few dispassionate jurors would have checked judicial dogmatism; it would have saved the accused and his counsel from always beginning the day in despair; and it would have abated the insolence with which respectable men were pointed out as unworthy, as their rejection by the court proved, to be trusted with the administration of justice.

There were some other peculiarities which, especially in appreciating the conduct of our criminal court, ought not to be lost sight of, because they can never exist without operating very unfavourably on the formation of the judicial character. One was that every proceeding of the court was absolutely final. There was no appeal to any other authority against any of its judgments,—not even that irregular and indirect, but pretty effective, appeal which consists of private conferences on different points with brother judges. There was not even a power of *reserving* a point of law for future consideration by the court itself. Everything done was done finally. No judge acted under the restraint or responsibility of any possible review. This was bad enough. But what was it when combined with this additional principle, that under the "*native vigour*" of the court, that tribunal could *create new crimes and apply to them any punishment short of death that it chose?* The first of these vices in the jurisdiction of the court exists in full force still. So does the second, though its absurdity has made it be timidly acted upon within these few years.

One of the unequivocal signs of the times was that these trials, though connected with great occurrences and principles, produced or elevated no eminent counsel. England blazed with Thomas Erskine. His, to be sure, was the blaze of success. But success was hopeless in Ireland; yet there

Curran made the victories of the accuser less splendid than the defeats of the accused. Clerk and Laing were not well qualified in manner for this field. But we had Gillies, and our own brilliant Henry Erskine, twin star to his brother; and there were others fit for the crisis, had they been evoked. Their services were sometimes declined by the accused,— a fact which, like many others, shows how useless professional aid was deemed. There was no fair audience of the middle class; no sympathy on the bench or in the jury-box for strenuous professional maintenance of the public principles connected with the trial; none of that outward public which, speak where he may, every orator addresses, and whose applause is his inspiration and reward. The doubly winnowed jurors appeared formally to acquiesce in the cold compliments paid by the court to "the learned gentlemen who have acted with such propriety for the prisoner," but inwardly they were pleased in the belief that the defence was not forgotten in considering the punishment.[1]

A great criminal judge would have shone in such scenes. He would have upheld the majesty of the law, but would have considered the violence of the

[1] "I despair altogether of making any impression by anything I can say,—a feeling which disqualifies me from speaking as I ought. I have been accustomed, during the greatest part of my life, to be animated by the hope and expectation that I might not be speaking in vain,—without which there can be no spirit in discourse. I have often heard it said, and I believe it to be true, that even the most eloquent man living (how then must *I* be disabled?), and however deeply impressed with his subject, could scarcely find utterance, if he were to be standing up alone, and speaking only against a dead wall." (Lord Erskine, on the Six Acts, 28th Nov. 1819, *Parliamentary Debates*, vol. xli. p. 441.)

times as an additional reason for administering it steadily. He would have compelled the people to respect his court by giving them reason to rely on its justice. His candour would have shamed others out of their partiality. He would have diffused his own purity and calmness over the troubles of the day.

Our judges were Robert Macqueen, the Lord Justice-Clerk, but better known then and still as Lord Braxfield ; David Rae, Lord Eskgrove ; Alexander Murray, Lord Henderland ; John Swinton, Lord Swinton ; William Nairne, Lord Dunsinnan ; and Alexander Abercromby, Lord Abercromby. Four of these, viz., Abercromby, Swinton, Dunsinnan, and Henderland, were, personally, mild, respectable men, and as judges perfectly honest. Henderland and Dunsinnan had done nothing to distinguish themselves. Abercromby (absurdly called by his friend Hume " the *ornament* " of the criminal bench) had written a few poor papers in the *Mirror* or *Lounger ;* and Swinton, the heavy and slow, had evinced in his writings on Trial by Jury in Civil Causes, on Entails, and on Weights and Measures, a thoughtful plodding in advance of his age. These men, though meaning well, and perfectly unconscious of doing ill, had no experience of political trials, or of such times, and were sincerely under the influence of fear, " the most unwise, the most unjust, and the most cruel of all counsellors." [1] Their political opinions and feelings were as abject

[1] Burke—*Correspondence*, vol. ii. p. 358.

as they generally were among the gentry from whom they had come. The scene was new to them, and none of them had been trained to look into it remotely. Nobody can be less safely trusted with discretionary power, especially on a bench whose proceedings are liable to no review, than a good, weak, inexperienced man in a fright.[1]

Eskgrove's only superiority to these four lay in his being a great feudal lawyer. But, besides having their public defects, he was an avaricious, indecent old wretch, whose habits and appearance supplied all Edinburgh with ludicrous and contemptuous anecdotes, and whose law was less connected with practical knowledge or common sense, than, except for his example, could be believed.

Braxfield was a profound practical lawyer, and a powerful man ; coarse and illiterate ; of debauched habits, and of grosser talk than suited the taste even of his gross generation ; utterly devoid of judicial decorum, and though pure in the administration of civil justice where he was exposed to no temptation, with no other conception of principle in any political case except that the upholding of his party was a duty attaching to his position. Over the five weak men who sat beside him, this coarse and dexterous ruffian predominated as he chose. He had the skill to conceal his influence by making what he wished, be said or done by his brethren ; but every-

---

[1] These four, being gentle and decorous, were no friends to Braxfield privately. His mere indecency was sufficient to debar much personal intercourse. Abercromby, in particular, abhorred him.

body who understood the scéne knew whose mind was operating. "*Bring me prisoners, and I'll find you law,*" was said to be his common answer to his friends, the accusers, when he learned that they were hesitating. Though he was much in my father's house, where these matters were very freely, and very rashly discussed, I never heard him utter, or recognise, such a sentiment. But I heard it often repeated, and never questioned, as his saying by his personal friends, who mentioned it as worthy of the man and of the times. Except Civil and Scotch Law, and probably two or three works of indecency, it may be doubted if he ever read a book in his life. His blameableness in these trials far exceeds that of his brethren. They were weak; he was strong. They were frightened; he was not. They followed; he, the head of the court, led.[1]

Hallam, the least violent of historical critics, in describing the condition of England under Charles the Second, says : "There was indeed good reason to distrust the course of justice. Never were our tribunals so disgraced by the brutal manners and iniquitous partiality of the bench, as in the latter years of this reign. The State Trials, none of which appear to have been published by the prisoners'

---

[1] Lest it should be thought indecorous, in a judge, to speak so irreverently of judges, I may protect myself by the authority of Camden, who, in delivering his opinion, as head of the Common Pleas, in Wilkes's case about general warrants, and referring to the weight due to the court in the case of the seven bishops, says, "Allybone, one of the three, was a rigid and a professed Papist ; Wright and Holloway, I am much afraid, were placed there for doing jobs ; and Powell, the only honest man on the bench, gave no opinion at all." (*State Trials*, vol. xix. p. 993.)

friends, bear abundant testimony to the turpitude
of the judges. They explained away and softened
palpable contradictions of the witnesses for the
Crown, insulted and threatened those of the accused,
checked all cross-examination, *assumed the truth of
the charge throughout the whole of every trial.*" (vol.
ii. p. 123, chap. xii.) In contrasting this with the
judicial character of subsequent times, he observes
that "There can be no doubt that State prosecutions
have long been conducted with an urbanity and
exterior moderation unknown to the age of the
Stuarts, or even to that of William ; but this
may by possibility be compatible with very partial
wresting of the law, and *the substitution of a sort of
political reasoning,* for that strict interpretation of
penal statutes which the subject has a right to demand. *No confidence in the general integrity of a
Government, much less in that of its lawyers, least
of all any belief in the guilt of an accused person,*
should beguile us to remit that vigilance which is
peculiarly required in such circumstances." (vol. ii.
p. 329, chap. xv.)

It would be unjust to impute the whole of these
defects to the Scotch judges of 1793 and 1794.
Except from Braxfield, who was, indeed, very coarse,
there was no *brutality* of manner. Nor was there
any other *turpitude* than what is implied in judicial
partiality. And there was no improper interference with witnesses. But *political reasoning*, and
confident assumption of the truth of the charge, were
always conspicuous. A headlong adoption on the

bench, of all the judge's feelings in society, was the chief source of their errors. It prevented their ever rising above the instincts of party men, dealing for party purposes with party adversaries. "All these men" (says Phillipps in his *State Trials*, and alluding to the victims of the Popish Plot, vol. i. p. 352)—"All these men, before their arraignment, were condemned in the opinion of the jury, judges, and spectators; and to be a Jesuit, or even a Catholic, was of itself a sufficient proof of guilt."

Hence, instead of thinking of maturing the law, what they were thinking of was, the conviction of the person accused. The principles, and the forms, of general justice were lost sight of in an exclusive and passionate eagerness about the existing crisis, and the victim at the bar. And even in dealing with the accused on this footing, they evinced utter ignorance of the art of managing political discontent. They plainly believed that men who were wrong could be made right, and bold men made timid, by mere legal severity. The idea of quieting by gentleness, or of trusting anything to the soothing of time, seems never to have occurred to them. That discontented men must be reconciled to the law by its cruelty, was their only impression. They agreed with Bishop Gardiner in *Henry VIII.*:—

> " Those that tame wild horses
> Pace 'em not in their hands to make 'em gentle,
> But stop their mouths with stubborn bits, and spur 'em,
> Till they obey the manage. If we suffer—
> (Out of our easiness, and childish pity
> To one man's honour)—this contagious sickness,

Farewell all physic : and what follows then ?
Commotions, uproars, with a general taint
Of the whole State ; as, of late days, our neighbours,
The upper Germany, can dearly witness,
Yet freshly pitied in our memories."

They had better have learned from Bacon that " shepherds of people had need know the calendars of tempests in State." And that "neither doth it follow that because these Fames are a sign of troubles, the suppressing of them with too much severity should be a remedy of troubles. For the despising of them many times checks them best, and the going about to stop them doth but make a wonder long-lived." (*Essays*—Of Seditions and Troubles.)

If there had been nothing but his own reason or conscience to restrain him, it is not easy to say what Braxfield would not have done. For in judging of him and his brethren, it must never be forgotten that the country, meaning by this the adherents of Government, applauded, and that parliament confirmed, their worst acts. Such support would not have misled, or satisfied, a good judge. But it was enough to make a bad one worse. If their style admitted of being worse, their merit in avoiding it was certainly greatly enhanced by the encouragement it received.

They were indirectly restrained, however, by the judgment of Henry Dundas, and the moderation of his nephew, Robert Dundas of Arniston, the Lord Advocate, both of whom, as is usual with responsible leaders, were more skilfully temperate than their followers. The Lord Advocate was a person of no professional consideration, of very moderate ability, and a poor brisk speaker. But he was a gentleman; lively and amiable in private life, and with a singularly animated and engaging look and manner. And in addition to political influence and personal attraction, he kept up (though only for his supporters) the old profuse hospitality of the house of Arniston. Power, agreeableness, and claret will make any man a favourite. Few could have exercised his half legal and half political office, in such times, without being excited into violence. But, beyond a little frothy warmth and weak declamation at the bar, he had no tendency that way. If the times and foolish friends had ever provoked it, it would have been checked by his uncle's sense, by his own humanity, and by his seeing that it was the curb, and not the spur, that his followers required. The true, and the very great, merit of both of these public officers is, that having nearly absolute power, they abused it so little.

Having got gentlemen transported for fourteen years to Botany Bay for a first conviction of sedition, it may well be asked what more they could have done? To which the answer is, that they might have multiplied the victims to almost any extent. It has been understood that if Hardy had been convicted, Government might, on the same evidence, have obtained capital convictions, even in England, against about 50,000 persons. This evidence would have applied equally to the discontented in Scotland, where prosecution had far less chance of being arrested by acquittals. Yet very few were indicted. Considering the temper of our court, and of our juries, this abstinence from prosecution is most honourable to our public accuser. Each conviction being hailed as a party triumph, no Lord Advocate ever gave up so much. He used to be applauded for the clemency of only charging sedition, when he might have charged high treason. But there was no ground for this praise. A trial for treason would probably have superseded Braxfield as head of the court, and it must have given the prisoner whatever benefit he could get out of the peremptory challenge, which, with a jury obliged to be unanimous, might have been considerable; and, after all, a single and speedy death was at least not worse than the many deaths that were then implied in the unnoticed and humiliating agonies of New South Wales.

Robert Blair, afterwards Lord President, was Solicitor-General. An admirable person; but, immersed in the very best professional practice, and with no taste for political management, he took as little charge of the public as he could. A good sound lawyer, of spotless moral purity, and high feelings of honour, he is one of the comfortable examples of the height to which character may elevate respectable powers. For without general knowledge, enlarged views, or any splendour of talent, and, for a person of his warm temperament, of great poverty of thought and diction as a speaker, Robert Blair, by mere dignity of character and manner, professional sense, deep integrity, and natural propriety of conduct, rose, justly, to be the legal god of Scotland. Whenever his office or his party forced him to come forward politically, he fell below himself, and got hot; which, indeed, was his prevailing temperament whenever he was roused from his favourite condition of calm, magnificent repose.

Thus, the only persons who conducted themselves in such a way as to place themselves on their trial historically, were the judges. Assuming the prisoners to have been guilty of the exact crimes with which they were charged, and it being certain that they had incurred the guilt of greatly and uselessly alarming society, still the criminality of a prisoner is no novelty. The prosecutors did their duty effectually, but mildly. The juries, though unquestionably prejudiced, were not more so than the circumstances round them can account for; and the mere honesty of their verdicts,—that is, the accordance of the verdicts with the jurors' views of the facts,—cannot be doubted. The public which witnessed, and in general, applauded the proceedings, only acted according to such light as its reason then had. And even though all these, under the impulse of improper feelings, had misconducted themselves, they would only have done what, though wrong, is neither very uncommon, nor very unnatural, in periods of violence. But *a court* can claim no charity from such considerations. It is set on an eminence above the world, where it ought to breathe pure air. It acts in the sight and for the benefit of all times. This, and its very function of justice, imposes upon it, above all duties, the duty of superiority to the intemperance of the hour. The more that the region beneath them is tempest-tost, the more ought the judicial atmosphere to be calm. Everything else in these trials might now be deemed insignificant, had the court kept itself correct. I wish I could believe that it had done so ; or that subsequent judges, instead of giving its errors importance by judicially adopting them, had suffered them to be forgotten.

SEDITION TRIALS.

I.—Case of JAMES TYTLER, 7th January 1793.[1]

THE accused did not appear, and was outlawed, without anything being said either by the prosecutor or by the court. The charge was that he had published " a *Seditious Libel.*"

II.—Case of JOHN MORTON, JAMES ANDERSON, and MALCOLM CRAIG, Journeymen Printers, 8th, 9th, and 11th of January 1793.[2]

The charge against these prisoners was, "The uttering seditious speeches, tending to create a spirit of disloyalty and disaffection to the sovereign, and to the established government; more especially when such discourses and speeches are addressed to persons in the military service of the country, whose *peculiar* province it is to protect the king and constitution as by law established, and uttered with a view to corrupt and withdraw them from their duty and allegiance," etc. And the facts set forth in support of this accusation were, that the prisoners had gone into a canteen in the Castle of Edinburgh,

[1] *State Trials*, vol. xxiii. p. 1.   [2] *Ibid.* p. 7.

and had there, in the presence of certain soldiers, drank "George the Third and last, and damnation to all crowned heads ; " and had told the soldiers that their pay was too small, and held "out the prospect of higher pay if they would join a certain description of men whom the said persons styled The Friends of the People, or a Club for Equality and Reform." All which was stated to have been done " with a seditious and wicked design," and in order "to seduce them (the soldiers) from their duty and allegiance."

The whole six judges were present.

The counsel for the prosecution were the Lord Advocate (Dundas), the Solicitor-General (Blair), and Mr. John Burnett, Advocate-Depute. Burnett, the author of the (bad) work on Criminal Law, was a laborious, dull, man, described by Henry Erskine as " the great manufacturer of indictments "—the crown-agents' drudge.[1]

The prisoners' counsel were Alexander Wight, the author of the book on Election Law, and a justly eminent person ; David Williamson, afterwards Lord Balgray ; and James Fergusson, afterwards a Commissary and a Clerk of Session ; all of the Tory party.

It was the fashion of those days to object to the relevancy of almost every indictment.[2] The inter-

---

[1] "The best apology for bestowing all this tediousness upon you is, that John Burnett is dinning into the ears of the Court a botheration about the politics of the magnificent ' City of Culross.' " (Letter from Scott to Richardson, 3d July 1810 : Lockhart's *Life*, vol. ii. p. 285.)

[2] A Scotch indictment is a sensible, fair, and handy instrument. It is, in its proper structure, not at all entitled to the praise said to be due to its brother of England, which is described as being so particular as to include all precision, and so general as to include all vagueness—that it appears to tell the prisoner everything, but in reality discloses nothing, and to pin the prosecutor down to certain specific points, while really letting him in to everything. Whether this be true of an English indict-

locutor fixing the relevancy was considered as a step against the prisoner ; and whether the charge was really liable to challenge or not, his counsel would have been thought deficient in zeal if he had allowed it to pass without some objection or other. In some cases it was a mere form ; but still, to object to the relevancy was a form rarely departed from. By our rational practice the relevancy of the charge is settled by the court before the evidence is adduced. We have no idea of trying a prisoner first, and then considering whether there was a relevant charge against him.

Mr. Fergusson performed the ceremony of objecting upon this occasion ; but what his objection was it is impossible to discover; for the substance of his statement is that the lads had gone into the Castle by accident, and that they had no bad intention, which were plainly matters of fact for the jury.

The libel was most properly found relevant. And it ought to have been so, simply upon the technical ground that the facts and the intentions

ment or not, the Scotch one is excellent. It is reasonably strict as against the prosecutor, and reasonably communicative to the prisoner.

It contains what is technically termed a major proposition, and a minor one. The major sets forth the law, the minor the facts. Thus, if it be a case of theft, the indictment sets out by stating that " whereas *theft is a crime*, yet you (the prisoner) *are guilty thereof*." After which the minor proceeds to tell how ;—thus, " In so far as you did, on such a day, and at such a place (naming them), theftuously take a purse from the pocket of A. B." The major is irrelevant if it announces that to be a crime which is no crime—such as witchcraft—or states what is a crime incorrectly. The minor is irrelevant if its facts do not amount to the crime charged in the major, or is defective in clearness, fulness, etc. If a major sets forth a murder, and a minor sets forth a forgery, or anything not a murder, that minor is wrong. In a case of sedition, the major should announce "*Sedition*" as the generic offence ; and the minor should disclose the facts someway thus : " In so far as you did, at such a time and place, wickedly utter the following words (quoting them), which words are seditious, by being calculated and intended to excite a spirit of disaffection," etc. The major proposition may set forth a plurality of crimes, and with aggravations. Thus : " Whereas mobbing, rioting, and assault, *are crimes*," etc., " yet you are guilty of the said crimes, or of one or other of them,"—so as to suit the evidence.

set forth were sufficient to sustain the charge; at least to sustain it *prima facie*, so as to compel the court to submit the whole matter to the jury. There was no necessity for the court descanting upon the guilt of the prisoners by anticipation—a proceeding which should always be avoided, if possible, because it tends to impress the jury with particular views before the facts are disclosed to them in evidence. *To a certain extent* this was then not easily avoided in our practice—at least not without great caution. Because one of the established topics in objecting to the relevancy of an indictment for sedition was, that the words charged exhibited no guilt. The simple answer to this ought, in ninety-nine cases out of a hundred, to be that, *in determining relevancy*, the words must be taken to mean that which the prosecutor undertakes to show that they mean. But after a preliminary harangue by the prisoners' counsel commenting on the innocence of the words, an incautious judge is apt to be tempted to follow, and to refute him; and is thus drawn into a premature disclosure of his views not only on the particular language, but on the whole collateral matter. The great evil of this, especially in seasons of prejudice, is that it obstructs the future candour of the judge, and prematurely gives a keynote to the jury. There may be some difficulty in a judge's hitting the exact line, but none whatever in his abstaining from lecturing from the bench on the political topics of the day, or anticipating what he thinks that the verdict must be. How far this was abstained from in this trial appears in the following judicial observations—all made before the evidence began.

The matter of fact for the jury to determine

was, whether the toast, if given, implied what was ascribed to it; and, if it did, whether this meaning was expressed from levity or from wickedness. But Lord Henderland seems to have settled this at once. Referring to the toast—" What," said he, " was this but covertly expressing a most wicked and flagitious wish that our gracious sovereign, *under whose mild and auspicious sway this nation has arrived at a pitch of prosperity unenjoyed and envied by most of the other parts of Europe,* should be damned?"—as if the seditious character of the words depended upon the personal character, or official conduct, of the sovereign. Would his Lordship have permitted the panel to attempt to prove, or even to state, the reverse of these opinions? " An impious wish that our beneficent sovereign, *distinguished by private and public virtues* — his sacred Majesty—the father of his people—would be damned! What could be more criminal?" On the Club for Equality and Reform, his Lordship sets out by saying, " *I can know nothing of these clubs in this place:* " a most proper sentiment. But unfortunately it is instantly followed by an ample discourse on their nature and tendencies, the reasoning and dignity of which might be forgiven, were not the whole harangue so misplaced. " I like not their names. The friends of the people, and a club for Equality and Freedom! What occasion for such associations with such names? Are not the people protected in the enjoyment of their constitutional rights, and in reaping the fruits of their industry? A club for Equality and Freedom! Freedom is a name we all revere, and we enjoy it. But if by equality be meant an equal division of property, it would be downright robbery

to introduce it. To say that all men have equal
rights when born, is a proposition from which no
consequence can be drawn. Or to maintain that
all men are equal is neither founded in truth nor
nature. *Scarce two children are born precisely alike.*
Among men, we differ in the simplest powers of
the body. *Few men possess the ability of walking
in such perfection as the celebrated pedestrian.* Has
every man abilities, natural or acquired, to qualify
him for a Minister of State? Or does the extensive knowledge of trade and commerce which so
eminently distinguish *a Hope of Amsterdam, or even
some of our own fellow-citizens here, who have, much
to their own honour and country's advantage, acquired large fortunes in the same way, belong to all
men?* "

It was perhaps a slight defect in the indictment
that it did not describe the " Friends of the People,"
or " the Club," as an association of a seditious
character, but merely calls them " a certain description of men." However, his Lordship first supplies
this by *assuming* them to be criminal; and then,
aware, apparently, that the panels had, by their
counsel, denied this, he takes the opposite view,
and assumes these associations to be *innocent.* "But
suppose the object of such societies to be no more
than to announce the above inconsequential proposition, or that their principles are *favourable to
order and government,* that they *mean to support
the Constitution;* what then?" Still " to withdraw,
or to attempt to withdraw, soldiers from such constitutional dependence and discipline, and place
them under any other influence or authority whatever, must be a crime." No doubt of it. A club,
though in other respects constitutional, is not

entitled to make soldiers mutiny.   But it does not
seem to have occurred to his Lordship that a club
that did this *could* not be an association " favourable to order and government," and " meant to
support the constitution." It seems an absurd case to
put. It is like talking of loyalty committing treason.

Lord Swinton agrees that the libel is relevant ;
and explains his views in a speech, which is unfortunate in two particulars.

In the *first* place, instead of leaving the circumstances stated in defence to be commented upon by
the presiding judge, or to be disposed of by the
jury, after the evidence, he goes into them at this
preliminary stage, and rejects the defence, not only
on the question of relevancy, but of *fact*.   He first
says that " The question is whether the articles
charged infer a felonious and criminal intent." And
then, in reference to the plea, which in truth formed
the sole defence, that the words were spoken in
convivial levity, he says, " Whether that construction can be put upon them, or whether liquor and
conviviality brought out the sentiments that were
uppermost (as *in vino veritas*) would depend on the
proof, which is not *hujus loci;* we are now only to
consider whether the charge is relevantly *laid*." All
this is correct.   But then he immediately proceeds
to do the jury's work by deciding that the words
and the sentiment imputed to the prisoners *must*
have been the result of seditious wickedness, and
not of thoughtlessness.   " They proposed to drink
to them (the soldiers) a toast, which if not importing
even a treasonable intent, certainly imported a most
seditious and wicked wish against our most gracious
and beloved sovereign—a sovereign not only ex-
emplary to monarchs, but to *private* men : a wish

that he might be the last of his race ; and at the
same time adding damnation to all crowned heads.
CAN *such a wish be called the loose and thoughtless
expression of juvenile conviviality? or does it not
rather import a seditious speech, intending* to inspire
disloyal sentiments into the minds of the soldiers ?
But the charge does not rest here. Interest is the
serious argument with mankind—*especially of the
lower rank.* The charge states that this was not
overlooked. The prisoners tell the soldiers their
pay was too small. What is sixpence a day to a
soldier ? You shall have higher pay if you will
join with the Friends of the People, or a club for
Equality and Freedom. *Friends of the people!
What are Friends of the people? Are the people
friendless? The people—who are they? No doubt
the common people. Is not this a clear innuendo that
the common people are friendless—have no friends
but this club ? "etc.* All this (to say nothing of its
taste) was plainly anticipating the result of the
evidence, not strictly deciding on the relevancy.
Accordingly, he distinctly says, " I am therefore
clear, upon the whole, that the particular articles
amount to the crime stated in the general charge,
viz., seditious speeches tending to create disloyalty
and disaffection to his Majesty, and to the established government, and *an attempt* to corrupt and
seduce the military from their duty."

In the *second* place, surely such allusions as the
following to the state of the times —especially on
topics as to which great political parties were daily
proclaiming their difference of opinion—might have
been spared. " The club for freedom too ! as if we
were not free! as if we needed this club to assert
our freedom ! Is there one here present who can

name a time when this nation had ever more freedom than now ; had more security for life, liberty,
and property, than at this moment, or indeed so
much ? *The state of the present times both at home
and abroad* [to which there was no allusion in
the indictment] *is the strong ingredient to make the
intent serious and manifest.*" Many good men had
quite different views on these subjects, and thought
our liberties in such danger that clubs and other
associations for their protection were indispensable. If it was proper in one judge to give his
opinion on these matters one way, it might have
been proper for another judge to express his opinion
in an opposite way ; and what an exhibition would
this have been for a court !

Lord Abercromby " adverted to the numerous
seditious meetings and associations in different parts
of the country ; " and " *considered the conduct of the
panels as appearing from the statement in the libel,
as of a very aggravated and seditious nature.*"

Possibly he only means that this is its nature
as set forth in the libel. If this was all he meant,
he was right. But it is a pity that he made his
meaning doubtful, by referring so directly to circumstances certainly not set forth in the libel ;
such as " the means that had been everywhere so
industriously employed by the members of such
associations to produce effects similar to what had
taken place in a neighbouring kingdom "—effects
which his Lordship characterised as the most oppressive despotism.

The *Justice-Clerk Braxfield* took the case out
of the hands of the jury altogether. For the only
point submitted to them in the defence was, that
the words had no seriously wicked design, but were

uttered carelessly. And his Lordship "observed
that it was no good defence to say that the words
here spoken were mere *verba jactantia*. They
were *obviously of a most wicked and seditious import*,
and *no plea of rashness, wantonness, or conviviality,
could be admitted as an excuse.*"

The correct speech for his Lordship to have
made would have been this : "I agree with your
Lordships that this indictment is relevant. The
words, taken as we at present must take them, in
their ordinary meaning, are seditious. It is competent for the prisoners, by evidence, or by argument, to satisfy the jury that a different construction ought to be put upon them ; or that they were
uttered in harmless levity—or that at least they
cannot be ascribed to any seditious or other wicked
intention. But all that the court knows at present
is, that the prosecutor, on the face of his libel, puts
a seditious construction upon them, and sets forth
expressly that they were uttered with the design
of infusing disaffection into the minds of certain
soldiers, and thereby withdrawing them from their
duty ; and all this he demands to be allowed to
prove. In this situation, I see no ground on which
we can withhold the case from the consideration of
a jury. This being the only point now before us,
I have no occasion to allude to other matters. I
say nothing about the state of the times, because,
though this subject may possibly be introduced
hereafter, it is not judicially known, or raised, to
us at present. I cannot permit myself even to
glance at the excellencies, real or supposed, of the
British Constitution ; or at any measures, by clubs
or otherwise, that may be said to have been adopted
or to be in contemplation, for remedying any of its

alleged defects ; and still less at a subject, always too delicate for discussion, and therefore always to be assumed—the public and private virtues of the sovereign. And I am especially anxious to protect the prisoners, by avoiding the expression, and even the formation of any opinion which may appear to imply their guilt, or to indicate any difficulty in their being able to reconcile the language imputed to them with their innocence. The jury ought to take their seats without any prepossession from the court on these matters. All I have to say therefore is, that I see no ground on which we can reject this indictment as absolutely irrelevant."

The relevancy being thus fixed, a jury was picked, and evidence was gone into on both sides.

The evidence is very imperfectly reported—indeed scarcely reported at all. The words charged are distinctly sworn to by one witness, who is said to have been corroborated by several others. The prisoners called witnesses to prove that their visit to the Castle was casual, or at least had no connection with politics ; "that they belonged to none of the societies called the Friends of the People ; and that their characters were unimpeachable."

They were unanimously convicted. And there seems to be no ground for questioning the propriety of this verdict.

They gave in a sensible and affecting written statement to the court in mitigation of punishment, setting forth their youth, their good characters, their aged parents, their conscious innocence of intention, its being their first offence, and their being connected with no political society. "We confess that we have been guilty of a piece of gross folly, and flatter ourselves that your Lordship will be sensible that the situation of the country makes it more criminal than it would otherwise have appeared."

Lord Henderland proposed the punishment. The prisoners had only been tried and convicted for sedition—certainly not a capital offence. Nevertheless the greatest portion of his discourse is occupied in showing that some other crime—it is not clear what—but of which the prisoners had not been convicted, was punishable by death. In support of this he refers to the Pandects, the Mutiny Act, a book called Bruce's *Military Law*, published in 1717, and the Emperors Arcadius and Honorius. He then says, " I ask pardon, my Lords, for this digression. I have been led into it by the novelty of the case, and the singular situation of the times." After which he proceeds to the proper business before them.

" We can only choose one of three punishments —either *transportation to Botany Bay;*—banishment, for sedition, to England, is out of the question— corporal punishment by whipping and imprisonment, or imprisonment alone. Were the panels aged and inveterate offenders whom there were little hopes to reclaim, be they of what profession they may—THE MORE LITERARY THE FITTER FOR SUCH PUNISHMENT— I should have had no scruple to deprive them of the enjoyment of this happy Constitution against which they had offended, and obliged them, by hard labour in an infant colony, to repair in some measure the injury they had done here. But it is a rule which a criminal judge ought ever to have in view, *exemplar cum severitate personam cum misericordia intuendam.* The panels are young ; their habits have been industrious, their former character peaceful." Therefore he was against Botany Bay. He is also against whipping, because "to punish by whipping, abandons them to despair, and disgraces their parents, one of whom is a respectable citizen." Therefore " wishing, in this part of my duty, *to follow the example and embrace the sentiments of our gracious sovereign,* who ever tempers justice with mercy, I wish to adopt the punishment of imprisonment alone." But he was not for making it long, because it could only be in the jail of Edinburgh; and "to make them denizens as it were of that unhallowed place, which is the sink of corruption,—where everything that is vicious, base and criminal, are huddled together,—where, if they preserve their health, they cannot for a long tract of time escape the contagion of vice and more sordid criminality—appears to me to be a measure which the necessity of example upon such persons in the present instance does not absolutely require."

The result was that they were sent to this sink of corruption for nine months, and thereafter, till they should find security to the extent of 1000 merks each for their good behaviour for three years,—a punishment which, considering the offence and the times, which last it was quite competent for the court to take into view upon common notoriety in this stage of the business, was not too severe.

Next to the references by the judges to the political circumstances of the day, and their commenting on the merits of the case in a way calculated to convey premature impressions to the jury, the most remarkable thing in this trial is the early indication of the taste for transportation. There was no Statute fixing this as the punishment, or as a possible punishment, for sedition. Nor had there been any judgment to this effect, nor any precedent, nor any judicial discussion on the subject. There had not been a single trial for sedition for nearly one hundred years. Yet without its being necessary for the case—for the court had plainly agreed that imprisonment was to be the punishment—and without one word of argument, the legality of transporting is at once judicially announced by Lord Henderland, and no doubt of this is expressed by any of the other judges. This was the state of the judicial mind under which the question was soon afterwards settled.

I have never heard how any of these young men turned out afterwards, or what became of them.

III.—Case of JOHN ELDER and WILLIAM STEWART,
10th January 1793.[1]

ELDER is designed in the indictment bookseller
in Edinburgh, and Stewart as a merchant in Leith.
They were accused of publishing a seditious writing
and two seditious medals.

Elder appeared at the bar, but Stewart did not.
Stewart being the person chiefly aimed at, the case
was adjourned, on the motion of the prosecutor, in
order that he might endeavour to apprehend him.
He does not appear to have succeeded in this,
however, for no further proceedings took place
respecting either panel.

Yet the case is curious now as an example of
what the accuser and one of the accused concurred
in believing that the court would hold to be sedition. The one testified his conviction by indicting,
the other by flying.

The words on one side of one of the medals
were " *Liberty, Equality, and an end to Impress
warrants,*" and on the reverse, " *The nation is
essentially the source of all Sovereignty.*" One side
of the other medal had the words, " *Liberty of conscience, equal representation, and just taxation;*" the
reverse the words, " *For a nation to be free, it is
sufficient that it wills it.*"

The writing, read under any feelings except

<hr>

[1] *State Trials*, vol. xxiii. p. 25.

those of that particular time, is still more innocent. It was a reprint of the " Declaration of the rights of man and of citizens, by the national assembly of France, which is agreeable to sound reason and common sense," and was as follows :—

" I. Men are born, and always continue free and equal in respect of their rights. Civil distinctions, therefore, can be founded only on public utility.

" II. The end of all political associations is the preservation of the natural and unprescriptible rights of man; and these rights are liberty, property, security, and resistance of oppression.

" III. The nation is essentially the source of all sovereignty; nor can any individual, or any body of men, be entitled to any authority, which is not expressly derived from it.

" IV. Political liberty consists in the power of doing whatever does not injure another. The exercise of the natural rights of every man has no other limits than those which are necessary to secure to every other man the free exercise of the same rights; and these limits are determinable only by the law.

" V. The law ought to prohibit only actions hurtful to society. What is not prohibited by the law, should not be hindered; nor should any one be compelled to that which the law does not require.

" VI. The law is an expression of the will of the community. All citizens have a right to concur, either personally or by their representatives, in its formation. It should be the same to all, whether it protects or punishes; and all being equal in its sight, are equally eligible to all honours, places, and employments, according to their different abilities, without any other distinction than that created by their virtues and talents.

" VII. No man should be accused, arrested, or held in confinement, except in cases determined by the law, and according to the forms which it has prescribed. All who promote, solicit, execute, or cause to be executed arbitrary orders, ought to be punished, and every citizen called upon or apprehended by virtue of the law ought immediately to obey, and renders himself culpable by resistance.

" VIII. The law ought to impose no other penalties, but such as are absolutely and evidently necessary; and no one ought to be punished, but in virtue of a law promulgated before the offence, and legally applied.

"IX. Every man being presumed innocent till he is convicted, whenever his detention becomes indispensable, all rigour to him, more than is necessary to secure his person, ought to be provided against by the law.

"X. No man ought to be molested on account of his opinions; not even on account of his religious opinions, provided his avowal of them does not disturb the public order.

"XI. The unrestrained communication of thoughts and opinions being one of the most precious rights of man, every citizen may speak, write, and publish freely, provided he is responsible for the abuse of this liberty.

"XII. A public force being necessary to give security to the rights of men and citizens, that force is instituted for the benefit of the community, and not for the particular benefit of the persons with whom it is intrusted.

"XIII. A common contribution being necessary for the support of the public force, and for defraying the other expenses of government, it ought to be divided equally among the members of each community according to their abilities.

"XIV. Every citizen has a right, either by himself or his representative, to a free voice in determining the necessity of public contributions, the appropriation of them, and their amount, mode of assessment, and duration.

"XV. Every community has a right to demand of all its agents an account of their conduct.

"XVI. Every community in which a separation of powers, and a security of rights is not provided for, wants a constitution.

"XVII. The right to property being inviolable and sacred, no one ought to be deprived of it, except in cases of evident public necessity, legally ascertained, and on condition of a previous just indemnity.

" *Quere.*—Would not the people of every nation in the world, by enjoying the above rational principles, be in a happier condition? They have but to insist on them and they will get them.

" *For a nation to be free it is sufficient that it wills it;*
" *And to love liberty, it is but necessary to know it.*"

Origin of Government.

"I. The nation is essentially the source of all sovereignty.
"II. The right of altering the government is a national right, and not a right of government.

" III. The authority of the people is the only authority on which government has a right to exist in any country.

" IV. Government is nothing more than a national association, acting on the principles of society.

" V. Government is not a trade, which any body of men has a right to set up, and exercise for its own emolument, but is altogether a trust from the people. It has of itself no rights, they are altogether duties.

" In every free country the artist, mechanic, and labouring man, has a right to bargain for his labour; and how is it that in Britain, which is called the land of freedom, they are by law deprived of their natural right? Why are they not as free to make their own bargains as the lawmakers are to let their farms and houses at what they deem their value?

" The great body of the people allowing these laws to exist, and that curse to liberty, impress warrants, at the caprice of government, to be issued, is tolerating the greatest rights belonging *to mankind* to be violated and kept from them.

" The first and noblest sentiments that ought to be engraved on the heart of every son of freedom should be

EQUAL REPRESENTATION,

JUST TAXATION,

AND LIBERTY OF CONSCIENCE,

and the opposers of those just and equitable principles should be considered by the people as tyrants, and ought to be treated as such by them.

" In a nation where the greatest body of the people have no right or voice in choosing their representatives, and are, at the same time, enormously taxed,

" *Quere*, Are they not treated in every respect as slaves or fools? Even to be the inhabitants of a conquered country would be as enviable a situation.

" *Quere*, If a nation chooses a certain number of men to represent them for a fixed period of years, suppose three, and that body, of their own will and accord, prolong their sitting to double the number of years for which they were elected, how far can such conduct be constitutional, or consistent with common sense, and the rights of the people who elected them?

" Can the people of Scotland reflect without indignation on the conduct of a certain *body* of men, and particularly so on the behaviour of Mr. D——, when the motion was lately made for a reform in the b——hs of S——d, and was rejected by them with the greatest supercility and contempt?

"From the free will and accord of such men the people of Britain have very little chance of getting their representation extended on a more rational and equal plan. Such a reform must be accomplished by themselves."

This writing, as well as the two medals, are charged as seditious, according to their plain and natural meaning. There is no innuendo set forth ; no reference to any peculiarity which made their circulation more dangerous then than it would have been at any different period ; no statement that any of their phrases or principles were the watchwords or tests of sedition among the people, or among the members of any party.

Now, giving the words ordinary fair play, I cannot discover any criminality either in the declaration or in the medals. There is abundance of abstract propositions about liberty, from which, as Lord Henderland says in the preceding case, "no consequence can be drawn." But this is usual in all declamations about freedom, and about the true sources and the proper limits of power ; and their inconsequentiality is the best evidence of their harmlessness. That such political mottoes as were engraved on these medals, and such political principles as were announced in the declaration, might tend to inflame, and that inflammation might end in insurrection, might be true, without sedition. It is possible for a country (Russia for instance) to be in such a condition that these results would follow from the enunciation of any principles of liberty whatever. The publication of Magna Charta or of the Declaration of Rights may, in certain circumstances, produce rebellion. But this will not found a relevant charge of treason or of sedition. And whatever may have been thought of these publications in Edinburgh, in the year 1793, there are few reasonable tories who would now think that they deserved prosecution.

Accordingly, if the trial had proceeded, it is possible that the indictment might have been found irrelevant. Only neither the accuser nor the principal accused expected this.

IV.—Case of JAMES SMITH and JOHN MENNONS,
4th February 1793.[1]

THIS case ended like the preceding one. One
of the accused (Smith) was outlawed for not appearing, and the prosecutor not choosing to proceed
against the other alone, the diet was adjourned,
and the matter was never afterwards moved in.

The major proposition is that "the wickedly
and feloniously printing and publishing, etc., any
seditious paper or writing tending to create a
spirit of disaffection to us, and of discontent with
the present excellent constitution of our kingdom,
and to excite tumults and disorders therein, or
which publicly express approbation of works of a
seditious and inflammatory nature—more especially when the practical use of these writings *is*
expressly recommended to the community, are
crimes," etc.

The facts set forth in support of this charge are
that Smith had produced certain written resolutions
to a meeting held at Partick, which, upon his
motion, were adopted, and that Mennons afterwards
printed and distributed them. So that the case
depended entirely upon the character of these
resolutions, which were as follows :—

"PARTICK, 22d *November* 1792.

" The inhabitants of the village of Partick and
its neighbourhood, animated with a just indigna-

[1] *State Trials*, vol. xxiii. p. 33.

tion at the honour of their town being stained by
the erection of a Burkified Society,[1] have formed
themselves into an association under the name of
the Sons of Liberty and the Friends of Man.   At
this meeting—from its number, equally hopeful to
the people, as formidable to the tools of tyrants—
the following resolutions were unanimously adopted :
—1st, That the Society do stand forward in defence
of the rights of man, and co-operate with the respectable assemblage of the friends of the people in
Glasgow, and with the innumerable host of reform
associations in Scotland, England, and Ireland, for
the glorious purpose of vindicating the native rights
of man,—Liberty, with a fair, full, free, and equal
representation of the people in Parliament.   2d,
That the Sons of Liberty in Partick, *having attentively perused the whole works of the immortal author
of ' The Rights of Man,'* THOMAS PAINE, declare it as
their opinion, that if nations would adopt the practical use of these works, tyrants and their satellites
would vanish, like the morning mist before the rising sun ! that social comfort, plenty, good order,
peace, and joy, would diffuse their benign influence
over the human race."

The only sedition that can be said to transpire
through these grand words consists in the adoption
of Paine's book.   It is therefore a defect (*perhaps*)
in the libel that it does not set forth, *technically
and substantively*, that this work was seditious, but
only intimates this *incidentally and indirectly*, by
mentioning " *the libellous and seditious book* or publication, entituled Paine's whole works," *as one of
the productions*.   Certain passages are selected from

---

[1] A society, I presume, for disseminating the principles of Edmund
Burke.

this book, and the attention of the accused is called to them by their being quoted among *the list of the articles to be brought forward as evidence.*[1]

How far the guilt of sedition is incurred by a general recommendation of a seditious book is a question not unworthy of being discussed, if such a charge shall ever be made again. The affirmative certainly cannot be laid down without some important qualifications, especially in reference to opinions expressed, or to recommendations given, by individuals privately. The point, I suppose, must always come to this,—whether the accused *promoted the inculcation* of the criminal writing ? or whether, by adoption, *he appropriated and published* its sentiments ? And this must be a question, on the whole circumstances, for the jury. If the private expression of individual opinion shall be held sufficient to warrant a conviction, an alarming field of justifiable accusation is opened to the prosecutor ; for it is an unfortunate fact that books are read, and have rash opinions expressed about them, nearly in proportion to their atrocity, and to the attempts to suppress them by penal law. There was no book more generally read, and more freely commented on, or more diffused by quiet sales, and by undisguised loans, than this very Paine's *Rights of Man.* But the peculiarity of this case was, that it was the *public recommendation,* for practical use, *of the most inflammatory and offensively seditious book of the age,* by a *numerous association, publishing its resolutions.*

---

[1] By our practice the prosecutor is not only obliged to give the accused a list of witnesses, but of all writings or other articles on which he means to found. These are termed the *Productions.*

V.—Cases of CAPTAIN JOHNSTON and of SIMON
     DRUMMOND, January and February 1793,
     and January 1794.[1]

THESE were not cases of sedition, but of contempt.
But I notice them, because they were ultimately
connected with the current proceedings against
sedition.

Johnston was the editor and proprietor, and
Drummond the printer of a newspaper called *The
Edinburgh Gazetteer*,—a vulgar, intemperate publication. Johnston, who lived in Edinburgh many
years after this, was a respectable man, and a
gentleman in his manners. The only fact against
him is, that he should have been connected with
such a newspaper; which, however, was polluted
by no such personal calumny as is now quite common, nor by anything that would now be thought
criminal intemperance; but was discreditable solely
from its being the popular organ, and from indulg-
ing in the vulgar declamation natural to such a
championship.

The trial of Morton, Anderson, and Craig had
begun upon the 8th of January 1793, and was
finished, by their receiving sentence on the 11th.
On the 15th there appeared in the *Gazetteer* what
professed to be a report of the proceedings, with a
speech, bearing to be in his own words, by the Lord
Justice-Clerk.

---

[1] *State Trials*, vol. xxiii. p. 43.

There can be no doubt that this was an inaccurate, and probably a wilfully inaccurate account of the trial. But in this respect it was not more partial than most party reports of similar proceedings; and had there been no offence except in the unfairness of the report, it is not likely that there would have been any complaint. But, as was notorious at the time, the true delinquency lay in the speech ascribed to the Justice, which made him personally vulgar and odious. Nobody who ever heard him speak could refuse to acknowledge that the Scotch imputed to him was rather softened than exaggerated; and everything he said during these trials shows that no injustice was done to his sentiments. In truth it was the general fidelity of the portrait, attested by its being long afterwards recited, even by the Justice's friends, as an excellent imitation of the diction and manner of the original, that made it so offensive. Still, a contempt may be committed by a ludicrous representation of judges, the truth of which, even if it could decently be inquired into, can never be established, or be expected to be admitted. The prudence of giving such things importance by noticing them, is always to be doubted. Accordingly attacks far more severe and weighty than this, but which it was not absolutely necessary to check, from their obstructing some actually current proceeding, have generally been overlooked by judges, who are aware that true dignity is generally able to protect itself. I do not recollect that Lord Mansfield thought it worth his while to take any judicial notice of Stewart for his merciless letters about his Lordship's conduct as a judge in the Douglas cause; and certainly Justice Best did not move judicially

against the excoriation by Sydney Smith on his
Lordship's opinions on the use of spring-guns.[1] The
impression at the time was probably correct, that
if it had not been for the temptation of crushing
the *Gazetteer*, and punishing its conducters, their
contempt of court would never have been noticed.

The proceedings began by a statement from
the Lord Advocate that the account of what had
passed at the late trial " was not only partial,
untrue, and unjust, but by imputing partiality
and injustice to the court, as well as from other
circumstances appearing in the paper itself, was
clearly and evidently calculated to lessen the regard
which the people of this country owe to the
Supreme Criminal Court."

Captain Johnston was ordered to attend; which,
after a delay of about a fortnight, occasioned by
his being ill of inflammation in the eye, he did.
He at once admitted that he was the proprietor and
editor of the newspaper, and that *as such* he was
responsible for what had appeared in it, which he
did not defend.   But he took no *personal* blame to
himself, because at the time the article was published, and for some time before as well as after,
he had suffered so severely from the disease in
his eye, that he had taken no charge of the paper
whatever, and indeed had been practically blind.
"From the commencement of January (says his
written statement) to the 16th (the day after
the article was published), the day I underwent
a severe operation in my eye, had the treasures
of the world been laid at my feet, I could not
have dictated, read, or wrote one line.   It is only
within these ten days I have been out of dark-

---

[1] *Edinburgh Review,* vol. xxxv.

ness." He ascribes the publication to the inadvertence of Simon Drummond, to whom he had intrusted the superintendence of the paper, and had given positive orders that he should insert nothing without his knowledge and approbation— an instruction which, in this instance, had not been obeyed; and that he had not heard of the contemptuous article till the 22d or 23d, and then only by accident. All intentional disrespect was disclaimed, and in rather fulsome language.

The complaint upon this was extended to Drummond, who had not been originally included in it. He was then twice examined, and gave a materially different account. For he says that he had received no instructions from Johnston, except that he should avoid the insertion of anything which should appear to him (Drummond) to be libellous; that it was " his invariable practice " to send a copy of the paper to Johnston by one of the boys in the office as soon as it was thrown off; that he called on him, and saw him on the 16th, the day after the publication of this number, and had a conversation with him on the subject of this very article, part of which he (Drummond) read to Johnston, who expressly approved of it. In all these particulars he directly contradicts his principal. He does not insinuate however that Johnston was privy to the composition, or original insertion, of the article. The manuscript could not be recovered; but it was neither in the writing of Drummond nor of Johnston; and Drummond's explanation is, that " he found the said manuscript among other packets which had been sent to the office; " that having read only a part of it, he put it into a bag, from which it was taken by a boy, and was printed without his knowledge;

but that *he read it, and added to it, before it was
finally thrown off.*

Legally, Johnston's statement could not be
affected by Drummond's contradictions; because,
when Drummond moved that he should be dismissed
unpunished on the ground that he had been taken
by the Crown as a witness, and therefore could no
longer be viewed as a panel, the court decided that
it was not as a witness, but as an accused party,
that his declarations had been taken ; and this being
his position, what he had said could only operate
against himself. *Morally*, the statements of the
master seem entitled to credit in preference to those
of the servant, and this on the following grounds :—

1. Drummond was improperly examined, and in
a way calculated to lead him to save himself, by
showing him the points on which he might contradict his superior. *What Johnston had said was read
over to him.* " And the former declarations emitted
by Captain Johnston, and the paper given in by
him to court, entituled Apology, etc., being, *at the
declarant's own desire*, read over to him, he of himself declares," etc. It is not usual, nor can it ever
conduce to fairness, to let one party know, before
making his own declaration, what a conjoined party
may have declared, especially when, as in this case,
no such opportunity was afforded to Johnston.
Drummond having desired it was only an additional
reason why it should have been refused.

2. He did not state the facts in which his contradictions consist at his first examination. That
first examination was taken *a day after* Johnston had
made his statement, so that he probably knew what
Johnston had said ; and this was at least known
to the accuser and to the court. Yet at his first

examination neither does he voluntarily contradict Johnston, nor do those whose object was the truth ask him any questions to enable him to do so. *He then applied, five days* after Johnston's statement, and *four* days after his own first examination, to be allowed to make a new declaration; and not only was this very properly allowed, but he was most improperly indulged, at his own request, with first hearing what Johnston had said. It is only *then* that the contradictions come forth, though the circumstances in which they consist must obviously have presented themselves to his mind, if they had been well founded, at the first; because their import is that he had been left to conduct the paper without any special instructions, and that the proprietor approved of the article almost the moment after its publication, so that little personal blame could be attached to himself.

3. The openness of Captain Johnston's original explanation, from which he never deviated,—his bad health, the 16th, the day on which he is said to have heard and approved of the article, being the very one on which he underwent a painful operation, and, above all, his character, render the assertions of Drummond by far the least credible.

However, it was a contempt of court, even on Johnston's own showing; but not nearly so bad a one as it would have been upon Drummond's.

The result was that the court (Braxfield all along absent) found that " the said publication is a false and slanderous representation of the proceedings in the said trial, and a gross indignity offered to this high court, calculated to create groundless jealousies, and doubts of the due administration of justice by the supreme criminal court of this part of

the united empire." They were both therefore sent
to jail for three months, and bound to find security,
Johnston to the extent of £500, Drummond to the
extent of £100, "*for their good behaviour*" for three
years.

This ended the first stage of the proceedings.

They were renewed about a year afterwards (20th
January 1794) by the Lord Advocate presenting a
petition for the forfeiture of the bond granted by
Captain Johnston and his sureties.

This application was, in substance, rested on the
statement, that the Convention of the Friends of
the People was a seditious association ; that this
fact was judicially known to the Court, because
William Skirving, its secretary, had, within these
few days, been convicted of sedition, chiefly for having been active in its proceedings ; that, nevertheless, Johnston had certainly attended one, and probably two, of its meetings ; that he had even spoken
there ; and that certain letters written by him to
Skirving showed that he had been in communication
with that person previously about the business that
was to be brought forward ; that "this conduct of
Mr. Johnston was highly aggravated, not only by
the consciousness, which he appears to have all along
felt, of the impropriety of his behaviour ; but that,
on this last occasion, the meeting or convention had,
by the change of its name, the form of its procedure,
the nature of the motions made, and the purport of
the debates and harangues which took place in it,
CLEARLY AND UNEQUIVOCALLY proved that the seditious, NAY, TREASONABLE, nature of its proceedings,"
etc., from all which the conclusion was, that he having
misbehaved, his bond should be declared forfeited.

Answers were lodged to this petition by Johnston

and his two sureties, one of whom, Mr. James Campbell, writer to the Signet, and afterwards solicitor
in London, was a whig, and the other, Dr. Francis
Home, physician in Edinburgh, and for many years
afterwards a professor in the University, was a very
decided tory. These answers were signed, and from
their style, I should think, must have been written
by Henry Erskine, who had then the honour of
being Dean of the Faculty, and about two years
afterwards the still higher honour of having been
dismissed, on account of his political principles, from
that situation.

The answers tear the complaint to tatters. No
refutation could be more triumphant. Upon the
absurdity of considering what Johnston had done as
accession to sedition, which was the sole ground of
complaint, but of which sedition he had never been
convicted or even indicted, it was unanswerable.

Accordingly, "no further procedure took place,
nor did Captain Johnston sist himself in court."

Three things are remarkable in this affair :—

One is, the commencement of that habit which
pervaded almost all the immediately subsequent
cases, of first describing aggravated sedition as
treason; and then violating the law by proceeding
against this treason as only sedition. The prosecutor
here states that the *treasonable* nature of the society's
transaction was *clear and unequivocal;* yet no step
was taken against it or any of its members for
treason, as such.

Another is, that Erskine never took up the point
that sedition, or even treason, was no legal ground
for forfeiting a bond for good behaviour which had
been granted in relation to *a contempt of court.* On
the contrary, by confining himself to show that his

client was not chargeable with all the guilt of the convention, he seems to have agreed with the prosecutor that a forfeiture would have been incurred by accession to that guilt. Where two such authorities concur, any third person may be rash in doubting. But are not all bonds, though for *general good behaviour*, to be taken as in relation, not perhaps to the *precise offence* for which they were exacted, but to the *class* of offences? Does a surety bind himself that his friend shall obey *the whole criminal law*? Would *forgery* be a ground for forfeiting a bond for good behaviour granted on a conviction for contempt? The terms of this bond, and I understand of all such bonds, were that "he, the said William Johnston, should *have and maintain a good behaviour* for the space of three years," etc. But does this, being interpreted, mean that he is to observe the whole moral law? Would bigamy have brought in the sureties?

The third is that the petition and the whole proceedings imply that it was the *court* that was to be convinced of his having committed sedition, and that it was upon the *judges* being satisfied of this, and not a jury, that his bond was to be forfeited. No objection is taken on this ground by Erskine, and all that Hume says in his statement of the law on contempts seems to suppose that this is the correct form and principle of all such complaints.

But when the King's Bench was about to bind John Horne over for "*good behaviour*" for three years as a part of his punishment for libel, he objected that he could not know what might be construed to be bad behaviour. Mr. Justice Aston explained that it meant "not to repeat offences *of this sort*."

" *Mr. Horne.*—Of this sort ?

" *Lord Mansfield.*—*Any misdemeanour.*

" *Mr. Justice Aston.*—Whatever shall be construed bad behaviour.

" *Mr. Horne.*—If your Lordships would imprison me for these three years I should be safer, because I can't foresee but that the most meritorious action of my life may be construed to be of the same nature.

" *Lord Mansfield.*—YOU MUST BE TRIED BY A JURY OF YOUR COUNTRY, AND BE CONVICTED." (*State Trials,* vol. xx. p. 789.)

This principle has not been acted upon by the Court of Justiciary, which, from the absolute and peremptory finality of all its proceedings, has no opportunity of discussion with other judges, and is therefore apt to get into unconsidered habits of its own. But the principle has never (so far as I am aware) been *rejected.* It has never been examined. When a proper case for settling the matter shall arise, great deference ought to be paid to Lord Mansfield's statement of the law of England, which looks very like the law of justice and of common sense. It is difficult to see how a person can be dealt with as guilty of sedition, or of any other crime, till he be convicted of it *by a jury.*

VI.—Case of WILLIAM CALLENDER, WALTER
BERRY, and JAMES ROBERTSON, January,
February, and March 1793.[1]

CALLENDER was outlawed for not appearing.

Berry was a bookseller; Robertson a bookseller
and printer; both in Edinburgh.

The indictment set forth that "the *wickedly
and feloniously printing,* or causing to be printed,
any *seditious* writing or pamphlet, containing *false,
wicked,* and *seditious assertions,* calculated to degrade and bring into contempt our present happy
system of government, and withdraw therefrom the
confidence and affections of our subjects; AS ALSO
the *wickedly and feloniously* publishing, circulating,
and selling *such wicked and seditious* pamphlet, *are
crimes,*" etc. And the facts specified in support of
this charge were not merely that they had printed
and published a pamphlet called *The Political
Progress of Britain,* but that this pamphlet was
seditious, and that they had printed and published
it *wickedly and feloniously.* The prosecutor first
gives the full and exact *title* of the pamphlet, which
he says was composed by Callender, and then he
attaches this quality to it: "which pamphlet is of
a *wicked tendency,* and contains, among other *wicked
and seditious passages,* the following," etc. Some
passages are then quoted, which are insulting to
parliament and to the sovereign, and are clearly

[1] *State Trials,* vol. xxiii. p. 79.

grossly seditious.   It is then stated that Callender
having delivered this pamphlet to Berry and
Robertson, they had printed and published " many
copies of the said *wicked and seditious* pamphlet,"
and that this had been done by them "*wickedly
and feloniously.*"   These two qualities, viz., of
wickedness in the pamphlet, and of wickedness in
the prisoners, are constantly re-asserted, and run
through every part of the libel.   But the pamphlet
itself is designated by its title so as to be distinguishable without these.

The counsel for the prosecution were the Lord
Advocate, the Solicitor-General, and Mr. James
Montgomery.[1]   Wight was counsel for the prisoners,
aided by Archibald Fletcher, one of the purest and
firmest friends of liberty then, or indeed at any
period, in Scotland.   Brougham states only the
simple truth when he says, " Among these eminent
patriots the first place is due to Archibald Fletcher,
a learned, experienced, and industrious lawyer ;
one of the most upright men that ever adorned the
profession ; and a man of such stern and resolute
firmness in public principle as is very rarely found
united with the amiable character which endeared
him to private society." (*Speeches*, vol. iii. p. 346.)

Fletcher objected to the relevancy of the libel,
upon no grounds whatever, and *in reference to the
objections urged*, it was most properly found relevant.
The language was by far the worst and the clearest
that had yet been complained of.

But was not this a point which might have
been maintained ?   The libel charges at least *two*
crimes.   It sets forth that what it charges "*are
crimes*," and asserts the prisoner to have been guilty

[1] I have noticed Mr. Montgomery in the case of *Gerrald*.

" of all and each, or *one or other*, of the aforesaid *crimes.*" Now, one of them is said to consist in the wicked *publication* of a seditious writing, which is certainly a relevant charge. But the other is said to consist merely in the wickedly *printing* such a writing. The two accusations are not only separated by being described as at least two crimes, but the crime of publishing is set forth as a new charge by itself, and is introduced by " *as also.*" Now, is the mere *printing* a seditious writing an offence ? I am not aware that it is, any more than the mere *writing* it. I suppose that a man may amuse himself by seditious composition, or by copying the seditious composition of others, with perfect innocence. In a trial for *publishing*, the fact of having written or printed, may operate *as evidence*, but the publication is the only crime.

This point was not taken ; but its importance appears in the verdict.

The evidence is not reported in the *State Trials*, nor anywhere else that I have seen.

The jury pronounced a special verdict, finding " it proven that the said James Robertson did *print and publish*, and that the said Walter Berry did *publish* only, *the pamphlet libelled on.*"

The prisoners maintained that no sentence could be pronounced on this verdict, because it was not a verdict of guilty, either in direct terms, or by necessary legal implication.

The court ordered minutes of debate, which proceed as if from the Lord Advocate on the one side, and from Wight and Henry Erskine on the other ; but Montgomery probably wrote for the prosecution and Fletcher for the defence.

The objections, and the answers to them, were

both extremely simple. Divested of superfluous
words, the argument on each side came to this :—

The prisoners maintained that the verdict merely
fixed the fact that they had printed and published
the pamphlet libelled on, which was a pamphlet
entitled *The Political Progress of Britain ;* but that
this did not imply their guilt, because—1st, The
jury had not found that this pamphlet was *wicked
or seditious;* and 2dly, Because even although they
had found this, they had not pronounced that they
had printed or published it *wickedly or feloniously.*
In short, their plea was, that they might have done
all that the verdict had found, without being guilty
of the offence charged.

The answer resolved, in substance, into these
two propositions—1st, That the jury, by referring
to the pamphlet " *libelled on,*" had used words
equivalent to " *as libelled,*" which was the usual
technical form of referring to any act with *all the
qualities attached to it* in the libel ; 2dly, That the
jury having found certain facts, it was the right,
and the duty, of the court to draw the inference
from these, as a question of law, as had been done
by the English judges in the analogous case of
Woodfall.

The court unanimously repelled the objections.

I am humbly of opinion that the court was
wrong.

The true principle is very well brought out in
the English case of *Woodfall,* in which the prosecutor pretended to discover something favourable to
his argument. (1770—*State Trials,* vol. xx. p. 895.)
Woodfall had been tried for publishing a seditious
libel. The precise words of the information are not
given ; but from what Lord Mansfield says they

must have been immaterial. The jury found the defendant, the prisoner, "*guilty of printing and publishing only.*" The Court of King's Bench determined that this was enough. *But why?* Because the jury, as the law of ENGLAND then stood, had no power, in cases of libel, to decide anything except the fact of publication. The character of what was published, and the motive of the publisher, were matters of *legal inference* for the court.

Accordingly, in delivering the judgment, Lord Mansfield said that he had told the jury, "as I have, from indispensable duty, been obliged to tell every jury, upon every trial of this kind, to the following effect :—That whether the paper was in law a libel, *was a question of law upon the face of the record;* for after a conviction a defendant may move in arrest of judgment, if the paper is not a libel, that all the epithets in the information were formal inferences of law from the printing and publishing." (vol. xx. p. 918.)   Hence his charge to the jury had directed them, " That *as for the intention,* the malice, sedition, or any other still harder words which might be given in informations for libels, whether public or private, *they were mere formal words,*—mere words of course,—mere inference of law, *with which the jury were not to concern themselves,*—that they were words which signify nothing, just as when it is said, in bills of indictment for murder, 'instigated by the devil,'" etc. (p. 901.)   This being the law, no wonder it was altered.   It was corrected by the Statute which made juries in England the judges both of the fact of publishing and of the writing being libellous, and libellously meant.   It made these cease to be words that signified nothing.   And even in *Woodfall's* case, the court *sustained* the objection that the verdict was *uncertain*, and ordered a *venire de novo*. (vol. xx. p. 921.) And this uncertainty must adhere to every verdict which merely finds the fact of publication.

But there was no need of such a statute in Scotland, because in this, as in a thousand other cases, our law was in advance of that of England, and had never fallen into the error which in England required the interference of parliament. With us the assertions by the prosecutor that the writing was seditious, and that it was wickedly or feloniously published, never were useless or superfluous words; they are assertions which the prosecutor *must* make in his libel, and *must prove*. Instead of being meaningless phrases, they point out matters of fact, which it is, and with us always was, the province only of the jury to determine, though no doubt the mere terms or import of the publication may warrantably be deemed by them to be sufficient evidence of its tendency and object. It is, in the law of Scotland, with libels as with any other crime, which is never held to be committed by a mere act, unaccompanied by a guilty quality in the mind of the agent; and there can be no conviction unless the jury find that quality established, as well as the abstract act, as, for example, in the cases of forgery or of perjury. What would be the legal value of a verdict merely finding that the writing uttered had been forged, the coin passed, counterfeited, or the statements sworn to, false, but without adding either in express terms, or by the use of some understood word, that the flaw was known to the prisoner? The questions actually put to the jury in this libel, and without putting which the libel would not have been relevant, were, whether this pamphlet was seditious? and if it was seditious, whether it had been feloniously published? Now the jury here found nothing proved beyond the fact of publication, of which a steam-engine might have been guilty. The insufficiency of this to warrant a sentence may be tried by this test. If the indictment had charged the mere publication alone, without averring either the seditious import of the pamphlet, or the seditious motive of the prisoners, could it have been sustained as relevant? The prosecutor admitted that it could not. " In one observation he perfectly agreed with the counsel for the panels, that it was *not the mere printing and publishing a seditious pamphlet* which was the offence imputed to the panels in the criminal letters under which they had been tried, but the printing and publishing it *with a wicked and felonious intention.*" (vol. xxiii. p. 95.)

Hume professes to think the judgment pronounced in this case right. His general ground is that "special verdicts are of two sorts, with respect to the duty which they devolve on the court. For sometimes the inference to be made by the judge is purely in point of law; and sometimes it *is an inference in point of fact!*" In illustration of this singular power of the court to supersede the jury by finding, or, which is the same thing, inferring, facts, he refers to two cases of murder, in which the juries, instead of finding the prisoners either innocent or guilty, found the mere abstract facts of violence inflicted, and of death following. The court, it seems, filled up what was wanting by this inferential process; and this Hume approves of. To me the precedents seem fully more questionable than the point they are brought to illustrate. Undoubtedly no such verdicts would be acted upon, or indeed received, in modern times. He then mentions the verdict against Robertson and Berry, and says, " In these instances the verdicts fix on the several panels the *fundamental* facts of killing, exhorting to kill, printing, and publishing, AS LIBELLED ; and nothing remains for the court but *to settle the conclusion in point of law,* whether, from the fact found, there arises a just *inference of that dole, or criminal intention which is essential to the crimes of murder and sedition.* The court accordingly *made that inference,* and gave judgment against the panels." (vol. ii. p. 457.)

The confusion of ideas and of words which pervades this passage goes far to make one suspect that the learned author felt that his friends on the bench had got into an awkward position.

First, the important words " *as libelled,*" which, *by adopting the whole libel,* would have prevented the point from arising, do not appear to have been in either of the verdicts in the two murder cases, and *certainly were not in the verdict against Robertson and Berry.* The jury refer certainly to " the pamphlet *libelled on.*" But this only identified the writing. It meant no more than if they had recited its title, *The Political Progress of Britain.* Suppose that a verdict were to bear that the accused had uttered the forged note *libelled*— not *as* libelled—that is, knowing it to be forged, but merely that a note identified by certain marks being described in the libel, he had uttered that libelled note. The utmost possible extent to which the words " libelled on " could be carried—but even this is quite unwarranted—would be to hold that they included the *seditious character* as an element of *the pamphlet.* The "pamphlet libelled on" must, in this view, be held to mean the *seditious* pamphlet libelled on. But, giving the prosecutor the benefit even of this stretch, the words can by no construction, and not even by any rational stretch, be made to include the seditious motive of the man. They do not find that he published *feloniously,* or *as libelled,* which is the established form in which a verdict generally includes, not merely the principal fact charged, but all its qualities.

Secondly, Since wickedness of mind is essential, it is, especially when disputed, a matter of *fact.* If so, on what ground is it that the court can supply *facts* which the jury have not found? Is it for the judges to draw "the inference of dole, which is essential to the crime?" If a jury were to find certain facts, and were *expressly to say* that they could not make up their minds as to whether there was dole or not, would the court quietly save them all trouble upon this score by itself determining this, *the most important question of fact in the case?*

Thirdly, How can the existence of these *facts,* viz., the wickedness of the writing, or the wickedness of the accused publisher, ever be settled "as *a conclusion of law?*

Lastly, Assuming the court to be competent to supply this inference, the jury had given no authority for it by "the fundamental facts" which they had found. The seditiousness of the pamphlet or of its publisher was not necessarily implied in the fact of publishing, or even made probable by it. The test of this is that there would have been nothing inconsistent with the words which the jury employed, if they had added that, though the pamphlet had been printed and published by the prisoners, it was a constitutional work; or that though it was seditious, their views in its publication were pure. The jury that tried Stein for bribery actually did this. They found that the prisoner gave Bonar £500, " but do not find the intention of seducing and corrupting the said John Bonar proven." The prosecutor in this case of Berry and Robertson argues that if this had been the jury's meaning in their case, they would have said so. But this is plainly begging the question. It assumes that they had not said so. I hold that they had said it by implication,—by the implication contained in the fact of their restricting their finding to the mere publication. But the true point is, whether the addition of such words as I have supposed would have been *absolutely inconsistent* with the actual verdict? I think it would not. And if there be no *repugnance* in the interposition of such words, or in the idea of their being there, was it not the duty of the court, under the rule of always giving a prisoner the benefit of the mildest interpretation, to supply them constructively, if it was to supply anything?

See what was done in England, this very year, (1793) in some precisely similar cases, after the libel law of that country had become the same with ours.

Daniel Eaton was tried (3d June 1793) before the Recorder of London, for " *unlawfully, wickedly, maliciously,* and *seditiously*" publishing " a *certain scandalous, malicious,* and *seditious* libel," entituled The rights of man. (*State Trials,* vol. xxii. p. 755.) The verdict was " Guilty of publishing, *but not with a criminal intention.*" (p. 780.) After a good deal of wrangling and professional fencing between the counsel and the Recorder, the legal import of this verdict was left to the determination of the twelve judges; but the result was that they gave no decision, and that no sentence ever followed. "The case in the King's Bench has never been mentioned since." (*State Trials*, vol. xxii. p. 822.)

In this case the jury positively negatived the criminal intention; and therefore the difficulties affected to be felt by some of the judges (p. 783) would be incomprehensible, were it not for the number of occasions on which, for a long while after the passing of the new libel law, almost every one of their Lordships testify their spite at that statute.[1]

But the same Daniel Eaton was again tried, on the 10th of July 1793, before Lord Kenyon, for publishing another libel; and on this occasion also there was the usual accumulation of epithets denoting criminality both in the writing and in the prisoner. The jury found him "*guilty of publishing the pamphlet in question.*" (vol. xxii. p. 822.) The attorney got leave to show cause why this verdict "should not be entered up *according to its legal import;*" but he never moved further in the matter, and no sentence was pronounced,—a result which can only be ascribed to his being satisfied

---

[1] See the singularly foolish remarks by Kenyon in the case of *Cuthell*, 21st February 1799 (*State Trials*, vol. xxvii. p. 674). "The law of libels has been alluded to in the course of the present trial. I certainly, in my legislative capacity, opposed the last bill that was before parliament upon that subject (the Libel Bill); not because *I thought that the bill introduced a word or syllable that was not law before*, but because it was unnecessary; and there was in it nothing to improve the minds, or *alter the duties of those who were to discriminate between the two jurisdictions of the court and jury.* And I am sure that *my conduct before the passing of the Libel Act was exactly conformable to the principles of that Act*, as indeed the law commanded it to be before this Act took effect. The truth is that in passing this bill through parliament, it was a race of popularity between two seemingly contending parties; but in this measure both parties chose to run amicably together."

It is odd how judges could be so averse to a statute, as to ascribe its passing to unworthy motives, even from the bench, when it did not introduce a word or syllable that was not law before.

that its legal import was an acquittal—or at least not a conviction.

The whole principle is demonstrated with irresistible clearness and force, by Erskine, in his beautiful speech for John Cuthell (*State Trials*, vol. xxvii. p. 655), where the defence was that he had only published *negligently*, and that negligence was not necessarily guilt. He asks what would be thought of an indictment which only charged negligence? It would certainly be rejected. And if so, can a *verdict* finding only negligence be sustained? If not, how can a verdict be sustained *as a conviction*, which merely finds the fact of publishing?—a fact consistent with even less blame than negligence—with unconsciousness or with accident. Cuthell was convicted, but was only fined in 30 marks, a nominality of punishment which Lord Campbell ascribes to the case being "*so revolting.*" (*Lives of Chancellors*, vol. vi. p. 519.)

Let us see whether our judges put their decision on better grounds than Hume has taken up.

"*Lord Henderland* thought that the verdict was to be understood as finding, with regard to Robertson, that the printing and publishing had been wicked and felonious, *the* malus animus *being necessarily inferred from the printing* AND *publishing;* but he thought the result was different in the case of Berry, who was found *only* to have published. One may utter a bank note not knowing that it was forged ; and so one may *publish* a book, while ignorant of its real tendency." And may not one *print* a book without knowing its real tendency? This reasoning shows how completely the judges were performing the duties of jurors. Instead of looking to the verdict, as the sole measure of the

guilt or the innocence of the prisoners, each of
them tries what other facts, beyond those that the
jury had furnished, he may extract out of it, and
upon what grounds. Lord Henderland thinks that
malus animus must be *necessarily* inferred from the
combined acts of *both* printing *and* publishing, but
he thought that *publishing alone* did not imply this.
So that each judge may make a new, or at least a
supplementary verdict, out of his favourite bits of
the evidence contained in the jury's verdict. This
is an absurd enough operation ; but when it is performed, it should be performed correctly. But,
publication being the evil, and printing, without
publication, being perfectly harmless, most men
will demur to the opinion of his Lordship, that the
one of these prisoners ought to be better off than
the other. No doubt anything that shows a greater
consciousness of the guilt of what is published in
one panel than in the other, or that gave him a
better opportunity of discovering its true character,
ought to weigh, *in evidence*, against that party.
But does printing do so ? A master printer (which
Robertson was) may have his types used without
his knowledge ; and though he had set them with
his own hands, he may not have observed the
latent sedition they were preparing for dissemination. If a court is to search amidst such circumstances for result of fact, it must go into them
much more minutely. The knowledge of the subject,
which a person prints or publishes, is of far more
consequence than these acts.

 Lord Eskgrove's opinion was in these words :—
" This is a special verdict ; and from the terms of it
a seditious intent is *necessarily* implied *in so far as
regards Robertson*, from the reference to the libel,

where the pamphlet was described as wicked and seditious." (The reference to the libel is exactly the same in the verdict as to both panels.) "The case is the same as if the jury had found Robertson guilty of printing and publishing a *seditious* libel." (Well, though they had, still the mind of the man need not have been seditious.) "This cannot be done without a *malus animus*"—(no! no accidental publishing of seditious matter!)—"every person being called upon to *consider* what he prints and publishes. There is more doubt as to Berry. *We have no law here as in England which makes the* PUBLISHING *and* SELLING *of a libel a crime.*" (Then Berry, who was merely convicted of publishing and selling, ought to have been at once acquitted. But no!) "*Therefore,* where there is a verdict of publishing, WE MUST DECIDE FROM THE CIRCUMSTANCES OF THE CASE ; and if the writing be very *short*, as a seditious handbill, a knowledge of its contents will be *necessarily* inferred from the publication ; but here the pamphlet being of *some size*, the same inference may not be warrantably drawn." Such an opinion is not a subject for serious criticism. Only it will be observed, that, here also, the principle is avowed, that the court is entitled to take the whole circumstances into its view,—not in applying punishment—but in giving a meaning to the verdict.

Lord Dunsinnan agreed with these judges as to "the difference between the two panels."

Lord Abercromby dissented from this difference. "Our law has always been different from the common law of England, where, in the case of libel, the jury, till a late period, were judges of the fact, but not of the law. With us, even in matters of libel, the jury have always determined both as to the law and the fact. In this case, if the jury had thought either of the panels not guilty, their verdict would have been in different terms." (This is not certain. But at any rate, they may have been *doubtful;* and may therefore have found all the fact that they could—*valeat quantum.*) " To publish a seditious libel is a crime at common law " (not surely unless it be done *wickedly ?*)—" every person being presumed to know the contents of what he publishes, *even although the book may be written in a language unknown to him."* (A plain confusion between criminal and civil responsibility.) " And in some respects the publisher is *more* guilty than the printer, the crime by his means becoming complete, and the injury to the public put beyond the possibility of recall." (So that they do not agree even as to their supplementary facts.) " The question here is, whether the verdict is altogether defective ? I do not think so. I cannot go to the proof. But I may to the indictment or libel ; and must consider the case in the same light as if the jury, instead of a reference to the pamphlet, *had recited it.* The jury might have found the seditious intent proved ; but in my opinion they did *better* by a special finding as to the fact, *leaving the court from thence to judge of the intent.* Nor can I distinguish between the two panels, so as to acquit Berry, against whom a finding as to the publishing only has been given," etc.

There are only two things worth noticing here. 1*st,* Suppose that the jury had, *in direct terms,* devolved the task of determining the wickedness of intent on the court, could the court have performed it ? 2*d,* Burnett (the poorest of all authorities, however) rests the judgment upon

Abernethy's idea that the verdict virtually *recites* the pamphlet. (*Criminal Law*, p. 243.) But suppose that the verdict had recited the whole of it —not virtually, but actually—and that it had even borne that the prisoners had published this pamphlet, it is clear that this does not advance the argument a single step. For reciting the writing neither fixes its criminality, nor the criminality of the publisher.

The Lord Justice-Clerk delivered his opinion in nearly the same words.

Three of them had thus declared in favour of Berry. But one, at the least, must have changed; otherwise, by the constitution of the court, he could not have been punished. One way or other, however, sentence was pronounced against them both— Robertson being ordered to be imprisoned six months, and Berry three, and each to find security to the extent of £100 for three years. An attempt was made to get the judgment reviewed by the House of Lords, but the petition of appeal was dismissed. Considering the times, and the grossness of the sedition, the comparative mildness of the sentence seems to indicate some misgiving in the court as to its dealing with the verdict.

VII.—Case of THOMAS MUIR, younger of Hunters-hill. August 1793.[1]

THIS is one of the cases, the memory whereof never perisheth. History cannot let its injustice alone.

Mr. Muir was the eldest son of a shopkeeper in Glasgow, who was also a small proprietor in Lanarkshire. Muir himself had recently been a member of the Faculty of Advocates, but had had his name struck off the roll on the 6th of March 1793, on account of his having become an outlaw for not appearing at a former diet to answer for the same charge of sedition for which he was now brought to trial. Distinguished by no superiority of talent, he was, except in the imprudence of getting himself into the position of a political prisoner in those days, a man of ordinary sense. His zeal for the promotion of what he thought Liberty, but especially of parliamentary reform, was quite free of that wildness of temperament which sometimes inflames reformers into absurdity of project and dangerous ardour of disposition. Thousands and tens of thousands of men, whose wisdom and virtue are above being either questioned or sneered at, went fully as far as he did, not only in their opinions, but in the open expression of them. His general character was excellent, both as a citizen, and in all the relations of private life, all which, however, may certainly concur in a seditious man.

[1] *State Trials*, vol. xxiii. p. 117.

Besides all the objections to the trial, there were a few candid political opponents who, almost at the time, were startled by the poverty of the *evidence* of guilt ; while all candid political friends were loud in their protestations that there was no evidence of it whatever. This is all that one reviewing the proceedings has to care about. But independently of the defect of proof, it was the opinion of all who could be dispassionate then, and has come to be the prevalent opinion of nearly everybody now, that he was really innocent.

The crime meant to be charged was sedition. But instead of using this direct and simple term, the accusation is expanded and multiplied into at least four separate charges. These are thus set forth :—

" Whereas, etc., the *wickedly and feloniously exciting, by means of seditious speeches and harangues, a spirit of disloyalty and disaffection* to the king and the established government ; more especially when such speeches and harangues are addressed to meetings or convocations of persons brought together by no lawful authority, and uttered by one who is the chief instrument of calling together such meetings ; As ALSO the *wickedly and feloniously advising and exhorting persons to purchase and peruse seditious and wicked publications* and writings, calculated to produce a spirit of disloyalty and disaffection to the king and government ; As ALSO the wickedly and *feloniously distributing or circulating* any seditious writing or publication of the tendency aforesaid, or the causing to distribute, etc. ; As ALSO the wickedly and feloniously producing and reading aloud in a public meeting or convocation of persons a seditious and inflammatory writing tending to produce in the minds of the people a spirit of insurrection, etc., and the publicly recommending, in such meeting, such seditious and inflammatory writing, are, *all and each, or one or other of them, crimes*," etc.

There are here four separate offences—1. The actually exciting disaffection by seditious speeches. 2. The wickedly advising the purchase and perusal of seditious works. 3. The wickedly circulating these. 4. The wickedly reading them in public.

These charges were explained and supported by the following array of facts :—

1. That the prisoner had attended two meetings, one at Kirkintilloch and one at Milton, of a society for reform, and had there delivered speeches, "in which speeches the said Thomas Muir did seditiously endeavour to represent the government of this country as oppressive and tyrannical, and the legislative body of the State as venal and corrupt ; particularly by instituting a comparison between the pretended existing government of France and the constitution of Great Britain *with respect to the expenses* necessary for carrying on the functions of government, he endeavoured to vilify the monarchical part of the constitution, and to represent it as useless, *cumbersome, and expensive.*" 2. That he had exhorted and advised John Muir, late hatter, Thomas Wilson, barber, and John Barclay, residing in Cadder, to buy and read Paine's *Rights of Man.* 3. That he had circulated, by distributing the works of Thomas Paine, " A Declaration of Rights," etc., by the friends of reform in Paisley, " A Dialogue between the Governors and the Governed," and *The Patriot*, and, in particular, that he " did *deliver and put into the hands of* " Henry Freeland

a copy of Paine's works. 4. That he read an "Address from the Society of United Irishmen," etc., to a meeting of the Convention of Delegates of the Friends of the People, and had there expressed his approbation of its sentiments.

It is needless to discuss this very crowded libel in detail. The multiplicity of its charges give it the appearance of an indictment against a person's general conduct ; but though this tended to diminish the chance of unprejudiced trial, it was not illegal. And there was unquestionably much relevant matter in it. Indeed, except on two points, the whole of it was relevant; and even on these two, whatever the presiding judge might have done after the evidence was closed, I do not think that the court could have rejected the libel as irrelevant. These points relate to the Dialogue between the Governors and the Governed, and to the United Irishmen's Address. I can discover no sedition in either of these papers. But still, though the judges had been in the same condition, they could not have ventured to act upon this *prima facie* opinion in considering the relevancy ; because the prosecutor asserts, and offers to prove, that both papers are seditious, and were seditiously used. For example, he sets forth in his libel that the address was " of a most inflammatory and seditious tendency, falsely and insidiously representing the Irish and Scotch nations as in a state of downright oppression, and exciting the people rebelliously to rise up and oppose the Government." The jury being the judges of the import of the paper, it is scarcely possible for the court to act upon its own view, taken up before evidence or observation, so far as to decide that almost any paper is innocent. It is not in this stage of the proceedings that the protection due to a prisoner accused of circulating a writing which appears innocent, even after it has been tried by proof and by argument, can be given.

The court therefore was right in finding the libel relevant. But it might have been done calmly, and without going into other, and exciting, matter, and without prematurely committing themselves on the possible extent of punishment—a question which could not be raised, except by consent, till after conviction, and on which the prisoner had not uttered one word.

Nevertheless, *Lord Henderland*, after telling, so far, what the indictment charges the prisoner with, continues thus :—" It charges him particularly with attacking kingly government, a pillar on which the Constitution hinges, and which, if undermined or pulled down, must give rise to the most serious consequences. Had he observed the history of this country he would have seen the pernicious consequences of the crimes laid to his charge ; or had he observed the situation of a neighbouring country, he would have seen that similar crimes had, like an earthquake, swallowed up her best citizens, and endangered the lives and properties of all. Sorry shall I be, if of such a crime a man be found guilty. I hope the panel at the bar may be able to exculpate himself. But if the charges libelled on are found to be true, they, in my opinion, must be found relevant to infer the pains of law ; *and these pains include everything short of a capital punishment.*"

" *Lord Swinton* said he had never heard such an indictment read, and he did not believe that in the memory of man there ever had been a libel of a more dangerous tendency read in that court. *There was hardly a line of it which, in his opinion, did not amount to high treason;* and which, if proven, must infer the *highest punishment the law can inflict.*"

Lords Dunsinnan and Abercromby coincided with the two last "as to the dangerous tendency of the crimes charged, and that if proven the *highest* punishment should be inferred."

Lord Eskgrove was absent.

The *Lord Justice-Clerk* said—" The crime here charged is sedition, and that crime is aggravated according to its tendency; the *tendency here is* PLAINLY to overturn our present happy Constitution,—the happiest, the best, and the most noble constitution in the world, and I do not believe it possible to make a better. And the books which this gentleman HAS *circulated* have a tendency to make the people believe that the government of this country *is venal and corrupt,* and *thereby* to excite *rebellion.*" So he thought the libel relevant.

The prisoner had asked Erskine to be his counsel; and Erskine, as he explains in a letter quoted in the *State Trials* (vol. xxiii. p. 807), agreed; but only on this most reasonable condition, that "the conduct of the case should be left entirely to me." This Muir had the folly to decline, partly from vanity, partly from despair. "He declined my assistance (says Erskine) on these terms. He pleaded his own cause,—and you know the result."

The prisoner gave in a written defence, the substance of which he also stated verbally. He admitted that he had exerted every effort for parliamentary reform and popular instruction, but denied all accession to sedition. "I am accused of sedition. And yet I can prove by thousands of witnesses that I warned the people of the danger of that crime,—exhorted them to adopt none but measures which were constitutional, and entreated them to connect liberty with knowledge, and both with morality. This is what I can prove. If these be crimes, I am guilty."

The presiding judge asked what exculpatory proof he meant to adduce. To which the prisoner answered that he "had been accused of seditious harangues, and of circulating improper books, and that he intended to prove the reverse." Instantly upon this, "the court desired to know, AS IT MIGHT SAVE TROUBLE," whether he ADMITTED *that he had recommended the particular books libelled?* To which he answered in the negative; but that he had advised reading books on all sides of the question. I am not aware of any other case in which the court attempted to extract, or would have even taken, an admission on a particular point, essential to the trial, from a prisoner, and least of all from a prisoner without counsel, and who had lodged a special written defence, which, of course, must be understood to contain all the explanations or concessions he chose to commit himself to.

The Lord Justice-Clerk then proceeded to pick.

The second person he called was Captain John Inglis of Auchindinny, who (I believe) afterwards commanded a ship of the line, under Admiral Duncan, in the engagement with the Dutch off Camperdown,—a gruff, honest sailor. This person, though as violent a hater of anything that might be called popular liberty as any of his two classes of country gentlemen or of naval captains, had the candour to state "that he was a servant of Government; that he understood that Mr. Muir was accused of a crime against Government; and that he did not consider it as proper that Mr. Muir should be tried by a jury composed of servants of Government; *that his mind felt scrupulous,—laboured under much anxiety,* and he begged leave to decline being a juryman." Instead of giving the prisoner, who had no peremptory challenge, the benefit of this conscientious delicacy, " Captain Inglis was informed that there was no *impropriety* in his being a juryman, although belonging to the service of Government," and, therefore, he was *compelled* to serve. That is, the rejection of the consideration he had submitted was a virtual compulsion. Now there was no *illegality* in his serving, but the *impropriety* stands on a different ground. Is it not improper to compel a person to take his seat as a juror who honestly feels a bias against a prisoner? Is it not improper in a court to expose the administration of justice to suspicion by *unnecessarily forcing* a prisoner to have his case judged of by such a juror?[1]

The prisoner, on being asked, according to the usage at that period, whether he had any objection to state to any of the first five jurors selected by the Justice, submitted an objection, the repelling of

[1] See the case of a juror who was challenged because he was *not indifferent*, the only proof of this being that he himself declared in court that *he felt not indifferent*. (*State Trials*, vol. xiv. p. 1100, anno 1704.) The court plainly thought the challenge bad, *as a legal challenge*, though this was not formally decided. The matter was got rid of with more sense and humanity than by deciding it. The *Attorney-General* says— " My Lord, we leave it to Mr. Pinfold (the juror) himself." *Chief Justice.* —" *Then, ask Mr. Pinfold.*" The court having sanctioned the arrangement, the Attorney-General put it to Mr. Pinfold, who said, " My Lord, I desire to be excused." *Att.-Gen.*—" *Then*, we excuse you."

See also the Irish case of *Rowan.* (*State Trials*, vol. xxii. p. 1038.) The court refused to recognise the fact, that a juror held an office under the Crown, as a ground of challenge for *legal cause.* But the propriety, or judicial decency, of the court, *in its discretion*, compelling a man to serve in spite of his conscientious scruples, or encouraging him to disregard them, did not arise.

which has been strongly condemned by the whig party, and lamented by most discreet men of all parties.

A meeting of the "gentlemen" of the city and county of Edinburgh had been held in the Parliament House on the 7th of December 1792, "for considering the present state of the country." Their first resolution was a mere general declaration of loyalty to the king, and of attachment to the Constitution as it was. They then "Resolve and do declare that we will jointly and individually use our utmost endeavours to counteract all seditious attempts, and in particular *all associations for the publication or dispersion of seditious and inflammatory writings,* or tending to excite disorders and tumults within this part of the kingdom." This was followed by the usual corollaries about cooperating with the magistracy; and the whole resolutions were ordered to be left for signature at the Goldsmiths' Hall, and a committee was appointed to carry them into effect.

Though no associations or writings were specified, there neither was, nor could be, any doubt that all this was pointed chiefly at Paine's *Rights of Man,* the Friends of the People, and the publication of their proceedings. There was nothing else to give the Goldsmiths' Hall Association, as it was termed, an object or a meaning. Their resolution was intended and understood as a denunciation of the convention, and of all its members, and eminently of Paine's book, and of those who dispersed it.

Accordingly the committee published this explanation :—" The committee for superintending the subscriptions hereby notify that in case any of the members of *those associations whose conduct has contributed to the alarm which gives rise to the present measure, and who have improperly assumed the description of Friends of the People,* or other like appellations, shall subscribe the resolutions now on the table, their doing so shall be considered an express renunciation of all future connection with associations of the above description."

Some of the members of the Friends of the People, and *Muir among the rest,* professing to be as loyal and constitutional as those of the association, went and subscribed the resolutions, but with additions meant to exclude the presumption of their having abandoned their own principles. On this the Goldsmiths' Hall committee showed who and what they meant to condemn, by adding to the preceding statement the following notice :—" However, on the afternoon of Thursday the 13th inst., some persons, after reading the above notice, having subscribed their names, with the additions of designations which seemed to the committee to express a resolution of still continuing members of the associations alluded to in the motion, they conceived themselves called upon to order their names, with the additions, to be deleted from the subscription book."

Muir's name was one of those thus struck out.

These are the facts, so far as I can discover them. They are stated as having been more strong and pointed by the prisoner, who asserted, and therefore must be understood as having offered to prove, that the proceedings had a particular reference to *him,* and that the association had even offered a reward for the discovery of any person who had circulated *the very writings* of which the circulation was imputed to him. But this would make little, if any, material difference on the import of what was done, or of what was meant, as appearing from the published explanation of the committee.

Every one of the five jurors were members of the association—that is, they had all subscribed the resolutions, and were all represented, in the act of erasing Muir's name by the committee.

The prisoner objected that these five jurors had prejudged his case, because they had not merely decided the fact of his having circulated certain writings, and belonged to certain societies, but that these *were seditious,* and that he was accessory to them *wickedly.* They had publicly denounced him on the very matters now laid to his charge. And these were not matters resolving into *fact,* such as compassing the king's death or levying war, but matters of *opinion,* such as the innocence of a pamphlet, or of a person's circulation of it.

Blair's answer to this was:—" The panel is accused of forming associations contrary to the constitution, and he presumes to object to those gentlemen who formed associations in its defence. With equal propriety might he object to their Lordships on the bench ;—their Lordships had sworn to defend the Constitution."

Now it is clear that this answer at least will not do. For, in the *first* place, the prisoner was *not* accused of forming associations contrary to the Constitution. There is no such charge in the libel. In the *second* place, his objection was *not* that any other persons had associated in its defence. It is no answer at all.

The prisoner stated his objection again, viz., that the jurors, identified as they were with the association, had already concurred in public acts implying his conviction of the very matters now laid to his charge.

The court was not more successful in its refutation of the objection. All that the *Lord Justice-Clerk* said was "that if the objections of the panel were relevant, *it would extend far indeed*. It would go to every person *who had taken the oaths to Government.*" *Lord Henderland* rests his opinion upon this :—" These gentlemen entered into a society for a particular purpose, and had the right of judging of the qualification of their members. They did not think Mr. Muir or his friends proper members." None of the other judges spoke.

So the objection was repelled, and the prisoner was obliged to submit his case to fifteen men, of whom there was *not one* (as he said without contradiction, and as has always been understood) who was not a member of the association.

There may, perhaps, be occasions on which it is absolutely impossible to obtain a fair, or even a legal jury. Such failures of justice are natural in revolutions, and in all civil convulsions which inflame one-half of the community against the other. Ireland and the civil wars, and perhaps even the year 1746, could possibly furnish examples. Whenever this occurs it is not a case to be remedied by a court, whose duty consists in merely administering the ordinary rules, with the ordinary machinery of the law. If a court has no means of acting, it must cease to act till these means be supplied. It is never justifiable in violating the law in order that it may proceed to dispense the law. If an objection to one juryman, therefore, be well founded, it is no defence for a court, in repelling the objection, that, if sustained, "it would extend far indeed." On the contrary, if it be well founded, the wider its application there is the more injustice done if it be not enforced.

Whatever force there may be in the objection taken by the prisoner, it is clear that neither the prosecutor nor the court met it. It was a mere evasion to say that it applied equally to the judges, or to every person who had taken the oaths to Government. Such persons had sworn to maintain the king and the constitution; and this may be held to imply that they had sworn to check, and to punish the wicked dissemination of seditious publications. But they had not sworn that any particular pamphlet was seditious; nor had they expelled an individual from their society because he had seditiously circulated that pamphlet. It is no legal objection to a squire being a juror in a poaching case, that he has joined a game association in a general denunciation of poachers. But could he lawfully, or decently, sit on the trial of an individual poacher, for whose detection he and his association had advertised a reward? No case, however, can be analogous, in this matter, to one of sedition; because in other crimes there is seldom any doubt except as to the external facts; whereas in sedition, the essence of what is to be inquired into generally is, whether a writing surveyed in all its parts and bearings, be of a given tendency, and whether its contents were disseminated from a given motive. To conduct this inquiry, especially in seasons of ardent faction, a tone of candour, utterly inconsistent with previous denunciations on the very subject of trial, is indispensable.

Notwithstanding all this, however, the question

whether these men were under a *positive legal disqualification*, is not free from doubt. But in estimating the spirit in which these trials were conducted, this is perhaps not very material. For assuming them to have been legally admissible, the friends of justice must surely regret that they were not merely admitted, but that they were *purposely selected*. After the first five had been objected to, and after the Court was thus aware of the facts, the next five that were chosen were liable to the same objection. But it was again repelled; and the third five were also taken from the association. So that the prisoner was put, by the presiding judge, voluntarily, into the hands of a whole jury of marked zealots—zealous, no doubt, for the best of all things, the Constitution, but zealous also against the prisoner as a supposed violator of it. The fact that the whole fifteen were members of the association I take from the prisoner's offer to prove it—from the absence of any denial by the prosecutor, and from statements made to me by persons still surviving who knew the whole circumstances.

I do not know the number of the members of the association, nor that of the jurors of the district. But I am assured by those who lived in those scenes, that there were abundance of qualified jurymen to be got, without selecting the members of the association; and this indeed can scarcely be doubted, for that confederacy, though it stretched into the country, was chiefly composed of the gentry from Edinburgh and its vicinity. Yet without making the attempt—without a moment's pause—without any expression of regret—were these fifteen persons put into the jury-box—not only without any grave judicial admonition to lay aside the prepossessions in that sacred place, but with undisguised intimations that these prepossessions rather fitted them the better for the duty before them. This was a case of sedition; and they, they were told, were the loyal. They had sworn to defend the Constitution; and who could be so well qualified to dispose of a prisoner who had feloniously endangered it ?[1]

The empannelling of this jury was virtually the pronouncing of the verdict. To be thoroughly understood the evidence must be all read and studied; and it cannot be quoted here. But its general import is clear.

That part of the indictment which charges the prisoner with having *uttered seditious speeches* WAS SUPPORTED BY NO EVIDENCE WHATEVER. On the contrary, the result, not merely of all the proof in defence, but of much of that for the prosecution, was, that his addresses were all strongly constitutional; urging reform, but deprecating revolution— recommending union and petitions, but dissuading from violence—praising France, chiefly on account of the cheapness of its government, and predicting the success of its arms, but uniformly preferring our own monarchy for us. Accordingly all that the Lord Advocate had to say on this branch of the case, in addressing the jury, was, that, asserting the superior *economy* of France, and *anticipating her military triumphs*, tended to make the prisoner's

---

[1] Many of the accounts of these proceedings mention it as another indecency in Muir's trial that the Justice put Mr. Rochead of Inverleith, in connection with whom there was an objection to his Lordship himself, upon the jury. But this proceeds upon a mistake. Muir was tried in August 1793,—Margarot, who *first* stated the objection to the Justice, in January 1794; and he said that the facts had only occurred "*in the course of last week.*" The objection could not have been stated when Muir was tried—nor till five months afterwards.

hearers like that country, and, so far, diminished their attachment to Britain, and thus provoked revolution. " The evidence I chiefly rest upon here is Johnston and Freeland, particularly Johnston ; and no evidence can be more distinct, connected, and clear. He and Freeland agree that the panel *spoke of the success of the French arms.* With what motive could he discourse on such a subject, to weak, uninformed, illiterate people, *but to fulfil his seditious intentions ?* " " He said that *their (our) taxes would be less if they (we) were more equally represented,* and that from the flourishing state of France they could not bring their goods to market so cheap as Frenchmen. *What could possibly be more calculated to produce discontent and sedition ?* "

This is substantially the *whole* case upon the first charge, even as put by the prosecutor.

The other three charges all resolve into one,— the wicked circulation of seditious publications, either by direct distribution, or indirectly by recommending or by publicly reading them. If there be any difficulty as to the *inference* to be deduced from the facts, there can be very little, if any, with respect to the *facts* themselves.

The prosecutor examined twelve witnesses upon these charges.

Of these there are four, viz., Alexander Johnston, Robert Weddell, John Brown, and John Barclay, who not only do not establish anything against the prisoner, but all concur in a description of the general tendency of his public speeches and private observations, even at the two meetings libelled on as having taken place at Kirkintilloch and at Milton, which throws great discredit on the probability of these accusations. Not one of them states a single

circumstance which can be made to support or to aid
any one of these parts of the libel.　On the contrary,
they all swear that, though the prisoner was an
ardent parliamentary reformer, his conduct was
uniformly constitutional, and even loyal.　The Lord
Advocate insinuated to the jury that these witnesses,
being fellow-labourers in the same cause with the
panel, were bad judges of these matters.　But they
were all his witnesses; they were uncontradicted;
it was not opinions, but facts, that they stated; and,
except for these witnesses, there would have been
almost no palpable evidence upon this part of the
case at all.

Other three witnesses—Robert Forsyth, advocate, James Campbell, writer to the Signet, and
James Denholm, writer—were only examined as to
what had passed at the meeting of the convention,
where the prisoner was said, in the libel, not only to
have, " *with a wicked and seditious design,*" produced
and read the United Irishmen's Address, but to have
" *wickedly and feloniously* " proposed that it should
be honoured with the thanks of the meeting, and
did " *wickedly and feloniously express his approbation
of the sentiments* contained in the said paper."　The
evidence of these three gentlemen, who were all
present in the convention, was the *only* evidence
upon this point.[1]

Now Campbell swears that all that the prisoner
did was to *read* the address.　He adds, " that after
Mr. Muir read it, *he said nothing more;* but before
he read it, *he spoke of answering it.*"　All that Denholm says is that the prisoner *read* the address, and

---

[1] Forsyth, after long and great practice, and the compilation of many
books, is still (1848) attending the Court.　Campbell became a successful
Scotch solicitor in London.

when this was objected to, said "that *he saw no harm in it.*" Mr. Forsyth alone says that Muir not only read it, but, when it was objected to, "*defended the paper*, and *proposed that it should lie on the table, and be answered.*"

This is the whole proof on this charge, exclusive always of the general circumstances which may be supposed to indicate the prisoner's motives. And it will be observed, *first*, that on the fact of his expressing approbation of the paper, Forsyth is a solitary witness, not corroborated, but contradicted in so far as the other witnesses did *not* hear this, they having the same opportunity that he had. *Secondly*, that even this approbation would fall far short of the exaggerated statement in the libel. And, *thirdly*, that these witnesses saw nothing done by the prisoner that impressed them with the feeling of his having been actuated by any improper motive. Indeed, this could not be expected, because they seem to agree with Forsyth that, though the language was too strong, he "did not think it a seditious paper." Denholm and Forsyth both state that the Convention had no object beyond parliamentary reform, and this only by lawful means ; and that Muir's whole conduct and language there were constitutional and moderate. If the paper had been so glaringly criminal, that it could not even be read without guilt, this evidence would be sufficient proof of that accession to its publication which reading implies. But though that address, or anything of that tendency, however innocent, was sufficient to alarm at this period, as any rumour, however absurd, alarmed in the days of Titus Oates, it must ever appear ludicrous to the eye of reason, to apply such a principle to this paper, unless it is to be

dealt with quite differently from the ordinary effu-
sions of popular eloquence in seasons of excitement.

There only remain five witnesses, viz., Henry
Freeland, William Muir, John Muir, Thomas Wilson,
and Anne Fisher.

Freeland was the person as to whom the libel
states that the prisoner " did *deliver and put into his
hands*" a copy of Paine's works. Now, what the
witness (a weaver) swears is to this effect : he
was at the meeting at Kirkintilloch ; Muir spoke,
predicting success to liberty in France, urging
reform in the Commons, and recommending the
reading of books in general, but naming none
except Henry's *History of England.* One, Robert
Boyd, mentioned Paine's book, when the prisoner
said "*it was foreign to their* purpose." All this was
at the meeting. After it was over he was sent for by
the prisoner, and had an interview with him. *The
witness " asked Mr. Muir* if ever he had read Paine's
book, and *what he thought of it.* Mr. Muir said
that *it had rather a tendency to mislead weak minds.*
The witness said he wished to see it. Mr. Muir
told him that it was in his greatcoat pocket, which
was lying on a chair in the room. *The deponent
then took it out* of the greatcoat pocket. He was
surprised that Mr. Muir did *not* recommend it to
him, because everybody else spoke well of it, and
was surprised that Mr. Muir *said it had a bad
tendency.*" "When he took the book, the leaves
were not cut open. The witness added again, that
he mentioned the book first to Mr. Muir."

Telling a person who asks for a book that it is
in one's pocket, and letting him take it, may, in one
constructive sense, be delivering it into his hands ;
but these are the circumstances in which it was done.

The fact of Freeland taking the book from the prisoner's greatcoat pocket is confirmed by *William Muir*, who adds, however, that he himself had got one copy of the Political Progress (*not libelled on*), and *eleven copies of " The Patriot "* from the prisoner, who bade him "show them to a society he was in, which was a society for the purpose of purchasing and reading books."

John Muir says that the prisoner "asked him if he had seen Paine's book, and the witness answered he had not, but would be much obliged to Mr. Muir for the loan of it; that the panel answered *that he had not the book, but that he might buy it*, on which the girl was sent out to buy it." Plainly a commission given to her *by the witness*, who accordingly adds that he "gave the girl the money with her." He says further that he would have read Paine if he had it, independently of this conversation, but that he would not have purchased it, if he could have got it to borrow. There is no instigation, or circulation here, by the prisoner.

Thomas Wilson was the prisoner's barber. The statement in the libel, as to him and others, is, that the prisoner did "wickedly *advise and exhort* John Muir, senior, late hatter in Glasgow, *Thomas Wilson*, barber in Glasgow, and John Barclay, to read Paine's *Rights of Man.*" Muir and Barclay contradict this statement. For all that they say is, that they having, in a conversation with the prisoner, asked about Paine's book, he said that he had it not, but that as it was for sale, they might buy it; upon which, Muir says, the girl was sent out for it for him. He stated the fact of its being to be got in the shops, but did not exhort, or even advise, to purchase it. Wilson goes further. For he swears

" that Mr. Muir having asked the witness if he had bought Paine's works, and on being told he had not, he *advised* him to get a copy, as a barber's shop was a good place to read ; but he did not *press* him to buy it. *That the witness did not purchase a copy,*" " *and never recollects of its being mentioned on any other occasion.*"

Anne Fisher had been a domestic servant in the family of the prisoner's father. It is upon her evidence, and the fact of Freeland getting Paine out of the prisoner's pocket, that the case, in so far as it proceeded on evidence, has been commonly supposed to have gone.

She knew nothing that had occurred at any meeting or society, but was asked solely about the recommendations of seditious books by the prisoner *in his own family.* But though this was the real object of the examination, yet in order to show that, generally, her master's son was addicted to dangerous politics, she was made to disclose all she had ever heard him say or do, *in the privacy of his father's house.* Yet even with this somewhat discreditable aid, no one opinion or expression is fastened upon the prisoner, which he ought to have been exposed to any legal trouble for avowing and repeating publicly.

Her evidence as to the books certainly goes the full length of charging the prisoner with recommending, and even procuring seditious publications. "She saw a good many country people coming about Mr. Muir's father's shop ; that Mr. Muir has *frequently said to these country people that Mr. Paine's ' Rights of Man' was a very good book ;* that she has frequently bought this book for people in the shop, and *this was sometimes at the desire of Mr. Muir.*" " That she knows Mr. Muir's hairdresser,

Thomas Wilson, and *she has heard Mr. Muir advising him to buy Paine's 'Rights of Man,' and to keep them in his shop to enlighten the people,* as it confuted Mr. Burke entirely, and that a barber's shop was a good place for reading in."

It is essential towards a sound judgment on the case, that it should be determined what credit is due to this witness, whose accuracy and candour were openly distrusted at the time.

Two circumstances will be observed.

1. That she uses terms, and is familiar with matters, as to which persons in her station are always quite ignorant, and very awkward when they are obliged to try to speak about them. She knew the exact titles of the whole pamphlets in the libel, Paine's *Rights of Man,* first and second parts ; The Declaration of Rights ; *The Patriot ;* The Paisley Declaration. She had heard, and remembered the words Burke and Volney, and knew that the prisoner "FREQUENTLY READ FRENCH LAW-books ;" she not only "heard him read *to his mother, sisters, and others,*" but knew that it was "The Dialogue between the Governor and the Governed ;" and in describing the prisoner's political views, as gathered from his overheard conversation, she mentions "the Constitution"—its being kept "*clean from encroachments ;*" giving "*new councillors to the king ;*" that "*France was the most flourishing nation in the world, and had abolished tyranny, and got a free government,*" etc. Whether she was doing more than reciting a prepared part, I do not know ; but it has never fallen to my lot to be acquainted with any *servant maid* who, untutored, could have given such learned evidence.

2. That in many vital points she is pointedly contradicted. Thus she says, "that John Muir was *much pressed* upon by the panel to purchase the book;" whereas Muir swears that there was not even an invitation, beyond simply stating the fact that if he wanted it, he must send to a shop for it, because the prisoner had it not to give him. Then she says that the prisoner frequently stated to the country people that the *Rights of Man* was a very good book,—a statement repugnant to the whole of the rest of the evidence on this essential point. For it is clearly established that the general tendency of his advice was dissuasive of this work. His statement to Freeland was: "It had rather a tendency to mislead weak minds;" to John Brown, "there were some things in Paine which would hardly do, and which were not constitutional;" to William Cliddesdale, that "there were some things in Paine's book which might be good in the sight of some men, but many bad; and that, for his part, he thought his system was impracticable; that he reprobated liberty and equality, as it implied violation of property, and assigned (asserted?) that a division of property was a chimera, which never could exist." His uniform advice was to read everything. And the books which it is unquestionably established that he did specially recommend, though very like those that would occur to a reforming Scotch advocate, were not like those that would attract a Jacobin thirsting for British revolution on French principles,—Henry's *History of Britain* (see Robert Weddell), Blackstone's *Commentaries*, Erskine's *Institutes* (George Weddell), and *Locke* (John Brock).

If this domestic spy is to be *discredited*, the

instigation to purchase seditious books, or their actual dissemination, is reduced to the advice given to Wilson, and to allowing Freeland to take a copy of Paine from his greatcoat pocket. If she is to be *believed*, then there is his further praising Paine to the country people, and occasionally sending a servant to buy it for customers in his father's shop. Deducting all the topics of mere prejudice, such as his being a parliamentary reformer, etc., this is the substance of the case against him.

It is unnecessary to do more than refer generally to the evidence on his side. It consisted of the testimony of about eighteen witnesses, who all concur in describing the prisoner as a person of constitutional views, a friend to our present frame of government, though not to all its abuses—moderate in the measures he recommended—not given to recommend or circulate any such books as were named or alluded to in the libel ; and in particular distinctly adverse to Paine. These witnesses seem to have been, at least several of them, in respectable stations ; and the prosecutor had nothing to say against them, except that they were all reformers, and therefore probably as bad as their friend at the bar.

Assuming the fact of his having recommended seditious books, and abetted their circulation, to the utmost extent said to be proved, the question arises, whether there was evidence that this was done " *wickedly and feloniously*," *in order to* " *excite a spirit of disloyalty and disaffection* "?

In determining this, the following points deserve the serious reflection of any one who is anxious for truth alone. 1*st*. The possibility of accounting for his conduct by other motives,—particularly that of inconsiderate zeal, and the temptation, nearly irresistible with all parties, but especially with an honest, popular reformer, to annoy their opponents by the propagation of principles, which, though perfectly lawful, are too strong for their adoption, and the rejection of which exposes them to odium. 2d. The general character and tendency of his opinions and measures, which are sworn to by all the witnesses, except Fisher, to have been temperate and constitutional. 3d. The state of the times, which admitted of no neutrality, and of scarcely any moderation, and which, therefore, encouraged excess on all sides, and suggests the unfairness of applying ordinary standards to a crisis so extraordinary,—a crisis during which, under these standards, verdicts might be pronounced by any one-half of the nation against the other. 4th. The difficulty of reconciling the idea of his being really actuated by a wicked desire to produce disaffection, with the small amount of guilt that, according to any just estimate of the evidence, can be said to be proved. If disaffection had been his principle and his object, is it conceivable that, watched and scrutinised as all his proceedings were, so very little of this tendency should have been detected? A person truly inflamed with this passion in those days would have gloried in displaying it in all his words and in all his actions. 5th. The familiarity with which books said to be seditious, but particularly all Paine's works, were read, and discussed, and lent, and sold, at this time. The French Revolution, the principles it evoked, and the spirit of inquiry it excited, made such productions almost the daily bread of the middle ranks.[1]

---

[1] My father had only lately ceased to be Sheriff of Midlothian, and was now a Baron of Exchequer. He was in the heart of all these scenes,

Accordingly, on the 21st of May 1792, this food had been denounced by a royal proclamation, which, as usual, only whetted people's appetites. Even Anne Fisher had read Paine, " as she was curious to see what was in it;" and Freeland, on being asked why he had requested the prisoner to lend him a copy, says, " because I was informed that the king's proclamation was directed against it, and I was curious to see a book that was so much spoken of." It was sold in all the shops openly, before the proclamation, and cautiously after it; and Anne Fisher had never further to go for it than to the shop of Brash and Reid, two of the most respectable booksellers in Glasgow. Nothing can be more conclusive, on this point, than what his sense of justice seems to have compelled Mr. Wylde to obtrude upon the court. Wylde was an advocate, and soon after Professor of Civil Law; a man of learning and talent; and so hostile to French principles and objects, that he is now chiefly known by his writings against them, and by the melancholy fact that this Scottish Burke afterwards lost his reason from alarm at them. When Freeland was mentioning that the prisoner had answered his inquiry about Paine's book by referring him to his greatcoat pocket, Wylde, who was present *as a spectator* at the trial, slipped a bit of paper into the prisoner's

into which he entered with the utmost fervour on the Government side; and, owing to our near relationship with the Dundases, the principal actors on that side were constantly in our house. Notwithstanding all this, there was a Thomas Dundas, then lieutenant of the " Lapwing " frigate in Leith Roads, and since (I believe) an admiral, a fierce loyalist, who first introduced me, *under the Baron's eye*, to the beauties of Paine. His Majesty's lieutenant was set to read, and did read, *every word* of the *Rights of Man*, on successive evenings, *to the whole family*, and such friends as happened to be there. The work was very freely discussed, and produced some argument and much mirth, but no feeling that we were seditious. The Baron was present at each reading.

hand. This seems to have occasioned some disorder; when " Mr. Wylde rose, and in a most
candid and manly manner stated that the note he
had given to Mr. Muir was simply mentioning that
a similar requisition was made to him, and *he would
have lent Paine's book, if he had had it in his possession.*" No honourable man could have hesitated to
attest that whether dangerous or not, this anxiety
to have, and this willingness to show, that book,
though not always avowed, was nearly universal.

No doubt there were other circumstances, which,
though it can now only excite surprise that they
were even alluded to, contributed powerfully to the
prisoner's ruin. He had gone to France, like
thousands of others. A French passport was
found upon him, for he could not travel without
one. He had been outlawed, because it was inconvenient to stand his trial when first indicted. He
had not only the words *Ca Ira* on a seal, but he bid
Anne Fisher tell a street organist to play that tune
—a tune played not only on the streets, but, from
its beauty and celebrity, on many tory pianofortes.
He was a member of the British Convention, a folly
in which many wiser men joined. And he even
belonged to the Society of United Irishmen, along,
at that period, with many of the safest men in
Ireland.

These incidental and collateral circumstances
were well fitted to secure a conviction; but, plainly
operating chiefly by prejudice, they were precisely
the circumstances against which, though their introduction could not perhaps be prevented, a right
court would have tried to protect the accused.
There was no evidence of the constitution or objects
of the Society.

But the nature of this court's protection may be judged of from some of the slighter incidents of the trial.

The libel charged the panel with exhorting people to read "*various* seditious pamphlets and writings, *particularly*," etc.; and then it specifies certain times and places where *certain named* books were so dealt with by him. The prosecutor asked Robert Weddell "whether *Flower's* book had been recommended." The prisoner objected that *no such book was alluded to in the indictment, or produced,* and that he could not be expected to be prepared, without warning, on all the seditious books in the world. The prosecutor defended his question on the ground of the general charge; and this, even although there was nobody mentioned to whom Flower's book had been recommended, and though, from *its not being produced, it could not be shown to be seditious!* The Justice-Clerk was in favour of the question, on the ground that "*Wherever art and part (i.e.* accession) *is libelled, there can be no objection to the generality.* It is a proper question. *It has a tendency to establish the major proposition.*" If everything having a tendency to establish major propositions be admissible, there seems to be no use of minors. This was too strong even for the accuser. And accordingly "their Lordships were going to give their opinions on this point, when the Lord Advocate *gave up the question.*"

Anne Fisher, among other domestic disclosures, was mentioning that the prisoner had spoken disrespectfully of the Court of Justiciary, and its circuits. The prisoner objected that he was not charged with contumely to judges or courts, or with impugning the administration of justice. The

answer was, that he was accused of exciting disaffection to the Constitution, and that courts of
justice were a part of it. This reasoning was
satisfactory to the whole bench, which agreed
with Lord Swinton, " that it was the general proposition of the libel that the panel went about sowing sedition ; and as the courts of justice were parts
of the Constitution, he was of opinion that reflecting
on them was included in the general charge." Now
he was not accused of sedition *generally*. The
accusation was that, *by certain specified acts*, consisting of speeches, or of recommending, or of circulating, seditious books, he had excited " a spirit of
disloyalty and disaffection to the king and the
established government." Let it be assumed that
these last words do not merely denote the *general
fabric* of the Constitution, but all and each subordinate part (a construction, however, which would
make it sedition to condemn the institution of justices of the peace, or any atom of the civil establishment),—still there was no fact in the minor proposition under which the obloquy of courts could
be included. The only things which the prisoner is
charged with having calumniated are " the *Government of the country, as oppressive and tyrannical,*
and the legislature of the State as venal and corrupt,"
and there is no statement of his having traduced
even these except in public harangues. The only
plausible ground on which the question could be
defended was, that it was competent to refer to the
prisoner's general conduct and language in order to
prove seditiousness of intent. But how did disrespect, or hatred, of the Court of Justiciary, or of
any other subordinate institution, even tend to
establish, or to evince a desire to produce disaffec-

tion to the king or government, seditiously, by means of wicked speeches or books ? Being a dissenter, according to this, tends to infer, or to indicate, sedition ; for it implies hostility to the Church.

It is not unusual with parties, whether prisoners or not, to let looks or expressions, distrustful or contemptuous, of an adverse witness, whom they think unfair, escape them. Courts generally abstain from observing these, or check them gently. But when this prisoner was asked if he had any questions to put to Anne Fisher, and answered, "*I disdain to put a question to a witness of this description*," Lord *Henderland* declared "that had Mr. Muir not been standing at the bar as a panel, *he would have ordered him into prison for the expression*"*!* No doubt, if a stranger—not a party—had said this, it would have been intolerable ; but, in this view, the anger of the learned Lord was misplaced ; so that it was plainly an explosion against the prisoner.

The report of the Lord Advocate's address to the jury, though short, is sufficient to convey its general tone and substance. As read now, it does not bear the impression of much of that gentlemanlike, spirited amiableness for which he was so justly beloved. But great allowance must be made for the heat of a very excitable temperament ; and far more for the violence which he was surrounded by, and which he addressed. His speech is unworthy of notice either as argument, or as commentary upon evidence.

It was an appeal, and upon the poorest grounds, to the most injudicial passions of the jury and of the day. The prisoner was a "*demon of mischief*," —his conduct was "*diabolical*,"—he was "tainted from head to foot, and *as unworthy to live under the*

protection of the law as the meanest felon," and " I
declare that in *the range of my official capacity,*
among *the numerous list of offenders whom I have
brought to this bar,* if there has been any one whose
actions *particularly* pointed him out for prosecution,
—whose conduct appeared *the most* criminal—who
has betrayed the *greatest* appearance of guilt—this
is the man "!!! The age tolerated this. And
when his Lordship, most unwarrantably, tried to
influence the jury by telling them that one of the
prisoner's letters was addressed to the Rev. T.
Fyshe Palmer, " *a man who is indicted to stand trial
at Perth in the course of a few days, and whom most
of you know,"*—although there had not been a particle of evidence of any such indictment, the court
tolerated this.

The prisoner defended himself with great spirit,
no inconsiderable talent, and occasional eloquence.
His exposition of the injustice of deducing the
general imputation against him, of a design to produce disaffection, from the circumstance of his having, *at the very worst,* encouraged the purchase or
perusal of Paine's book twice or thrice, out of a
long course of free and watched conduct, and of the
party hostility to which the prosecution might be
much more easily ascribed, is extremely powerful.
" I smile at the charge of sedition. I know for
what I am brought to this bar." " I will give you
little trouble. I will prevent the lassitude of the
judges ; I will save you, the jury, from the wretched
mockery of a trial,—the sad necessity of condemning a man, when the cause of his condemnation must
be concealed, and cannot be explained." " What
has been my crime ? Not the lending to a relation
a copy of Mr. Paine's works ; not the giving away

to another a few copies of an innocent and constitutional publication; but for having dared to be, according to the measure of my feeble abilities, a strenuous and active advocate for an equal representation of the people, in the House of the people ; for having dared to attempt to accomplish a measure, by legal means, which was to diminish the weight of their taxes, and to put an end to the profusion of their blood."

The Lord Justice-Clerk *spoke* to the jury; but it would be an abuse of the term to say that he made a judicial *charge.*

After stating the question before them to be, whether, "on the whole of the proof, taken in connection, you think the panel guilty of sedition or not?" he says, "Now, in examining this question, there are two things which you should attend to, which require no proof. The first is, that the British constitution is the best in the world. For the truth of this, gentlemen, I need only appeal to your own feelings," etc. "The other circumstance, gentlemen, which you have to attend to is, the state of this country during last winter. There was a spirit of sedition and revolt going abroad," etc.

After this introduction, he proceeds to justify the prisoner's assertion that the advocacy of parliamentary reform was his real crime, by not only introducing that topic, but plainly telling the jury that THE PROMOTION OF THAT MEASURE, IN THE CIRCUMSTANCES, WAS OF ITSELF SEDITION. " I leave it for you to judge whether it was *perfectly innocent* or not, in Mr. Muir, at such a time, *to go about among ignorant country people,* and among the lower classes of people, *making them leave off their work,* and inducing them to believe that a reform was absolutely necessary to preserve their safety and their liberty, which, *had it not been for him, they would never have suspected to have been in danger.* You will keep this in remembrance, and judge, whether it appears to you, *as to me, to be* SEDITION."

He then saves himself and them the trouble of examining Paine's book by informing them that " Sedition in England, gentlemen, must be sedition here, and sedition here must be sedition in England ; and it would be right, in forming your opinion, to *have an eye upon the judgments of the English courts, who have condemned the publication of that work.*" *No such judgments had been given in evidence, or even quoted in argument from any report ;* and although they had, the seditious import of a writing was a matter of *fact*, which this jury were bound to have ascertained for themselves from a personal consideration of the actual writing.

The circumstance of the prisoner having made a temporary visit or retreat to France is thus dealt with :—" Mr. Muir has attempted to set up an apology for his non-appearance. But I would ask why, at such a crisis, he should go to France ? Independently of that, he should have recollected that an *Embassy to a foreign country without proper authority is a species of* REBELLION. *This proves* that he was *supposed* to have considerable influence with these *wretches*, the leading men there, and *establishes* his connection with them. And what characters are these ? *I never was an admirer of the French, but I can now only consider them as monsters of human nature.*"

He then almost closes with these words :— " Mr. Muir might have known that *no attention* could be paid (by parliament) to such a rabble (the petitioners for reform). *What right had they to representation ?* He could have told them that the parliament would never *listen* to their petition. How could they think of it ? *A Government in every country should be just like a corporation ; and, in this country, it is made up of the landed interest,* WHICH ALONE HAS A RIGHT TO BE REPRESENTED. As for the rabble, who have nothing but personal property, *what hold has the nation on them ?* What security for the payment of their taxes ? They may pack up all their property on their backs, and leave the country in the twinkling of an eye. But landed property cannot be removed."[1]

This was the language of a man holding the office, and professing to perform the duties, of a British judge, uttered at that stage of a criminal trial, for a political offence, at which the jury generally bends in reverence to the court, expecting their errors and their prejudices to be cleared away by the correct relevancy, the apt pertinence, the considerate candour of the bench.

The jury of course unanimously found the panel " guilty of the *crimes* libelled,"—that is, of the *whole* crimes.

It is common for the court to thank juries for their attendance and their attention. But in this case the Lord Justice-Clerk "informed them that the court *highly approved of the verdict* they had

[1] This language is so outrageous that it might be ascribed to inaccuracy or hostility in the reporter, were it not that it is the same in all the reports, even those by the most ardent party friends ; and though severely commented on in parliament, *was never disclaimed.* Howell says (vol. xxiii. p. 117, *note*), that he compiled his *State Trials* out of *all* the reports, which, however, did not differ materially, and were " *in no instance contradictory.*" The truth is, such passages were those by which their Lordships thought that they were best performing their duty, and they were always the most emphatically delivered.

given." (*State Trials,* vol. xxiii. p. 232.) In every political case this expression of sympathy had better be avoided, were it for no other reason than that it saves the judge from the risk of disclosing political zeal. Its tendency is shown in the trial of some of the Popish Plot prisoners, where Chief-Justice Scroggs told the jury, on their coming in with a verdict of guilty, "You have done, gentlemen, like very good subjects and very good Christians—that is to say, like very good Protestants; and now much good may their 30,000 masses do them." (*Phillipps,* vol. i. p. 353.)

Then came the great question whether the court could or would transport. But their Lordships soon settled this ; because without a moment's pause, instantly after the verdict was given in, they pronounced a sentence of transportation. Not a word was said by the prisoner. He was not invited or provoked to say a word, by being directly informed at this stage that this was the sentence in contemplation. He was silent till it was too late to speak.

So the first of these transportation precedents was obtained *without discussion.* For this reason, this is not the fittest occasion for examining the legality of such a sentence.

But even if lawful, transportation was certainly not necessary. The punishment was discretionary. Yet, exercising a discretion, the court sentenced a person in the rank of a gentleman, convicted of a first offence, and this offence sedition, to transportation *for fourteen years.* The judges have given their reasons to history.

Lord Henderland informed his brethren that " We have our choice of banishment, fine, whipping, imprisonment, and transportation. Banishment would be improper, as it would only be sending to another country a man dangerous to anywhere he might have the opportunity of exciting the same spirit of discontent, and sowing with a plentiful hand sedition. Fine would only fall upon his parents, who had already suffered too much by the forfeiture of his bond. Whipping was too severe and disgraceful, the more especially to a man who had borne his character and rank in life. And imprisonment, he considered, would be but a *temporary* punishment, when the criminal would be again let loose, and so again disturb the happiness of the people. There remains but one punishment in our law,—transportation. It was a duty he owed to his countrymen to pronounce it, in the situation in which he sat, as the punishment *due* to his crimes. I am sorry; it *wrings my very heart*," etc. The audience had given way, at the conclusion of the prisoner's address, to one of those expressions of applause which may be either accounted for from approbation of his principles, from sympathy with his fate, or from mere admiration of impressive speaking. His Lordship declared that he did not "seek to aggravate the offence committed by the panel by the misconduct of his deluded friends." If so, it was unfortunate that he should have mentioned an incident, certainly far from being unprecedented; for as he says that it "*proved to him that the spirit of sedition had not as yet subsided*," it may induce a reader of the trial to suspect that the severity of the punishment and this "indecent applause, unknown in that high court," had some connection.

Lord Swinton set out by laying it down that the offence of which the panel had been convicted was

" a crime of the most heinous kind, and *there was scarcely a distinction between it and high treason,* as, by the dissolution of the social compact, it made way for, so *it might be said to include every sort of crime, murder, robbery, rapine, fire-raising, in short, every species of wrong, public and private."* Then, after some melancholy stuff about the people and petitions, he proceeds in these incredible words :—
" With regard to the punishment, I observe that the maxim that the severity of punishment ought to be in proportion to the atrocity of the crime, *does not hold in our law;* for that with us punishment is not revenge nor atonement. *If punishment adequate to the crime of sedition were to be sought for, it could not be found in our law,* NOW THAT TORTURE IS HAPPILY ABOLISHED." Of course he who thought torture the only adequate punishment of sedition must be credited when he declares transportation to be not only a " mild," but *" the mildest,"* punishment for the offence ; for which opinion, moreover, he quotes an authority from the law of one of the Roman tyrants : " By the Roman law, which is held to be our common law, where there is no statute, the punishment was various, and transportation was among the mildest mentioned. Paulus, L. 38, Dig. de Pœnis, writes : ' Auctores seditionis et tumultus, populo concitato, pro qualitate dignitatis, AUT IN FURCAM TOLLUNTUR, AUT BESTIIS OBJICIUNTUR, AUT IN INSULAM DEPORTANTUR.' We have chosen the mildest of these punishments."

Lords Dunsinnan and *Abercromby* concurred ; the latter observing that " if anything could add to the improper nature of the panel's *defence,* it was his pretended mission to France, *and the happiness he expressed in the circle of acquaintance he had* there.

It was evident that his feelings did too much accord with the feelings of those *monsters*."

The rugged Braxfield had the hypocrisy to pretend to be *considerably affected* by the prisoner's situation; but cheers himself by reflecting that his crime " borders on *treason;* and perhaps it is owing to the humanity of the Lord Advocate that the panel had not to stand trial for his *life*." He then alludes to the applause of the preceding night, but, unlike Henderland, had no scruple in avowing that he made that circumstance, for which the prisoner was not responsible, and which happened after the evidence and his address was over, a ground of aggravation against him : " *This circumstance had no little weight with him when considering of the punishment Mr. Muir deserved*." After expressing his concurrence with his brethren that " transportation was the *proper* punishment for such a crime," he mentions that he was only troubled by a solitary doubt—" he only hesitated whether it should be for *life,* or for the term of fourteen years."[1]

Nothing short of the concurring evidence of all the reports could make history believe that such speeches could have been delivered from any supreme bench in Great Britain at the close of the

[1] Lord Dreghorn, one of the civil judges, attests that one of the criminal ones told him at the time that the Justiciary judges thought Muir's " crime so great, that they might HAVE ADJUDGED HIS SERVICES without being over-severe"!!! that is, they might, besides transporting, have made a *slave* of him ; for to adjudge a convict's services was to give him up by compulsion to a taskmaster. Such a thing was certainly competent, *if transportation was competent*, under the 25th of Geo. III. cap. 46, and was sometimes done when the transportation could not otherwise be carried into effect. But these judges (according to Dreghorn, or his informer) saw no over-severity in doing it to a gentleman convicted of sedition ! The truth of Dreghorn's remark, that this would have been " a most *democratic* determination," had not occurred to them. (Dreghorn's *Works*, vol. ii. p. 65.)

eighteenth century. But history must recollect that parliament was so prostrate at this period, as not only to let the judges remain unimpeached, but to protect and to praise them for the uttering of these very speeches.

Muir was sent to Botany Bay, which, and the voyage to which, were very different in 1793 from what they are now. He escaped, and died in France.

The recent edition (1849) of Allen's *Inquiry into the Prerogative* contains a "biographical notice of the author," by Sir James Gibson-Craig, who not only lived, but acted, in these scenes, and is still alive, in the vigorous possession of his memory and of all his mental powers. This notice contains the following statement relative to Muir's case :—" He was found guilty, and sentenced to transportation. All were thunderstruck with the extreme severity of the sentence, and none more than the jury. They met immediately after the court rose, and unanimously expressed their opinion that the sentence was beyond all measure severe. They thought Muir's guilt had been so trivial that a *few weeks' imprisonment* would be a sufficient punishment, and they resolved to prepare a petition to the court, and to meet next day for the purpose of signing it. But when they met, Mr. Innes of Stow produced a letter he had received, threatening to assassinate him for his concurring in the verdict of guilty—on which the jury separated, considering it impossible for them to interfere. Of this I was informed by my uncle, Mr. Balfour of Pilrig, who had been clerk to the jury."

This fit of squeamishness seems to have affected no subsequent juries.

About thirty-five years after the trial, I asked one of the jurymen how, on looking back, he could account to himself for his conduct. His answer was, " *We were all mad.*" A poor apology for a jury; none whatever for a court.

In the recently published memoirs of his own life, Sir Samuel Romilly says, in a letter from Edinburgh to Dumont: "I have been pleased with everything I have seen in Edinburgh, and about it, except the persons of the women—I mean those of the lower ranks of life—which are certainly very plain; and the administration of justice, which I think detestable. I am not surprised that you have been shocked at the account you have read of Muir's trial. You would have been much more shocked if you had been present at it, *as I was.* I remained there both days, and think I collected, in the course of them, *some interesting materials.*"

I dare swear he did !

And in the still more recently published memoirs of Bentham, there is a letter to Bentham from Romilly, dated "Edinburgh, 2d September 1793," in which there is this passage : "I am passing my time here very pleasantly; principally, however, in a society which you would not at all relish —lawyers. Indeed, I doubt whether this would be a very safe country, just at this moment, for you to be found in; for *I heard* the judges of the Justiciary Court, the other day, declare, with great solemnity, upon the trial of Mr. Muir, *that to say the courts of justice needed reform was seditious,* highly criminal, and betrayed a most hostile disposition towards the Constitution, of which the courts of justice form a most important part." [1]

[1] Vol. i. of the Memoirs, and xix. of the Works, p. 295.

VIII.—Case of THOMAS FYSHE PALMER, September 1793.[1]

MR. PALMER was born and educated in England.
After obtaining a Fellowship in Queens' College,
Cambridge, and a curacy in Surrey, some conscientious scruples about the Trinity made him forego
very favourable pro'spects in the Church of England, and descend to the position of an Unitarian
preacher, in which capacity he unfortunately set
foot in Scotland. A scholar, a gentleman by family
and manners, and of the purest moral character, he
was highly esteemed by an extensive class of friends.

His trial took place at the Perth Circuit in September 1793, before Lords Eskgrove and Abercromby. The prosecution was conducted by Mr.
John Burnett, assisted by Mr. Allan Maconochie;
the defence by Mr. John Clerk and Mr. John
Haggart.

Burnett I have already mentioned. Mr. Maconochie was raised to the bench in March 1796,
under the title of Meadowbank, the name of his
estate in Midlothian; a singular person—able and
learned—his ability greater than his soundness, and
his learning more varied than accurate; a wretched
speaker; and the whole man, notwithstanding the
force and richness of his powers, made somewhat
ridiculous by a constant display of metaphysical
and argumentative ingenuity, and a strange manner

and appearance. Clerk (afterwards Lord Eldin) was just beginning the long, successful, and honourable professional career which lay before him. Eloquence was not his field; but talent, boldness, and freedom of political principle, were. His opinions and conduct were so daring, that though certainly never violating the law, he was one of those (not a small class) whose not being sent to expire in New South Wales was owing solely to his not being accused of what was then called sedition, which he committed every hour. Haggart's presence was a disgrace to any cause. Without any power except that of vulgar impudence, the lowness of his character stained every scene he acted in, and made degradation his natural position. His ascent, however, to that zenith of disreputableness, which he afterwards reached, was only commencing at this time.

Two technical objections were stated in bar of the panel's being obliged to plead. These were, that the word Fyshe in his name was wrongly spelt in the indictment, and that in the copy of the libel served upon him there was a misrecital of the word *your* for *our*. Both were properly repelled.

The indictment contained two charges : *First*, That the prisoner had wickedly and feloniously *written or printed*, and *Secondly*, that he had wickedly and feloniously *circulated* a seditious writing. The words are, that whereas, etc., " the wickedly and feloniously *writing or printing*, or the causing to be written and printed, any seditious or inflammatory writing, *calculated to produce a spirit of discontent* in the minds of the people against the present happy constitution and government of this country, *and to rouse them up to acts of outrage and*

violence BY *insidiously calumniating and misrepresenting the measures of Government, and falsely and
seditiously justifying and vindicating the enemies of
our country with whom we are at open war :* As ALSO
the wickedly and feloniously *distributing and circulating any* seditious or inflammatory writing, are
crimes," etc.

The statement in support of both of these
charges comes just to this—that the prisoner's having
composed and written an address to their fellow-
citizens, by the Friends of Liberty at Dundee, afterwards got it printed and distributed, which address
was "*of a wicked and seditious* import," and
"*seditious and inflammatory.*" It is not said to be
calculated to produce the particular spirit of discontent *specified in the first branch of the major proposition, nor by the means* there described. The
address, upon the import of which the whole case
turned, was in the following terms :—

"Friends and fellow-citizens ! You who by your
loyal and steady conduct in these days of adversity,
have shown that you are worthy of at least some
small portion of liberty, unto you we address our
language and tell our fears.

"In spite of the virulent scandal, or malicious
efforts, of the people's enemies, we will tell you
whole truths. They are of a kind to alarm and
arouse you out of your lethargy. That portion of
liberty you once enjoyed is fast setting, we fear, in
the darkness of despotism and tyranny. Too soon,
perhaps, you, who were the world's envy, as possessed of some small portion of liberty, will be sunk
in the depths of slavery and misery, if you prevent
it not by your well-timed efforts.

"Is not every new day adding a new link to our

chains ? Is not the executive branch daily seizing
new, unprecedented, and unwarrantable powers ?
Has not the House of Commons (your only security
from the evils of tyranny and aristocracy) joined
the coalition against you? Is the election of its
members either free, fair, or frequent ? Is not its
independence gone, while it is made up of pensioners
and placemen ?

" We have done our duty, and are determined
to keep our posts ; ever ready to assert our just
rights and privileges as men, the chief of which we
account the right of universal suffrage in the choice
of those who serve in the Commons House of
Parliament, and a frequent renewal of such power.

" We are not deterred or disappointed by the
decision of the House of Commons concerning our
petition. It is a question we did not expect
(though founded on truth and reason) would be
supported by superior numbers. Far from being
discouraged, we are more and more convinced that
nothing can save this nation from ruin, and give to
the people that happiness which they have a right
to look for under Government, but a reform in the
House of Commons, founded upon the eternal basis
of justice, fair, free, and equal.

" Fellow-citizens ! the time is now come, when
you must either gather round the fabric of liberty
to support it, or, to your eternal infamy, let it fall
to the ground, to rise no more, hurling along with
it everything that is valuable and dear to an
enlightened people.

" You are plunged into a war by a wicked
ministry and a compliant parliament, who seem
careless and unconcerned for your interest, the end
and design of which is almost too horrid to relate

—the destruction of a whole people merely because they will be free.

"By it your commerce is sore cramped and almost ruined. Thousands and tens of thousands of your fellow-citizens, from being in a state of prosperity, are reduced to a state of poverty, misery, and wretchedness. A list of bankruptcies unequalled in any former times, forms a part of the retinue of this quixotic expedition; your taxes, great and burdensome as they are, must soon be greatly augmented; your treasure is wasting fast; the blood of your brethren is pouring out; and all this to form chains for a free people, and eventually to rivet them for ever on yourselves.

"To the loss of the invaluable rights and privileges which your fathers enjoyed, we impute this barbarous and calamitous war, our ruinous and still growing taxation, and all the miseries and oppressions which we labour under.

"Fellow-citizens! the friends of liberty call upon you, by all that is dear and worthy of possessing as men—by your oppressions, by the miseries and sorrows of your suffering brethren, by all that you dread, by the sweet remembrance of your patriotic ancestors, and by all that your posterity have a right to expect from you—to join us in our exertions for the preservation of our perishing liberty, and the recovery of our long-lost rights."

The prisoner objected to the relevancy of the indictment; but before stating the objection he took, I may repeat another which it occurs to me that he might have taken.

It relates to the first charge, which is for "WRITING OR PRINTING" a seditious libel of *a very particular description*. It is not for writing or printing *any* seditious libel, but solely for writing or printing a seditious libel, calculated to produce a *specified effect*, and this solely by *specified means*. It is a libel calculated "*to produce a spirit of discontent in the minds of the people, etc., and to rouse them up to acts of outrage and violence.*" And this result is to be accomplished "*by insidiously calumniating and misrepresenting the measures of Government, and falsely and seditiously justifying and vindicating the enemies of our country.*"

Now, in the *first* place, I have ventured (in Muir's case) to doubt, whether the mere *writing or printing* anything be indictable. The *publication* forms the subject of the second charge ; and there is nothing in the first one except the writing or printing. Now, may not a person who does not publish, but chooses to keep his compositions to himself, amuse himself by writing or printing almost anything he pleases ? There is no sedition surely in one's desk.

In the *second* place, assuming the relevancy of a charge for mere writing or printing, there is no statement in the minor proposition fitted, or apparently even intended, to support this part of the charge. It is said, generally, that the address is "*seditious and inflammatory,*" and "*of a wicked and seditious import ;*" but it is not set forth that it is calculated *to produce discontent, and to rouse the people to outrage*, and, of course, it is not set forth that these consequences were to be produced by its calumniating Britain or praising France. It may possibly be true that the writing really was calculated to effect these results, and by these means. But, according to the correct structure of our indictments, this is not enough. The prosecutor is bound *to make his averment*. When he charges murder, it is not sufficient that he first announces this to be a crime in the major proposition, and then narrates facts, in the minor, from which its commission may, or must, be inferred. He must say, in words, that, by these acts, the deceased was murdered. Here he first puts a peculiar and precise accumulation of qualities into the description given in his major proposition of the exact offence he intends to charge; and then, in support of this charge, he merely quotes a writing without averring that it exhibits, or proves, any one of these qualities.

I do not at present see a good answer to this objection; though, perhaps, there is one. And it is not unimportant. Because if this matter be held to be excluded, a great portion of what the prosecutor plainly thought the best part of his argument on the general merits, becomes irrelevant.

The objection which the prisoner's counsel did take was, that the address was not seditious. In order to show this, Mr. Haggart went into a full and minute examination, critical and political, of the whole address, paragraph by paragraph, and almost word by word—interpreting, glossing, and colouring it all, so as to make it suit the defence; after which, Mr. Maconochie performed the same operation on behalf of the prosecution.

It seems to me to be clear that there was sedition in the paper, though not nearly so much as was said. The Court, therefore, was right in repelling the objection, but it went on a wrong ground.

The proper principle to have acted upon was, that so long as the case stood in this position—that the prosecutor *ascribed* sedition to the paper, and a seditious intention to its publisher, and the prisoner denied that these were *facts*,—there was nothing to warrant the Court in interposing itself between the jury and the parties, by deciding disputed matter of fact—that is, putting its own construction on the contested documents, and thus deciding the fact, especially when the soundness of the prosecutor's imputations can never be properly judged of without his being let in to a full exposition of his evidence and argument. Unless, therefore, the prosecutor's construction be *palpably* groundless — so plainly groundless as to be *absurd*—a court ought never to prevent the case from going to the jury in the first instance. It is enough to warrant its letting the case proceed, that there is nothing *obviously ridiculous* in the charge. And it is only by adopting this principle that the evil can be avoided, of juries beginning their acquaintance with the case under the prepossession that the court is clear of the seditious import of the writing. All that they need know is, that the court thinks this a matter *not unfit for their consideration.*

But this was by no means the ground taken up by the judges here, nor in any of these trials. On the contrary, their Lordships seem always to have been afraid of trusting the jury, without a series of preliminary expositions of the atrocity of the case they were to try. It appears as if their object had been, under the form of delivering opinions on the relevancy of the charge, to impress the jury with a feeling that the charge was well founded. And accordingly they uniformly decide that the language or the conduct impugned was clearly seditious, not merely *as stated*, but *in fact ;* and also, that it could obviously have been employed solely from a seditious motive.

Thus *Lord Eskgrove* goes over the whole paper, sentence by sentence, with a running commentary of premature imputation and one-sided construction, exactly as he might have done after conviction. His criticisms are unworthy of being examined. The result to which they led him contained the greatest sum of extravagance which could possibly have been extracted from the occasion. It was not merely that there was sedition in the paper, but that it was *all* seditious. " I am of opinion that it (the charge) is perfectly relevant ; that there is no occasion to separate it, and to say, This is seditious, or that is seditious ; but that the *whole* of it is seditious ; and *I believe there is scarce anything in it but what is seditious.*" Indeed in a previous part of his opinion he seems to acquiesce in the statement of the prosecutor that "it approaches very near to *treason.*" The reasoning, or rather the ignorant and unjust assertions, by which he arrives at these conclusions, are truly humiliating. Commonplace abuse of the French—idle encomiums on the admitted excellencies of our own Constitution—in order that these may be regularly followed by horror of reformers, and an inversion of the principle of always giving an unconvicted prisoner the benefit of the mildest possible interpretation—these, with vulgar diction and the profoundest political ignorance, form the substance of this judicial display.

The judicial condition of his Lordship's mind indeed was disclosed in a few collateral incidents, which cannot be passed over. The prisoner's counsel exemplified the licence of expression and of discussion tolerated in this country by quoting a number of strong passages from the speeches and writings of great men ; and among others mentioned Burke's statement, that "kings were naturally lovers of low company." On which Eskgrove observed, " *Then low company should like kings* "—a remark which no one would have objected to if it had been meant as a joke, especially as it would have been one of his Lordship's very few efforts in that line. But it was intended, and spoken, as an insult to the prisoner. He had nothing to do at this stage of the proceedings with the prisoner's personal history, or with the facts of the case. Yet he could not help anticipating the evidence, by observing, " All nations are liable to have *bad men* among them ; but I own I am little obliged to strangers who, coming here *under the pretence* of preaching what they call the Gospel, should preach sedition among the people." In the same style he goes out of his way to sneer at the idea of parliamentary reform ; and because Haggart had said something in favour of a qualification of £100 Scotch yearly, in land, and the address happened to be *dated* from a Berean meeting-house, though the Bereans had nothing to do with it, his Lordship does not feel it beneath his dignity to insult this sect. " I was surprised to hear my friend Mr. Haggart, at the bar, in place of an universal suffrage of the people, limit the right of voting to £100 Scots a year. *I rather suspect there is not one in all the Berean congregation who could boast of so much property.* This society therefore need not distress themselves about a suffrage which even Mr. Haggart does not seem disposed to allow them." In order to show how Mr. Palmer was accustomed to spell his name, the title-page of an Unitarian publication of his was referred to. Instead of simply saying that this could not be admitted as evidence of the fact in dispute, his Lordship could not omit

the opportunity of rousing what was then the most
easily excited of all prejudices among the people of
Scotland, by mentioning the book as " this publication of his, *denying the Divinity of Jesus Christ.*"
Palmer had no more to do with the Bereans or their
place of meeting than his Lordship had ; yet he
blames the prisoner as a stranger who first comes
here to preach, and then, "instead of doing that,
turns *his meeting-house into a house of sedition,* for it
states it as dated from the Dundee Berean Meeting-
house." But indeed I suppose it may be taken for
certain that his Lordship did not know the difference between the Bereans and the Unitarians, and
in all probability took them to be the same.

Lord Abercromby probably did not intend to
adopt all these judicial episodes ; but on the proper
matter of the relevancy he not only declares his
concurrence, but adds, " I believe there is not within these walls one man of common understanding—
whose mind is not warped by some strange bias, by
some unaccountable prejudice—who does not concur
in the opinion given by your Lordship."

The relevancy was accordingly sustained.

The forty-five jurors were nearly equally divided
into those who appear on the face of the list as
lairds, and those who do not. As I read it, there
were twenty-two of the former class, and twenty-
three of the latter. Of the fifteen, as selected by
the judge, eleven were lairds, two merchants, and
two law-agents.

It is needless to analyse the evidence, because
its true result admits of no doubt. The prisoner
was not the person who suggested that there should
be an address, nor was he the original composer of
this one, which was written by George Mealmaker,

a weaver. But he was consulted about its terms, and advised alterations, to a sufficient extent to make him be fairly held accessory even to the composition. Though he saw nothing criminal in it, prudence made him fear that its publication might, in these times, bring them into trouble, and therefore he discouraged its circulation. But being outvoted as to this by the Society, he undertook, and performed the task of getting it printed and distributed.

The facts, of accession to the composition, and of publication, being established, the question arose, Was he guilty of the charge? And this, as usual, depended on the two other questions—Was the address seditious? and, Was it published from a seditious intention?

Burnett's address to the jury for the prosecution was the plain, commonplace discourse of an Advocate-Depute trying to make out his case; with no original remark, no able view; regularly admitting the constitutional privileges of free statement, even of supposed grievances, free discussion, and a free press; and then, according to use and wont, as regularly imposing limits upon each of these, which must make its exercise impracticable or useless; and imputing to each sentence the meaning and the dangers then ascribed by his party to every expression of popular opinion. There was nothing that any person in his position might have more safely relied upon than the prejudices of the jury, and therefore it was very unnecessary to inflame them. But parties who require the aid of such feelings, generally think it right to give them the air of judicial sanction. Burnett therefore tells them that sedition, "when all the evils attending upon

popular *fury and insurrection* are considered, I am
confident all of you will join me in thinking to be
one (an offence) which *stands* FOREMOST *in the list
of human crimes."* This being laid down, the consequence follows. " He, therefore, that is the
author and instrument of sedition, *in whatever way
it is applied,* ought rightly and properly to be considered as the author and the committer of *all those
crimes that sedition naturally begets;* and he that
attempts to commit it is guilty of an offence of
that *atrocious* nature which every civilised state in
Europe must, and does, punish with the *utmost*
severity." So, because sedition begets insurrection,
and insurrection treason, he who is guilty of sedition
should be punished as a traitor; just as intoxication
should be punished as assault or murder, because it
is the daily parent of both. This poor trash might
easily be forgiven. But it is more difficult to
excuse his taking up Eskgrove's hint, and repeating
an intolerant and disgraceful allusion to the religious opinions of the prisoner. " Nor will it turn
out to be a circumstance in his favour that he is
by profession a clergyman; *but a clergyman of that
description whose principles are as hostile to the
religion of his country as to the established Government of it. He does not, however, stand at your bar
for his religious principles."* Why then introduce
them?

Clerk's speech for the prisoner was admirable,
but probably not the better of having the report of
it corrected by the speaker himself, at the distance
of nearly twenty-five years, which Howell says was
done for him—an operation which generally impairs
the naturalness and freshness of a speech, and sub-
stitutes in its place the regular structure of a

written discourse. However, the excellencies of this argument are substantially preserved. It is able, manly, and direct, full of constitutional views, and applies less ingenuity to the examination of the address than fairness and common sense. He is particularly successful in his exposition not merely of the right of stating and remedying supposed grievances, but of the collateral excesses which often accompany the practical exercise of this right, and which must be mildly dealt with.

Lord Abercromby's charge, upon the whole, was fair and judicial. Its only defect, perhaps, was, that in explaining to the jury the exact points they had to consider, he did not lay sufficient stress upon the necessity of their being convinced, before they could convict of the wickedness of the prisoner's intention. On the contrary, he sometimes directs them that all they have to make up their minds upon is, whether the prisoner published the address, and whether it was seditious. However, there are other passages, particularly towards the close, which do convey the idea (though certainly not with due plainness) that they must moreover be satisfied that the writing was not sincerely *meant* for the purpose of procuring a petition for reform, to which, and not to a desire for popular disaffection or outrage, it had been ascribed. The defect of the whole summing up is, that it never once warns the jury of the duty of candour in appreciating the conduct, and particularly in appreciating the *motives* of others; nor attempts to guard them against mistaking their own fears and prepossessions for evidence and sense. The horrors of the French revolution, though already impressed so painfully on their imaginations as to affect their reason, are emphatically recalled to their recollections; while the apologies for men of certain temperaments being seduced by the splendour of its dawn, and by the contagiousness of free opinions, into an admiration of this revolution, and into a consequent intensity of ardour in pursuit of reform, are never so much as alluded to. And his unfitness to preside over any trial for sedition is disclosed in one unfortunate part of his charge, in which he copies Braxfield in denouncing every effort in favour of universal suffrage as, in itself, illegal. " Gentlemen, the right of universal suffrage is a right which the subjects of this country never enjoyed; and were they to enjoy it, they would not long enjoy either liberty or a free constitution. *You will therefore consider whether telling the people that they have a just right to what would unquestionably be tantamount to a total subversion of this Constitution is such a writing as any person is entitled to compose, to print, and to publish.*" He ought surely to have known that the Constitution, aware what benefits it had derived, and was constantly deriving, from the free suggestion of improvements, tolerates the honest exposure of every supposed defect, and the honest maintenance of every supposed remedy ; and that, therefore, no judge is warranted in obtruding his particular political opinions upon juries, as indisputably and eternally sound ; or to claim deference to these, in opposition to the opinions of equally wise and good men. I can never help wondering what these tory judges, who so constantly introduce their political principles, would have said, if there had been a whig judge on the bench who imitated their example.

Although putting everything to the jury in the

form of only instructing them to consider it, his charge was strongly against the prisoner, both on the import of the paper and on the guilt of his design.

The truth of the case appears to me to be neither entirely with the one party, nor entirely with the other. That part of the address which asks, and virtually asserts the affirmative—"Is not the executive branch daily seizing new, unprecedented, and unwarrantable powers? Has not the House of Commons (your only security from the evils of tyranny and aristocracy) joined the coalition against you?"—is seditious. It imputes a criminal usurpation of authority to the executive; and a criminal accession to this usurpation to the popular branch of the Legislature; and these it states as *facts*. This was sedition—if it was seditiously done. The passage also was seditious where it is said that "that portion of your liberty you once enjoyed is fast setting, we fear, in the darkness of despotism and tyranny." The same must be said of the passage where the people are said to be "plunged into a war by a *wicked ministry and a compliant parliament*;" and of the statement that every day is "adding a new *link to your chains.*"

Undeterred by the declarations of *Maconochie* and *Abercromby*, who both defy any person "in the use of reason and common sense" to doubt that the *whole* paper is seditious, I profess that, except in these passages, I can discover little, if any, sedition in it.

The people,—the lowest of the people,—the very beggars, as Clerk said,—have a right to form and to express their honest opinions on the defects of all our political institutions, and not only to sug-

gest, but to urge, the adoption of what they think
the proper remedies. They cannot, either with
wilful falsehood, or with what a court must presume
to be falsehood, ascribe such guilt to authority as
necessarily deprives it of respect and due obedience ;
and, therefore, all assertions of perfidy by either
branch of the Legislature in the exercise of their
constitutional functions, and especially every insult
to the Sovereign, are criminal. But it is not
criminal to believe that any institution—even the
Legislature, collectively, or in its separate branches,
is so constituted as that it has certain injurious
tendencies ; or to explain what these are, how these
tendencies arise, and how their causes are to be
removed. The constitution of parliament, in particular, is not only a legitimate subject of discussion,
but is the subject that has been, and is, and, so long
as we are free, will continue to be, more freely
discussed than any other public matter. To hold
that the House of Commons is ill constituted is
the right of every one ; and he who thinks that the
defects of its constitution lead to extravagant taxation, unnecessary wars, and a disregard of popular
privileges, and that nothing can correct all this
except a more extensive suffrage, though it should
even be what is called universal, is entitled to say
so, nor is he bound to say it timidly, and as if conscious of guilt, and terrified for an indictment. He
may say it plainly, directly, and fearlessly, and with
all the vehemence that honest men are in the habit
of using when urging important opinions. If the
sentiment be lawful, the law troubles itself very
little about the rhetoric.

Burnett was quite correct in saying that the
paper " is written in a style which marks the school

from which it came ; it is *violent, hyperbolical, and declamatory.*" But violence, hyperbole, and declamation are not sedition. Criticisms, however, on detached parts of any writing, which must be judged of as a whole, are seldom of much use. And taking this address as a whole, I think that Clerk's description of the school it belonged to was just. "The language employed by the promoters of reform was pointed, zealous, acrimonious ; imputing corruption, in plain terms, to the system of which they demanded a reform ; but it was the language of controversy, not the language of sedition. It was the language of freemen, who had a right to complain of their grievances, for the purpose of having them redressed. It was the language of discontent, and it had a tendency to spread the discontent. But still it was not seditious, nor in any other respect illegal. He who speaks or writes to raise [1] discontent or disturbance, or to bring the Government into hatred or contempt, is seditious ; and he whose speeches or writings *have that tendency* is seditious, *unless* in either case the speaker or writer *has a legal object in view.* But *non injuriam facit qui jure suo utitur*—men may have *a right* to complain, and to complain loudly, though their complaints should be discreditable to Government. If they, *bona fide*, seek reform, or anything else relating to their rights, whether public or private, they do no wrong, though their exertions in defence of those rights which they still possess, or the recovery of those of which they have been unjustly deprived for a time, should raise disturbances or discontents." This (though a most uncandid construction was afterwards put by the

---

[1] He means, he who does this *merely in order* to raise discontent ; that being his *design*.

court on the argument) is the true, and to a certain extent a satisfactory, defence of parts of the address.

The views both of the prosecutor and of the judges were all tainted by two material errors.

In the *first* place, they always considered the mere production of *discontent* as in itself criminal. Maconochie gets quite animated (vol. xxiii. p. 287) in his indignation at that part of the address in which it is said that the people had lost some valuable privileges which their ancestors had enjoyed; for, says he, this is a falsehood, and a *seditious* falsehood, because "there is nothing that *tends* more to kindle *discontent* in the minds of the lower classes of people than the idea of being deprived of what their ancestors had purchased, and endeavoured to transmit to them." And even Abercromby directs the jury that the point they have to decide is, "whether it is an innocent publication, or whether it was not a publication *tending* to *raise a spirit of discontent* in this country." They put the criminality of the paper on its mere *tendency* to produce *discontent*,—as if any popular grievance could ever be remedied, except by pointedly calling attention to its existence, and the possibility of removing it, and in this way stimulating discontent. According to this the whole working of our Constitution must be changed. The popular soul, in which there is always passion combined with reason, and which expresses itself in cheers and curses as well as in calm words, must be extinguished. If all that has been legally gained to liberty, by popular discontent, purposely excited, be struck from the Constitution, what would remain?

Yet Eskgrove carries this so far that he holds
the statement in the address about the people being
lethargic as an aggravation of the prisoner's guilt ;
because why rouse people who are quiet ? "This
paper (says he) goes on to say, ' We will tell you
whole truths ; they are of a kind to alarm and arouse
you out of your lethargy.' Here this writer is supposing that his auditors are in a state of lethargy,
which implies a state of contentment ; they *are in a
pacific, contented state.* But this writer is to *awaken*
them from their lethargy." So that the more stupi-
fied by slavery slaves are, the more it is the duty
of a good citizen to leave them in that condition.

In the *second* place, they utterly rejected the
relevancy, even as an extenuation, of all reference
to the language generally used on similar occasions by men of unquestionable wisdom and public
virtue. And indeed the *practice of the nation*
has been often disposed of not only here, but in
England, by the judge saying that one libel cannot
be defended by another. "If," said Eskgrove,
"there are a thousand instances of crimes that go
unpunished, is that an argument to be used by a
lawyer ; and because persons are guilty of equal
crimes, and have not been punished, therefore a
Supreme Court is to stamp an authority upon
crimes brought before them ? Let us suppose for a
moment that a murderer were brought to this bar,
what should we think if a counsel should plead that
many murderers, ay, murderers of title and respectability, had passed unpunished—let this man go !
That is the strangest argument I ever heard." (vol.
xxiii. p. 297.) This sentiment, though common
with courts trying sedition, is utterly inapplicable
to such cases.

The law, *when known*, must no doubt be enforced; and its having been violated with impunity by one man is no legal ground for letting it be violated with impunity by another. And there are cases in which the exact rule admits of being always clearly seen and inflexibly applied. When the law exhausts itself by positively prohibiting a plainly described act—as when it enjoins a fiscal regulation —this law is capable of being enforced with absolute precision, and it must be so enforced. It is idle to speak of moral innocence, of successful evasions, or fortunate escapes. There is no equity in whist,— as Lord Glenlee once said when such considerations were urged to him against the application of a clear and positive principle in a civil cause. The game must be played according to its rules. But there are other, and far more numerous cases, in which even the legal principle is far from being distinctly conceived,—in which, when distinctly conceived, it is very inaccurately expressed; and in which combined clearness of both conception and expression only make both the principle and its application depend the more entirely on the varying circumstances of national habits and of individual motives. Even in the comparatively simple case of murder, the practice of the law is often very materially affected by the public manners and usage. It is easy for judges to tell jurymen that duellists are only "murderers of title and respectability" (though even on the bench this is always said with a softening tongue), but for centuries, jurymen, *with the approbation of the country and of parliament*, have uniformly refused to exclude the moral and personal considerations by which the law is evaded, from their view.

But in cases of sedition the law is meaningless or impracticable, except in reference *to those political habits of the country, which are the only true exponents of the understood, practical, working of the Constitution.* Supposing the first point which must occur in every trial for sedition—namely, the mischievous *tendency* of the act or language complained of—to be settled, the far more difficult and important point, of the innocence or wickedness of the prisoner's *intention*, remains to be ascertained. Now, when the prisoner is not charged with mere insult to high authority, but is accused of promulgating dangerous principles, or of making too exciting appeals to the people, what defence can be more relevant or conclusive than the fact that he has only acted or spoken according to established usage? Even when juries in England had no power except to determine the fact of publication, it was idle in courts, determining the rest as matter of law, to profess to disregard what had been generally done by others in positions analogous to that of the prisoner. But from the moment the juries had to dispose of the whole case, it was extravagant to tell them that the manner in which all other persons were in the practice of exercising their right of being discontented, and of availing themselves of the discontent of others for the redress of supposed grievances, should be altogether left out of view. According to this, neither place nor time are elements in the case. They are only to look at the particular act or expression before them, and though the very same act or expression have been long habitual to the whole people, they are to judge of it just as they might have done had they been obliged to decide upon such things if they had been attempted

under Henry VIII. Suppose that Mr. Palmer had
put into this address, that kings were naturally
lovers of low company, it would, to a certainty,
have formed a text for a copious discourse on the
insolence of his sedition ; and yet if he had produced
the exact thought, or even the very words, from
the loyal and constitutional Burke, this would have
been totally unimportant! It is always forgotten,
that when the people are exercising a right, *for the
exercise of which the law has prescribed no precise
form*, an individual has scarcely any other guide,
either in the mode of preferring his claim for redress,
or in the intensity with which he expresses it, than
generally prevailing, and never punished, custom.
No doubt this introduces an element of great delicacy into trials ; because in a free country there are
precedents for everything. But it is the business
of the court and the jury to appreciate them. Their
disregarding extravagance, absurdity, or guilt, the
raving of the street orator or of the crazy libeller, is
no reason why they should equally disregard sense,
moderation, and constitutional boldness : the written wisdom of the patriotic sage ; the speech which
was eloquent chiefly because it was high-minded ;
the unchecked public declarations of great parties ;
or the unindicted exhortations of eminent men. As
the rule is commonly delivered from the bench, it is
nothing in favour of a prisoner that he can show that
if he be wrong, Locke and Hallam might have sat
at the bar beside him. And the injustice of this is
generally shown the very next moment. For if
what the prisoner has done can be paralleled by
nothing as bad, the solitude of his guilt is said to
be the best evidence of its greatness ; and wherever
the prosecutor can discover the same criminality

among dangerous people, he is sure to be allowed by the court to declaim on the badness of the prisoner's company. It was correct in Burnett (it seems) to tell this jury that the address was violent, hyperbolical, and declamatory, and written in a style *which marked the school it came from;* but it was not correct, or at least it was useless, in the pursuer to prove, by quotations from De Lolme, Hume, Burke, Grattan, Fox, Pitt, and the proceedings of parliament, that this school was that of the philosophers and statesmen who are our acknowledged constitutional oracles.

Assuming the writing to have been, either wholly or partially, criminal, there was no evidence of the prisoner's guiltiness of intention, except his publishing a guilty address. His having used secrecy in getting it printed is founded on. But there is nothing in this ; because men had reason to be afraid at that period of doing anything whatever in furtherance of the popular cause. No prudent man would have openly published anything, however innocent, against Government, if he could have done it covertly. There was no conscious guilt, or illegal object, sworn to by any witness. On the contrary, they all concur substantially with the account given by George Mealmaker of the purpose of the publication. " The meaning of the society was, if I rightly understood them, that in the present situation of the country, and in the part that we had taken in the affair, we were determined to call upon our fellow-citizens by a spirited address. We meant nothing in the world but to make way to their *feelings,* and not to their *passions.* We had no idea of sedition in it; and if there was, it was from want of knowledge in us ;

our ignorance was to blame. What we expected from it was, in the course of our prosecution to cause a reform, we thought it necessary to put forth a paper of that kind, *to animate* our fellow-citizens to go on in getting that redress which we had not yet got." (vol. xxiii. p. 307.) Accordingly the evidence of criminal intention consists solely in the promulgation of a criminal writing. And as men are justly presumed, *where there is nothing to the contrary*, to intend that what they do shall have its natural effects, this evidence is sufficient wherever the guilt of what is published *is too obvious to be mistaken*. Whether it was probable that this prisoner could fail to perceive the criminality of the paper, must depend on each person's opinion of that criminality. Those who, like Maconochie, not only thought the *whole* paper *grossly* seditious, but some of it *treasonable* (p. 283), must hold that the publisher could not be blind to such glaring iniquity. Those who, like myself, think a great deal of it was innocent, and that there was nothing sufficient to exclude the construction that reform was the object, will find little difficulty in believing that a man of his good character and ardent temperament might have no object except to exercise his constitutional right, and no idea that he was exceeding his privilege. But certainly there was nothing unreasonable in the opposite view. The only thing unreasonable was in the court's *confidence* that the *whole* case was *clearly* against the prisoner.

The jury convicted him. But they did so in very peculiar terms. They unanimously " find the address mentioned in the libel to be a seditious writing, *tending* to *inflame* the minds of the people ; find that the panel was art and part guilty of

writing the said address, and that he is guilty
of causing the said address to be printed, and that
he is guilty of distributing, and causing to be
distributed, the said seditious and inflammatory
writing."

Eskgrove complimented the jury for having
" returned a *clear and accurate* verdict, which I
am persuaded will prove a lasting blessing to your
country." And no objection to sentence passing
on this verdict was taken by the prisoner. Yet
the verdict seems exposed to a very formidable
doubt.

The charge is, that the panel composed, printed,
and published the seditious address " *wickedly and
feloniously;* " and all that the jury find is that the
writing is seditious, and that he wrote, printed,
and distributed it. They do not say that he did
these things wickedly ; nor do they find him guilty
as libelled, or guilty generally ; or use any other
term or form of reference, which necessarily implies
a conviction of anything beyond publishing a seditious address. The verdict goes a material step
beyond those in the preceding case of *Berry and
Robertson*, and in the English case of *Woodfall;*
because it decides that the paper is seditious.
But is a conviction of publishing a seditious paper
enough, *under this charge?*

I do not think it is ; simply because a seditious
paper may be published innocently. There is no
absurdity in the idea of a *special verdict* which
should find a writing seditious, and that it was
published by a prisoner, who nevertheless, in consequence of his ignorance, or good intentions, should
be acquitted. Where a person is accused of any
crime under its technical name—such as murder,

theft, or treason—a verdict of guilty is sufficient; because the technical name implies and includes within it all that personal wickedness which is necessary to constitute the offence. But where a prosecutor avoids the known technical title, and prefers a specification of particulars, he necessarily exposes himself to the risk of the jury being against him upon some of them, or, by mistake, omitting some of them from their verdict. For example, suppose that in place of charging murder by the employment of this word, he sets forth that "whereas, etc.," the feloniously shooting a man through the head, in consequence of which he dies, and is murdered, is a crime, etc. ; and that the defence consists in first denying the averment of shooting, and in then saying that, although this averment be proved, the prisoner was legally entitled, as by duty or in self-defence, to kill the deceased, so that he did not act feloniously; and that the verdict is guilty of killing,—I presume that it will not be said that any sentence could pass on such a verdict.

Such a case seems to me to be analogous to the present one. This very prosecutor admitted in the discussion with *Berry and Robertson* that the mere publication of a seditious libel would not be sedition. Now what more does the jury find here? Accordingly, suppose that an indictment were to set forth no more than this verdict finds—that is, suppose it were to charge the mere publication of a seditious pamphlet, without stating that this was done *wickedly*, I consider it certain that it would be rejected as irrelevant. But if this would have been an indictment on which no trial could follow, it must, *a fortiori*, be a verdict on which no punishment could follow. Of course, I presume that the verdict is to be taken as the jury give it, and is not to be changed into something more injurious to the prisoner, by the supplementary introduction of new facts by the court. It is not difficult to discover why no motion was made in arrest of judgment. The same judges had concurred with the rest of the court in rejecting a similar objection in the much stronger case of *Berry and Robertson;* where they did not merely supply the words " wickedly and feloniously " as applied to the prisoner, but the word " seditious " as applied to the writing. After this it was in vain to renew the discussion.

In proposing that the prisoner should be transported, *Lord Abercromby* describes his guilt as deepened by three aggravations. One of these— namely, his being a man of superior station and talents, which it was the more criminal in him to employ the influence of in order to lead poor and ignorant people into mischief—was certainly an important feature in the case, and justly operated against him. The other two were of a very different character.

One of them was that *the country was quiet.* Muir's sedition was committed in the autumn of 1792; and throughout his whole trial it was conspicuously urged as an aggravation against him that at that time the people were in a state of dangerous political frenzy. Palmer's was committed in June and July 1793; and one of Lord Abercromby's aggravations against him is that at this time the *frenzy had entirely ceased!* He first mentions " with what industry, and with what uncommon assiduity, a spirit of discontent, of groundless discontent, and of sedition, was attempted to be excited in this

country not many months ago." And then he goes
on thus : " My Lord, by the virtuous exertions *in
every corner of the country of men of every rank and
of every description all uniting in one voice of loyalty
and attachment to the country and the constitution,
that spirit of discontent which, some months before,
had so violently raged, was in a great measure subdued.* My Lord, *in the month of July last this
country was enjoying peace and tranquillity.* ALL
ALARM HAD CEASED." Yet, on the ground that it
was so much the worse to disturb the public repose,
he converts the circumstance which of all others
renders sedition harmless, into a special reason for
punishing it the more severely. So Muir suffers
because the people were in a state of excitement ;
Palmer because they were not.

The other aggravation proceeds on a stupid misapprehension of a part of Clerk's speech. Clerk had
maintained the obvious, ordinary, and well-founded
argument that the case of a person *honestly* seeking
the redress of what he truly believed to be a political
grievance, was entitled to a more favourable consideration than that of one whose alleged sedition
arose out of no such exercise of a constitutional
right. He did *not* argue that sedition *could not be
committed* in the course, or even in the very act, of
petitioning parliament ; and a *pretence* of petitioning,
or of doing anything, was a case he put in no plea
of favour for whatever. The whole substance of
what he said was that toleration must be extended
to the honest exercise of constitutional privileges,
without which they could not be exercised at all ;
and that though sedition might be committed in the
course of exercising them, this made a separate and
more mitigated case.

Now his Lordship first mistakes all this, and then turns what, even according to his own view, was the error of the counsel, into an aggravation against the prisoner, who had not spoken a single word. " My Lord," said he, " were I not unwilling to load the unhappy man at the bar with all the aggravations that might be mentioned, I might add that even the nature of *the defence set up by him yesterday is an aggravation of the crime charged against him.* For your Lordship knows that that defence principally rested upon a bold and confident vindication, which he set up in the face of his country, of that very writing, and of those very measures, which he had pursued. My Lord, we were told that by the law of this country every subject and every citizen was entitled, *under the* PRETENCE of canvassing the measures of Government, and the conduct of ministers, to publish, to circulate, and to paste upon the walls of every town in the country, *seditious* writings, NAY, TREASON ITSELF ; for if public measures only be canvassed, *there is no crime.*" ! ! !—(p. 373.)

Lord Eskgrove's view of the case rests on the same considerations. He " perfectly coincided with the sentiments just expressed. I lament particu- larly that it should have been thought necessary for the panel's defence to have advanced doctrines which were *heard with astonishment, and which I consider with detestation,*—I mean that doctrine to which your Lordship has just alluded. *We live in a country where we are told* that every man is at liberty, *under* THE PRETENCE of censuring the mis- management of ministers, to paste up and circulate that which tends to inflame the people, and *to excite them to insurrection and rebellion,* and *to do it*

by expressions of the grossest falsehood; that it is
LAWFUL TO STIR UP SEDITION EVEN BY FALSEHOOD.
To *assert our Constitution* TO BE WORSE THAN IT IS,
although the consequences can be merely insignificant to the world at large, *is a false attack upon
the King, the Parliament, and the Constitution;* and
still the law of this country is so defective as that
this shall pass with impunity. This is a doctrine
entirely new to me." So that it is criminal to
assert the Constitution to be worse than it really is,
however excellent it may be admitted to be; or even
to praise it, if the praise do not come up to the full
measure of its deserts.

Burnett, whose ponderous book on criminal law
is much occupied with his own self-reported experience as a depute-advocate, seems to sanction (p. 246)
these outrageous paraphrases of what Clerk had
said. But they were *utterly* groundless. There is
not a word or an idea to justify, or even to excuse,
them in either of the two trials published at the
time, or in Howell's compilation. And that Clerk
never expressed the sentiments imputed to him
may be considered as fixed by the *real* evidence of
this fact, that he was neither mad nor a villain.
No counsel who was honest and sensible—no counsel
who was not insane, and did not mean to sacrifice
his client—*could* have spoken such nonsense, with
such an obvious operation against a prisoner relying
on his reason and honour. And the principle that
he really did maintain was quite sufficient to create
misapprehension, or to provoke misrepresentation, in
a quarter where the open assertion by a respectable
advocate of such a popular privilege as Clerk con-
tended for, was the most alarming of all sedition.

Abercromby got so tender-hearted that he closed

by exhibiting himself in the attitude of a suitor before his soft brother. " I shall therefore conclude with *humbly soliciting* the *mildest punishment* which, under all the circumstances of this case, it appears can with propriety be inflicted "—being transportation. This appeal was irresistible. Indeed, Eskgrove declared : " My Lord, I *always shudder* when it is incumbent upon us to pronounce a punishment of this nature against a person such as the panel at the bar." But in truth there was no need for the shudder here, but rather for a sensation of joy at the painful duty they had escaped ; because his Lordship adds that the prisoner had been " but *little* short of going the length that your Lordship has pointed out, which might have called upon us, in certain circumstances, to have pronounced the sentence of *death*." The idea of fine and imprisonment seems never to have occurred to them. Eskgrove appears to think that if they did not transport, they had no alternative but to banish from Scotland ; and "how should I reconcile it to the Judge of my conscience, to send a seditious incendiary from the country of Scotland to the country of England, to propagate the same mischievous principles." Therefore transportation has this recommendation (which death would have had also), that " by sending him to foreign parts beyond the seas, *we shall be taking as much care of our neighbours as of ourselves*."

The result of all this was that he was sentenced to endure "the mildest punishment" for seven years.

An error in the terms of the sentence, which had occurred in the previous case of *Muir*, and was repeated in the three subsequent cases of *Skirving*, *Margarot*, and *Gerrald*, was committed also on this occasion. The 25th of Geo. III. c. 46, in express reference to which all the sentences were pronounced, attaches the penalty of death to the offence of a convict being found at large, without some lawful cause, "within any part of the kingdom of Great Britain *or Ireland*," before the period of his transportation shall have expired. But all of these sentences merely certify that the prisoner shall be punished capitally if he be found at large " within any part of *Great Britain*." I infer that this was a mere error from the fact that, after being first pointed out in parliament on the 10th of March 1794, it was corrected in the very next case, being that of *Mealmaker*, in 1798.

But was it an error fatal, as has been maintained, to the whole sentence? That it was fatal to the *certification* is tolerably clear; because that was entirely a matter of statutory provision, and such a statute must be literally observed. What power had the court to limit the capital punishment to the case of the convict's returning to a *particular place* within the statutory sphere? Could they have declared that he should be executed if he should be found at large *within Scotland*, or within *Edinburgh?* But the difficulty is whether the rest of the sentence—as, for instance, the transporting part of it—was vitiated?

The prisoner closed the proceedings by the following manly declaration of the feelings under which he had acted, and of the hopes by which he was even then upheld:—" My Lords, I can appeal with conscious sincerity to the great Searcher of hearts for the good intentions and uprightness of my conduct. My life has for many years been employed in the dissemination of what I conceived

to be religious and moral truths—truths which I
supposed to be of the greatest importance to mankind. My friends know with what ardour I have
done this; at the total sacrifice of all my worldly
interests. But during the late great political discussions that have taken place, it was entirely,
naturally, impossible, in a man of my sanguine
disposition, to remain an unconcerned bystander.
I felt as all around me felt. I caught the general
impulse. I thought, too, that I perceived that
politics were a great branch of morals, if they did
not comprise the whole of our duty to our neigh-
bour. For, my Lords, would but our superiors—
would but all the world—do to one another what
they, in like circumstances, would wish to be done
to themselves, our petitions would have been
answered, and every grievance redressed. I trust
that my politics is the cause of common justice—
the cause of benevolence and of human happiness.
It was under the influence, I protest, of these considerations that I was led to enter myself into the
society of the Friends of Liberty. I thought, my
Lords, that a parliamentary reform would enhance
the happiness of millions, and establish the security
of the empire. For these reasons it was, and with
these views only, as God is my Judge, that I joined
that society of 'low weavers and mechanics,' as
you called them, at the Berean Meeting-house at
Dundee; and for these reasons too, and to gain
these ends, that I assented to the publication of
this handbill; for the declaration and the test of
the society, and all their endeavours, so far as I
have been able to learn, were solely confined to
that one object of parliamentary reform, and a more
equal representation of the people.

" It is not, my Lords, the first time that I have suffered in endeavouring to benefit others. For this I have borne shame, odium, reproach, and a great diminution of fortune. I hope and trust that it is my utmost ambition, and all who know me will agree with me that it has been the tenor of my life, to endeavour to add, if possible, to the sum of human happiness. And, my Lords, if I should be called again to the like or more severe trials—if I should be called again to suffer in what I cannot but think the cause of men in general—the cause of human happiness—I trust that I shall be able to bear my sufferings, not only with fortitude, but with cheerfulness—with the hope, my Lords, that my sufferings will not be wholly lost, but will, by the blessing of that Great Being whom I serve, be rendered efficacious to the good of my fellow-creatures."

In ordinary cases my experience of their falsehood and impudence prevents me from placing any reliance whatever on asseverations of innocence by fairly convicted prisoners, even though made on the very edge of eternity. And even in cases which have been so far political as that public principles or objects may have been involved, but where common atrocities were perpetrated or designed, guilt has often been denied, or tried to be justified, by dying lies. But little as such protestations can be regarded so long as they rest solely on the assertion of the prisoner, they deserve the deepest consideration when they coincide with other probable facts. In reference to the sincerity of his declaration, especially respecting the feelings under which he acted, his character is a fact of the greatest importance. And if the guilt be political purely,

and therefore, from its not being stained by contemplated accession to ordinary crime, may be
incurred by an otherwise good man, it would be
not merely ungenerous, but unjust, to discard every
protestation merely because it proceeded from one
against whom a verdict had passed. The political
scaffold, and many of its finest historical scenes,
would testify against such a conclusion. Everything depends on the circumstances. Those who
think a prisoner not merely guilty, but properly
tried and properly punished, for an offence implying
personal immorality, will not be moved by a parting
speech. Those who think that he was tried hardly,
and punished cruelly, for an offence which might be
fairly ascribed to mere inconsiderate ardour, will
listen to his last words with respect, and may never
be able to get them out of their ears. And in
reference to the fitness of the punishment, the
very loftiness of the sentiments, as they disclose the
nature of the man, are, if believed to be genuine,
material.

I cannot help thinking that he must be a hard
man, or must be swayed by very hard views, who,
on looking back to this Perth Circuit, can now
think it creditable to the country that a person
capable of uttering the preceding sentiments *sincerely* was sentenced to be transported for seven
years for a first conviction of sedition. When we
consider what he was—the habits of his life, his
intellectual attainments, respectable friends, and
high character—and follow out a single day of the
hulk, with its convict dress and its irons—of the
transport, with its felons and capricious master—or
of Botany Bay, where even the governor's kindness
could not save such a convict from severe and

degrading personal toil—the heart sickens even at
the feeble conception which our fancy can form of
the base suffering to which he was doomed.

After being kept some weeks in Perth jail, and
some months on board a hulk, he was sent to New
South Wales, where he served out his full time.
He left that region, homeward bound, in a vessel
of which he himself was the principal owner, in
January 1800 ; but, after many disasters, was
obliged to put into a place called Guam, an island
in Eastern Seas belonging to Spain, with which
Britain was then at war. After being detained a
prisoner of war there from January 1801 till June
1802, death finally released him.

IX.—Case of ALEXANDER SCOTT, 3d February
1794.[1]

No proceedings took place in court against this
man, except outlawing him for not appearing.
He was the printer of the *Edinburgh Gazetteer*,
and a member of the British convention. The
substance of the indictment is, that the convention
was a seditious association,—that it was the scene
of seditious harangues,—that it passed seditious
resolutions,—that the accused took part in all this,
or acceded to it ; and that he published the proceedings in the *Gazetteer*.

[1] *State Trials*, vol. xxiii. p. 383.

X.—Case of WILLIAM SKIRVING, 6th and 7th of January 1794.[1]

MR. SKIRVING was a Scotchman, educated originally for the Secession Church, but afterwards a farmer; a person of good character.

His case, and those of *Margarot* and *Gerrald*, by which it was succeeded, open a new scene in these prosecutions. These trials involve the constitution, proceedings, and objects of the association called The British Convention, their accession to which was the principal thing charged against these three prisoners; and the interest of their cases is increased by the circumstance that the guilt, or the innocence, of the convention was a material point in the memorable trials of Hardy, Tooke, Thelwall, and others, which occurred in England about this period. The coincidence of trials, to a great extent on the same matter, in both parts of the island, affords the judicial student an opportunity of observing the different styles in which similar legal proceedings may possibly be conducted.

The whole minutes of the association, both in its original state as " *The General Convention of the Friends of the People,*" and as afterwards enlarged into " *The British Convention of the Delegates of the people associated to obtain Universal Suffrage and Annual Parliaments,*" are published in the *State Trials* (vol. xxiii. p. 391), and some witnesses were

[1] *State Trials,* vol. xxiii. p. 391.

examined in the cases of *Skirving, Margarot,* and *Gerrald,* as to the structure and designs of these two bodies,—which, together, seem only to have endured about a month—*the life of the British Convention having, apparently, been only about fourteen days.*

A person anxious for truth will obtain little satisfaction from either of these sources. The minutes, though apparently honest, and even rashly open, are meagre, abrupt, desultory, and confused, and read as if they had been written as jottings amidst the noise and interruptions of each sitting. And the witnesses, instead of being required to explain fully, and in their own way, what the conventions really aimed at, are chiefly examined on detached points or occurrences, and plainly give their evidence under the reluctance naturally produced by its having been laid down on the bench that trying to obtain annual parliaments and universal suffrage, which were the professed objects of the convention, was not only illegal, but was nearly, if not absolutely, conclusive as evidence of sedition. The introduction of French terms and forms, the denouncing and inflated declamation, the desire of mystery, and the tone of authority, all tend to give the proceedings a strange and suspicious appearance. But neither these incidents, nor any plainly announced principles, nor any explicit declaration, enable us to see exactly what it was that the members, or rather the leaders, truly meant. This may be *gathered;* for universal suffrage, and annual parliaments—and these alone—transpire through all their language and all their acts. But this was said to be a pretence, and a cover. And if it was so, then no other object is to be found, either distinctly announced, or incidentally disclosed, in the minutes.

In this situation I know no source of information to which we can safely recur, except to the opinions of fair and sensible men, who, though greatly disapproving of the convention, were privy, from personal acquaintance with its more respectable members, and from living in the scene of its transactions, to its real designs. And such intelligent and neutral spectators did exist. The convention, though now associated in our minds with the idea of vulgarity and extravagance, contained some members who had friends deeply interested, for their sakes, in ascertaining, and well qualified to appreciate, its genuine objects. The tories could not be expected to know anything personally of these matters ; but there were many even of the higher order of whigs to whom, from their general sympathy with reform, notwithstanding their condemnation of the convention, the plans of the leaders were freely opened, and with whom they were habitually canvassed.

Now, I have repeatedly discussed the subject, many years after its prejudices were over, with persons of intelligence and candour, who were acquainted with the very innermost recesses of the convention, and I never heard one of them give any other account of it than this : That universal suffrage and annual parliaments were really its sole objects ; that it proposed to effect these reforms, not by overturning the Constitution, or by any other violence, but by discussion and agitation ; that their system of agitation included, as it commonly does, those arts of organisation, of control over remoter adherents by central dictators, and of fierce denun-

ciation of opponents, which are usual in seasons of
great excitement, with all parties advocating popular
claims ; that in the existing condition of the popular
mind, such ends, and such means, though possibly
not criminal, warranted the utmost jealousy of
Government, and made the convention be justly
condemned by all the prudent friends of liberty ; to
whom, in particular, the mimicry of the convention
in France, intended, as it partly was, for the culpable purpose of terrifying their adversaries, was
peculiarly offensive, and was the folly that chiefly
frightened these adversaries into the retaliation of
such cruel punishments.

It may be difficult to agree with Lord Erskine,
who, in his address to the jury for Thomas Hardy,
says that the statement, that the convention meant
" to assume and maintain, by force, all the functions
of the State," which was the charge imputed to it,
was not " *within the compass of human belief,*" and
that if a man were offered a dukedom and £20,000
a year for trying to believe it, he could not succeed.
(*State Trials*, vol xxiv. p. 940.)[1] But certainly a
reasonable mind may, after every possible inquiry,
remain unconvinced that the convention had either

---

[1] " To return to this Scotch convention : Their papers were all seized
by Government. What their proceedings were, they best know ; we can
only see what parts they choose to show us. But from what we have seen,
does any man seriously believe that this meeting at Edinburgh meant to
assume, and to maintain, by force, all the functions and authorities of
the State ? Is the thing within the compass of human belief ? If a man
were offered a dukedom and £20,000 a year, for trying to believe it, he
might *say* he believed it—as what will not man say for gold and honours ?
But he never in. fact could believe that this Edinburgh meeting was a
parliament for Great Britain. How indeed could he, from the proceedings of a few peaceable, unarmed men, discussing, in a constitutional
manner, the means of obtaining a reform in parliament ; and who, to
maintain the club, or whatever you choose to call it, collected a little
money from people who were well disposed to the cause—a few shillings
one day, and a few pence another ; I think, as far as I could reckon it
up, when the report of this great committee of supply was read to you,
I counted that there had been raised, in the first session of this parlia-

this, or any other, criminal design ; and, beyond all question, there was no sufficient *evidence* of this traitorous project *produced* at any of the Scotch trials ; while history will probably hold *the existence* of such evidence as refuted by the acquittals which terminated all the trials, depending partly on this matter, in England.

The Scotch cases, *as trials*, must depend on their own evidence ; but the character of the convention *as an historical fact*, may be established otherwise. Now its character was unfolded, by evidence, in the English trials, far better than it was in the Scotch ones, chiefly because its English connections and proceedings were disclosed, while in the Scotch trials they were left entirely out of sight. The English evidence really makes Erskine's assertion not very extravagant. Still the trials in Scotland must be considered, each according to its own proof. Actual and judicial truth are not always identical. Courts must be tried according to the light in which they did act, or ought to have acted.

In examining this case of *Skirving* it will be convenient to postpone the account of the incidents of the trial till we endeavour to ascertain the nature of the guilt that was charged, and of the evidence by which the charge was supported.

It was maintained by sound lawyers at the period, and the opinion has not lost strength since, that *according to the view of the facts taken by the prosecutor and the judges*, Skirving, and the other leaders of the convention, were guilty of *high treason;* and that therefore it was incompetent in

---

ment, £15, from which indeed you must deduct two bad shillings, which are literally noticed in the account. Is it to be endured, gentlemen, that men should gravely say that this body assumed to itself the offices of parliament ?" (*State Trials*, vol. xxiv. p. 940.)

the public accuser to charge them, *in respect of their accession to the convention*, with any inferior offence, or in the court to permit the trials, except in so far as they depended on other matter, to proceed as for sedition. Next to the legality of the sentences, this is the most important general question connected with these proceedings.

It may be assumed (I suppose) that an act plainly amounting to high treason cannot be tried as any inferior offence. This, as I understand, is what is meant to be laid down by all the leading authorities. And this construction of these authorities is strikingly confirmed by the following entry in Lord Eldon's anecdote-book, made in order to record his reason for not charging the English prisoners with mere misdemeanour, which would have had a better chance of success than charges of treason : " They, too, who were lawyers and judges, having stated their opinion that these were cases of high treason, I could not but be aware what blame would have been thrown upon the law officers of the Crown, if they (the prisoners) had been indicted for misdemeanour and the evidence had proved a case of high treason ; which proved, *would have entitled them to an acquittal for the misdemeanour.*" (Twiss's *Life of Eldon*, chap. xii.)

Upon consulting living English lawyers of great authority, I am informed that, practically, the rule is, that neither the Attorney-General nor the judges consider themselves bound to be *inquisitive* in order to detect treason lurking in other charges ; but that where it *stands prominently out*, it must be seen, and an acquittal on the inferior accusation directed ; and that courts or prosecutors aggravating a charge of sedition *by openly proclaiming it* to be, in truth, a case of high treason, would not be tolerated.

This principle is not only implied in the preceding private memorandum by Eldon, but in his public management of the trials he refers to. The connection of these English prisoners with the convention was put forth as one of the strong facts against them. One of the answers to this circumstance was, that accession to the convention could not be treason, because in Scotland it had only led to charges and convictions of sedition, which could not have been the result if the existence of treason had transpired. Now the reply to this never is that this was not the law ; but that, in point of fact, the treason had not transpired, because the evidence of it was only obtained after the Scotch trials were over. This was a virtual admission, both by the prosecutor and by the court, of the principle that *plain* high treason, or high treason that is declared to be plain, cannot be prosecuted as anything else.

This being assumed, does a conspiracy, or an association, for the purpose of *overturning the Government, and of usurping its function,* BY FORCE, imply the guilt of high treason ? All the judges of those days, both English and Scotch, said that it did ; because a scheme of such universal public disorder implied the violent abolition of the kingly office, and a consequent invasion of the royal person, which was the clearest overt act of compassing the king's actual death.   Erskine did not dispute, or at least only disputed feebly, that in most, if not absolutely in all cases, the actual, or the imagined death of the king was, *in point of fact,* involved in any conspiracy, either directly to depose him, or to effect such a forcible change in the Constitution that his

deposition must form a part of it.   But his great
point was, that all this was for *the consideration of
the jury;* and that *in law* there was no such constructive treason—no treason by compassing the
death, except a compassing of which the *natural*
death was the *primary* and *direct* object.   He
agreed with the judges to this extent, viz., that
where *the jury* was convinced that the death of the
king *must* have been in the contemplation of the
conspirators, as necessarily involved in their project,
this was treason.   The difference between him and
them was, that the judges held that changes, by
violence, amounting to the total overthrow of the
Government, were not merely *evidence* of a compassing of the death which *ought* to satisfy a jury, but
that they implied it by *legal necessity.*   The difference is essential and immense; but they both
concur in this, that such violent and utter changes,
such forcible revolutions, do amount to treason;
only they arrive at this conclusion by materially
different roads.   Phillips, who is justly said by
Mackintosh to "survey the most contested, the most
obscure, and the most bloody proceedings in our
history, with the sagacity, probity, and sincerity
of the wisest magistrate" (*History of England,*
chap. iii., note), gives his reasons and authorities
for thinking that Eyre and others, who laid down
this doctrine of legally constructive treason, were
wrong. (Phillipp's *State Trials,* vol. ii. p. 79.)

But in appreciating our Scotch trials, it is fair
to give our judges the advantage of holding that
their English brethren were right.   Now the
doctrine of the English bench was, that a conspiracy to effect by force a revolution so great that
it involved the subversion of the whole political

system, and consequently of the monarchy, was treason in law.

Thus Chief-Justice Eyre lays it down to the grand jury in his charge previous to the case of *Hardy*, that "if a conspiracy to depose or imprison the king, to get his person into the power of the conspirators, or to procure an invasion of the kingdom, involves in it the compassing and imagining of his death; and if steps taken in prosecution of such conspiracy are rightly deemed overt acts of the treason of compassing and imagining the king's death,—need I add, that if it should appear that it has entered into the heart of any man, who is a subject of this country, *to design to overthrow the whole Government of the country*—to pull down and to subvert from its foundations the British monarchy, that glorious fabric which it has been the work of ages to erect, maintain, and support—which has been cemented with the best blood of our ancestors— to design such a horrible ruin and devastation, which no king could survive, a crime of such a magnitude that no lawgiver in this country has ever ventured to contemplate it in its whole extent,[1]—need I add, I say, that the complication and the enormous extent of such a design will not prevent its being distinctly seen that the compassing and imagining the death of the king is involved in it—is in truth, of its very essence?" (*State Trials*, vol. xxiv. p. 203.)

Another passage of the same charge is still more deserving of attention; because the facts which his Lordship there states hypothetically are almost exactly those which our public prosecutor asserted had

---

[1] If this be the fact, how is it treason, under the 25th of Edward III.? See Godwin's powerful *Cursory Strictures* on this charge, republished in the *State Trials*, vol. xxiv. p. 210.

actually distinguished the convention. " I presume that I have sufficiently explained to you, that
*a project to bring the people together in convention,
in imitation of those national conventions which we
have heard of in France, in order to usurp the
Government of the country, and any one step taken
towards bringing it about—such as, for instance, con-
sultations, forming of committees to consider of the
means, acting in those committees—would be a case
of no difficulty—that it would be the clearest high
treason.* It would be compassing and imagining
the king's death; and not only his death, but the
death and destruction of all order, religion, laws,
all property, all security for the lives and liberties
of the king's subjects." (vol. xxiv. p. 207.)

And in his summing up to the jury on the trial,
when it was his duty to be still more guarded and
precise, he directs them that "the conspiracy to
depose the king is *evidence* of compassing and
imagining the death of the king, *conclusive in its
nature; so conclusive that it is become a presumption
of law,* which is in truth nothing more than a
necessary and violent presumption of fact, *admitting of no contradiction.* Who can doubt that the
natural person of the king is immediately attacked
and attempted, by him who attempts to depose
him?" (vol. xxiv. p. 1361.)

Erskine, and all the whig lawyers doubted it.
They did not contest that a design to depose was
admissible evidence to prove a design against the
life, but they maintained that it was the duty and
the right of the jury to determine—1*st*, whether the
existence of any such overt act was established, and
2*d*, whether a design against the king's natural life
was the proper inference to be drawn from such act.

It is the exposition of this principle that covers Erskine's defence of Hardy with the brightest forensic glory. He places it in every variety of light conducive to its being clearly seen; and its illustration and maintenance pervade the whole course of an oration which will not owe its immortality so much even to the beauty of its calm and earnest dignity, as to the demonstrative character of its legal reasoning. But though this proposition be the matter of the whole defence, he, at proper pauses, concentrates his argument into short and striking summaries.

Thus, "the charge of a conspiracy to depose the king is therefore laid before you to establish that intention (to kill). Its *competency* to be laid before you *for that purpose* is not disputed. I am only contending, with all reason and authority on my side, that it is to be submitted to your consciences and understandings, whether, even if you believed the overt act, you believe also that it proceeded from a traitorous machination against the life of the king. I am only contending that these two beliefs must coincide, to establish a verdict of guilty. I am not contending that, under any circumstances, a conspiracy to depose the king, and to annihilate his regal capacity, may not be strong and *satisfactory evidence* of the intention to destroy his life; but only that in this, as in every other instance, it is for *you* to collect, or not to collect, this treason against the king's life, according to the result of your conscientious belief and judgment, from the acts of the prisoner laid before you; and that the establishment of the overt act, even if it were established, does not establish the treason against the king's life AS A CONSEQUENCE OF LAW; but, on the contrary, the overt act, though punishable in another shape as an independent crime, is a dead letter upon this record, unless you believe, *exercising your exclusive jurisdiction over the facts laid before you*, that it was committed in accomplishment of the treason against the *natural life of the king.*" (*State Trials*, vol. xxiv. p. 895.)

Now the question that arises on the Scotch cases is, whether, according to *either* principle, the facts, *as professed to be viewed by our public prosecutor or the judges*, did not warrant, and therefore require, that treason should have been charged?

In order to judge of this, let us look at the indictment, as expounded by the prosecutor's commentaries.

The major proposition of the libel sets forth no crime except sedition. The facts set forth in the minor in support of this charge are, in substance, these: 1. That the prisoner (Skirving) had circulated the Dundee paper, for his connection with which Palmer had been already condemned. 2. That he had been an active member of the society called the Friends of the People, and had, as its secretary, circulated a seditious handbill, part of which is quoted. 3. That he had been equally involved with that society after it assumed the new name and character of the convention of delegates of the people associated to obtain universal suffrage and annual parliaments. 4. That in both associations he had made seditious speeches and motions. 5. That after the convention had been dispersed by the civil magistrate, he, who had previously resisted, endeavoured to reassemble it.

There has never been any question that, with the exception of the circumstances connected with the convention, these statements justified a *charge* of sedition. The doubt only applies to the convention; deducting which, however, the case becomes unimportant. It was the convention that was chiefly meant to be prosecuted, that forms the conspicuous subject of discussion, and that gives its peculiar interest to the trial.

Now, in reference to this part of the case, the indictment, and indeed the whole proceedings, are full of statements and allusions to recent occurrences in France, like other current public events. And the two facts for which that country is particularly referred to are, that the people had first become republicans, and then regicides. And from this it is concluded not in loose talking, but in judicial, and even technical statement, that imitation of France implied republican and regicide designs here.

Thus the indictment sets forth, with considerable minuteness, that, " In particular, the members of the said association, under the names and denominations aforesaid, did, in the months of October, November, and December 1793, at Edinburgh aforesaid, in imitation of the proceedings of the said French Convention, call each other by the name of ' citizen '—divide themselves into ' sections ' —appoint committees of various kinds, such as of ' organisation,' of ' instruction,' of ' finance,' and of 'secrecy'—denominate their meetings ' sittings,' and inscribe their minutes with the first year of the British Convention." (vol. xxiii. p. 475.)

Now why was all this said to have been done ? For this special purpose, viz., because the society " having presumptuously and seditiously arrogated to themselves the name of The British Convention of the Delegates of the people associated to obtain universal suffrage and annual parliaments, did, *in the whole form and manner of their procedure, as well as in the principles it publicly avowed and propagated, clearly and unequivocally demonstrate, that, under the specious pretext of reform, their purposes were of the most dangerous and destructive tendency, hostile to the peace and happiness, as well as to the constitution of this realm, and too plainly indicating the same rebellious maxims which have governed, and do still govern the proceedings of the convention of France,* the public and avowed enemies of this country, and with whom this nation is at present at open war." (vol. xxiii. p. 475.)

This intended introduction into Britain of those particular principles and measures of the French, whereby they had murdered their king, and erected a republic on the ruins of their monarchy, is the main and peculiar fact charged against the convention, both as a substantive offence, and as furnishing the true key to all the other circumstances. Except with reference to their proceedings as republicans and regicides, the mention of France is meaningless. It is not rebellion *in general* that is charged; but that particular rebellion which consisted in the recommendation, adoption, and proclaimed resolution to act upon the rebellious maxims and objects *which had governed the French convention.*

Now could the recent French rebellion have been imitated, or been attempted to be imitated in Britain, without the treason of levying war against the king; or without that of compassing his death? No matter whether this compassing was implied in the imitation by what the

English judges held to be a presumption of law ; or whether, as Erskine maintained, it was only to be inferred by a strong presumption of fact. Could the proceedings of the French Convention have been copied here, without what, on either principle, would have been treason ? Chief-Justice Eyre answers this in his summing up in *Tooke's* case. " If this convention was a convention on the plan of the convention in France, *to take the government of the country upon them, any one measure taken to bring forward that convention would clearly be an overt act of high treason in compassing the king's death.*" (*State Trials*, vol. xxv. p. 737.)

Our public prosecutor, who ostentatiously adopted the treason law as laid down by the English judges afterwards, answers this question also.

The Solicitor-General made an opening speech, the object of which seems to have been, to show that the course of the convention in France had been a mere career of sanguinary treason. He calls them " scenes of *anarchy,* scenes of *rapine,* scenes of *bloodshed,* of cruelty and barbarity, hitherto unknown to the world, which have desolated that unhappy country, and disgraced it among the nations of the earth." And the guilt of the British convention consists in this, — that they " *have chosen to form themselves on that wicked model.*" " We find them constantly departing from the language of this country, and adopting foreign language, which, when connected with those scenes that it has produced, *show a wish to adopt a model,* which I am surprised that any person in this country could have thought of." (*State Trials*, vol. xxiii. p. 487.)

The Lord Advocate revised his address to the jury, and gave a copy of it to the editor of the

State Trials. (vol. xxiii. p. 536, note.) And in this deliberate report by himself of his own argument, reconsidered after the doubt of the propriety of his having charged only sedition had become familiar to lawyers, and been finally given to history, he teems in almost every passage with assertions and reasonings intended to show that *the utter subversion* of the Constitution, which he constantly calls treason, was the sole, and the scarcely disguised, object of the convention. But besides these merely general and declamatory imputations, he distinctly and anxiously sums up, and reduces his charge to the exact offence of treason.

Thus : " Every mode of their (the British Convention's) proceeding, every resolution which they adopt, is framed directly and positively upon the model of the French Convention ; and I desire you to take this along with you when you consider this subject, that although this meeting was illegal in every part of it, YET THE MAIN POINT OF MY CHARGE AGAINST THEM is this—that being a convention *formed upon the model of that at this moment existing in France,* and a nation with which we are at war, the panel, who was their secretary, and all those who engaged in it, *have proved,* if not *totidem verbis, most clearly and unequivocally, by every circumstance of their conduct,* that their *sole purpose and intention was,* not a reform, BUT A SUBVERSION OF PARLIAMENT,—not a redress or cure of grievances, imaginary or real, in a legal, peaceable, and constitutional way, but *a determined and systematic plan and resolution* TO SUBVERT THE LIMITED MONARCHY *and free constitution of Britain,* and to substitute in its place, BY INTIMIDATION, FORCE, AND VIOLENCE, A REPUBLIC OR DEMOCRACY as wild, as cruel, as despotic, and as abominable as that which at this moment desolates France." (vol. xxiii. p. 544.)

In another passage his Lordship brings the crime, which he declares that he understands himself to be charging, still nearer the *person* of the king. " If, *as my opinion is*, their purpose was to assemble a convention of delegates representing, as they say, thousands of people, then the conclusion is INEVITABLE, that the purpose for which this convention met, was, *to join those persons whom, we know, within these few months, have dared to hold out in their own country, that they* WOULD LAND AN ARMY IN THIS, and establish what they pleased in it—would punish London, the proud metropolis of Britain, for its interference and defending itself as it has done— you will be of opinion, with me, that they meant to lift the *hand of rebellion against their sovereign*, the constitution of their country, and the liberty of their fellow-citizens." (vol. xxiii. p. 556.)

Nor were these merely the unguarded expressions of a prosecutor eager for his case and warm with its statement. Hume's *Commentaries*, published several years afterwards, were the work of an ardent and avowed apologist of all that was done by the crown or the court in all of these trials ; and he, in describing this prosecution, with the cautious gravity of a jurist instructing posterity, says (vol. i. p. 547) that the cases of *Muir* and *Palmer* " were followed in the succeeding year by the conviction of William Skirving, Maurice Margarot, and Joseph Gerrald, for their several parts and proceedings in the meeting termed the British Convention—an assembly which arrogated the character of the representatives of the inhabitants of Great Britain, and in that capacity took measures for debàuching the affections of the people, AS WELL AS TO DEFY THE LEGISLATURE, *and* RESIST *any attempt which might be made* by statute, OR OTHERWISE, to suppress them." The English judges could not for a moment have doubted, that taking measures by force to defy and resist the legislature, including the sovereign as a part of it, was treason ; and there is no ground to suppose that Hume differed from them.

Burnett, who was not only engaged in this particular trial, but was well acquainted with the whole views entertained by the public accuser and his party on all these proceedings, is more precise. " By this name, and under the pretext of obtaining a reform in parliament, this notable association held their meetings in Edinburgh, and *by the whole tenor of their proceedings* showed EVIDENTLY that their PURPOSE was of the most seditious and EVEN TREASONABLE nature. They assumed the language and imitated the forms of the National Convention of France, that grand committee (as it was termed) of general insurrection for the purpose of overthrowing every existing government in Europe, etc. Their whole proceedings, indeed, evinced that their OBJECT was, not reform, but a change and SUBVERSION OF THE WHOLE FRAME AND CONSTITUTION OF GOVERNMENT ; dictated *evidently* by French principles, and, there was too much reason to presume, by French influence." Subversion of the Government is elsewhere described, in express words by this author, as treason. After explaining what he calls sedition, he laid it down as indisputable that " *a total change or subversion of the existing system,*" if really intended, is treason. In other words, high treason was the crime of the convention.

His explanation of the failure to charge treason is this :—"THOUGH LITTLE DOUBT COULD EXIST OF THE TREASONABLE NATURE OF THIS ASSOCIATION, still their object and purpose it might be difficult to establish by satisfactory evidence. It was *therefore* judged better to bring the leading members of it to trial for sedition." (pp. 247-8.) And in another passage (footnote, p. 256), he says :—" THE LAW OFFICERS, THEREFORE, IN THIS COUNTRY, THOUGH THEY WERE SATISFIED OF THE TREASONABLE PURPOSE OF THE BRITISH CONVENTION, acted wisely in not bringing the members of it to trial for high treason."

The view thus taken of the real guilt of the convention by the legal advisers of the Crown in Scotland was confirmed by that taken by their brethren in England. The only difference was that those in England acted on their view, while those in Scotland did not. Accession to the convention was set forth as one of the overt acts against the English prisoners for treason. The doctrine of the Attorney-General uniformly was that "the design of conspiring to assemble persons who are to act as a convention of the people, claiming all civil and political authority ; or claiming power to alter, against its will, the constituted legislature ; or a meeting to form the means of bringing together such a convention so to act, is an attempt to create a power subversive of the authority of the king and parliament—a power which he (the king) *is bound to resist at all hazards*. But it will not rest here. This will be sufficiently proved. But evidence will likewise be offered to you as satisfactory to prove that the express object of calling this convention— the express object of appointing a committee of con-ference and co-operation, which was to devise the means of constituting such a convention, was ultimately and finally, and *in their prospect*, THE DEPOSITION OF THE KING." (*State Trials*, vol. xxiv. p. 266.) Hence he, consistently, charged treason.

And Erskine, with equal consistency, uses the fact of the leaders of the convention having been tried only for sedition in Scotland as conclusive against the Crown that accession to the proceedings of that body could not be treason. The Solicitor-General (Sir John Mitford, afterwards Lord Redesdale) has no other answer to this, except that the Scotch prosecutor was not in possession of the full evidence of the exact intent of the association. The Attorney-General makes the same defence of our proceedings. He first says (speaking in the case of *Hardy*, tried about nine months after Skirving), that if the Scotch prisoners "had been tried for high treason, they would have had *no right to complain*. (vol. xxiv. p. 334.) And then, in the trial of Tooke, a few weeks after the date of this observation, he justifies our law officers for not so trying them by saying that the undoubted treason of the convention had *not been known* when the Scotch trials took place. Since English juries acquitted even in spite of all the discoveries that had been since made, it "would have been a bold thing," he says, in the Lord Advocate to have charged treason. But if, says he, "the interests of the public had been committed to me upon that case, *as I knew it* when I so expressed myself (alluding to a speech in parliament), I should have thought it my duty to ask a jury whether it was not a case of high treason." (vol. xxv. p. 546.)

This may be all quite correct *in his view of the Lord Advocate's information.* But,

In the *first* place, it has never been explained, and it is very difficult to conjecture, what the Lord Advocate's defect of information, or what the subsequent discoveries, consisted in. Even in the English trials there is no material, if indeed there be any perceptible, difference, *in so far as the character and objects of the convention are concerned,* between the proof there and the proof here.

In the *second* place, this apology for the Scotch charges, which, after being suggested in England, was at once adopted here, seems to me to be quite irreconcilable with the facts as stated by our prosecutor himself. For how can it be said that there was any defect of evidence as to the treasonableness of the convention's intent when the prosecutor himself declares that " EVERY CIRCUMSTANCE OF THEIR CONDUCT MOST CLEARLY AND UNEQUIVOCALLY " shows that their object was to " subvert our limited monarchy, and to substitute in its place, by INTIMIDATION, FORCE, AND VIOLENCE, *a republic or democracy* " ? What further evidence could remain to be discovered, after the public accuser stated responsibly in court, and to the last made the statement a ground for demanding a verdict, that "the *conclusion was* INEVITABLE," that the convention meant "TO LIFT THE HAND OF REBELLION against their sovereign"? Nor were these idle words. He was excluded by the terms of his own charge from holding any other language. His indictment did not merely state, but mainly depended on the statement, that an invasion of the kingly authority, and a repetition in this country of the regicide rebellion in France, was the "*pur-*

pose" of the convention, and that this purpose was "CLEARLY and UNEQUIVOCALLY DEMONSTRATED by the WHOLE FORM and MANNER of their PROCEED-INGS." Even if their proceedings had been secret, this would have been immaterial; for not only their substance, but their whole form and manner (as his Lordship informs the court), had been dectected. But there could be no secrecy in the conduct of a society which is said to have made audacious publicity one of the means by which it debauched the affections of the people towards the monarchy, and defied all that monarchy's power.

Burnett's two statements, viz., that the law officers of the Crown "*were satisfied* of the treasonable purpose of the convention," and yet acted wisely in never charging treason, are irreconcilable, except on the single supposition that there was an absence of *evidence*. Even this would leave the public prosecutor in an awkward position; because where there is no evidence to warrant his directly charging the commission of a crime, he is the very last person who ought even to insinuate it. He ought to keep his private belief to himself. On the present occasion there was enough of prejudice without its disclosure. Yet he inflamed the case against a merely seditious prisoner by vehemently exaggerating it into a case of treason. And no wonder he did so. For his own depute, afterwards the institutional expounder of his master's views in these very trials, informs his readers that "very *little doubt* COULD *exist of the* TREASONABLE *nature of the association*," and that "the WHOLE TENOR *of their* PROCEEDINGS showed EVIDENTLY that their purposes were of the most seditious and even *treasonable* nature." The official blunder of the prosecutor consisted in his not following this fact out to its legal consequences—the judicial blunder of the court in not compelling him either to do so or to disavow it. One way or other the prisoners ought to have either had the increased protection which the form of trial is supposed to give to a prisoner accused of treason ; or ought not to have had what was preferred against them solely as an accusation of sedition, indirectly aggravated by its being represented as amounting to treason.

There have been other hypotheses, besides the want of evidence, to account for the course that was followed. One is, that it avoided the inconveniences of trials for treason, while it did not mitigate the result of convictions of treason ;—another, that there was no real belief that the guilt of treason, *correctly speaking*, had been incurred, but that its vague imputation was merely rhetorical. A third, to which I give more credit, is forced upon myself by what I saw take place in the case of *Mackinlay* in the year 1817. Mr. Grant (now one of the Supreme Court Judges at Calcutta), who had been for above twenty years at the English bar, objected to an indictment for administering unlawful oaths, that its facts amounted to treason, and that, therefore, it was incompetent to try them as any inferior offence ; and he explained and defended this principle in an able printed argument. The court had no occasion to reject the principle, because, assuming it, they were of opinion that it was inapplicable. But they certainly did not recognise it. Nothing could be more evident than that its idea was a novelty to the minds of ordinary Scotch lawyers, insomuch that if Grant had not been much more of an English lawyer than a Scotch, the defence would never have been stated. The very phraseology in which it was expressed in the English authorities —such as the treason drowning the sedition, or the sedition merging in the treason—was treated as a subject of merriment, and sneered at as incomprehensible and English. It is not probable that the older judges had been better educated in treason law than their successors of that day.

Indeed, their ignorance, or disregard, of the legal necessity of never sinking treason, where the facts show it to have been committed, in any minor charge, is incidentally disclosed in one of Lord Abercromby's remarks in giving his opinion on the relevancy of Skirving's indictment. The Solicitor-General had announced that the convention had resolved to join the French if they should land in this country—that is, that they had resolved to adhere to the king's enemies; and he stated this *judicially, as a part of the case against Skirving.* Abercromby saw that this was the statement of a case of treason. Yet, instead of at once adopting the right conclusion, his observation is this:— "Nay, my Lord, if a fact which the Solicitor-General stated should come out in evidence, that the British Convention, as it is called, determined and resolved that, in case of a French invasion, a convention of emergencies was to be called,—*of course to assist that invasion,*—I think, if that be a fact, the public prosecutor MIGHT have laid his charge as high treason. But that is not the charge before us. It is a charge of sedition only." (*State Trials,* vol. xxiii. p. 512.) His Lordship does not appear to have seen that the public prosecutor *must* have laid it as treason ; or that, *on the strength of his own statement,* it was the duty of the court to compel him to do so. It is quite plain that if, instead of this treason, the prosecutor had taken any other,—as, for example, if he had imputed to the convention a scheme for *murdering the king*, but had only set this forth as an aggravation of sedition, this judge must, in consistency, have allowed the trial, though only for sedition, to have proceeded.

If it was a case of treason, or ought to have been considered as such, the whole proceedings were wrong from the first to the last.

Viewing it as a case of sedition, the evidence against Skirving consisted, on all the material points, of the written documents referred to in the libel. Sixteen witnesses were called, and the examination of most of them was necessary in point of form ; but their testimony does not affect the real truth of the case. Thus :—

1. Alex. Morren,
2. John Kidd,

Were called to prove the circulation of the Dundee address, and the prisoner's accession to it.

3. Joseph Mack.
4. John Dingwall.
5. William Scott.
6. Harry Davidson.
7. Provost Elder.
8. Mr. M'Vicar.
9. Mr. Coulter.
10. James Laing.

These eight prove the prisoner's declarations, the seizure of papers, the dispersion of the convention by the magistrates and by the sheriff, and such things.

11. William Ross.
12. Alex. Aitchison.
13. Geo. Ross.
14. David Downie.
15. James Robertson.
16. Will. Lind.

These six establish handwriting, and the proceedings in the convention ; on which last matter they, in substance, merely corroborate or explain the minutes.

As to all this there was really no dispute. The important evidence consisted of the writings charged as seditious, and the minutes of the Friends of the

People, and of the convention. The case is somewhat perplexed by what seems now to have been a very needless attempt by the prosecutor to prove consciousness of guilt by the suspiciousness of certain blanks in the minutes. This, so far as it is now intelligible, appears to be a very unsuccessful effort; because though there be certainly no want of blanks, these are not more frequent, nor in more important places, than what are generally to be found in the first draught of the accounts of the transactions of much higher, and less numerous, and perfectly innocent meetings. It is rather surprising to find these minutes so full and so rashly honest. But they record the transactions of men who were fearless and rash. The most dangerous parts of their proceedings were the parts they were proudest of. At any rate, if these minutes did not disclose their acts and their designs, nothing else brought forward at this trial did.

The question in reference to the prisoner's guilt is not as to the facts, but as to the conclusion to be deduced from them. In order to arrive at a sound result it is necessary to examine the charges separately.

I. The first fact set forth against him is his publication of the Dundee address.

I have spoken of this paper already in discussing the case of *Palmer*, and have only to repeat here that I think there was clearly sedition in some parts of it.

II. The convention was originally called together by an advertisement which invited certain descriptions of persons to join it, and it was argued that there was sedition in that part of the call which was addressed to the lowest of the people. The words are these : " The landholder is called upon to coalesce

with the Friends of the People, lest his property be
soon left untenanted ; the merchant, lest the commerce of the country be annihilated ; the manufacturer, whose laudable industry has been arrested
in its progress ; the unemployed citizen ; the great
mass of labouring and now starving poor ; and finally
all the rabble—are called upon by the remembrance
of their patriotic ancestors, who shed their blood in
the cause of freedom, and to whose memories even
the enemies of that cause are compelled to pay an
involuntary tribute of applause." It was conceded
that the landowner, the merchant, and the manufacturer, having all property, might lawfully be
courted ; and that the citizen, though unemployed,
and even the poor, starving though labouring, had
hopes which might be appealed to without crime ;
but it was held that the *rabble* could only be invited
for their physical strength, which disclosed a design
to use force if necessary ! "Calling upon the
rabble ! (exclaims *Lord Swinton*)—How are the
rabble to do it ? can they do it any other way than
by outrage and violence ? Is there any other instrument in their hands than that of outrage and
violence ?" (vol. xxiii. p. 511.) Since his Lordship
was not shocked at the starving poor being invited,
it is not easy to understand his horror of the rabble.
But in those days there was no tolerance for the
assumption of any opinion by the lower orders.
The very term *the people* was used sparingly, and
always with aversion. The *public* was the word for
the middle ranks, and all below this was the *populace*, or the *mob*. As an element in the constitution,
as the holders of lawful power, or as a respectable
portion of the public, *the people* were not recognised
in the thoughts or in the language of the loyal in

Scotland. They were called the rabble as a *sneer*, and it was by a retort of this sneer that the advertisement invited them.

III. There was still worse sedition discovered in the following passage of the same paper : " Had certain gentlemen countenanced this association last year, instead of pledging their lives and fortunes to prompt a corrupt and ambitious ministry to engage in a war which can only bring guilt and ruin on the nation, we might have been still enjoying uncommon prosperity, and a happy understanding among ourselves as brethren ; and now, if they will not retract that very impolitic step, and immediately join their influence to the only measure which can prevent further calamity, if not anarchy and ruin, *their pledge may be forfeited, and the friends of the people will be blameless.*" The meaning extracted out of this was, that if the loyal addressers, who (as usual) had pledged their lives and fortunes in support of the war, did not retract that pledge, the Friends of the People might *take their lives* without guilt, because the pledge had been forfeited. How few loyal addresses have failed to pledge life in support of the throne ? And of how few of them has it not been said that they had been broken ? Yet was it ever discovered before that this imputation was anything beyond a mere factious insult, and implied an instigation to murder the addressers ? If, however, this statement had the meaning imputed to it, it was worse than sedition. It was an invitation to murder.

IV. Being assembled, the convention did, as the libel states, " in imitation of the proceedings of the said French convention, call each other by the name of *citizen*, divide themselves into *sections*, appoint committees of various kinds, such as of *organisation*, of *instruction*, of *finance*, and of *secrecy* —denominate their meetings *sittings*, grant *honours of the sittings*, and inscribe their minutes with the *first year of the British Convention.*"

This imitation of the convention in France was also founded upon against the prisoners in the English trials, but in a very different tone and with a very different view. It was only employed there as a *circumstance of evidence*. Chief-Justice Eyre instructs the grand jury before whom the bill against Hardy was to be presented, thus : " In the course of the evidence you will probably hear of bodies of men being collected together, of violent resolutions voted at these and at other meetings, of some preparation of offensive weapons, and of the *adoption of the language and manner of proceedings of those conventions in France* which have possessed themselves of the government of that country. I dwell not on these particulars ; because I consider them, *not as substantive treasons, but as circumstances of evidence* tending to ascertain the true nature of the object which these persons had in view." (*State Trials*, vol. xxiv. p. 207.)

But in Scotland the fact is formally set forth, even in the indictments, not exactly as a substantive charge—for there is no charge except sedition—but as a circumstance of evidence *that is conclusive*. The Solicitor-General maintained, and the court supported the sentiment, that "*the very name of British Convention carries sedition along with it.*" (vol. xxiii. p. 486.) The word, or the assumption of the title of *Delegate* is uniformly treated as equally criminal. Yet, as was remarked in answer to this straining for seditious signs, both in the Scotch trials and the English ones, these are two ancient and innocent terms in the law of Scotland, indicating nothing either unusual or alarming. Not only had a *Convention of Delegates*, composed of men of high station and acknowledged loyalty, sat undisturbed and unsuspected in Edinburgh shortly before this very period, for the promotion of burgh reform ; but our royal burghs were directed by statute to elect their representatives in the House of Commons by means of *delegates;* and for above three centuries these burghs had annually assembled at Edinburgh in their municipal parliament as a *convention*, in which, except as a delegate, no member could be received.   The idea that an imitation of the terms and forms used in the French convention *necessarily*, or even *probably* implied an intention to imitate French king-killing and massacre, must seem strange to any one who observes the openness with which this imitation was practised ; or who recollects the tendency of all little societies to give themselves importance by mimicking some greater association.   Could the republicanism of an American be justly suspected because he wished his national Congress to copy the forms or phrases of the British monarchical House of Commons ?   Noticing this adoption of the machinery of the French Convention was perfectly fair ; and, *as a symptom*, it was an important circumstance *if proved*.   But it certainly ought not to have been considered as almost justifying a disregard of everything else in the case.

And all this part of the case is liable to an important observation, equally applicable to some others of these trials, and which it may be as well to state here, once for all.

Skirving's indictment, as well as those of Margarot and Gerrald, sets forth several averments of *terms and usages* peculiar to the new government of France, and of *events* that had recently occurred there —such as the murder of the king—the subversion of the monarchy—the existence of a body called the convention—their being at war with Britain, etc. These matters do not arise *incidentally* in the course of the trials, nor are they introduced by way of illustration, or explanation. They appear as parts of *substantive charges or statements in the indictment.*

Now *there is never even an attempt to prove any one of them.* They were all assumed without a vestige of evidence.

If, as I conceive, they required to be proved, these verdicts are all without evidence on the most important facts.

Certain public facts may be assumed, and are so in every trial, without being formally established by evidence. But they ought not to be assumed when they form *matters of charge, or appear in the libel as matters which the prosecution engages to establish.*

These French terms and occurrences are dealt with *as notorious,* without proof, in the corresponding cases of *Hardy* and others for treason. But *only as incidental* matter. The indictments do not set it forth; nor is it treated as matter of substantive charge; or as matter which, by announcing it as such, the prosecutor gives the accused reason to believe that his defence as to this matter is made out by the mere failure of the accuser to prove it. The indictment against Wakefield does set forth statements connected with invasion; and therefore though invasion, or the threat, and the fear of it were as universally notorious as the meridian sun, still, being interwoven into the body of the charge, a witness is called to swear that " at the commencement of last year there was a rumour of an invasion of this country by the French." (*State Trials*, vol. xxvii. p. 703.)

If this objection be well founded, it vitiates large and important departments of these trials.

V. It was resolved in the convention that " in case the minister bring into the Commons' House a motion for a convention bill, such as was passed in Ireland, it shall immediately be noticed to the delegates." And the object of this notice was explained, in a subsequent resolution, to be, that there should be what was termed " A Convention of Emergency ; " that " a secret committee of three and the secretary be appointed to determine the place where such Convention of Emergency shall meet ; that such place shall remain a secret with them, and that each delegate shall, at the breaking up of the present session, be intrusted with a sealed letter containing the name of the place of meeting ; this letter shall be delivered unopened to his constituents, and preserved, etc., until the period shall arrive when it shall be deemed necessary for the delegate to set off ; " and that " the moment of any illegal dispersion of the present convention shall be considered as a summons to the delegates to repair to the place of meeting." (vol. xxiii. p. 476.)

The Lord Advocate maintained this to be sedition in its most aggravated degree. In speaking of it, indeed, he calls it sedition and treason indiscriminately ; but his assertions, as to the real meaning of the resolution, make it clear treason in law. It was " the first step in that system of *anarchy and disorder which they wish for*, and which has taken place in a neighbouring country." (vol. xxiii. p. 554.)

This is too strong an inference. But there can be no doubt that it was a criminal resolution. The explanation given by the prisoner was, that the introduction into parliament of a bill for putting the convention down was a matter which they had a right to resist by constitutional means; that therefore they were obliged to meet about it; and that they concealed the intended place of assembling in order to avoid obstruction. However plausible this might appear to them, it naturally seemed to others much liker a project for defying an anticipated statute, or for overawing parliament from passing it. It was by far the worst fact against the convention, and most clearly seditious.

VI. It is stated in the indictment that when the provost and sheriff wished to disperse this body, the prisoner and his associates did "*resist* the authority of the said magistrates, and refused to depart unless they were compelled to do so by *force;* upon which the said provost, or some other magistrate then present, was obliged to lay hold of the person of him who was then acting as president, and *forcibly to draw him from his seat.*"

This is scarcely worth noticing except as a specimen of exaggeration. For, 1st, no such force was either necessary, or used. The magistrates all concur in stating that the members of the convention, holding themselves to form a lawful assembly, refused to depart without force; but Mr. Macvicar (soon afterwards provost) swears that the chairman said that " any SIGN of force was sufficient" (vol. xxiii. p. 522), and that accordingly the provost " went up to the chair, took Mr. Browne by the hand, and *gently* pulled him away." (p. 522.) The nature of this pulling is explained by the puller,

who says that he went to the chair "to *hand*
Mr. Browne out." (p. 520.) And in describing a
subsequent dispersion, next night, he (the provost)
says that they went away at once, " only, *as on the
evening before, desiring some* force to be used *by way
of etiquette.* " 2*d.* Their not dispersing would neither
have been seditious, nor evidence of sedition ; but
rather the reverse. It showed that they thought
their meeting lawful. If they had done anything,
in convention, after this, their being dispersed by
the magistrates might be used as a fact which
deprived them of the power of pleading ignorance of
the illegality of the meeting. But *the convention
never met again ;* and hence the only use to which
the prosecutor tries to turn the resistance to dispersion, consists in applying it as evidence of the guilt
of the convention's *previous* proceedings ; which is
absurd. But indeed, in reason, the whole thing is
utterly insignificant.

It is so insignificant, that it is not worth while
inquiring into an otherwise very material point,
which the prosecutor and the court always assumed.
This is, Whether the magistrates had *a right* to
disperse the meeting ? It was a meeting not said
to be committing any *breach of the peace.* Now,
under whatever *responsibility* men may assemble,
and speak, can their meeting, or their speeches, any
more than their writings, be *prevented*, or *suppressed*,
so long as the public peace is safe, and merely because
their proceedings may be reasonably suspected to be
seditious ? If a book cannot be prevented from
being published because it is to contain criminal
matter, can a speech be prevented from being spoken?
And if one man may speak, may not many ? And
if many, why may they not meet to speak ? It

would be idle to examine this bit of law here, for, either way, the law is immaterial. But to show that it is not so clear as the court assumed it to be, I may refer to a letter from Lord Eldon to his brother Lord Stowell, in August 1819, where he says : " An unlawful assembly, *as such merely*, I apprehend cannot be dispersed ; and what constitutes *riot* enough to justify dispersion is no easy matter to determine, where there is *not actual violence begun* on the part of those assembled." (*Eldon's Life*, vol. ii. p. 339.)

VII. After their dispersion, a proclamation and interdict was issued by the magistrates against their reassembling ; and it is set forth in the indictment that the prisoner repaired to the place where an intended meeting was to have been held ; where, " in place of only reading or notifying the judgment of the magistrates to those convened," it is said that he read a paper of the following tenor :—" Members of the Committee of the Friends of the People,— The magistrates of the city having forbid your legal and constitutional meeting, called this day by advertisement ; and by their proceedings to prevent it, having given occasion to a great concourse of people, which may issue in tumult, and must hinder your deliberations, it is judged proper to adjourn the meeting, and to lay the business of it before the several societies for their separate determination. It is therefore proposed to you to give place to the violence used against you. You will thereby convince the public that you did not deserve such treatment ; and now that your delegates have a permanent existence, your several societies will be multiplied greatly, and means will be used to lay the business before each society individually." (vol. xxiii. p. 479.)

This is in the same situation with the last charge. In itself it is immaterial; and as evidence of previous sedition, it is inapplicable. The magisterial order *as described in the libel* was directed exclusively against the *particular* meeting which it had been announced was to be held *that evening* in Edinburgh. The prisoner's paper had certainly no tendency to make *this* meeting be held; and its encouraging others is no evidence of any consciousness of the guilt of the convention. The proclamation neither made the convention illegal, nor necessarily extinguished the prisoner's belief of its innocence. Wise magistrates are generally too glad to see popular bodies disperse, to be offended or alarmed at the protestation about oppression and patriotism with which they generally go off; and to see such a circumstance so seriously brought forward, in such a case as this, compels us to suspect that, the prosecutor was less confident in the weightier matters of his charge than he professed to be.

VIII. The prisoner was also charged with having made or patronised certain inflammatory and dangerous motions, the statement of some of which really makes one stare. (vol. xxiii. p. 477.)

One of these was, " That the convention expresses its ardent desire *to cultivate a more close union with the societies in England,"*—there being no statement as to the names, or nature, or objects of any such societies. It seems to have been taken for granted that the Court of Justiciary in Scotland was accurately and judicially aware of all the sedition in England.

Another (which does not seem to have been carried) was, " *that delegates from the country who*

may run short of money from the prolongation
of the business of the convention, *shall be supplied
by the treasurer.*" (p. 426.) The convention only
existed about a fortnight, and so far as can be
detected, its funds never amounted to beyond a few
pounds sterling. So it was not the act of giving a
hungry country member his breakfast that was
criminal—for this never was done—but the pro-
mising it.

A third motion ascribed to Skirving in the
indictment, but which was made by Margarot, was,
that "all the members both of the convention and
of the primary societies should subscribe a Solemn
League and Covenant." (p. 477.) The Solicitor-
General's commentary on this is in these safe
terms :—" I am sure no words are necessary to
satisfy your Lordships that this was *most* illegal
and *most* seditious." (p. 488.) A Solemn League
and Covenant *in Scotland!*

IX. There are very few societies, lawful or unlawful, which do not require, or at least encourage,
their members to attend. The convention felt in
this respect like other clubs ; and therefore the
advertisement which called it together closed with
this *nota bene :* " *N.B.*—Those members who do not
attend or send an excuse will be publicly called upon
to give their reasons for absenting themselves." (p. 475.)
This most reasonable intimation actually raises the
Lord Advocate's horror to nearly its highest pitch.
Nothing places us so much within the very scene,
and lets us feel its heat so freshly, as that the
simple and ordinary notice that they would ask
their absent members why they had not been
present, should produce this burst of tolerated
absurdity. " Mr. Skirving tells you, in this

advertisement, that those members who do not attend, or send an excuse, will be publicly called upon. Those men, therefore, who choose to retract or alter their opinions—who choose to come back and join the majority of the country, to be faithful and loyal to their king, and attached to their constitution—had this menace held out to them, that they would be publicly called upon, in as public a way as this paper is circulated, to account for their conduct; intimidating them from following the dictates of their conscience, and exciting them to join in forming an arbitrary government, worse than the despotism of which a neighbouring country affords an example; domineering over the minds and bodies of their countrymen, and owning no authority but that which they mark with atrocious acts of injustice and cruelty." (vol. xxiii. p. 542.) What an exponent of the court is the fact that the prosecutor felt that this would be effective!

I am aware that in appreciating a criminal case the circumstances cannot be separated, but that the whole must be judged of under the light thrown on it from its various parts. For though every atom of irrelevancy or insignificance impairs the force of a complex case, the importance of the insignificance or irrelevancy can only be ascertained when the facts are viewed in combination. They may be all arranged by a meridian.

The meridian here is the convention. If it was innocent, the guilt of all the rest, even if it existed, was nearly immaterial. If the convention was guilty, there is much of the rest which must partake of its guilty character.

Now we have a better chance of having the existence, and the extent of its guilt safely appreciated, under the correct and decorous considerateness of English justice, than under the spirit which then excited the criminal tribunal of Scotland. And the way in which the matter was treated in England was this :—

1. It was conceded that a popular effort to obtain a reform in the constitution of parliament was not illegal, even though it should be conducted by an organised association,[1]—nay, even though this association should call itself, and should be, what was termed a convention. To refer to any particular passage in evidence of this would weaken the force of an admission which pervades the whole doctrines of all the prosecutors and of all the judges throughout the whole of the English trials. In Scotland, the court, besides expressly concurring in the sentiment of Blair, that the " very name of convention carries sedition on the face of it," uniformly held out this title as a sufficient foundation for inferring guilt.

2. It was not held that the attempt to reform parliament, though made by a convention, became illegal, even because the proposed reform consisted in annual parliaments and universal suffrage. All the English judges gave it as their opinion that such a reform was dangerous, and that it was connected with dangerous matter, and that it was absurd, and utterly repugnant to the genius of the British constitution as hitherto understood. But not one of them either lays it down as law, that the promotion of such a reform was illegal, or encourages any jury to hold the fact as conclusive evidence of sedition. Even Justice Rooke, who seems to me to have had

[1] The statutes against political societies with affiliated branches, secret committees, etc. did not pass for some years after this.

the nearest affinity (except, perhaps, Buller) to the least offensive of his Scotch brethren, only says this: " As to universal suffrage, we know, for three centuries past, we have had a legislative condemnation of universal suffrage in this country ; and in no country on the earth has universal suffrage ever prevailed. In a neighbouring country, after having tried it, they found it would not do.[1] In no country has it obtained; and it is, at this moment, contrary to the law of this country. After hearing that, whoever would, BY ANY OTHER MEANS THAN FAIR DISCUSSION, ENFORCE the doctrine of universal suffrage, is *a mischievous member of society.*" (*State Trials*, vol. xxv. p. 1150.) No doubt neither this, nor any other, reform can be legally enforced except by fair discussion. But in the Scotch court the principle was, that there could be no fair discussion on such a subject ; for the *end* was held to be criminal. *I think* that it was uniformly laid down from the bench, that at all times, and in whatever way advocated (except by petition to parliament, which was placed beyond the jurisdiction of the courts), the promotion of universal suffrage and annual parliaments was, *in itself*, not merely illegal, but criminal ; just as it was held that a proposal to abolish the monarchy would have been. But *indisputably* it was held that the urging of such a reform *at such a time* was criminal, and was conclusive evidence of the particular crime of sedition. Now this was clearly not held in England. So long as this reform — wild, dangerous, and ill-timed though it was — was urged only by fair discussion, and was not a cover for concealed guilt, the urging of it,

[1] Where was this ? In France, where it was never tried ? Or in America, where it succeeded ?

though by a convention, was there deemed innocent.

3. But it was not entitled to legal protection if
it was a mere *pretence ;* and whether it was a pretence or not, was a question of fact for the jury.
" I told the defendant " (says even Rooke) " that
you (the jury) should be apprised of what I considered to be the right of every man in this country,
—namely, that he has a right to discourse upon
speculative plans of reform; with this proviso, that
he shall not endanger the peace of his country.
For whenever speculative men are not contented
with, but go beyond, their abstract speculation, *it
is for a jury to determine whether they do not* MEAN
to do something more—so as to disturb the public
mind—to bring the Constitution into discredit,"
etc. (vol. xxv. p. 1149.)

All this being settled, the English judges always
put it to the juries—not in form, but in sincerity—
whether, upon the whole, the real design of the
convention was reform or revolution. And instead
of merely appealing, on this question, to the juries'
prejudices, or passions, or terror, or party interests,
they discuss it calmly, by observation and reasoning,
as a matter of fair judicial doubt ; and endeavour to
lead themselves, and those they are addressing, into
right conclusions, by accurate examinations of the
evidence, and candid general views ; " because one
great object of this prosecution must be, *that the
country may be satisfied,* and may see that the public justice of it has taken its fair course." (Eyre's
charge in *Hardy's* case, vol. xxiv. p. 1383.)

In this truly judicial spirit, these judges, though
all of them were party men, and personally would
have rejoiced with their party, in the conviction of

the prisoners, were so much better trained, that
they never mocked the juries, by first telling them
formally that they were to weigh the evidence, and
then giving them and the audience to understand
that they must be fools, and almost as criminal as
the prisoners, if they were accessible to the slightest
doubt ; but, seeing that the cases had two sides,
they gave fair play to each, and left the results
truly in the hands of the juries as dispassionate men.
As dispassionate men! No doubt the results were
left in the hands of the Scotch juries ; but were
they so left *as in the hands of dispassionate men ?*

Thus Eyre, in his beautiful charge in the trial
of Tooke, puts the case of the prosecutor, in so far
as it depends on the convention, thus :—" On the
part of the *prosecution* they say that they (the
prisoner and his associates) ought to be taken, upon
this evidence, to have called this convention for the
purpose of usurping the powers of the Government,
because they have proclaimed to the world that their
object was to have such a convention, and to put
this country upon the footing of a neighbouring
country, in which there is such a convention, which
has usurped the powers of Government. And they
say, for the prosecution, that after that declaration,
coupled, as it is, with all that conduct tending to
prepare the way for overthrowing monarchy and
aristocracy and all the orders of the State, they have
a right to insist that it is not enough for those persons, who are charged with high treason, to insist,
and to bring witnesses to say, that that was not their
intention, but that their intention fell far short of
it ; for that they ought to be tried by their conduct
rather than by their professions, and that their conduct marks that this was their object ; their con-

duct in respect of their general publications—their conduct in respect of the National Convention of France—their conduct in respect of the Scotch Convention,—leaving out all the smaller intermediate parts of the evidence, from whence a great deal of matter might be picked out, some of it affording grounds of suspicion, some going a great way beyond suspicion, and fairly affording a ground to collect this intent.

"Gentlemen, *this is the strong part of the prosecutor's case; and here I think he must leave his case,* for I do not see myself that he has carried it any further than to show that the conduct of these societies has been the conduct of determined republicans; that they have taken all occasions to countenance the idea of a revolution here, to be effected by a national convention, which was to be the form of government to be established in the place of the existing government of the country; and that they had irritated the public mind by every artifice that they could possibly use, in order to prepare them for such a crisis, and to make such a use of the national convention, wherever that national convention should in fact be formed. And, gentlemen, it is certainly true that if you look at this case, IN THE EXTERIOR OF IT, and upon the outline which I have stated, there is *great ground* to impute this to those societies; and it would be difficult for this prisoner in particular to take himself out of that implication." (*State Trials,* vol. xxv. p. 738.)

Having thus stated the case on the one side, observe the fair spirit with which he immediately proceeds to give a similar general view of it on the other.

"But that this conduct may yet be explained, and that, when the question is with the jury, whether

that which all mankind might be justified in suspecting, *does really turn out to be sufficiently founded
in fact, and to be so distinctly proved as to warrant
a jury who are bound to acquit if there remains any
doubt upon the case in finding a verdict of guilty, is
quite another consideration.*

" Gentlemen, I consider everything beyond the
outline I have stated—*which outline I consider as
the prosecutor's evidence*—I say I consider everything
beyond that as evidence on the part of the person
accused. This inquiry has let us into a great deal
of the interior of these societies ; and it has produced
a discovery, I cannot say very much to the honour
of their leaders, that *they have magnified their
numbers and their strength*—for a purpose which
every man must see—*very much beyond the truth.*"
(He gives two examples.) " There was an ostentatious display of force, of strength, and of consequence, which they really had not, with a view to
mislead the public. But however that may be, yet
the true state of these societies, and of the Constitutional Society in particular, will certainly have a
material effect upon the question of fact, whether at
the time this national convention was proposed, they
really had it in their minds to use it to usurp the
government of the country? because it is a very
essential thing to inquire, when a great end is proposed, what are the means by which it is to be
effected? It appears upon the evidence that the
Constitutional Society had neither numbers, money,
nor even zeal, according to the evidence. Sinclair
complained very much that he was abandoned when
he was in Scotland. Very often their committees
would not, and did not, meet. I am not speaking at
present of Mr. Horne Tooke, the prisoner, personally.

But that seemed to be the general conduct of the Society. They seem to have had no resources such as men naturally furnish themselves with who engage in desperate enterprises. From all the examination, we have not been able to trace any direct conspiracy, pointed to this object, by individuals who can be named. Nay, the contrary is proved, as far as the evidence goes. They say that this man, and that man, and the other man, and every man that they had any knowledge of, were not involved in any such conspiracy; and there certainly is a difficulty upon this evidence in that respect, admitting that the general outline I have stated would warrant very strict conclusions; yet upon whom to fix this conspiracy seems to remain a thing of difficulty." (*State Trials*, vol. xxv. p. 739.)

I give these as mere examples of the judicial state of his mind, and of the impartial and reasoning frame into which, in spite of his strong political feelings, he must have brought the jury. Similar examples present themselves in every page; and it must be impossible for any age to follow the progress of some of these trials without feeling the presence of a JUDGE—of an eminent person, by no means devoid of partialities, nor superior even in legal learning, and far inferior in talent to many with whom he was acting; but trained by professional habit, controlled by a powerful bar and an independent public, and attracted by high official taste, towards the ambition of doing his duty well; and thus, so presiding over scenes of great political importance, and of ardent and difficult civil conflict, that every person around, from the prisoner opposed by the Crown, to the attorney-general wielding the whole of the Crown's legal force—from the counsel of the accused, tempted and privileged to sacrifice almost everything to the safety of their client, to the audience, composed indiscriminately of the friends and the enemies of both parties—from the witnesses by whom, under a severe, and often offensive, process, the facts are stated to the jury, separated from the world, by whom these facts are to be appreciated, —all feel that they are in a temple of justice, and are all impressed with a disposition to do homage to that justice by which they are conscious that they are all controlled, and protected, and guided.

The result was that all the English treason prisoners were acquitted, by verdicts which show well-conducted trial by jury in a magnificent light, and saved this country from possible proscription and from speedy revolution. Yet it was not the acquittals that were chiefly valuable. It was the fairness of the trials. Convictions would have done great mischief; because above one-half of the community had previously committed itself in a manner that would have placed it entirely at the mercy of a terrified and triumphant party. But still even convictions, *if preceded by such trials,* would have been less mischievous than acquittals got by trials that were unfair. Nothing stills a people, even under a revolution, so surely as their confidence in the administration of the law; and therefore no evil is so great as judicial injustice, or as even these deviations from the manner and appearance of justice, which custom has gradually introduced as essential to its reality, and with which the public reverence is associated.

Whether these English prisoners would have been acquitted if they had only been charged with sedition, or whether the Scotch ones charged with sedition ought to have been convicted, or would have been so if tried in England, is a different question. But applying the principle and feelings which breathe through the English trials to the Scotch ones, it does not seem to me to be possible for any candid legal critic to doubt that an honest and rational jury might have either acquitted Skirving and his associates (whose cases were substantially all the same), or might to a certain extent have condemned them. The great fact that is quite certain is that each prosecutor and each prisoner *had a case;* and that crushing and revelling over the accused, confidently and peremptorily, under the forms and the phraseology, but without the genuine spirit of trial, was not merely indecorous, but was utterly unwarranted by the nature of the matter with which the court had to deal.

If I, with my present views, had been a juror on these Scotch *convention* trials, I would have been clear for convicting the prisoners of *something*, and of something *serious.* I never could have concurred in a general conviction on all the matter said to be seditious, but must have held some of it to be innocent and some absurd. In particular, I could not have believed that the convention meditated the treason imputed to it, or meant to do more than to promote that reform which consisted in universal suffrage and annual parliaments; and this not by force or revolution. As little, however, considering the times, could I have thought the prisoners entirely innocent. Much of their language was too disdainful of authority, and was plainly used in order to diminish the people's awe of authority. And some of their resolutions justified the belief that they wished to shake the people's confidence in the legislature for the purpose of fixing it on themselves—not certainly from the crazy and incredible hope that the convention was able to supersede parliament in its own favour, but from the policy, or rather the instinct, which makes every opposition party, especially during great struggles, try to strengthen itself by attracting reliance, and to startle power by the prospect of its own danger. Their worst acts in this way consisted in their arranging, or rather in their announcing that they had arranged, a general convocation of their members all over the country by means of sealed letters and a committee of emergency, etc. ; for the execution of which the introduction of a convention bill into parliament by the minister was to be the signal.

In short, the attainment of their favourite reform was impossible without popular support ; this they could not secure without convincing the people that they would never have their grievances redressed by parliament constituted as it was ; in this position they were obliged to cry parliament down, and to cry themselves up ; and in violent times sedition is almost inseparable from the practical solution of the party problem with which these men had to deal. In all this there was nothing new. Many of the wisest and the best men conducting the most loyal parties, in their obstructed efforts for reforms of demonstrable necessity, have been placed in the same situation.

A correct trial, succeeded by a discriminating verdict, and ending in a rational and legal, though rather severe punishment, would have satisfied justice, and saved the court.

But how were they tried? how were they convicted? and how were they punished?

As soon as Skirving's indictment was read, a proceeding took place for which, so far as I know, there had been no precedent in any Scotch criminal trial. The Solicitor-General rose and addressed the court in a full speech, in which he went at large, and of course with the usual exaggeration of counsel, into all the circumstances of the case and of the times. This speech, though professed to be only intended to *explain* the charges, was powerfully calculated to make the jury *believe* them. *Prisoners* have sometimes, though very rarely, made such preliminary addresses, partly from indulgence, and partly because it is then, for the first time, that they have an opportunity of letting the judges or jurymen know what the defence is to be. And if they were not allowed to explain this in a speech, they would only require to write it, and then to read it as their formal defence, as is usual at this stage. But though with these considerations in its favour, such speeches are very rare even from prisoners ; and I cannot discover any other example of one by a prosecutor, whose charge, in all its details, is in the hands of the judges before the trial, and is read publicly to the jury. Nor had anything occurred to provoke a speech on this occasion. In particular, neither the court nor the accused had said anything against the libel, the relevancy of which was the only point then properly under consideration. But the Solicitor avowed that he spoke " *for the sake of the jury who are to try this case*"—being the very reason why he should have been stopped.

Nor, with all my reverence for Blair, can I say that there was anything worthy of him in this speech, even as an address to the jury. He was allowed at this stage to reconcile the jury to inattention and premature confidence, by letting them know that their task was to be a very easy one, as "the very name of British convention carries sedition along with it." (vol. xxiii. p. 486.) Universal suffrage "is an idea that never entered the head of those who framed the Constitution," "*nor was it ever maintained or even thought of by anybody else;*" "an idea never adopted in any country, ancient or modern ; at least in any government of the extent of Great Britain it was never tried, except indeed in one instance,—a modern experiment,—and one which I should have thought that no nation in the world would choose to repeat—I mean the experiment of France." (vol. xxiii. p. 487.) He had forgotten the successful experiment of America, which, though not confirmed by time in 1794, was at least less modern than the French one. " The law (he says) is always the same—immutable, but the crime (sedition) is of that nature that the circumstances of the time must operate very strongly " (vol. xxiii. p. 489) ; which position he thinks it worth while to illustrate by an example which was deemed striking at the time, and has been repeated by Alison and others since. The firing of a shot or two on the Castle Hill by a few persons with white cockades would have been harmless, he says, five or six years before, but would have been treason in 1745. Did anybody ever doubt that the criminality or the innocence of a political act was liable to be affected by the political circumstances of the times ? But his inference, which is that the state of France was *conclusive* of the guilt of the convention, is plainly unwarranted. For where British subjects are exercising a constitutional privilege, though in an imprudent way, and for the attainment of an extravagant, but still a legal object, their conduct, however imprudent, cannot be made criminal merely by the contagious dangerousness of what is passing in a foreign country. Are we to lose every right which foreign politics make it dangerous for us to exercise? The establishment of a republic in France would probably make the principles, and even the ordinary language, of British freedom too exciting to many of our own people ; but would this render the use of it illegal?

As soon as this ill-timed novelty was over, the Justice-Clerk went out of his way, in his turn, to impress it the more on the jury, and apparently to invite its prolongation. "You have given us (said he, addressing himself to the Solicitor) a *very good commentary* upon the indictment, but there is one part which you have not read, and *I want to hear your commentary upon the words* of it." His Lordship then read the following sentence from the convention's address : "And now if they will not manfully retract that very impolitic step, and immediately join their influence to the only measure which can prevent further calamity, if not anarchy and ruin, *their pledge may be forfeited, and the Friends of the People will be blameless.*" The Solicitor's explanation of this passage is—"That whatever mischief happens, the blame is not to be laid on the Friends of the People, because they have so good a cause." Instead of merely listening to this in silence, as to the statement of a party, and waiting till the opposite, and by legal presumption, the innocent party could give his interpretation, his Lordship publicly announces his own opinion ; for an opportunity of declaring which it is plain that all this preparation had been made. "*Lord Justice-Clerk.*

—I suppose the Friends of the People *might cut our throats with impunity*—they would not be blameable." (vol. xxiii. p. 490.)[1]

Skirving, who had chosen to be his own counsel, then read a written address on what he supposed, or professed to suppose, was the relevancy ; but which, like the speech that had preceded his, was just a premature discussion of the facts. His worst enemy could scarcely have furnished him with a discourse better fitted to aggravate the hostility of those who were to try him, or worse fitted to ingratiate a defence even with a jury that was unprepossessed. Mere trash.

The libel was found relevant, after speeches from the bench in the usual style.

The prisoner repeated the objection to all the jurors who were members of the Goldsmiths' Hall Association ; of course, after the judgment in Muir's case, without effect. But Skirving's objection was not nearly so strong as Muir's ; because though he also had been expelled from the association, or had rather been denied admission into it, this had not been specially connected with his having dissemi-

---

[1] This is something like Chief-Justice Scroggs in the case of *Stayley*, where, as fair trial was endangered by prejudice against the Catholics, Popery should either not have been alluded to, or the prevailing panic about it should have been guarded against. But Scroggs told the jury, who were all Protestants, that the Catholic principle was that " whoever are not of their persuasion are heretics ; and whoever are heretics may be murdered (if the Pope commands it), for which they may become saints in heaven. This is what they have practised." (*State Trials*, vol. vi. p. 1510.) Nothing is more common than thus mistaking a sect for a crime. *See* Lister's remark in his *Life of Clarendon*, vol. ii. p. 512, on the case of *Keach*. This person had published a child's primer, containing doctrines chiefly about infant baptism and the Millennium, inconsistent with the liturgy and the creed of the Church—a nonsensical charge, but quite suited to the times (Charles II.), and a trial most disgraceful to the court. (*State Trials*, vol. vi. p. 702.) But the prisoner happened to be a Fifth Monarchist, and, in truth, it was for this, and not for his theology, that he was persecuted. In the same way, though the political doctrines of these Scotch prisoners were thought dangerous, the great sin of the men consisted in their belonging to the reforming party.

nated Paine's works; nor did such dissemination form the principal charge in his trial. He had been rejected merely because his general politics were offensive. Muir had been condemned by the associates for the precise fact for which as jurymen they tried him.

The judicial manner of disposing of the objection was very characteristic. Whether it was well or ill-founded, the prisoner had at least stated it clearly and inoffensively. His words—and his *whole* words —were : " I object in general to all those who are members of the Goldsmiths' Hall Association. And, in the second place, I would object to all those who hold places under Government, because it is a prosecution by Government against me ; and therefore I apprehend they cannot, with freedom of mind, judge in a case where they are material parties." It is scarcely credible that this legal objection should have been instantly represented and rejected, by men acting as judges, thus. " *Lord Eskgrove.*—This gentleman's objection is that his jury ought to consist of the Convention of the Friends of the People ; that every person wishing to support Government is incapable of passing upon his assize. And *by making this objection the panel is avowing that it was their purpose to overturn the Government.*" *Lord Justice-Clerk.*—" Does any of your Lordships *think otherwise ? I daresay not.*" *Mr. Skirving.*—" The ground of my objection to these gentlemen was, not that they belonged to that association : by no means ; but that they have prejudged me by striking my name out of their society." *Lord Justice-Clerk.* —" I remember the same objection was stated by Mr. Muir, and was overruled." (vol. xxiii. p. 513.)

Fifteen jurors were then picked. I afterwards knew them all except two, James Craig of Seton

Hall, and Edward Innes, confectioner. The thirteen whom I knew, and I have no doubt these two also, were very good men, and as fit to try this case, as an assize of honest and frightened Episcopalians, selected by Lauderdale, would have been to try a Covenanter. The favourite answer of the prosecutor and of the bench in this, and in all these cases, to the imputation of prejudice, was, that the country was divided into the friends of the Constitution and its enemies, and that the prisoners had no claim to be tried only by the latter. " Is the sheriff (said the Lord Advocate), in returning his roll of forty-five names, on the assize, to inquire previously who are attached to the Constitution, and who revile and conspire against it, and to return only those of the latter description? and to exclude all the former? Are traitors only to sit as jurymen on trials for high treason ? Long, I trust and believe, will this pre-judice, of which the panel complains, subsist in full force and vigour." (vol. xxiii. p. 538.) This was quite satisfactory at the time ; and the principle was steadily acted upon. Since those who were deemed traitors, *but had not been convicted of treason*, were unfit to try persons accused of that offence, and since those who reviled the Constitution could not be trusted with cases of sedition, the sheriff was encouraged, if not obliged, to inquire, *as it was most notorious that in point of fact he invariably did*, into political opinions, before making his return. He was led by the principles laid down for his guidance by the Crown and by the court, independently of any inclination of his own, to return those only who were considered right men ; and the presiding judge would have thought himself contemptible if he had scrupled to adopt, and to avow the operation of the same principle in his far more decisive selection. It is, unhappily, true, that it would not have been easy to have produced a perfectly fair jury on such subjects, in Scotland, at that period. But had it not been for this ostentatious *preference*, by the court and the public accuser, for the *prominent* men of their own party, it could not have happened that they always succeeded in filling the box with the greatest possible amount of unfairness. There were calm and respectable men, on both sides, liable to serve ; a slender infusion of whom would have been conducive to justice, and to its appearance ; but they were necessarily excluded by the avowed principle that those only could be trusted who, as the Lord Advocate stated, " were PREJUDICED *in favour of the British Constitution* " *!* (vol. xxiii. p. 538.)

I have already said all that is necessary about the evidence.

The prosecutor's speech to the jury was at least better than the prisoner's. The prisoner's, indeed, was as wretched as the one he had already delivered himself of ;—ignorant, tedious, powerless, offensive without effect, even in the offensive line ; and desultory without variety ;—the speech of a vulgar man who did not know the strength of his own case, and had not mind to feel the force of the appeal which most political prisoners who are harshly tried may successfully make to the public and posterity.

Braxfield's charge was worthy of himself.

I am one of those who think that, in Scotland, where prisoners have always counsel, and their counsel speaks last, the occasions are few on which a criminal judge can do his duty by summing up, without indicating his opinion of the prisoner's innocence or guilt. And there is a good deal to be said in favour of the view which goes even beyond this, and requires a criminal judge not merely to *indicate* his result, but to feel such responsibility for the verdict as to state his opinion openly and plainly, and even to give it the weight which is imparted to the judgments of any sensible man by the grounds of them being explained; and thus to lead the jury, by the same process that operated on himself, to the same conclusion. This, however, requires to be very cautiously done; for it certainly borders upon the dangerous line of the judge's superseding the jury altogether, or letting them feel that they need not exercise their own intellects, but may repose passively upon the authority of the court. Dangerous, however, as this system of charging may be, it is one which is not infrequently practised by many good Scotch judges.

And there are some circumstances which naturally lead them into it, and led their predecessors still more. The absence of civil juries deprived the old criminal judges of all experience of jury business except in the Court of Justiciary.[1] And the cases have long been so well prepared, by the public prosecutor, for this court that they are generally clear, which tends to generate a habit of confident negligence. Everything done in that court is done finally and irreversibly; so that no Justiciary judge remarks, or directs, or decides, under any fear of legal correction in any form. The spirits, too, of the old judges were exhausted, and their tempers pretty well tried, by the whole evidence, in cases inferring death or demembration, with all its wranglings, being taken down in writing.[2] To these men,

---

[1] Jury trial in civil causes was only introduced in 1815.
[2] This was only abolished by the 23d Geo. III. cap. 45.

whose opinions of the case had probably transpired involuntarily, and fretfully, a dozen of times in the course of the day, the summing up, besides being the approach of relief, was the occasion for their justifying all their previous rash disclosures, and they naturally made it one-sided and positive,—a tone that was perfectly safe where the picking had excluded obstreperous characters from the jury-box. The radical defect was the finality. They were not only undisturbed by any vision of any motion for a new trial—which it would not be easy to engraft on any part of the British criminal system—but they were, and, unfortunately, still are, freed from any reference to other judges, or even to themselves, on reserved points. The tendency of this is somewhat corrected now, by their training in civil causes, and its consequent occasional exhibition of the possibility and extent of judicial error. But still the absolute finality is a great evil, and hurt the old judges to a degree which can scarcely be estimated at present.

But even when a judge really means to secure a particular verdict, or thinks it his duty to reduce juries to be chiefly instruments in his hands, there are certain arts by which decorum and skill may prevent this from being seen, and may diminish its impropriety by hiding its indecency. Mildness and seeming deference will allure a jury, which it would be unsafe to attempt to drive. Elaborate exposition, and minute collation of evidence, interspersed with good commentary, will overpower unpractised minds by apparent superiority in dealing with legal proof. And the dexterous candour of appearing to leave everything to their better judgment,— but not till this judgment has received an impression only the deeper that it has been conveyed by insinuation,—flatters them into harmony with the court by the very delusion that they are independent of it.

These arts are oftener practised than avowed. And they may sometimes be useful, especially where there is a popular prejudice against innocence. But they will never be stooped to by a great judge, who, maintaining the law, and yielding, after fairly instructing them, to the jury on the facts, will have more weight by wisdom and simplicity, than could be derived from the deepest use of the nicest skill. Where a judge is determined, however, no matter for what reason, that the verdict shall be his, these arts suggest the forms in which this usurpation may be practised with the least injury to the character of the court. They were, therefore, all despised by Braxfield, who, devoid of all conception of what constituted a court's character,—sure of his times and of his jury,—and eager for victims, proceeded in this, and in all his charges in these cases, on the coarse and audacious principle that the jury were ready to have given their verdict as soon as they had taken their seats,—that all that they wanted being the countenance of the court, they could not get it too plainly, and that everything that suggested doubt, or consideration, or candour, or recognised the case as susceptible of more than one view, was needless, since none of these feelings truly existed. Accordingly, instead of trying to elevate them to a purer region, above the interests and contentions of the world they ought to have left, the tendency of all that he said was to keep them sunk into the position of party men, and to let them know that the court would back them.

He sets out in this case of *Skirving* by instructing the jury what sedition is, and his definition—*the whole of it*—is in these words : " I take the crime of sedition *to be the violating the peace and order of society;* and it is attended with different degrees of aggravation, according to what is the object of it ; when sedition has a tendency to *overturn the constitution of this country* it *borders* upon high treason; and if it goes that length it loses the *name* of sedition, and is buried under the greater crime of high treason ; and a very little more than is contained in this indictment would have made it the crime of high treason." (vol. xxiii. p. 589.)

Sedition is " *the violating the peace and order of society* "—a description which omits all the qualities by which a person charged with this offence is protected by law, and includes all the circumstances by which he is apt to suffer from prejudice. Innocence of intention is nothing. The exercise of constitutional right is nothing. The liability of society to be endangered almost to occasional dissolution by legal struggles for its improvement is nothing ; and the jury are instructed that he of whom the abstract fact can be truly stated, that he has violated the peace of society, is guilty of sedition—a doctrine which can only be appreciated when we recollect the tendency of men to believe that their party is society.

Instead of attempting to allay the party feelings which he knew well were most likely to warp them, he inflamed them by these purely political words and allusions : " Gentlemen, in considering this case, one thing occurs to me, and that is, the conjuncture under which these facts are alleged. It was during the time when this nation is engaged in a bloody war with a neighbouring nation, *consisting of millions of the most profligate monsters that ever disgraced humanity; justice will never enter into their ideas, but they swallow up all before them;* and I say, gentlemen, that *the greatest union in this nation is necessary, in these circumstances, to support us under this war.* And therefore, gentlemen, *supposing,* in short, that this nation has been feeling some grievances from any imperfection attending the Constitution, I say, under these circumstances, *this is not the time to apply for relief;* and I appeal to your own feelings, and your own good sense, if *it would not be brought forward better at any other time;* and that we should employ all our force to get rid of that foreign enemy, upon which the safety and the happiness of the country does in a great measure depend." (vol. xxiii. p. 589.)

This made the jury's task abundantly easy, for it brought all opposition and all reform under the ban of sedition. It gave them up their whole political adversaries, comfortably and legally, to be dealt with as seditious, the misfortune of which for the prisoners was that little else was needed for conviction in those days.

He had made the *supposition* that we had grievances ; but in order to correct any error that this might lead to, he immediately explains that this was a mere argumentative assumption, and that in truth no man could seriously assert that our grievances were so great as to endanger the country (which was the genuine belief of many) without furnishing evidence of his own sedition by that mere fact. "*Every one must admit* that of all the nations under the sun, Great Britain is the happiest ; and that under all the imperfections that may attend their Constitution, it is the most complete system of government that ever existed upon the face of this earth, with all its imperfections. I am sure, gentlemen, you must be sensible that you enjoy your lives, and your properties, and everything that is dear to you, in perfect security. Every man is certain that he will not be deprived of anything that belongs to him ; and there is no man, let him be as great a grumbletonian as he will, if he is asked where he is hurt by the imperfections of the Constitution, he cannot tell you, but, on the contrary, that he is living happily under it. *Gentlemen, when that is the case, what construction must you put upon the proceedings of a society who represent this country as on the very brink of destruction ? I submit to you whether that is the work of the people who have a real regard for society.* And if you are of opinion that these meetings are of a seditious nature, and of a seditious tendency, when the question comes home to the panel at the bar, you *must* find him guilty." (vol. xxiii. p. 590.)

The frightfulness of this principle will be perceived by those who observe the *historical fact*, that there never has been, and probably never can be, any animated struggle for any reform in which the reformers, especially when they are quite honest, rest their claim, or can rest it, on any other ground except that the evil complained of is bringing the country to destruction. What else secured the Revolution, the Protestant succession, the libel law, the repeal of the Catholic disabilities, and Test Acts, the abolition of the slave-trade, the reform of Parliament, or any other of the great changes which are now parts of the law ? On Braxfield's principle, he must have recommended a Bristol jury to condemn Wilberforce for predicting, if not invoking, the vengeance of heaven on Britain for adhering to the slave-trade ; and would have brought both Burke and Chatham within the talons of his definition, for their speeches (out of Parliament), against the American War—speeches which did not merely assert the speedy extinction of this country, but did what they could to produce this result, by applauding the revolt that was to accomplish it. These men did not ungird their loins, and relapse into silence, and give their respective mischiefs another long lease of toleration, because we were at war, or because their agitation might alarm the friends of abuses, or even shake society.

Referring to the resolution about forfeited pledges, he repeats to the jury the calm and elegantly expressed construction which he had previously announced, that he thought the only one of which it was susceptible. " What is the construction of that language ? Why, *certainly* that the people would be *bound* to rise, and that they were *at liberty* to destroy such tyrants ; and that their lives and property would be forfeited, and these friends of the people *would do no harm*, in the cause of liberty, *by cutting their throats*. That is the plain English of that paragraph. I can see no other." (vol. xxiii. p. 592.)

There was no evidence produced of Palmer's conviction. There could be none properly, except by the production of the record of the conviction, which does not seem to have been exhibited. Indeed, it was not libelled on as a production. And if it had been tendered, though it might have established the fact of a conviction of a person called Palmer, it could not have established the seditious nature either of the address or of any other fact, for which he was punished, *as a circumstance against Skirving in the present trial.* Skirving's jury was not bound, and not even entitled, to be decided, or even to be influenced, by the opinion of a different jury, in a different trial, respecting the guilt or the innocence of a paper or of a fact. The same matter may occur in separate trials; but —and especially where the accused are different— it must be gone over again in the second; for one jury, or court, is entitled to approve of what a separate court or jury, or even the same court or jury, in a different trial, may have condemned. Even the *guilt* of Palmer was not a relevant fact against Skirving; for the intentions of the two men, and the circumstances in which they acted, might be different.

Notwithstanding all this, the *Lord Justice-Clerk* refers to Palmer's conviction as morally, if not legally, conclusive against Skirving. "Gentlemen, Fyshe Palmer's publication, *of all that I ever read* (!) is of the *most* seditious tendency, and a more wicked publication it *was not possible for human invention to devise* (!); and accordingly Palmer was very justly indicted for that composition, and he was found guilty at the last circuit at Perth by a most respectable jury; in consequence of which he is condemned to banishment by transportation." (vol. xxiii. p. 591.) Had there been any evidence of the charge against Palmer, and of his conviction—which, however, I cannot discover that there was—all this might be tolerated, because the paper itself was produced, and the jury could judge of it. But observe the use which he makes of Palmer's conviction, *as conclusive against Skirving.* "Palmer was justly found guilty of sedition, because he allowed it (the address) to go out to the world ; and *I say Skirving is equally guilty of the pains of law with Palmer."* (vol. xxiii. p. 591.) This (*as usual*) was going beyond the prosecutor, who had told the jury (p. 539) that notwithstanding Palmer's conviction, they were bound to read and to construe it for themselves.[1]

The Lord Advocate and the Justice-Clerk, and indeed all the judges, uniformly lay great stress on the circumstance that Skirving was *secretary* to the convention ; and treat this as sufficient of itself to make him responsible for all it did. This however was not the English view. Hardy was secretary to the Constitutional Society, but Eyre tells the jury that this was immaterial. " Had he acted *only* as secretary, it might be said, he might have been misled in a great many things ; he might have written many things which he did not understand, or which he had not time to weigh ; as a man might write whole

[1] In the trial of Sydney, Chief-Justice Jefferies allowed the conviction of Lord Russell to be read as evidence against the prisoner. (*State Trials*, vol. ix. p. 859.) In Skirving's case the record of the conviction of Palmer was not read, and, since it was not specified as an intended production, it could not be read. But independently of these technical defects, Phillipps's criticism is unquestionably sound. "The conviction of Lord Russell could not, on any legal principle, be admitted as evidence against Sydney, who was a stranger to those proceedings, and had no opportunity of controverting them, or of making his defence against them. Nor, on the other hand, if Lord Russell had been acquitted, would the proof of his acquittal have been legitimate evidence in favour of Sydney. For the opinion of a jury on a former prosecution, as to the innocence or guilt of a prisoner (which must be supposed to have proceeded on the evidence then produced), could not afford any reasonable inference to guide the judgment of a different jury, on a different state of facts, as to the guilt or innocence of another person." (Phillipps's *State Trials*, vol. ii. p. 115.)

This error was corrected in the subsequent case of *Hampden ;* against whom Sydney's conviction was not allowed to be produced. (*State Trials*, vol. ix. p. 1078 ; *Phillipps*, vol. ii. p. 119.)

Hardy's *acquittal* was allowed to be given in evidence for Horne Tooke ; *but only because Hardy's guilt was set forth in the indictment as a fact against Tooke* (see *Phillipps*, vol. ii. p. 115).

sheets without having any idea of the sense after he had written them. *It was therefore very much in his favour to consider the prisoner only as a secretary."* (*State Trials*, vol. xxiv. p. 1372.) Nor does he apply this remark to the case of a person *not a member*, who is brought in merely to write, for Hardy was a member. But he goes on to deduce guilt from his having acted as principal—holding the *additional secretaryship*, even of this influential member, as insignificant.

There was never any want with Braxfield of the *phrases* of a charge. " Gentlemen, I leave the case in your hands." " It is for you to say ; " " It is you who are to be satisfied ; " " If you have a doubt, the prisoner is entitled to the benefit of it." These judicial *forms of speech* are all duly sprinkled over what he called his summings up. But the judicial *spirit* in which they were used may be estimated from the nature of the discretion which he gives the jury to understand that they may exercise. There is no case in which any prisoner has so strong a claim to that protection, and even to that chance, which the Constitution supposes to consist in his being left liberally in the hands of a jury, as when he has the Crown for his adversary, in a trial for a political offence. Dictation by the court is never so offensive as there. Yet the charge of this supreme criminal judge teems with observations amounting to sneers at the idea of innocence, and with many things very like invitations to convict, and defiances to acquit. Thus he pretends to exhibit a correct view of the evidence, and then suggests the very result for the loss of which his heart would have been grieved. " IT WOULD BE VERY DIFFICULT FOR ME TO CONCEIVE IT POSSIBLE THAT THIS MAN, NOW AT THE BAR, CAN

BE FOUND NOT GUILTY." (vol. xxiii. p. 591.) And guilty of every *article* charged ; of all the facts, in all their details. " Gentlemen, I will not run through all the other evidence ; *for indeed almost* EVERY ARTICLE *of this libel is proved.*" (vol. xxiii. p. 591.)

He was right—in the opinion of the jury. They unanimously found him guilty " of the CRIMES libelled."

There was only one libelled—sedition. Therefore they could only mean that the prisoner was guilty of all the *acts* charged. But this was an inaccurate verdict ; at least a verdict inaccurately expressed. No advantage was attempted to be taken of this blunder ; and probably none could have been taken. Whatever merit the jury might have had in other respects, however, they certainly did not deserve the Justice-Clerk's compliment, in so far as correctness was concerned. " Gentlemen (said he), you have returned a very proper verdict ; and I am sure you are entitled to the thanks of your country for the attention you have paid to this trial." (vol. xxiii. p. 593.)

Then came the vintage.

Lord Eskgrove held the verdict to have established—which it certainly did—that " this man is guilty in *general*—that he is guilty of *the whole* indictment " (p. 596), " of one and all the *facts charged against him in the minor proposition.*" (p. 595.) His Lordship was " always very sorry to pronounce sentence upon any of my fellow-subjects *for sedition ;* of the heinousness of which I had flattered myself, from two late instances, every man was so thoroughly sensible that I should not have occasion again to sit upon a trial of that kind." (p. 594.) But then the crime of which the prisoner had been convicted was that " of attempting to imitate the example of the late revolution in a neighbouring country, in which country now exists everything that is horrible in nature—bloodshed, massacre, murder, the throwing off the belief of a God, the abolishing the Christian religion" (p. 595), which two last circumstances seem to appear, in this trial, for the first time in his Lordship's speech. He objects particularly to the prisoner having joined in calling " upon the rabble to remember their patriotic ancestors who shed their blood in the cause of freedom." " I do not know what knowledge this panel has of the pedigree of the ancestors of the rabble who shed their blood. I think it is very plain that if the rabble are to assist in the reformation of the country the shedding of blood should have been omitted, unless it was to tell them that that was the way of reform, by shedding of blood." (vol. xxiii. p. 596.) After this judicious sarcasm he comes to the result, which is, that as Muir was transported, so should Skirving. " Your Lordship did pronounce a sentence of banishment by transportation against that gentleman (Muir) ; and I cannot, from the whole tenor of this indictment, find that the crime of which this man is convicted is one whit less ; and therefore I think the court is called upon to place him under the same circumstances." (vol. xxiii. p. 597.)

Lord Swinton concurred in the result of this opinion, which he describes as " very full and very solemn." Holding the verdict to convict the panel " of all the particular charges contained in the indictment" (p. 597), "the question comes to be what punishment the crime deserves. I conceive nothing less than that which was inflicted upon Mr. Muir. I do not know but the crime deserves *more;* but we

cannot do *less* than punish the same crime by inflicting the same punishment." (p. 598.) It is rather
a curious example of the superiority in some respects
of Swinton—a thinking, dull man—to the unspecu-
lating bigotry of his brethren, that though he be
absolute against universal suffrage, he admits that
something may be said in favour of annual parliaments. " In this case they wished for universal
suffrage and annual parliaments. One of these is
a most ridiculous and absurd doctrine—universal
suffrage. Nothing can be so absurd. Annual parliaments, or a shorter duration of parliaments, *may
be a matter of argument.*" (p. 597.) I think I hear
Braxfield's grunt, and see the stare of Dunsinnan's
large vacant visage, at this frightful concession.

Dunsinnan considered the punishment suggested
as a *"moderate* and proper punishment, and I *most
heartily* concur with your Lordship." (p. 598.)

Lord Abercromby makes the important and (for
him) the unexpected admission that these societies
had contained many good men. It is only their
leaders that he blames. " The object which these
societies held forth to the public at first was a
general reform, without specifying the nature or
extent of it ; and, my Lord, I am disposed to
believe that at that period *there were many well-
disposed persons in every part of the kingdom who
joined these societies without any wicked purpose,
believing that their sole object was to render our Constitution, excellent as it is, still more perfect, without
entertaining the most distant idea of overturning that
Constitution.* My Lord, whatever the views of these
persons—of these deluded persons—may be, every
thinking man, every man of common discernment,
might see what was the object of the *leaders* of this

society; and that under the pretext of reforming the Constitution, they intended to overthrow it. About the beginning of the year 1793 it was well and justly observed *by a person who, I fear, had but too good reason to know the real views of these societies*, that if the friends of freedom, as he termed them, could obtain the reform in parliament which they were then demanding, that, my Lord, it would immediately have been followed by the abolition of the monarchy, and the total overthrow of our Constitution." (vol. xxiii. p. 599.)

Who the person here alluded to was I cannot discover. Whatever may have been the tendency or object of what the leaders did, I cannot ascertain which of them it was who *admitted* that what they wished, if conceded, would immediately overthrow the monarchy. But it seems that there was *no secret* as to this being their object. For his Lordship states that " after they had been dispersed by the magistrates, they had a meeting at the Cockpit ; and, my Lord, *they ventured to declare to the public at large,* and to their fellow-citizens, that *their sole and only* OBJECT is to overturn the present happy Constitution which we now enjoy." (vol. xxiii. p. 599.) Where the evidence of this declaration is to be found I do not know. It is not in this trial.

His Lordship declares himself to be satisfied that what the convention really desired was annual parliaments and universal suffrage ; but it is *exactly from this fact* that he deduces evidence, not merely of the political danger, but of the *indictable guilt*, of that association. " The *name* which they assumed to themselves denotes in the clearest manner that that (the overthrow of the Constitution) was their sole object ; for they assumed the name of the British Convention of the Delegates of the People, associated to obtain universal suffrage and annual parliaments," and then he goes on to remark that these imply revolution. (p. 599.)

The conclusion he arrives at is that the prisoner ought clearly to be transported. " I think that no man—I THINK THE PANEL HIMSELF—cannot think that this punishment is too severe." (vol. xxiii. p. 600.) No criterion, certainly, could be more fair than this. But it is not recorded that the panel intimated his concurrence.

The *Lord Justice-Clerk* seems to have been discomposed by a foolish opinion, which the prisoner had read after his conviction, of an English counsel about the law of sedition, and most of what he says relates to this subject, which makes a now insignificant speech. He " feels very much for the situation of the panel." As " to the punishment to be inflicted, as I have always considered sedition as THE MOST DANGEROUS CRIME that CAN BE committed, I think we cannot discharge our duty to the country unless we inflict for that crime a severe punishment. Mr. Muir was transported for fourteen years ; and *the only hesitation in that case was whether it should be limited to fourteen years* or not. I have no inclination to go beyond it in this case ; but I think it is impossible we can, consistently with the justice of the country, pronounce a less sentence upon this panel than we did upon Mr. Muir." (vol. xxiii. p. 601.)

Lord Henderland was absent.

For these reasons William Skirving was sentenced to fourteen years' transportation, and was sent accordingly to Botany Bay. Of his history after leaving this country I can discover nothing accurate. It has always been stated by his friends that he was treated cruelly on his outward voyage by the shipmaster, and that he died soon after landing.

He quitted the bar with this remark : "My Lords, I know that what has been done these two days will be rejudged ;—that is my comfort and all my hope." (vol. xxiii. p. 602.)

END OF VOL. I.

AN EXAMINATION

OF THE

TRIALS FOR SEDITION

WHICH HAVE HITHERTO OCCURRED

IN SCOTLAND

BY THE LATE

LORD COCKBURN

ONE OF THE JUDGES OF THE COURT OF SESSION

"When our ashes shall be scattered by the winds of heaven, the
impartial voice of future times will rejudge your verdict."
MUIR's *Speech to his Jury.*

VOLUME SECOND

EDINBURGH: DAVID DOUGLAS

MDCCCLXXXVIII

CONTENTS OF VOL. II.

SEDITION TRIALS.

XI.—Case of MAURICE MARGAROT, Jan. 13, 1794.[1]

MARGAROT was an Englishman. The Crown counsel try to aggravate his guilt, in the course of the trial, by representing him as an attorney. (vol. xxiii. pp. 636-697.) But their own indictment describes him as a merchant, and I believe that this was the truth. He had come to Scotland as a delegate to the British Convention, and had the fatal honour of being elected one of its presidents. It was for accession to the proceedings of this association that he was tried. And therefore his case, though distinguished by a few occurrences of its own, does not differ in its substance except in one not very material matter, from that of *Skirving*.

In examining it, it will be convenient to discuss the main body of the trial first, apart from its incidental peculiarities.

The crime charged was *sedition;* and all the material circumstances resolved into these facts, viz., that the convention was criminal, and that the prisoner was responsible criminally for what it did. But in describing the legal guilt of the convention, facts and designs are imputed to it, which must compel a lawyer to entertain even stronger doubts

than in the case of *Skirving*, of the competency of
having charged any offence short of high treason.

The indictment sets forth that the convention
had held meetings, "which, though held under the
pretence of procuring a reform in parliament, were
evidently of a dangerous and destructive tendency,
WITH A DELIBERATE AND DETERMINED INTENTION to
disturb the peace of the community, AND TO SUB-
VERT THE PRESENT CONSTITUTION OF THE COUNTRY;
WITH WHICH VIEW they imitated, BOTH IN THE FORM
AND TENOR of their proceedings, that Convention
of People, the avowed enemies of this country,
who at present USURP the government of France."
(vol. xxiii. p. 609.) Both the prosecutor and the
court held that this fact implied treason, and would
have *warranted* a charge of this offence; and indeed
the lenity of the accuser, in having refrained from
such a charge, attracts the admiration of the judges,
and was gently professed to be scarcely reconcilable
with his public duty by the Lord Advocate.

His Lordship explains his case thus :—"If by
aping and imitating the example, the language, and
the forms of a French convention—a country with
which we are involved in war—they (the convention) demonstrate their intention of following its
footsteps in *revolution and in blood;* if, as I shall
prove to you must have been the case, their *intention* was *to overawe the legislature* in the free and
independent exercise of its functions, by combining
a majority of the people TO RISE IN ARMS AND IN
REBELLION against any measures which the wisdom
of parliament might direct for the public security
and safety; if, in the event of that invasion from
abroad with which the public enemy has menaced
us, they, in place of resisting, were to JOIN THE

INVADERS, (for notwithstanding all the professions of the panel and his associates to the contrary this day in the course of the trial, such, on the sound construction of the evidence, and in common reason, I shall show IS THE ONLY CONCLUSION POSSIBLE to be drawn from the past and uniform tenor of their conduct and language,) then is the crime of *sedition* as clear and unequivocal as ever occurred in the criminal practice of this, or of any other civilised country." (vol. xxiii. p. 681.)

But what he meant by sedition was successful rebellion. Animadverting on the statement by the convention, that it represented a majority of the people—" If true (says he), what is the *unavoidable* inference?—that *insurrection and* TRIUMPHANT, IRRESISTIBLE, REBELLION was in their hands and under their control, and that, in no distant or improbable event, they were to exercise it." (vol. xxiii. p. 695.)

No wonder that, after this exposition, his Lordship should ask the jury " to check the evil in its bud, etc. ; to mark your sense of the proceedings, and to stop them, while their guilt still remains with a *feature* of sedition marked upon it—verging upon treason,—*with such a trifling distinction that it is almost impossible for a lawyer to find the difference* [!!] It is so little, that when the indictment was preferred against Mr. Margarot, had it not been for the *promptitude* with which it was necessary to bring him before you, I should have laid the case before the King's Council in England, as to the appointment of a secret committee, *whether that per se was not sufficient to ground the charge of high treason.*" [1] (p. 701.) But *his own* opinion was,

---

[1] This speech was revised for the *State Trials* by his Lordship (p. 679, note).

that it was sufficient. Nothing prevented him from charging high treason, except that this crime could not be tried so *promptly* as sedition.

The very same view of the legal character of the guilt implied in the facts set forth was taken by the court. The prisoner had chattered a deal of nonsense about the relevancy; and in disposing of this, which was unworthy of notice, *Lord Hender-land* gave it as his opinion that the libel was relevant, because, whether truly or falsely, it charged the prisoner with having taken "an active and distinguishing part in the deliberations of a society, met WITH A DETERMINED PURPOSE TO OVER-TURN THE CONSTITUTION," etc. "The criminality does, to be sure, consist in this, that they met with a determined purpose to overturn the Constitution." This, he says, "*approaches* to high treason;" and in evidence of this he quotes an English indictment for treason,[1] where "the charges laid against the prisoners were very little different from those contained in the present indictment." (p. 623.) His Lordship was mistaken in his supposed analogy; because in the case referred to there was a direct charge of a design to depose the king; unless indeed he meant, as is probable, to say that a similar charge was virtually contained in the libel against Margarot.

Lord Eskgrove's opinion was to the same effect, and on the same grounds, but he takes occasion to say: "My Lord, *it is not the province of such men as these* to take upon themselves the amendment of the Government. The intention of their meeting, they say, was to obtain universal suffrage; or, in other words, to establish that every man living in

---

[1] Against Francis Townley. *State Trials*, vol. xviii. p. 333.

this country is to have a vote to choose a representative in parliament,—a thing that never did
obtain, and does not now obtain, and that *never can*
obtain, in this country." (p. 624.) It would not be
worth while noticing this observation if it merely
expressed the political opinion or speculation of this
judge; but it is another of the many examples of
their Lordships always considering universal suffrage or annual parliaments as at once so dangerous and so hopeless, that they were in themselves
seditious objects.

Lord Swinton introduces another topic. Of all
the French imitations, nothing excited such ludicrous horror on this supreme criminal bench as the
word " *Tocsin* " (which Eskgrove invariably pronounced *Tock-Fin*). There was a discussion in this
trial between the prisoner and the court, whether it
was one French word, or two Chinese ones, referring
to a motion made in the convention, of which the
prisoner had said, " It is an excellent motion ; the
event it alludes to ought to be the Tocsin for the
friends of liberty to assemble." " My Lords " (says
Swinton), " *this is a very ill-chosen word.* What is
this ' Tocsin ' ? It is an instrument made use of by
the people of France to assemble. It is borrowed
from a place from which I would wish to borrow
very little." (p. 625.) But neither the nature, nor
the uses, nor even the very existence of this imple-
ment were established by any attempt at evidence.
If ever the notorious fact of the existence of a war,
or of a threatened invasion, require to be proved
when made matter of charge, or of substantive statement, surely the nature of a particular bell required
to be so. But the existence and purposes of this
terrible instrument, like the political character of a

tune called Ca Ira in *Muir's* case, were all taken for granted.

The libel was properly found relevant.

The evidence was, in substance, the very same with that against Skirving. Five witnesses, Mr. Davidson, Mr. Scott, Mr. Mack, James Lyon, and John Macdonald, proved the declarations, the seizure of papers, and the dispersion of the convention,—the last being effected by the mere "appearance" of force; for the sheriff states that he said at the time that "he supposed anything that had that *appearance* would be satisfactory." (p. 635.) Six other witnesses,—Thomas Cockburn, Alexander Aitcheson, George Ross, William Ross, John Wardlaw, and Samuel Paterson, prove certain proceedings in the convention, but not better than they were proved by the minutes. They disclose no new or concealed enormities. The prisoner examined five witnesses, with no effect, and apparently with no object, except to hurt himself by offensiveness.

The only visible differences between this case and *Skirving's* were in these two points : *first*, Margarot was not charged with the circulation of the Dundee address ; *second*, there was an alleged proceeding in the convention charged against him, which was not charged, or at least was not set specially forth, against his brother reformer.

This proceeding, as described in the indictment, was, that on the 28th of November 1793 it was resolved, "that this convention, considering the calamitous consequences of any *act of the legislature* which may tend to deprive the whole or any part of the people of their undoubted right to meet, either by themselves or by delegation, to discuss any matter relative to their common interest, whether of a public or private nature ; and holding the same to be totally inconsistent with the first principles and safety of society, and also subversive of our known and acknowledged constitutional liberties—do hereby declare before God and the world that we shall follow the wholesome example of former times, *by paying no regard to any act* which shall militate against the Constitution of our country; and shall continue to assemble, and consider of the best means by which we can accomplish a real representation of the people, and annual election, *until compelled to desist by superior force.*" (p. 611.)

There can be no doubt of the criminality of any resolution by a number of persons to resist a statute; but I see no sufficient evidence that such a resolution was adopted.

The mere fact that it was not brought forward against Skirving makes its having been adopted extremely improbable ; especially as the Lord Advocate says (p. 694) that he knew of the resolution before any of the prisoners were apprehended, and that it was his knowledge of it that made him direct the meeting to be dispersed. Accordingly the evidence, even as explained by his Lordship, is quite unsatisfactory. His case is, that the words are proved by the minutes and by the *Gazetteer ;* that their substance was repeated by Margarot on the 5th of December ; that the terms of the motion, as passed, and as originally set down in the minutes, were altered, but enough of their import retained to preserve the truth ; which is confirmed by two witnesses, Ross and Cockburn. (vol. xxiii. p. 695.) But there seems to be an error in almost every part of this representation.

No such motion, nor any motion of this tendency, is in the minutes. This is certain. But there happened to be a blank in the minutes, which was left as the secretary, George Ross, swears (p. 661) in order that a resolution then passed might be afterwards entered ; and the question is, What was this resolution ? The prosecutor's case required him not merely to assert (which he did excellently) but to prove, that it was the resolution charged. His *argument* is that it *must* have been so, and that it was conscious guilt that made them leave the blank. But his *evidence*, when applied to the exact point, resolves into mere fancy. It consists entirely in his gratuitous assumption that the unengrossed resolution was identical, or inseparably connected, with the one about the committee of emergency, and the meetings which were to be held at places only to be disclosed by the opening of sealed letters. But this last resolution was not adopted on the 28th of November ; and, besides, the two were essentially different in their objects. All this, however, is really immaterial. Because whatever the blank *ought* to have been filled up with, it was not filled up at all ; and therefore whatever inference the omission may warrant, nothing at least can be made *of the minute itself.*

Then as to the *Gazetteer :* no doubt it was, in one sense, the paper of the convention ; for it professed to promulgate the sentiments and proceedings of that body, of which George Ross, the principal clerk in the *Gazetteer* office, was a member, and occasionally acted as its assistant secretary. (p. 659.) This newspaper was therefore patronised by the convention. But the convention did not control or superintend the editing of the paper, and "never furnished anything towards the expense of the printing." (p. 667.) It was conducted at his own discretion, by Mr. Scott, the publisher, who sent two persons (the Rosses) to the convention to take notes, which they did, with the usual accuracy of unpractised reporters. But though they wished to be correct, they will not swear that they succeeded ; and their reports were never revised by any one for the convention. The newspaper " was carried on totally independent of the convention." (p. 667.) I do not know what the *Gazetteer* stated to have been the motion, because its words are not given. But the credit, and indeed the admissibility, of the newspaper as evidence, depends entirely on the proof of its accuracy ; and therefore all this resolves into the testimony of the witnesses. Now although the reporters meant their reports to be accurate, and believed them to have been so, they could not swear that they actually were so. And, in particular the prosecutor's statement about *resisting* the statute, receives no corroboration either from them or from any other witness. The two Rosses, Aitcheson,[1] and especially Cockburn, who is chiefly relied on by the Lord Advocate, all remember that, in the events specified in this part of the indictment, the convention was to meet, but they expressly

---

[1] It has very often been said, and generally by those who had good means of knowing, that this Aitcheson was secretly betraying his associates. The style of his evidence certainly looks very like that of a man who, under the appearance of boldly defending the prisoners, was in reality trying to make their case as offensive as he could. He calls Margarot " a *second Sidney* " (p. 653), and Gerrald " *a second Lycurgus* " (p. 923), and professes that he would " much sooner appear here as the panel at your Lordship's bar, than as a witness ; " and in Gerrald's trial he treated them to impudent and foolish discourses in defence of the convention's terms of citizen,—" Liberty Stairs," etc., till Braxfield roared, " Put him out, then ! put him out ! " (Pp. 926-927.) Notwithstanding all this, two circumstances make me disbelieve in his perfidy, or at least not comprehend it. One is, that the prosecutor always treats him very contemptuously, and not at all in the way in which penitent or divulging accomplices are generally used ; and it is absolutely certain, from their characters, that neither Dundas nor Blair, nor any of the advocates-depute, could assume this tone insincerely. The other is, that no suspicion of him ever escapes any of the prisoners. On the contrary, they plainly consider him a bold and true friend.

negative all intention, or understanding, of resistance. They were to meet *to assert their rights;* which George Ross swears was to be done *by drawing up a remonstrance to parliament.* And when Cockburn is asked whether the resolution said " anything about paying no attention to a Convention Bill if it should pass," all the length that even he can go, is merely, " I *think* there was a *mention* of *something similar* to that." (p. 648.)

Accordingly, the resistance is merely an inference by the prosecutor. " Combining all this evidence (says he), written and parole,—weighing and considering it fairly and impartially,—can you hesitate in believing that *rebellion against the legislature* of this country was the *avowed and real purpose* of this assembly, and of this panel at the bar in particular ? " (vol. xxiii. p. 695.) It may be fair enough to deduce a particular *design* from such a complex mass of circumstances and considerations ; but the *terms, or exact import of a specific resolution,* require very different evidence. The prosecutor's belief may be very well founded ; for the boast, or threat, that they would disregard any statute which was intended to extinguish them was not out of character with these people, in the temper they were then in. But in reference to criminal evidence, the proof is at the best very questionable.

The Lord Advocate addressed the jury. Speeches, upon temporary subjects by ordinary men, can scarcely be appreciated by those who only read them after the casual interest and allusions are weakened by time. But it surely evinces some want of perception, or singular fidelity in reporting, that in revising this address, his Lordship did not

omit a number of passages which the partiality of
friendship cannot now avoid being distressed by.

Such, for example, as his aggravation of sedition,
which is a greater crime, it seems, when committed
by an *attorney* than by anybody else. " It tends
to aggravate the crime of this man, that if he was
an attorney, which I do not know that he was, *he
has made an ill use of his profession;* his criminality
is without excuse; his guilt is, indeed, of a more
atrocious nature." (p. 697.)

It may sometimes be excusable to refer, on such
occasions, to the general circumstances of the times,
without any other evidence of them than that which
it is supposed that no one can live without possessing. But *special,* and particularly *local,* facts can
never be introduced safely, unless they be regularly
established, and be thus subjected to scrutiny both
as to their relevancy and their truth. It would
therefore have been going far enough if his Lordship
had only alluded to two tumultuous assemblages
which he asserted had recently alarmed Edinburgh,
but as to neither of which had there been a single
particle of evidence. But not content with alluding to these occurrences, he uses them as established facts, tending to support his primary charge.
" Compare you that, gentlemen, with what has
passed within these few days past in this city ; with
the attempts to excite tumult and disorder which,
on the trial of Skirving, disturbed, at a late hour of
night, this supreme court of criminal justice in which
we now sit; compare it with the mob assembled
this morning to conduct this man to his place of
trial with triumph, and with shouts, and clamour, and noise, and violence, clearly directed to
intimidate court and jury and prosecutor in the dis-

charge of their duties ;—that clamour, indeed, nobly
and honourably met, resisted, and put down by the
spirit of the loyal and well-disposed inhabitants,
turning out in support of their insulted magistrates
and courts of justice ; *and then doubt, if you can, as
to the seditious, not to say treasonable, purposes of
this person with whose guilt or innocence you are now
charged.*" (vol. xxiii. p. 696.) It is certainly possible that the fact of there having been one popular procession at the close of Skirving's trial, and
another at the beginning of Margarot's, may have
been quite satisfactory to that jury as evidence that
the person they were trying for sedition had, in
truth, been guilty of treason. But, 1*st*, ought not
facts so detached from the other matter of the case,
and so conclusive, to have been put into the indictment ; and, 2*d*, should they not have been proved ?

Margarot, though said to have been rather a
clever man, made a long and injudicious harangue
in his own defence. No enemy, anxious to deprive
him both of hope of acquittal, and of sympathy in
conviction, could have made a worse. He does not
appear to have had the remotest conception where
the strength, and still less where the weakness, of
his case lay ; nor did he state or reason it, even
according to his own view, with any force, sense, or
plausibility ; and throughout he was defying without
formidableness, and insolent without effect.

But there was certainly nothing to justify the
rude and cruel criticism of the Justice, who, the very
instant that Margarot was done, and immediately
before he himself began his summing up, interposed
this observation : "You have gone on for four
hours, and I would not allow you to be interrupted.
If you had not been a stranger I would not have

heard one-third of what you have said in four hours ; *which was all sedition from beginning to end.*" (vol. xxiii. p. 763.) Even if this statement had been true, which it was not, and even although it had not implied an admission of his Lordship's own incorrectness, in quietly listening to the commission of a crime in his own court, it was a coarse advantage for a Judge to take of any prisoner in making what he thought his defence. But it was a hint to the jury.

His Lordship then proceeded to charge ; that is, he proceeded to do what, when properly done, amounts to this,—that the judge instructs the jury on the law, lays down the points of fact necessary to be ascertained in reference to the accusation and to the defence, and directs their attention to the evidence bearing on these facts on both sides, and states his own impression of the result, if he thinks this proper,—the most delicate and important task this that a judge has to perform, even on ordinary occasions, but one which raises him into a position requiring the calmest reflection and the most sacred candour, where it is a case with the Crown on the one side, and a subject, accused of a political offence, and on trial before a jury of known prepossessions against him, on the other.

His Lordship professed to give only " *the general idea of the case.*" This plan of a charge easily enabled him to make his summation a mere exhibition of his own political opinions, and an intimation to the jury that they might safely act upon theirs.

Neither the indictment, nor the verdict, nor the sentence against Skirving were made evidence on this trial, or were known judicially to the jury. Yet, such was their Lordships' habit of introducing all the popular occurrences of the day, that he tells

them " a very material circumstance, which you will
have under your observation in forming your judgment, and it is this,—that that society (the convention) stands upon the records of this court, not
above six or seven days old, to be a seditious
society ; when a person, a secretary to that society,
was found guilty of the crime of sedition, and has
been, by a judgment of this court, condemned to
transportation for fourteen years. *That is a pretty
strong circumstance to show that this was not an
innocent meeting.* If it was a lawful meeting, I am
afraid that that poor man Skirving has suffered
very unjustly. In the *first* place, there was an
unanimous verdict, of a *most respectable* jury, against
him ; and, in the *second* place, the *court pronounced
judgment* upon that verdict." (vol. xxiii. p. 764.)
Now, *no particle of this had been proved.* It could
not have been so. Skirving's verdict was dated on
the 7th of January 1794, and Margarot was tried
on the 13th of that month, and, consequently, had
got his indictment before the record against Skirving could have been specified as one of the articles
of intended evidence.[1] And though this obstacle
had not been in the way, it is clear that the whole
of these facts were irrelevant and inadmissible.
What was Skirving's case to Margarot ? He was
not on his trial upon Skirving's evidence, or before
Skirving's jury. If Skirving had been *acquitted*,
would the court have allowed Margarot to produce
the verdict as evidence either of his innocence or of
the convention's ? The mere *illegality* of this refer-

---

[1] By the law of Scotland a prisoner, besides a list of witnesses, is
entitled to notice, in the body of the indictment, of every article of docu-
mentary evidence that is to be produced by the prosecutor against him,
and he must receive a copy of the indictment at least fifteen days before
the day of trial.

ence to the opinion, and possibly to the error, of a
different jury, or a different case, was by no means
its worst feature.   It tended to instruct this jury,
that they need not trouble themselves by taking the
nature or objects of the convention into their consideration, because this vital point was already fixed, and
that as Margarot's connection with the society was
not disputed, the trial before them was a mere form.

His Lordship then gives them his doctrine of
the legal nature of sedition.   He first instructs
them that a design "to overturn the king and
parliament by *mobs* and *violence*," is not necessary,
which is certainly correct ; and then proceeds to the
more delicate task of explaining the case in which
the crime consists in the mere expression or promulgation of opinion.   This subject, which borders
on the most important constitutional privileges, and
the exercise of the most useful rights, he exhausts
at once by the following tremendous principle :—
" I apprehend, in some sense, the crime of sedition
consists in *poisoning* the minds of the lieges—which
may naturally, IN THE END, HAVE A TENDENCY
to promote violence against the State, and in *endeavouring* to create a DISSATISFACTION in the country,
which NOBODY CAN TELL WHERE IT WILL END.   It
will very naturally end in overt rebellion ; and *if it
has that tendency*, THOUGH NOT IN THE VIEW OF THE
PARTIES AT THE TIME, yet *if they have been guilty
of poisoning the minds of the lieges*, I apprehend
that that will constitute the crime of sedition to all
intents and purposes." (vol. xxiii. p. 766.)

This doctrine, viz., that the guilt of sedition may
be incurred by the mere *remote tendency* of the acts
composing it, to create a *dissatisfaction* which *may
end* in rebellion, *though this was not in the view of*

the accused at the time, is one of the most monstrous that has been uttered from any modern British bench. It makes, or may make, the questioning of any supposed defect, the challenge of any fancied abuse, perhaps all discussion of constitutional principle, criminal. It may truly be said of every such discussion that "*nobody can tell where it will end.*" And this combined uncertainty and remoteness of the result, instead of excluding the idea of sedition, which in law requires the specific wickedness of *intending* the production of a certain degree of public and nearly *immediate* mischief, by measures *plainly calculated for this end,* is, it seems, all that is wanted to constitute the offence. Everything, according to this, has been sedition that has ever produced hostility, however gradual, to government, though only by the natural progress of thought. All that is now law was once innovation, says Bacon ; and all that was ever innovation was once sedition, adds Braxfield.

The qualification that the distant and unmeant rebellion must be brought about by mental *poison* is no extenuation of the doctrine, partly because, except where the delinquency consists in mere negligence, there can never be guilt in any result which is produced so unintentionally and so remotely that it was never contemplated ; and partly because scarcely two people ever agree as to whether what is administered be poison or medicine. Hume's toryism is poison to the palate of a whig ; Brodie's detection of Hume to that of a tory. The dissenter holds the mind of the people to be poisoned by a harangue in favour of establishments ; the churchman by a harangue against them.

The sound law is well laid down by Erskine in

his speech to the jury for Hardy,—a speech which, though only the pleading of a counsel, is a model to all judges of the highest excellencies of a judicial charge :—" The doing an act, or the pursuit of a system of conduct which *leads, in probable consequences,* to the death of the king, *may legally affect the consideration of the traitorous purpose* charged in the record ; and I am not afraid of trusting you with the evidence. How far any given act, or any course of acting, *independently of intention,* may lead, probably or *inevitably,* to *any natural or political consequence, is what we have no concern with.* These may be curious questions of casuistry or politics ; but *it is wickedness and folly to declare that consequences, unconnected even with intention or consciousness, shall be synonymous in law with the traitorous mind;* although the traitorous mind alone is arraigned as constituting the crime." (*State Trials,* vol. xxiv. p. 880.) Every word of this is applicable to Braxfield's unintentional sedition.

His Lordship then reduces his principle to practice ; and very correctly. Since the production of *dissatisfaction,* which *may* end in rebellion, though nothing rebellious was in the contemplation of the author of the dissatisfaction, constitutes sedition, this offence is necessarily committed by any effort to obtain any reform, at least by any appeal to the people in seasons of agitation ; because reform implies defect, and the disclosure of defect creates dissatisfaction ; and nobody can tell where dissatisfaction will end. The Justice therefore told the jury, and, in consistency with his principle, was compelled to tell them, that the mere fact of the prisoner's having in these times been a reformer of the Constitution, was, if not absolutely conclusive, yet strongly against him : "I submit to you whether a man that *wishes well to his country* would come forward and insist upon a reform, *parliamentary or not parliamentary*, at such a crisis, which *would create discontent* in the minds of the people, when every good subject would promote unanimity among the lieges to meet the common enemy. I say, in place of that, to bring forward a great reform in parliament *is a thing totally inconsistent with the Constitution of this country.* I say bringing it forward at that period IS A STRONG PROOF that they were not well-wishers to the Constitution of this country, *but enemies* to it. I say that no good member of society would have taken these measures. I appeal to you all, that you are living under a happy Government, in peace and plenty, in perfect security of your lives and property, the happiest nation upon the face of the earth. And when that is the situation of this country, I appeal to you whether I have not given a fair and just description of it—for a set of men in that situation to raise a faction in the minds of the lower order of people—*to create dissatisfaction to the Government, and consequently make a division in that country.* I say that *these things appear to be, from the very conjuncture at which they are brought forward, sedition of a high nature.*" (p. 766.)

This was exactly the doctrine on which the Attorney-General claimed a conviction of the seven Bishops. "There is not any one thing that the law is more jealous of, or does more carefully provide for the prosecution and punishment of, than *all accusations and arraignments of the Government.* No man may say of the great men of the nation, much less of the great officers of the kingdom, that they act *unreasonably* or *unjustly;* least of all may any man say any such thing of the king. For these matters *tend to possess the people that the government is ill administered; and the consequence of that is to set them upon desiring a reformation; and what that tends to, and will end in, we have all had a sad, and too dear bought experience,"* (*State Trials*, vol. xii. p. 281)—a principle, as Mackintosh justly observes (*James II.*, p. 277), " subversive of all political discussion." Accordingly, the part of Lord Clarendon's intolerant " *Five Mile Act*," which has always been condemned as the worst, is that in which nonconforming clergymen are compelled to swear "that they will not, at any time, *endeavour any alteration of government in church or state.*" If this was tyrannical, it was a tyranny of which the principle is approved of by every one of the judges in these Scotch trials. (See Campbell's *Chancellors*, vol. iii. p. 220.) And in this even Thurlow deserts them. When, at this period, Government wanted severer laws against sedition, he objected (being out of office), and asks, " Was it fitting that a man should be subject to such penalties for saying it was an abuse that twenty acres of land below Old Sarum Hill, without any inhabitants, should send two representatives to parliament ? All were to be punished who attempted to create a dislike to the established Constitution of which this renowned rotten burgh is a part."

The Justice made two or three other immaterial observations ; but what I have quoted forms the real import of all the summing up.

The rest of the charge consists in telling the jury that the convention " IS ALREADY DETERMINED to be a meeting of an illegal nature," and that the prisoner is proved to have taken a lead in it ; after which he closes by repeating the certainly conclusive principle that, in these times, reform was sedition. " He took up four hours in a defence which was sedition from beginning to end ; *finding fault with the Constitution;* and I think a speech of a very seditious tendency." (vol. xxiii. p. 767.)

Thus directed, the jury unanimously found the prisoner " guilty of the *crimes* libelled."

The prisoner then renewed some objections which he had taken at an earlier stage, and which, having been repelled or disregarded then, were of course dealt with in the same way now. But he also stated another objection, which is disposed of by the court as a new one. It was, that one James Carlisle had got access to the witnesses, and conversed with them, while they ought to have been all locked up by themselves. If this had been stated in due time, it might have been an awkward occurrence, according to our notions about witnesses which prevailed at that time. But being only brought forward after conviction, the objection was properly repelled. But not contented with deciding the point that had actually arisen, the Lord Justice-Clerk decides a much more important point that had not arisen. " I am entirely of the same opinion. And I will tell the panel that if the court were to sustain the objection, *it would not avail him as an absolutory from the crime* with which he is charged, even if it would make null and void all the proceedings ; because *he would be liable to be tried over again."* (*State Trials*, vol. xxiii. p. 771.) No doubt, anything that made all the proceedings *null and void*, must leave any prisoner liable not to be tried *again*, because what is null and void is no trial, but to be still tried. But it is a different case entirely, where, after conviction, but before sentence, an objection occurs which arrests judgment. The proceedings here would not have been all made null and void; but a part of the evidence—viz., that which consisted of the testimony of the witnesses who had been talked to—would have been found contaminated. Suppose it is discovered, before sentence, that a witness had been bribed. Probably, with us, this would be no ground for an arrest of judgment. But if it was a ground, would this imply that because the verdict was inoperative, the prisoner could be re-tried?

After what had passed at the immediately preceding trials, the sentence could not be expected to be anything except transportation for fourteen years; which accordingly was pronounced.

There was no discussion either as to its legality or propriety. But *Lord Henderland* declared—" I know no other way which I could discharge my duty to God, to my country, or to my own conscience, but by proposing that this man should be *banished* forth of this kingdom *by transportation,* or in common language, should be transported, for fourteen years."

Lord Eskgrove approves. " The court can do no less than make use of the power which the law gives them, to send him to *a place where he can do no harm."* (vol. xxiii. p. 774.)[1]

Lord Swinton thought that sedition " is worse, in one respect, than most other crimes. Many other crimes are committed from the sudden impulse of passion or heat. But this crime is committed with a premeditated, felonious intention, by deliberating on the means of *overturning our Constitution.* They begin with seditious and inflammatory discourses,

---

[1] The other world would have been a better place, on this principle.

endeavouring to draw simple, and perhaps well-meaning, people after them, *by pointing out imperfections*, which will be in every Government whatever, and *placing them in a strong light;* and, in the next place, by seditious writings." (p. 774.) But the real guilt certainly consisted in the horrid practice of placing imperfections in a strong light—thereby causing dissatisfaction—and "no one can tell where it will end."

Lord Abercromby agreed with all his brethren in considering "the circumstance of this panel being a *stranger* to this country as an *aggravation* of his crime;" and thought the punishment "the *mildest* which, under all the circumstances, ought to be proposed." (p. 776.)

The poor Justice was in a very distressing situation. He was a lover of mild punishments. "I have always *more pleasure* in inflicting a mild punishment than a more severe one." Both gave him pleasure, but the severe one least. An ordinary judge would have yielded at once to this weakness, and selfishly enjoyed his favourite gratification. But Braxfield was moved by a higher principle—a calm sense of duty; and sedition "is OF ALL CRIMES KNOWN AMONGST MANKIND, of the MOST heinous nature." Therefore it "well merits the HIGHEST arbitrary punishment that this court can POSSIBLY inflict." Hence "the moment I heard the verdict, *I revolved in my own mind* the circumstances attending this case," and the result was, that "the only doubt that occurred to me was *whether we ought not to go* FURTHER" than had been done on the two preceding occasions. (p. 776.) But, on the whole, the allurements of humanity prevailed, and his Lordship solaced himself with only fourteen years.

Margarot was the only one of these early sedition prisoners whom I saw. I was sitting one day—
a Monday, I think—in Swanston's writing-school,
which was on the third or fourth floor of a house on
the south side of the High Street, opposite the
Cross, when I observed a crowd coming out of the
Parliament Close, following a little, black, middle-
aged man, who was put into a coach, from which
the people instantly proceeded to take off the
horses. Several of us boys ran down the stair, and
heard that it was Margarot, whose name was familiar to us, though we understood nothing of his story,
except that he was one of the Friends of the People
—a title terrible in our ears—and was to be sent to
Botany Bay. This, I think, was on the Monday
before his trial actually took place. But as he had
gone into the Parliament House (on the morning of
Skirving's trial, I suppose), and was seen coming
out again from a place from which no seditious
prisoner was supposed to have any chance of escap-
ing, the cry had arisen that he had been let off; and
some of the populace drew him in triumph to his
lodgings in the Black Bull, at the head of Leith
Walk. I ran alongside the carriage, and, when I
could get near enough, thought it excellent enter-
tainment to give an occasional haul; for which I
afterwards got as severe and serious a rebuke from
the Lord Advocate as if I had committed some base
immorality, although my horror of the Friends of
the People, like that of all boys, sons of the gentry,
was fully equal to his own.

In about a week Margarot came from the Black
Bull to be tried, attended by a procession of the
populace and his convention friends, with banners
and what was called a tree of liberty. This tree

was in the shape of the letter M, about twenty feet high and ten wide. The honour of bearing it up by carrying the two upright poles was assigned to two eminent conventionalists, and the little culprit walked beneath the circular placard in the centre, which proclaimed liberty and equality, etc. I was looking out of a window in the old Post-office, which was then the northmost house on the west side of the North Bridge. I think I see the scene yet. The whole North Bridge, from the Tron Church to the Register Office, was quite empty at first ; not a single creature venturing on that bit of sand, over which the waves were so soon to break from both ends. The Post-office and the adjoining houses had been secretly filled with constables, and sailors from a frigate in the roads (I think the "Hind," Captain Cochrane), all armed with sticks and batons. No soldier appeared, it being determined that this civic insurrection should be put down by the civil force, unaided at least by scarlet.

As soon as the tree, which led the van, emerged from Leith Street, and appeared at the north end of the bridge, Provost Elder and the magistrates issued from some place they had retired to (I believe the Tron Church), and appeared, all robed, at the south end. The day was good. There was still not one person—I doubt if there was even a dog— on any part of the space, being the whole length of the bridge, between the two parties. But the rear of each was crammed with people, who filled up every inch as those in front of them moved on. The magistrates were in a line across the street, with the provost in the centre, the city officers behind this line, and probably a hundred loyal gentlemen in the rear of the officers. The two parties advanced steadily towards each other, and in perfect silence, till they met just about the Post-office. The provost stepped forward about a pace, so that he almost touched the front line of the rebels, when, advancing his cane, he commanded them to retire. This order probably would not have been obeyed; but at any rate it could not have been obeyed speedily, from the crowd behind. However, all this was immaterial; for, without waiting one instant to see whether they meant to retire or not, the houses vomited forth their bludgeoned contents; and in almost two minutes the tree was demolished and thrown over the bridge, the street covered with the knocked down, the accused dragged to the bar, and the insurrection was over. The execution was entirely by the civil and naval arm; but the rebels, however formidable they looked as they came on, fled the instant they were attacked.

The popular idol in this scene was a little, dark creature, dressed in black, with silk stockings and white metal buttons, something like one's idea of a puny Frenchman, a most impudent and provoking body. Burnett, quoting Thurlow's words against Horne (*State Trials*, vol. xx. p. 779), describes his conduct as "a paradeful triumph over justice"—not a good expression as applied to Margarot; for in court there was little parade and no triumph. It was mere baffled impertinence. Abercromby's observation was much truer, that "from the moment he appeared at the bar, till the instant he was carried out, his whole conduct was of the most indecent kind." (vol. xxiii. p. 775.) Some allowance, however, must be made for the provocation he received, and for a pragmatical Englishman's contempt of all courts, and all forms, and all phrases, except his own.[1]

He flew out before ever the diet had been called, and first objected to the jurisdiction of the court because the Lord Justice-General was absent ; and then insisted that the court should grant him a caption to compel the attendance of the Duke of Richmond, Mr. Dundas, and Mr. Pitt, who were in England, as witnesses, and that the trial should be delayed till they should appear. It is needless to say that both of these proposals were justly disregarded.

But he made other objections which the court ought not to have been provoked by his offensiveness to treat with contempt.

According to our undoubted law, courts of justice ought to be open to the public, especially on criminal trials, in which the public generally are, and ought to be, much interested. Hence it is only in virtue of a statute that our court is entitled to proceed with closed doors, in one description of

---

[1] For the finest examples of panels' impudence we must go to the trials of Horne Tooke. When at the bar as a supposed traitor in 1794, he was generally quiet, because he was in the hands of Erskine. But when he was his own counsel on two trials for libel in 1777 (*State Trials*, vol. xx.), his genius in this line was very conspicuous. His respectful insolence to Mansfield, Chief-Justice ; his teasing contempt of Thurlow, Attorney-General ; his sneers at the law ; and the provoking self-possession and cheerfulness with which he frets and defies everybody else, are excessively entertaining. Hone's audacity, which, it is said, killed Ellenborough, was powerful, but coarse. He struck with a rusty cleaver. Tooke cut with a bright lance. The strength of both, as of every person who is disrespectful with effect to a court, arose from their being to a certain extent right. Tooke was struggling against the unjust and nonsensical rule which then virtually deprived a person, tried in England for libel, of the benefit of trial by jury ; and he had Thurlow, a bully, for his opponent. Hone was rising above the usual lowness of his character and public habits by the manliness with which, unassisted, he bore up against, and thrice baffled, the cruelty of compelling him to go to trial, for separate offences, on three successive days, although he sought some delay, however short, from the fact, visible to every one, that he was exhausted both in body and mind.

cases. It is notorious, however, that where there
is any unusual demand for places, the door-keepers
take advantage of this, and demand admission
money. But still the court is filled; and this very
exaction enables a respectable class of spectators to
be comfortable, who would otherwise be crushed or
excluded; and no complaints are made. But where
complaints are made, it is a very dangerous thing
for the court to avow that it leaves the lieges to the
mercy of its officers. Margarot stated that money
was exacted at the door, and said, "I demand that
the doors of this place may be opened, in order that
the people may partake of what passes." To which
the answer, by the Lord Justice-Clerk, was, "It
would be a very pretty opening, I think." Margarot
said : " The doors are shut, and I understand it is the
custom of the door-keepers to take money, which is
contrary to the law of the land!" To which the
reply by the Justice is, " That *you have no business
with!*" (vol. xxiii. p. 630.) But has an accused man
no business with the legal publicity of his own trial?
—no interest in the presence of friends who may
think him innocent, or whose appearance may cheer
and console him though guilty? Is he obliged to
submit, without even asking the protection of the
court, not only to have all his own friends excluded,
but to have the court crowded at the discretion of
mercenary officers, by the friends of the prosecution? Lady Russell, according to this, might have
been debarred from the trial of her husband, and
this would have been no business of Lord Russell's !

When asked, according to the old mockery,
whether he had any challenge for cause to any of
the first five jurymen selected by the presiding
judge, he said, " I have no personal objection, but I

must beg to know by what law you have the picking
of them ? " (p. 632.)   This most reasonable question
was answered, with solemn folly, by Abercromby.
" His Lordship is *not picking, but naming* the jury,
according to the established law, and the established
constitution of the country ; and the *gentleman at the
bar has no right to put such a question.*" (p. 632.)
Did his Lordship really suppose that it was the word,
and not the thing, that the prisoner was startled
with ?   And surely it was no unnatural question for
an Englishman to put, who had never seen, and
probably never fancied the jury, in a political case,
being selected by the presiding judge.[1]

After the prisoner had entered upon his evidence
in defence, and had examined the sheriff and the
provost, he introduced a matter which made a great
impression at the time, and gave rise to the following scene :—

" *Mr. Margarot.*—Now, my Lord, comes a very
delicate matter indeed.   I mean to call upon my
Lord Justice-Clerk, and I hope that the questions
and the answers will be given in the most solemn
manner.   I have received a piece of information
which I shall lay before the court in the course of
my questions.   First, my Lord, are you upon oath ?

" *Lord Justice-Clerk.*—State your questions, and
I will tell you whether I will answer them or not.
If they are proper questions, I will answer them.

" Did you dine at Mr. Rochead's at Inverleith
in the course of last week ?

" *Lord Justice-Clerk.*—And what have you to
do with that, sir ?

---

[1] Margarot had the impertinence to tell the jury that if not *packed*,
they were at least *picked*.   He would have been more correct if he had
said that the first had a tendency to be implied in the last.

" Did any conversation take place with regard to my trial?

" *Lord Justice-Clerk.*—Go on, sir.

" Did you use these words : What should you think of giving him a hundred lashes, together with Botany Bay ; or words to that effect?

" *Lord Justice-Clerk.*—Go on. Put your questions if you have any more.

" Did any person—did a lady—say to you that the mob would not allow you to whip him ? And, my Lord, did you not say that the mob would be the better for losing a little blood ? These are the questions, my Lord, that I wish to put to you at present in the presence of the court. Deny them, or acknowledge them.

" *Lord Justice-Clerk.*—Do you think I should answer questions of that sort, my Lord Henderland?" (vol. xxiii. p. 672.)

There can be no doubt of the relevancy of the fact here virtually announced by the prisoner. If the Justice had spoken as was imputed to him, it was plainly improper in him to try a case he had so prejudged. There can be as little doubt, that the prisoner, if he could establish the fact, threw it away by his manner of using it. It ought to have been stated at the outset, as a disqualification of the judge ; and the other persons, said to have been of the dinner party, should have been called as witnesses to prove it. Instead of this, he allowed the Justice to preside, so far, without objection ; and then introduced the objection to him as a part of the defence. And besides the dangers of relying on the answers he might get from a person supposed to be capable of such misconduct, he could scarcely expect a judge to submit to such interrogation upon the bench.

The incorrectness of the court's treatment of the matter is equally clear. They quashed the whole inquiry on grounds so plainly untenable, that their resorting to them creates a strong suspicion that they were afraid of the truth. *Lord Henderland* answered the Justice's request that he would tell him whether he should answer questions of that sort, by saying, " No, my Lord ; *they do not relate to this trial.* Questions as to facts *material to the charges contained in this indict-ment,* my Lord Justice-Clerk is obliged to answer, but not otherwise." (vol. xxiii. p. 672.) *Lord Eskgrove* says : " What may have been said *in a private company* cannot in any way affect this case as to the panel at the bar ; it certainly cannot throw any light on the subject. I am of opinion, therefore, that you ought not to answer questions of that sort, which cannot involve the fate of the trial. I think, therefore, that it is not consistent *with the dignity of this court,* and cannot be beneficial to the panel." (p. 672.) *Dunsinnan* and *Swinton* rest their opinions on this, that " the answer to none of these questions *can tend to exculpate him,* or alleviate the offence of which he is accused. Not one of them are proper, not one of them are competent ; and ought not to be allowed to be put. And were he not a stranger to this country, I should look upon it as an insult offered to this court." (p. 673.)

It is not easy to give their Lordships credit for being unconscious of the fallacy of the principle on which they thus threw their shield over their chief. They might have held that the challenge came too late ; or that the Justice was not bound to submit to interrogation ; or that he was not obliged to criminate himself ; or they might have invited the

MARGAROT. 31

prisoner (he being a stranger who required direction) to establish his charge otherwise. These might, no doubt, have proved awkward suggestions ; because the prisoner might have called other witnesses ; or might have put the Justice to the necessity of declining to answer ; or subsequent prisoners might have been warned not to let the proper time for stating the objection pass ; all very awkward. But still these were the only courses legally open to the court ; and almost anything would have been better than appearing to shelter one of themselves. But the irrelevancy of the fact *as a defence for the prisoner*, which was the ground they went upon, clearly implied no irrelevancy in it *as a charge against the judge*. What if the prisoner had offered to prove that his Lordship *had taken a bribe* for trying to obtain a conviction ? Could the court's saying that this " can neither tend to exculpate the prisoner, nor to alleviate the offence of which he is accused," be considered as anything except a determination to exclude inquiry ? The conclusion which the prisoner drew from this ground of decision was perfectly correct. The Justice asked him, " Have you any other witnesses ? " He answered, " It is needless, my Lord, when I am told that the answers to such questions could neither exculpate me, nor alleviate the charges against me. But it would have gone to show the jury that I *was prejudged before my trial came on*." (vol. xxiii. p. 673.)

This mode of getting rid of the subject was by no means satisfactory to the public, even at the time. It was generally understood that the Justice really had uttered the sentiments imputed to him, which certainly were not at all out of character, and that a lady had incautiously repeated them. Mr.

Rochead, at whose table the words were said to have been spoken, kept a luxurious bachelor's table at Inverleith, his property. According to the prevailing custom at the time, he had a dinner-party almost every Sunday, and very much with the same people. My father, Sir Robert Dundas, soon afterwards my brother-in-law, the Lord Advocate, and the Justice-Clerk, were established guests. Rochead's mother lived with him, and this introduced a few ladies. I heard the matter often talked of at my father's house, by the persons who had composed this party, though never in the Justice's presence. These friends never talked of it in such a way as to show that even they doubted that his Lordship had been rash. They rather enjoyed it as not a bad sentiment for the times, and laughed at Margarot's impudence and defeat. Accordingly it is remarkable that there was never any authoritative denial by those who had been present ; and even Braxfield made no protestation of innocence, even in the form of expressing his belief that he could not be expected to stoop to the refutation of such a calumny. And when the objection was renewed, at the proper time, on the subsequent trial of Gerrald, and offered to be established by evidence independent of the judge, his brethren still refused to allow it to be gone into —a proceeding which it is difficult to reconcile with any hypothesis except one.

Margarot's sentence was carried into effect. Both during his voyage to New South Wales, and while there, it has always been said, and I believe truly, that he behaved very ill, particularly towards his companions in misfortune. He was the only one of them who ever saw Britain again. He returned about 1810 ; and was examined before a committee

of the House of Commons on Transportation in 1812.
His account of the state of the colony at that
period, and the fact that to bring himself, a wife,
and a servant, home, cost about £450, give us some
idea of the nature of the punishment inflicted on
these men. He revisited Edinburgh, when he was
surprised to find his friend Braxfield, and all his
other judges, dead ; and all his jurors either dead
or not to be found, except one, to whom he gave a
supper. But by this time the juryman had become
a whig, and the convict a tory. He died in 1815.

XII.—Case of CHARLES SINCLAIR, February
and March 1794.

I DO not know whether Sinclair was Scotch or
English by birth, but he had certainly been resident
in England, and was another of the persons who
came here to distinguish himself in the convention.

With the exception of a speech which he himself is charged with having delivered there, his indictment is founded on the same facts, and in all
material parts is in the same words with those
against Skirving and Margarot.

Henry Erskine and Archibald Fletcher appeared
as his counsel. Both are too well known to require
anything to be said of them here.

They made three objections to the relevancy
of the indictment. 1. Burnett (p. 249) states the
first (or one) of them to have been that sedition was
not a crime at common law. It may possibly have
been so, but nothing of the kind appears from
the report. The first, as there described, was that
the libel did not specify the exact law, *whether
common or statutory*, on which the prisoner was
accused. 2. That the indictment was *uncertain*,
in so far as it did not set forth whether it was *real
or verbal* sedition that was meant to be charged.
3. That it concluded for the pains of law generally,
without specifying what these were.

These were all justly repelled. It was clearly
an indictment for sedition at common law; this

covered every species of the offence; and no indictment specifies the punishment that is to follow a
conviction.

The whole objections, indeed, were apparently
taken merely as a mode of raising the discussion
about the power of transporting. How such a point
was permitted to be raised at such a stage I cannot
comprehend; for nothing surely can be more premature than to discuss the punishment before
there be a conviction; and all the objections to the
relevancy might have been stated, even though it
had been conceded that transportation was illegal.
However, it was raised and decided. The court,
which had already committed itself, both by its
opinions and its sentences, could scarcely be expected to see its error now, though the matter was
for the first time seriously argued by distinguished
counsel. I shall not examine the argument here,
because a better opportunity will arise in the next
case, that of *Gerrald*. But some things connected
with it deserve to be noticed.

Some curious specimens were exhibited of the
vagueness of even lawyers' notions of the legal
nature of sedition.

Assuming the facts to be as set forth in the
libel, Fletcher maintained that as there had been
no *commotion*, it was only *verbal* sedition; and that
this being the same with *leasing-making*, it could
only be punished under the Act of 1703 by fine, imprisonment, or banishment, which last did not mean
transportation. The shortest answer to this, I
should have thought, would have been that there
was no distinction *in law* between verbal sedition
and real; and that though these might be convenient
terms for denoting aggravated or mitigated cases,

the law knew only the single offence of sedition. But the Lord Advocate's chief answer was that the indictment made it plain, "and must certiorate the panel that the crime founded on is *real* sedition." (p. 790.) Between these two stood Blair, who agreed with neither of them, but declared that " the facts charged amount to BOTH *verbal and real* sedition." (p. 786.)

After thus differing from his chief on the meaning of their own charge, it is not wonderful that Blair should think that "to give a definition of sedition would be difficult, *perhaps impossible;* but *I have no hesitation* in giving this definition of it, viz." He then gives his definition ; and his success may warn all sensible men to abstain from attempting to define that (and without hesitation), of which the definition is difficult, or perhaps impossible ; for the definition thus confidently given is, "that the act charged must be unauthorised by law, and must be done with an intention to disturb the peace of the community." (p. 786.) According to this, many treasons are seditious, and so is every mob, and every riot, and every breach of the peace.

The power of transporting was often defended in those days on the ground that sedition was equivalent to leasing-making—that by the Act 1703 leasing-making warranted banishment, and that this word justified transportation. But in this case of *Sinclair* it is remarkable that the application of the Act 1703 to sedition is pointedly disclaimed. *Lord Eskgrove* (who, by the way, says that "sedition is clearly a common law offence, *mentioned even in the scriptures,*"—p. 796) declares that "as the offence here is not leasing-making, *the Act* 1703 *is entirely out of the question.*" (p. 797.) "The Act 1703 (says *Aber-*

cromby) does in no shape apply to the case before us." (p. 799.) And the *Lord Justice-Clerk* says, " I am clear that the Act 1703 has nothing to do with this case." (p. 800.)

The only statute supposed to be applicable being thus excluded, the principles on which their Lordships proceeded were that the case was to be regulated by common law; that as under this law the Court of Justiciary has an inherent authority to declare new crimes, so it can introduce and apply what it conceives to be appropriate punishments; and that the only doubt that can be reasonably entertained of the appropriateness of transporting was whether it was not too mild. This reasoning assumes the legal existence of this extraordinary authority.

Abercromby's exposition of it is as follows :— " We all know that the manners of a people cannot be stationary. New manners necessarily give birth to new crimes. In some countries doubts may arise in what way, and by what law, such new crimes are to be punished; whether they require a special enactment, or may be punished by the common law of the country. In Scotland no such doubt can arise ; because *the supreme criminal court here has always been understood to be possessed of an inherent and radical jurisdiction to punish every offence that can be denominated* a crime *upon the principles of sound reason and morality.*" (p.798.) He means that can be so denominated—by *us, the Court of Justiciary.* What *our* principles of morality and sound reason lead us to denominate a crime, that we can legally so denominate ; and having thus added it to the catalogue of public delinquencies, we can punish it as we think proper. To the same purpose, the *Lord*

Justice-Clerk says : " I have always held it [the court]—*and every lawyer must be of the same mind* —to possess a common law jurisdiction to the effect of inflicting ANY punishment, according to the quality of the offence, *less than death,* for every crime the punishment of which is not specifically defined by statute." (p. 800.)

It may be conceded that this power of inventing punishments is a necessary consequence of the power of creating new crimes, because, without the one, the other is useless. And hence, I see no reason, except that carrying the principle to its full extent would show its extravagance, why they stop short of death, where death happens to be what they think appropriate. But these judges apply their principle of suiting the penalty to the delin- quency, even to old crimes. Their doctrine is, that wherever their discretion is not *excluded* by a statute, the punishment, even of offences long practised and punished, is entirely in their hands ; —a monstrous principle, which leaves the court un- fettered even by its own precedents, and prevents the people from knowing the exact consequences of criminal acts. But it is a principle necessary for the justification of what the court did with sedition ; for seditious acts were no new offence, but were never punished by transportation before.

The truth is, however, that the possession of such authority is a mere justiciary delusion. Hume does not merely assert the existence, but praises the expediency, of such a power, which he terms " *the native vigour* " of the court. But it would be mere idleness to enter upon any serious discussion of such a subject. The very pretension must be incon- ceivable to those who are aware of the tendency of every court to extend its own jurisdiction, and of the facility with which the habit of saying a thing comes to be taken as evidence that the thing is true. It is a pretension which supersedes the legislature; and this on the subject the most important for the public policy and the safety of the people; and erects six judges into an absolute and practically irresponsible tribunal, for pronouncing any action to be criminal, and any punishment less than death to be adequate. This is a claim so dangerous, and so unconstitutional, that it would scarcely be sustained by the open and unquestioned usage of a hundred years. But at present it rests upon nothing except the assertions of the usurping judges, followed by no *exact* precedent except the single and recent case of combination—the most unfortunate in its history of any case that could have occurred for justifying the exercise of this judicial legislation. For parliament differed from the court upon the " sound reason and morality " of the question, and upheld, as just and necessary, what a majority of their Lordships had condemned as criminal and injurious. Accordingly, though this pretension has not been quashed by any judicial determination, or yet put down by any statute, the judges now talk seldom and timidly about it; no public prosecutor appeals to it, and the public unanimously scout it.[1]

The indictment was found relevant on the 17th

---

[1] It is now many years since the preceding pages were written. I grieve to be enabled to say that a case (*Greenhuff*, 19th December 1838) has since occurred, where a public prosecutor did appeal to the "native vigour," and the court re-asserted its existence, praised it, and acted upon it. Being then on the bench, I raised my solitary voice against this. It was a case which, unfortunately, made no noise, and in which there could, in Scotland, be no sympathy with the accused. If such another proceeding shall occur, I do not think it will be possible for me to resist bringing the principle before the public, for discussion and condemnation.

of February 1794. But instead of proceeding with the trial, the case was continued till the 24th. On the 24th it was again continued till the 10th of March ; and on the 10th to the 14th, the day of Gerrald's trial, when the prosecutor got the diet deserted *pro loco et tempore,* and the proceedings were never renewed.

Burnett explains this result by saying that " the trial proceeded no further against Sinclair, *he not being deemed a leading offender."* But, in the *first* place, *judging from the indictment,* he was fully as bad as any of the others. The minutes attest his activity in the convention, and the indictment does not merely charge him with all the general sins of that body, but with a violent speech and resolution of his own. In the *second* place, if his not being a leading offender was a good reason for not trying him, it was a much better one for not indicting him.

The *truth* is, that he had become a Government spy,—as Mr. Fletcher, whose openness and enthusiasm exposed him to the artifices of any villainy which made its advances in the form of zeal for liberty, or of suffering in its cause, had the best possible means of knowing, and always attested.

XIII.—Case of JOSEPH GERRALD, 3d, 10th, 13th, and 14th of March 1794.

NONE of these cases made such an impression at the time, or has sunk so deeply into the heart of posterity, as Gerrald's—not however so much from his superior innocence, as from his character and heroism. He was an Englishman, a gentleman, and a scholar ; a man of talent, eloquence, and fidelity to his principles and associates ; the rashness of whose enthusiasm in the promotion of what appeared to him to be the cause of liberty, though not untinctured by ambition or vanity, was the natural result of the political fire which at that time kindled far less inflammable breasts. The purity of his intentions was above all suspicion.

He was at large upon bail when he heard of the resolution to bring him to trial. Dr. Parr and other friends advised him not to go to Scotland. But having, by his example, encouraged others to join the convention, he held himself bound in honour to prevent the impression which his keeping away might produce, and heroically put himself into the hands of those whom he knew would destroy him. Nothing can be nobler than the high-minded courage with which he met his fate ; or more affecting than the agitation of his excellent friends, who knew what awaited him, but could not shake his constancy.

Dr. Parr gives the following account [1] of one

[1] In a letter to Mr. Laing, and lately, if not still, in the possession of Thomas Thomson, Esq., Depute Register.

interview in which he told Gerrald that his bail
would be paid, and urged him to withdraw. " He
heard my proposal attentively, but with no emotion
of joy.   At first he paused ; and then, after calmly
discussing with me the propriety of the proposal, he
peremptorily refused to accede to it ; and finally,
after hearing my earnest entreaties, closed our conversation in words to the following effect : 'In any
ordinary case,' said he, 'I should, without the
smallest hesitation, and with the warmest gratitude,
avail myself of your offer. I readily admit that my
associates will not suffer more that I suffer less. I
am inclined to believe with you that the sense of
their own sufferings will be alleviated by their
knowledge of my escape. But my honour is pledged,
and no opportunity for flight, however favourable,
no expectation of danger, however alarming, no
excuse for consulting my own safety, however
plausible, shall induce me to violate that pledge.
I gave it to men whom I esteem, and respect, and
pity ; to men who, by avowing similar principles,
have been brought into similar peril, by the influence of my own arguments, my own persuasions,
and my own example. Under these circumstances,
they became partakers of my own responsibility to
the law ; and therefore, under no circumstances
will I shrink from participating with them in the
rigours of any punishment which that law, as likely
to be administered in Scotland, may ordain for us.'
He uttered the foregoing words emphatically, but
not turbulently ; and finding him fixedly determined
upon returning that night to Scotland, I did not
harass his mind by any further remonstrance. He
was very calm before we parted ; and I left him
under the strongest impressions of compassion for

his sufferings, admiration of his courage, and moral
approbation of his delicacy, and his fidelity."

His behaviour in Edinburgh was equally mag-
nanimous. On the evening before his trial, Mr.
Laing and Mr. Fletcher went almost on their knees,
imploring him to withdraw. But he was inflexible
in following what he considered as the honourable
course. The last free hour he ever had was passed
at Fletcher's, where he breakfasted before going to
be tried. Mrs. Fletcher [1] tells me that he was again
urged to withdraw, which even then could have been
managed—but in vain ; and that he took leave of
them with the calm and affectionate demeanour of
a good and firm man going to meet his death.
His conduct throughout his trial was distinguished
by the same noble superiority to his fate. The
manner and tone of no prisoner ever contrasted more
strikingly with that of his judges. The feebleness
of his health, which obviously left him no chance of
surviving the anticipated sentence, gave his case the
only additional interest of which it admitted.

He appeared at the bar with unpowdered hair,
hanging loosely down behind—his neck nearly bare,
and his shirt with a large collar, doubled over ; so
that on the whole he was not unlike one of Vandyck's
portraits. This was the French costume of the day.
His adopting it on this occasion gave great offence
to the judicious, even of his own party, and has not

[1] Brougham says of this lady, that "His (Fletcher's) zeal for the
maintenance of these principles, and his anxiety for the renovation of
British liberty, were, if possible, still further excited by the matrimonial
union which he entered into with a lady of whig family in Yorkshire ;
one of the most accomplished of her sex, who, with the utmost purity of
life that can dignify and enhance female charms, combined the inflexible
principles and deep political feeling of a Hutchison or a Roland."
(*Speeches*, vol. iii. p. 346, Introduction to speech on Burgh Reform.)
This is quite true, so far as it goes. But besides these public virtues,
she is one of the most amiable of women in every domestic relation.

been forgotten yet. It was foolish certainly ; for no one in his position should do anything which may be supposed to savour of affectation. But it must be recollected that he had lived much abroad, and that this dress was one of the symbols of his party. And, no doubt, he appeared in it, partly from a desire to show his opponents that he did not shrink from displaying the outward badge of his principles, even in that extremity. A Quaker is honoured for his hat now, and did not suffer in the estimation of the reflecting even when his sect first put it on. Powdering, or not powdering, the hair was, at this time, one of the established tests of opinion. The heads of the loyal were polluted with white dust ; he who meant to proclaim his admiration of France did so by natural ringlets ; or, if he was very intense, by a short crop.

The proceedings began (3d March 1794) by his stating to the court that " as I am totally ignorant of the laws of this country, being a native of England, I applied to several gentlemen of the profession to advocate my cause, (but) *they unanimously refused.*" (vol. xxiii. p. 803.) Malcolm Laing indeed authorised the fact of his refusal to be intimated. (p. 807). Erskine explains (Letter to Howel, vol. xxiii. p. 806), that the only ground on which he ever declined, was, when he was not allowed to conduct the case in his own way. But some counsel declined even when this most reasonable condition was acceded to, as it was by Gerrald. Erskine was not applied to by him; but Laing never disguised that his reason, and that of his brethren who acted as he had done, was, their aversion to hurt clients by helping to produce the semblance of fair trial, where the reality was absent.

However, as Gerrald said that he wished for counsel, the court agreed to appoint any he chose, and advised him to name four, that he might be sure of obtaining at least two. He named Erskine, Laing, Gillies, and Fletcher. But the court said that it could not interfere with Erskine's numerous and important engagements. The trial was put off till the 10th, when the prisoner returned with Clerk, Fletcher, Gillies, and Laing. The two last, however, took the whole ostensible charge of the defence.

Gillies had only been about seven years at the bar; but, even then, had given earnest of the formidable powers that afterwards raised him into very extensive practice. He was promoted to the bench in 1811. A plain, or rather coarse manner, strong sense, and direct, manly, unadorned speaking, joined to the reputation of a friendly, generous nature, made him a very powerful counsel. Laing was better fitted, both by his faculties and his tastes, for study than for practice, and this was almost his solitary important case. Of great force of intellect and the sternest probity, he carried these qualities into all his pursuits; and is now known as the most original and honest of the historians of Scotland.

The first thing done was, to renew the personal objection, which had been repelled in Margarot's case, to the Lord Justice-Clerk's judging in this trial. But Gerrald stated it in a way which removed the obstacles against its success when it had been formerly brought forward. In the *first* place, it was stated at the very commencement of the proceedings, and before the Justice had done anything except showing, by taking the chair, that he meant to preside. In the *second* place, instead of having no evidence except the testimony of the challenged Judge, he offered to prove the fact on which his objection rested, by other named witnesses.[1] In the *third* place, instead of stating it verbally, he set it forth in a minute, which was made part of the record.

This minute was as follows :—" Joseph Gerrald stated that before proceeding to trial, he must take the liberty of declining the Lord Justice-Clerk, as having disqualified himself from judging in the present question, by having prejudged it. In order to show that this objection was not made at random, Joseph Gerrald offered to prove that the Lord Justice-Clerk had prejudged the cause of every person who had been a member of that assembly calling itself the British Convention ; inasmuch as he had asserted, in the house of James Rochead of Inverleith, that ' the members of the British Convention deserved transportation for fourteen years, and even public whipping ; ' and that when it was objected to by a person in company, that the people would not patiently endure the inflicting of that punishment upon the members of the British Convention, the said Lord Justice-Clerk replied, ' that the mob would be the better for the spilling of a little blood.' I pray that this may be made a minute of court." (vol. xxiii. p. 808.)

Upon this being read, the Justice left the chair, which Henderland took.

The prisoner "desired to have the matters alleged substantiated by evidence." This, however, was not allowed, because it was held that the allegations were *irrelevant*.

---

[1] See vol. xxiii. p. 825 for the names.   Except the Justice and Miss Ainslie, I knew them all well afterwards.   All were regular fixtures at the Inverleith dinners.   It was a lady (but I don't say Miss Ainslie) who was supposed to have peached.

In considering their relevancy, their truth must be assumed.

Now, although being a member of the convention was an important circumstance, there was no necessary guilt in this mere fact. It was always admitted by the prosecutor, and assented to by the court, that it was possible for a person to have joined this association innocently. To make it criminal, the addition of a *criminal intent* was necessary; and accordingly such an intent was always charged. And as the existence and degree of this intent could only be inferred from the whole circumstances, the case of each prisoner differed, or might differ, from that of all the rest; so that no fair opinion could be formed of any one case, without a due consideration of all its peculiar facts.

But the charge against his Lordship was, that without waiting to be informed judicially of the circumstances of the case now before him, he, *in the immediate contemplation of these trials*, had announced it as his opinion that the mere fact of having belonged to the convention deserved transportation, if not whipping. Now the indictment in his hand set forth accession to the acts of the convention as one of the facts charged against Gerrald; and there was no reason, from the experience of the past trials, to suppose that he would deny this to be a fact. His Lordship therefore had prejudged the identical case; that is, he had made up his mind, or professed to have made it up, that the prisoner, *whatever his intent, or his peculiar circumstances, might turn out in evidence to have been,* deserved transportation, at the least, on account of this single undisputed fact. He had prejudged the case, both on the guilt, and on the punishment.

The words having been uttered in the confidence of private society, only makes their sincerity the more probable. The levity of loose conversation was not suggested, either by his Lordship or his apologists, as his explanation. And it could not have been so, because there was no levity in these times, on such subjects. And, at any rate, a judge has no right to harden his mind against the reception of judicial views, or to depress prisoners, by talking lightly of the results of their trials.

If the Lord Justice-Clerk, or his brethren, therefore, had been wise, he would have avoided, or been made to avoid, all discussion on this subject, on the best pretence, and with the best grace, that he could, unless he had a good case on the truth of the objection; in which event he ought to have insisted on the prisoner being indulged with the freest proof. But since the facts were offered to be proved, and the challenge was insisted on, and was disposed of judicially, it humbly appears to me that its relevancy ought to have been sustained. And no lawyer can fail to be confirmed in this opinion, by seeing the grounds on which it was rejected.

Lord Henderland being in the chair, laid the matter before the court in the following terms :—
" Your Lordships have heard the minute of the court concerning the respectable judge who has the honour to preside as vice-president in this court in the absence of the Lord Justice-General.[1] My Lords, it is a thing perfectly new in the annals of this court ; nor is there one instance to be found in our records upon the books of adjournal. My Lords,

[1] The Lord Justice-General was then the head of the court *nominally*, but never acted. He was not a lawyer.

you have heard the nature of the complaint, which is as extraordinary as it is unprecedented ; and it will become you, my Lords, well to weigh what is the import, and what ought to be the legal effect, of such an objection, offered in such extraordinary circumstances, *and at so early a period* as this. You had it in a different form indeed in the case of *Margarot.* But you will consider it in this new form, in this new guise, which it has assumed. You will consider how far it is important in its nature, or how far it is the same that was offered in the case of *Margarot.* You are not prohibited from forming a different judgment upon it now from what you might have done then ; but I thought it necessary to bring these matters under your Lordships' view before you proceed to give your opinion upon this so unprecedented and extraordinary a minute. It is now submitted to your consideration." (vol. xxiii. p. 809.)

Eskgrove's opinion proceeds entirely on a misrepresentation of the ground of the declinature. " I do not observe," says he, " that this gentleman says *his name was ever mentioned* in that conversation, or that anything was said of him *individually."* (p. 809.) This was true ; but surely a man, or his case, may be mentioned by description. " He says it was an expression in common conversation, importing that honourable judge's opinion that the members of the British Convention should be transported for fourteen years, and even publicly whipped. *I do not conceive what interest this gentleman has in it; he has not yet acknowledged himself a member of that convention."* But was he not charged with being so ? and had he not denied it by pleading not guilty ? " My Lord, *one man's conduct may be*

different from another's in that assembly. As to
the expression, it *could* only import, *hypothetically,*
that IF that convention *was guilty of the crimes
stated against them*—of that attempt to overthrow
the Constitution of the country—to create rebellion
and insurrection in the country—*then* the punishment adapted to such an offence was, in his opinion,
transportation and public whipping. What is there
in that more than in the opinions given in this
court already in causes of this kind," etc. " I think
it was nothing more than a *general* opinion, given
upon the nature of the offence *as charged,* that it
was a convention of persons meeting to overturn
the happy Constitution of this country, and giving
it as his opinion that such an offence merited that
punishment. I am sure that can be no disqualification from sitting in this court, where the same
opinion has been given by all your Lordships."
(p. 810.)

Now, taking it even in this last view, the impropriety of the Justice's alleged observation is
clearer than ever ; for it amounted to a prejudication of the *very case under trial,* the case " *as
charged.*" But it cannot be taken in this view ;
for Eskgrove is plainly not addressing himself to
the fact offered by the prisoner to be proved. The
Justice was *not* declined for saying that all men who
attempt to overturn the Constitution should be
transported, but for committing himself prematurely
to the opinion that this was the object of all the
members of the convention. He was not, in the
situation of a judge who should say that a murderer
deserved death, but of a judge who, on the eve
of trying certain soldiers for firing on the people,
should say that every man in that regiment should

be hanged. The *hypothesis* is a mere friendly invention by Eskgrove. Braxfield seldom dealt in
anything so fine as hypothesis. What Gerrald
wanted to prove was the expression of a positive
and absolute opinion, directly applicable to his particular trial.

Eskgrove had set out by saying that the objection " is a novelty in many respects ; and I do not
think this panel at this bar is well advised in
making it. What could be his motive for it I cannot perceive. He has the HAPPINESS of being tried
before one of the ablest judges that ever sat in this
court. But he is to do as he thinks fit. *I am sure
he is to obtain no benefit if he gains the end he has
in view.* And therefore I cannot perceive his motive,
unless it be an *inclination, as far as he can, to throw
an indignity upon this court.*" (p. 809.) It was something for the prisoner to get rid of Braxfield ; and
it is natural for every prisoner to like to disparage
the court that is to condemn him, especially when
the ground of disparagement is one which, by showing
prejudice in the presiding judge, may render the guilt
of the accused less unquestionable. But if a party,
either criminal or civil, has an objection that is well
founded, it is not usual either to withhold the law
from him, or to sneer at him for stating it.

This insinuation against the prisoner's motives
passed unnoticed by him. But he interfered when
it was repeated more offensively. After disposing
of the observation that the people would not submit
to the infliction of corporal punishment on the
members of the convention, *Eskgrove* said : " I can
ascribe it (the prisoner's statement of it) to nothing
but *malevolence and desperation.*" This produced
the following exhibition :—

" *Mr. Gerrald.*—My Lord, I come here not to be the object of personal abuse, but to meet the justice of my country. Had I been actuated by such motives, I am sure I should never have returned to this country.

" *Lord Henderland.*—I desire you will behave as becomes a man before this high court ; I will not suffer this court to be *insulted.* [!]

" *Mr. Gerrald.*—My Lord, far be it from me to insult this court—

" *Lord Henderland.*—Be silent, sir !

" *Mr. Gerrald.*—My Lord—

" *Lord Henderland.*—I desire you will be silent, sir !

" *Mr. Gerrald.*—My Lord, I am sure that my coming to this country shows that I was actuated by the purest principles of justice.

" *Lord Eskgrove.* — If I have said anything wrong, I will very readily retract what I have said. But *I was making* AN APOLOGY [! ! !] *for this objection*, that I cannot ascribe it to a solid objection of counsel, none of whom have stood up to support it. I meant nothing more by what I was saying. I am very sorry for the expression I made use of, and I ask the gentleman's pardon." (p. 811.)

It does not elevate a tribunal in one's imagination that one judge makes an apology for what another tells the prisoner that he insults the court by seeking. Why none of the counsel maintained the declinature after the use that was thus made of their silence, I have not been able to learn.

Lord Swinton's opinion was that there were no legal grounds of declinature of a judge except those mentioned in the Statute, and that these were only two—*interest or capital enmity*, neither of which existed here. Interest was out of the question. And as to enmity, it is "absurd." "I never heard of this man's name in my life before he came into this country, and I dare say his Lordship never did. And what interest he can have, except that of compassion for a man in that unfortunate situation, I cannot tell, and I appeal to the feelings of every man. I say it is *impossible*." (p. 812.) This opinion exhausted the question, and there was no need for having said anything more. But his Lordship had permitted himself to begin with these words : " My Lord, an objection of this kind, coming from any other man, I should consider as a very *high insult upon the dignity of this court*. But coming from him, standing in the peculiar situation in which he now stands at the bar, charged with a crime little less than treason, the *insolence* of his objection IS SWALLOWED UP IN THE ATROCITY OF HIS CRIME." (p. 811.) Not swallowed up in the atrocity of the prosecutor's charge, but of the *prisoner's guilt*. Yet the trial had not begun ! And what a symptom is it of a court, when the judges treat a declinature of one of their number, on a ground of supposed legal or of supposed personal impropriety, as an insult !

Abercromby admitted that wherever " a judge is guilty of a breach of the sacred trust reposed in him, he is amenable to the laws of his country, and may be *impeached* for that offence." But when addressed to the *court*, he gives it as his opinion that " THERE IS NO SUCH THING AS A COMMON LAW DISQUALIFICATION OF A JUDGE," in reference of course to any individual case. " But, my Lord, that [impeachment] is not the shape in which this objection comes before you. It comes in the shape of a

disqualification. Now, my Lords, I KNOW OF NO
CIRCUMSTANCES WHATEVER WHICH CAN DISQUALIFY
A JUDGE FROM SITTING TO DISCHARGE HIS DUTY,
EXCEPT THOSE IN THE ACT OF PARLIAMENT." So
that if Braxfield had drawn the indictment, or
taken a bribe, or given a written pledge to Government that he would do all he could to obtain a
conviction, or had committed any other crime for
which he might have been degraded by parliament
ultimately, this would not have entitled the prisoner to object to him in the meantime, unless the
partiality which had produced these improprieties
had sprung from what an old Scotch Statute calls
interest or *capital enmity*—that is, pecuniary interest in the trial, or deadly hatred of the prisoner
personally. The specific case of judicial partiality
arising from political disapprobation is excluded.

He agrees with Eskgrove that the objection
stated, if well founded, reaches them all as well as
the Lord Justice-Clerk. " Upon every occasion
when I have had an opportunity of giving my
opinion on the subject, I have never hesitated to say,
that I considered the British Convention as a conspiracy of a most dangerous and of a most criminal
nature.' (p. 812.) No doubt. But his Lordship
forgets that the declinature of the Justice was not
founded on his having condemned *the convention*,
but on his having condemned *every individual*
member of that body, the prisoner, of course, included, merely on the solitary fact that he had
belonged to it. And by condemning *the convention*,
Lord Eskgrove could only mean that he *strongly
disapproved* of it, and to the extent of deeming it
criminal. But what Braxfield was accused of was,
not merely his condemning *individuals*, but his

condemning them *as on their approaching trials.*
There could be no *whipping* except under an *anticipated sentence.*

His Lordship concluded by an observation which
has too much the appearance of a desire to intimidate the prisoner in his defence. After acknowledging that he " is presumed to be innocent of the
charges laid against him till he is found guilty by
a verdict of his country," he proceeds, in the very
next sentence, to anticipate the verdict, and to
cheer the panel by its consequences. " But I have
no hesitation in saying now, in the presence of that
man, in the presence of his counsel, and in the presence of this audience and of your Lordships, that
IF he should be convicted of the crime charged
against him in this indictment, I *shall* say that even
fourteen years' transportation is *too slight* a punishment for an offence of such magnitude. My Lord,
in the case of *Margarot* I had a doubt. But that
doubt was whether fourteen years' transportation
was not too slight a punishment for the offence,
aggravated as it was by a variety of circumstances,
and, in particular, by *the very improper and indecent
conduct of that man to the court in the course of his
trial, which, for his own sake, I hope the panel at the
bar will not do,"* (p. 813)—a pretty significant hint
to a prisoner who had only declined one of the
judges, though in perfectly respectful terms, and
whose single interruption of the bench was so
just, that the interrupted judge made a personal
apology for having provoked it. Judges should be
very cautious in making the misbehaviour of a
prisoner at the bar a ground for increasing the
severity of his punishment. This misbehaviour is
not the offence for which he is tried ; and when it

consists of disrespect to the court, the equanimity even of judges is not unapt to be so ruffled, as to make the aggravation be appreciated rather by their temper than their reason. Where a *new crime* is committed at the bar, it had better, in general, be punished separately ; and perhaps the only misconduct that may be correctly visited in the sentence pronounced in the principal case, is where it evinces *bad character*. But even this is doubtful.

Lord Henderland puts the point at first correctly enough. He states it to be, whether the language ascribed to the Justice implies prejudication ?—and he thought that it did not. " It appears to have been a transient conversation *with respect to the crime of sedition*, and the punishment due to *it;* but is that a ground for declining a judge ? I appeal to the feelings of any man who has conversed on this subject. *I appeal to the feelings of every juryman who has tried these cases; I appeal to the feelings of every juryman who will try these cases;* would he think himself bound, in the smallest degree, by such a conversation ? Would he think the case prejudiced one iota ? " " My Lords, taking it in this point of view, the words said to be expressed— in the manner in which they were expressed, and the occasion on which they were expressed—must all go together ; and IT IS ADMITTED THAT THEY ARE, SO FAR, FAIRLY TOLD YOU. It is not said that was a judicial opinion given by this learned judge ; and *therefore* was not anything like a prejudication of what he might do in this court ; and we are to judge whether, by fair inference, it ought to be held so,— whether, by consulting the common sense of mankind, for that is the test of all criminality." (p. 813.)

This is true. The common-sense of mankind is

the test of all criminality. But it is not equally true that courts are always correct exponents of this common sense. Very few men, off the bench, will agree with this judge, either in his representation of the ground of declinature, or in his reason for rejecting it. The very essence of the prisoner's objection was, that it was *not* a *conversation* about *sedition* and *its* punishment, but the expression of a positive opinion by the Lord Justice-Clerk, on the particular case of Joseph Gerrald, as one of a class, who were all included in that opinion. And if it be sound that because the opinion was not given *judicially,* it "was not anything like a prejudication of what he might do in this court," then there can never be any extra-judicial prejudication.

His Lordship then proceeds to try his declined brother by the test of the common sense of mankind. And his manner of doing so is a fair example enough of the degree of accuracy with which this matter was reasoned. Immediately after mentioning "the test of all criminality," he proceeds thus : " And here, my Lord, a respectable judge — an honour to his profession and abilities, whom I know to be a man of the highest honour and the strictest integrity—is to be tried before us. For we are his jury. And we are called upon by our great oaths, as judges, and laying our hands upon our hearts, to say that this respectable judge, by what is here alleged, is to be *rendered incapable of sitting in this chair,—to be degraded from his office, and held unfit to judge in the most important trials in this country,* where his abilities, steadiness, and knowledge in the law are most required. I cannot go to such a length." (p. 814.) Who had asked him to do so ? He was not moved to go one-tenth part

that length. The plea of the prisoner only went to
exclude the justice from acting in *this particular
trial;* and a judge may disqualify himself, by accidental rashness, from interfering in a single case,
or in a single class of cases, without incurring any
general disability. At any rate, if the plea was
well founded in reference to the individual trial, its
tendency, even though it had led to the official
extinction of the judge declined, ought to have been
utterly disregarded.

Treated as the challenge was, *Dunsinnan's*
opinion was perhaps the wisest of them all. The
whole of it was in these words : " My Lords, this
objection is new, and not a little extraordinary. It
very much surprised me. I shall enter into no
observations upon his conduct ; and I think your
Lordships *ought to pay no attention to it, either in
one shape or in another.*" (vol. xxiii. p. 812.)

The declinature being thus repelled, the Justice
resumed his seat—with what feelings those who
best knew him can best tell.

The indictment was then read. In its structure
and substance, it was nearly identical with those
of Skirving and Margarot. The only new matter
introduced consists of three speeches said to have
been made by the prisoner ; two in the convention,
and one when it was dispersed. The last, however,
was rather an exclamation than a speech, and merely
amounted to an expression of indignation, or of
resistance, against the dispersion. One of the
addresses in the convention was in favour of universal suffrage ; the other, on the statute passed
shortly before for suppressing such societies in
Ireland. They are both, of course, more declamatory than wise. But they are both so clear of sedi-

tion, that if it were not for certain remarks made upon them from the bench, I should have held that this vice was not imputed to them even in the indictment. Because all that it says of these harangues is, that they were delivered, "*wickedly and feloniously*," in the convention, an "*illegal and seditious meeting.*" It is not said that these speeches are, *in themselves*, seditious. Accordingly I read the indictment as mentioning these addresses only as acts showing that the prisoner was an active member of the society—a character in which it might have been wicked and felonious to make even a speech not seditious. But this is not the construction put upon the libel by the judges; for they almost all select different passages of these speeches as seditious. They are too long to be quoted at length; but I may perhaps notice hereafter some of the passages objected to, which we may be sure are the worst. Meanwhile, this indictment is, in other respects, the same with the two preceding ones, and therefore requires no new observations.

Gillies addressed the court in a full speech, both on the relevancy and on the legality of transporting. He was ably answered by Mr. Montgomery, eldest son of the Lord Chief Baron—a remarkably sensible, gentlemanlike, well-conditioned person, who would certainly have risen high in his profession, if this had been necessary for his comfort. But a baronetcy, a large estate, a secure seat in parliament, and an agricultural taste, impair a wise man's relish for the *Dictionary of Decisions.* He therefore brought his legal career to a respectable close by rarely seeing the Parliament House after he ceased to be Lord Advocate, which he had been for about a year, when the whigs came into office in 1805. He represented his own county of Peebles long after this ; and good sense, good conduct, and good manners, secured him respect in every situation. Blair followed on the same side, and Laing replied for the prisoner.

This seems to have been an excellent discussion. The counsel for the prisoner strike me as having shone the brightest; but this may be a prejudice from my admiration of the spirit with which they maintained offensive doctrines—a merit which their side alone admitted of, and from that side being the one towards which I rather lean. But the whole discussion was good. It forms one of the very few scenes in these trials, where the air of a court of justice is felt.

I cannot understand, however, how the legality of any particular punishment was allowed to be argued at this stage. It could only be so hypothetically ; for an acquittal would have rendered the whole discussion useless. The only explanation that Gillies can give me is, that it was arranged with the court that this would be the most convenient time for the argument. But, except upon the ground that a conviction might be very safely anticipated, it is difficult to comprehend how such an arrangement could be acceded to in any quarter. I shall not follow the example ; but shall reserve anything I may have to say on the sentence till the verdict be pronounced.

Both Laing and Gillies allude, plainly enough, to the existence of the depressing feeling that their efforts must be hopeless. *Gillies* mentions the difficulty "of directly and strongly maintaining that other views ought to have guided your Lordship's judgment formerly, and that other views ought to guide it now. Added to this is that *firmly rooted and widespread notion of the guilt of all those who stand at this bar accused of sedition.* The temper of men's minds, from many obvious causes, is such, that they consider a person at this bar, *under this accusation,* as already condemned ; that it is almost unnecessary to plead for him, except as going through the forms ; while he whose fortune it is to undertake such a cause *is considered as, in effect, a sharer of the crimes imputed to him whom he defends,* and by doing his duty may incur all the consequences that ought only to follow his not doing it. As to the panels thus brought before you, the public considers them as the personal enemies of us all. Our properties, our lives, our all, are represented as the objects of their violence ; and against danger so near, and danger so dreadful, *we should not be scrupulous about our means of defence.*" (vol. xxiii. p. 827.) *Laing* says that he had at first declined the case, " *not only from personal considerations, which I forbear to mention,* but because my recent avocations have been very different from the pursuits of this bar." (vol. xxiii. p. 869.)

As to the relevancy, strictly considered, the argument, when stripped of its husk, comes to this kernel.

It was maintained for the prisoner, that there was nothing criminal in any number of persons meeting in a society called a convention ; that though the attainment of any given reform of parliament, particularly of annual parliaments and universal suffrage, was the object of the convention, this object did not render the convention criminal ; that all the acts of the British Convention, and all the speeches delivered in it, in so far as these were challenged in this indictment, were innocent; that therefore there was no sedition set forth at all; but that if there was, then, as it was not said to have produced any popular rising or commotion, it was verbal sedition, and not real, and therefore the relevancy could only be sustained to this extent; or that, if the statements in the libel were meant to describe real sedition, its reality consisted in there having been a scheme for the overthrow of the Government, and that this being high treason, it could not be tried as sedition.

The answer to this was that the general charge of sedition in the major proposition entitled the prosecutor to bring out any form of the offence in his minor; that the case exhibited in this minor, though bordering upon treason, did not actually amount to this crime, as introduced into Scotland at the Union; that the mischief described as intended, plainly amounted to what the prisoner chose to call real sedition; but that real and verbal, though convenient as terms to indicate the import of the circumstances of two classes of cases, were not known to the law as denoting generically different offences; that the convention was a seditious association, and sedition was the character and the object of the acts it did, and of the speeches it heard; and that even though the court should, on the first impression, concur with the prisoner's counsel in their construction of all these, still the prosecutor was entitled to have an opportunity of supporting his own view of them by evidence and argument before a jury.

The court repelled the objections, and found the libel relevant. And, except in one particular, this was right. I am strongly impressed with the idea that, *ex facie* of the indictment, and still more as the indictment was explained, the matter presented itself as a case of treason. But, holding this view to be excluded, there was plainly no such palpable irrelevancy as could have warranted the court in refusing to send the case to a jury. The truth is that the leading objection, as is very common in cases of sedition, was not so much to the relevancy of the libel, as to the groundlessness of the charge. It resolved into this, that the convention, in its constitution, objects, acts, and words, was innocent. But how could the prosecutor be held concluded as to all these without being allowed to adduce his evidence? I should therefore have held the indictment relevant, even though I had acquiesced in all the criticisms of the prisoner's counsel.

But it is for this very reason, namely, because the objections to relevancy involved the consideration of the merits, that a cautious judge, in delivering his opinion on relevancy, will never say more than what may be absolutely necessary to enable him to dispose of the precise matter then before him. It may require some skill and more forbearance to hit the right line, but the *principle* is to leave the whole matter, if relevant, to the jury, *entirely and truly*, subject always to judicial direction and observation at last, but free from all confident opinions, hypothetical anticipation, and positive constructions, from the court at first.

This is a principle, however, which it must be presumed that our judges of 1794 did not acknowledge, because they certainly did not practically adopt it. They went into the case in all its minuteness, and let the jurymen know before they took their seats that the seditiousness of the convention,

and of all its proceedings, and of the prisoner's
speeches there, was so clear, that in truth there was
nothing to be ascertained except the facts, or rather,
that since these were admitted, there was nothing
to try at all. Not that the prisoner might not show
all these to be legal, for *in words* this privilege was
most fully and most formally reserved to him ; but
then they expressed their concurrence in the prosecutor's constructions and imputations, not hypothetically, but absolutely, and virtually reversed the
rule by sending the prisoner to trial under an obliga-
tion to prove his innocence. Each judge seems to
have spoken nearly exactly as he might have done
if he had been summing up.

Henderland indeed seems in one part of his
opinion to have so far forgotten his position as
actually to address somebody he supposed to be the
jury : "*Gentlemen,* as to the particular activity of
this panel at the bar, you have his speeches." It
had not at this time been proved that he had ever
made any speech. Then, after quoting one of his
supposed speeches, his Lordship makes this commentary :—"This at least, to push it no further,
shows his conduct and his activity in this resolution,
which *I must, in sound construction of common sense,
consider as seditious. Gentlemen,* I will not run
over the different proceedings of this convention.
They divided themselves into sections, departments,
and so on. They *also had sittings, committees of
organisation, instruction,* and *finance.* And, *taking
all those into consideration,* I am at a loss to find out
the necessity of such a form of government if they
only intended to petition parliament." (vol. xxiii.
p. 892.) He might properly enough have saved
some of this, in reference to the averments by the

prosecutor in the indictment. But it is plain from his whole strain that he was speaking from his recollection of the facts proved before him in the previous trials, and was telling (unconsciously perhaps) what he thought of the real *truth of the charge.*

Eskgrove goes over all the leading facts, accompanying each with a commentary decisive against the prisoner. I shall only quote one passage in further evidence of the important fact that the court did not recognise the clearly constitutional right of every British subject to propose whatever reform he chose, provided he did so honestly, and proposed to effect it by lawful means. Throughout all these trials the judges uniformly held that certain reforms, as for example universal suffrage and annual parliaments, were criminal objects *in themselves,* were not only hurtful, *but necessarily carried with them their own evidence that mischief was the intention* of their promoters. Thus *Eskgrove* says : " They were endeavouring to obtain universal suffrage and annual parliaments. My Lord, as to universal suffrage, I never heard that it had obtained in the British Constitution, and therefore, though it may be lawful to obtain A change, *yet if it is a change* OF THAT SORT, *it goes to show that it was not their intention to improve the Constitution, but to subvert and overthrow it.*" (p. 895.) Yet this change has not only been advocated since, but had been advocated then with impunity by many unquestionably well-intentioned and eminent men, and it is now one of the ordinary subjects of unchecked public discussion—which shows how careful a judge should be not to assume his own political principles to be eternal truths, or to hold everything to be clearly wicked which alarms him.

One of the speeches ascribed in the libel to the prisoner contains the following exposition of the principle of all representation, whether universal or not : —"If you appoint a man to act as your agent, and make his situation such that he has every temptation to betray you, without incurring the danger of being called to account, the probability is that he will sacrifice your interest to his own. It is therefore that a free suffrage of the people is what every man ought to desire, as that alone can make the interest of the representative and his constituents the same. The great art of government is that all should be governed by all. But unhappy is the country where men are called upon by every interest to act in opposition to their duty." (vol. xxiii. p. 816.) It is not constitutionally correct to hold the representative to be a mere agent; and there may possibly be other errors of a similar kind in this passage. But it could scarcely occur to anybody now-a-days that there was anything in it to excite the horror of a judge coolly deciding a question of relevancy. Yet this apparently very harmless text produced the following discourse from *Swinton* :—

"The gentlemen who have appeared and displayed so much ability for the panel have taken a great deal of pains to fritter down what is meant by universal suffrage. My Lords, I maintain that it is not only inconsistent with the British Constitution, but inconsistent with every constitution or government that ever did exist, *or ever can* exist, that every mortal who has arms and legs and head—(and we are all equal, all of like passions and like judgments with one another)—that every one of them shall have equal suffrage—in what ? Not only in the election of legislators, but of magistrates, of

ministers, and of judges too. *Universal suffrage,
according to their meaning, is a suffrage to rejudge
what judges may do* [!]; also to judge whether they
will obey an Act of Parliament or not; and whether
the Acts of these annual parliaments are agreeable
to their mind or not. I will tell you what : annual
parliaments are inconsistent with any government
at all; because if these parliaments should pass an
Act which these universal suffragants disliked, they
have a right from nature to meet and say, this is a
wrong Act; we did choose these people, but they
have gone contrary to our universal suffrage, and
we have a right to rejudge them, and overturn what
they have done. And I will give it you in the
prisoner's own words,—if it be true as charged in the
libel,—in his own speech." His Lordship then reads
the words above quoted, and proceeds thus :—
" Now mark this : the great art of government, I
apprehend, is that all should be governed by all.
That is to say, that the whole of the suffragants,
the whole voters, shall be governed by the whole
voters. What is this but saying that the mob
shall be governed by the mob, the multitude shall
be governed by the multitude? *Who would be
chosen a judge by such governors? Because they
would rejudge him* [!]. There has been one instance
in France where the revolutionary tribunal and the
jury having found that the people were innocent,
these suffragants, these general voters, thought the
judges did wrong, and they judged them over
again; and, if the account we have be true, every
one of them were carried to the lamp-post. *So the
plan is that there should be an eternal appeal from
the guillotine to the lamp-post—that is the plan of
this universal government* [!!]. He (the prisoner)

says : 'Were all mankind to assemble in public meetings, one of two things must follow—either they will behave properly or improperly ; if properly, their meeting will tend to do good ; if improperly, it carries its own cure along with it. The people will soon be brought into a better method by a sense of self-preservation, by which they will correct the errors into which they have fallen.' *That is to say, they would cut one another's throats, and the few that remained would see their folly* " [!!] etc. " But, my Lords, you need only to read these things ; *they do not need argument.* I am, THERE-FORE, clearly of opinion that it is sedition, not only tending to overturn the British Government, but every Government, and that it is most clearly relevant to infer the pains of law." (p. 898.)

The gentleness of the prisoner's subsequent apology for this harangue well entitles him to the praise of forbearance. He repeated his own words and re-asserted the sentiment in his defence, and quotes Sir William Temple as an authority for the principle that " the only skill or knowledge of any value in politics was the secret *of governing all by all ;*" " words," says he, " which his Lordship thought proper to ridicule, *because he did not understand them.*" (vol. xxiii. p. 975.)

Dunsinnan, Abercromby, and the Lord Justice-Clerk say nothing, except generally that they think the indictment relevant, which was the best course they could adopt.

The prisoner objected to two of the persons selected by the Justice-Clerk to serve as jurors.

The objection to Mr. Rankin, that he held the honorary appointment of tailor to the king, was clearly bad in law—that is, as a challenge for cause.

But it is equally clear that since the prisoner doubted his having a fair trial if this person served, it was harsh in the Justice to persist in having him. There were so many other jurymen, indeed, who could be very safely trusted, that, had it not been for the jealousy with which, during the days of picking, every interference with the picker was received, no doubt Mr. Rankin would have been dispensed with. So his Majesty's tailor was allowed an opportunity of punishing the imputation on his candour by being put into the box.[1]

The other objection, which was to Mr. Creech, bookseller, though repelled, seems to me to have been relevant. I do not know what the exact English rule is, but I see several cases in which, whenever it was ascertained, especially if by a proposed jury- man's own admission, that *he had given an opinion upon the subject of the trial,* he was dispensed with. They frequently dispute whether he should be with- drawn by consent, or challenged, or held rejected for cause ; but, one way or other, they seem always to get rid of the man. (*See,* for example, *State Trials,* vol. xxii. p. 1039, case of *Rowan.*)

Now, the objection to Mr. Creech was that "he has repeatedly declared in private conversations *that he would condemn any member of the British Convention, if he should be called to pass on their assize.*" (vol. xxiii. p. 901.) It is not easy to con- ceive more distinct prejudication, or a spirit less becoming a juror. And what were the answers to it ? The prosecutor said nothing. But *Henderland* said that "if he (Creech) had said that he would

The only juryman who was for convicting the Seven Bishops was Arnold, "the brewer of the king's house." (Mackintosh, James II., p. 274.)

condemn them *whether they were guilty or not*, it would have been a good objection." " But it is not stated that he said he would do so, whether they were guilty or not." (p. 901.) This formal addition, however, was immaterial. He was accused of having said that he would condemn on the mere fact of a prisoner having been a member of the convention, obviously implying that, to him, this fact would be conclusive of guilt. All the other judges, however, adopt the same ground. *Eskgrove* observes that the juror is not stated to have said " that he would convict Mr. Gerrald *whether right or wrong;*" and besides, "if it was only in common conversation that he *had such an opinion of the intentions of the British Convention*, it is not a good objection." (p. 901.) Nobody was interfering with his opinion of the British Convention. But it was admitted on all sides that that institution might contain innocent members ; and the objection was that, notwithstanding this, he had declared that he would convict on the mere fact of membership, and, of course, whether right or wrong, though he did not use these words.

Braxfield (who rarely did things by halves) gives his opinion in these very considerate words : " As this objection is stated, I HOPE *there is not a gentleman of the jury, or any man in this court, who has not expressed the same sentiment*"[! !] (p. 901.) Gerrald then restated his objection, and explained it to be, not that Mr. Creech had said generally that he would convict *all disturbers of the public peace*, but all members of the convention,—*though the illegality of this association was one of the very points to be ascertained;* and that thus " he had prejudged the *principles* on which I am to be tried." But their Lordships said no more. It was unfortunate for the Justice's *hope* that Creech had the audacity to protest that it was *impossible* he could ever have uttered such a sentiment. But the Justice did not leave him out, as in consistency he ought to have done, on this account.

The evidence was very short, and a mere repetition of what had been given in the previous trials. Its object was to prove that the prisoner was an active member of the convention, which was the scene of all the guilt imputed to him. The speech ascribed to him was not very satisfactorily proved ; but instead of denying it, he admitted, and defended it.

The Lord Advocate was in London attending his duty in parliament, where the conduct of the Court of Justiciary in relation to these trials was at this very period under discussion. The jury was therefore charged for the prosecution by Blair, the Solicitor-General.

His speech has nothing in it of the slightest permanent interest or attraction. But still, for the case, it was a powerful and respectable prosecutor's address—the different points well arranged, and well put, and not with much more frequent or stronger appeals to the terrors or the party feelings of the jury, than what were excusable in his situation. His argument is, that the constitution, language, and resolutions of the convention show it to have been a seditious association ; that the prisoner was an active member, and, consequently, responsible for what it did ; and that, besides this constructive guilt, his own speeches involved him in sedition personally. All the circumstances, sentiments, and expressions are worked up in support of these propositions clearly and forcibly. There are some things, however, that will strike a modern reader with surprise.

He repeats his notion that there was sedition in the very title of a "Convention of *Delegates* of the People," because this was an usurpation of the character and authority of the House of Commons. (p. 935.) Burnett thinks it worth his while to record that the merit of this idea is due to Blair. (p. 248.) And the steadiness with which the Solicitor-General recurs to it in every one of these trials makes him appear more pleased with the conception than might have been expected from so sensible a man.

He expresses his strongest possible concurrence with the court in the opinion that seeking universal suffrage is not only dangerous, and inconsistent with the nature of our government, but *seditious*. It is " a complete subversion of that form of government under which we live ;" and this form of government having been fixed at the Revolution, such a change can *never be advocated* without carrying with it its own evidence of seditious intention. (p. 936.)

This could not be maintained without suggesting to his mind the case of a well-disposed man maintaining any given form as a speculative theme, and the constitutional right, as generally conceded, of every individual to propose even dangerous innovations, provided he does so honestly; and it is distressing to find such a case—being the one on which the whole privilege of public discussion depends—disposed of by a man like Blair on such shallow and incorrect views. He holds that the Revolution settled the government; that we owe what he calls "*allegiance*" to the *government as thus settled*, including all its parts ; and that, therefore, the recommendation, though even as a mere speculative

opinion, of any change inconsistent with the settlement, is seditious.

His words are these : "But we are told that
universal suffrage is a speculative opinion with
respect to government; that wise men differ upon
it; and that it is a part of the freedom which we
enjoy to have the liberty of fairly discussing every
political subject, and this among the rest. Gentle--
men, *this is a proposition which I will take the liberty
to deny.* I will take the liberty to say that the
maintaining the freedom of discussion of political
questions to the length which *is* [not which is *meant
to be*, but which *is*] *subversive of the Constitution, is
most illegal*, and most unconstitutional. For what
is the situation in which we stand? We are not
here in a state of nature; we are not savages, and
now for the first time to choose a constitution for
ourselves—not like a man shipwrecked upon a
desert island, free to choose any mode of government
we please. No; we are all of us born subjects of
the British Empire—subjects of Great Britain—
which is the most inestimable blessing, and the most
inestimable birthright, that can be bestowed upon
us. *From our birth we owe allegiance to the Constitution established at the Revolution, and we are
not to venture to say that another constitution would
do better in its place.* I say by law we owe allegiance to it from our birth, and by law we are bound
to prevent *it* being *encroached* upon; and that no
body of men have a liberty to say *that we will
indulge in speculation,* and there is no harm in
speculation. Now, gentlemen, I ask, was universal
suffrage any part of the constitution established at
the Revolution? Gentlemen, I shall only suppose
that in place of associating themselves for the pur-

pose of obtaining universal suffrage, as they tell us, suppose they had entitled themselves an association in order to obtain a demolition of kingly power and of nobility. To be sure, they might have told us it was mere matter of speculation, and that many good men had thought we were much better without kings and without nobles. But I am sure, living in this country, and under the constitution of Great Britain, *any* proposition of that kind, maintained by *any* body of men, would be illegal and seditious." (p. 936.)

No wonder that reformers were easily convicted, where such a doctrine was openly and responsibly propounded by a public accuser, and with the cordial assent of the bench. Its plain result is, that all reform, at least where it amounts to material organic change, must be seditious. We are always to go back to the year 1688, or thereabouts, and to take the structure of the government, and consequently of its essential parts, as we then received them, and every subsequent change implies sedition. There is to be no talking of expediency. All considerations of the kind are excluded by our allegiance to the original government, exactly as they are in relation to the sovereign, by our allegiance to him; and this rule is given us in the one case, as it is in the other, by the mere fact of British birth; and this for the very purpose of precluding even speculation on a subject so dangerous to be touched, or to be even reasoned about. The Revolution settlement fixed that there should be three parliaments, one for each of the three divisions of the empire; that each English one should endure only three years; that all Catholics should be excluded from either sitting in any of them, or from voting at elections; that there should be no popular representation in Scotland; that the number and the distribution of members, and the qualifications of electors, should be as then recognised; and that juries should have no right to decide upon the guilt of defendants on their trial for libel. Yet all of these vital and organic forms and principles of the Constitution, as adjusted at the Revolution, have been changed. And many others, such as universal suffrage, annual parliaments, vote by ballot, the inexpediency of an Established Church, the exclusion of bishops from the House of Lords, and the policy of even the institution of hereditary nobility, have not only been discussed, as political speculations, by philosophers, but have long formed subjects of common popular argument.

This may be all very dangerous, but its legal criminality is a very different matter. The misfortune (as some would call it) is, that under a government not absolutely despotical, we cannot arrest the progress of thought; and wherever speculations, strange to our habits, come, in the progress of thought, to be familiar to the public mind, the only safety is in letting them have free vent. Blair's error consists in his not perceiving that susceptibility of improvement, and consequently the right to suggest it, *are parts of the Constitution*. We would never have got out of the heptarchy upon his principle. What he ought to have said was, that to constitute sedition, there must be both immediate and intended public mischief or danger; that the important element is the evil design; that this does not always require external evidence, but may, in the discretion of the jury, be inferred from intensity of language, or outrageousness of project;

and that the prisoner's conduct supplied such evidence. But instead of thus leaving the objects of the convention to be judged of by the jury, as one of the circumstances from which public danger or evil intention is to be deduced, he, and the judges still more, lay it down in such a way that the jury must understand it to be *matter of law*, that there are certain reforms, the urging of which no purity of intention could prevent being criminal, and that annual parliaments and universal suffrage were two of these.

The sensitiveness of people's alarm at any doubt of the absolute perfection of every part of our system, is evinced by his observation on Gerrald's statement, that the Constitution was not so pure now as at the Revolution. This may have been a very erroneous opinion, but it would scarcely occur to any calm man that it was criminal, even though the Government at the one period should be compared to a living body, and at the other to a carcase. Yet when Gerrald's speech said that "the present form of government, in my opinion, no more resembles the Revolution, than a dead putrid carcase does a living body," Blair is at the trouble to make this commentary, "which is just saying, in other and more florid words, what is stated in the minutes, that the blessings obtained by the Revolution were now *totally done away*." (p. 941.)

But it was dangerous to question even the policy of the Union, though this was, at this very period, as well as long both before and after, one of the ordinary questions for discussion at all Scotch debating societies. Gerrald had said (in the speech libelled on) "that it was justly observed by citizen Callender that soon after the union of the crowns" [he clearly meant kingdoms] " of England and Scotland, the people of both countries were deprived of some of their most valuable privileges. It was from that period that the greatest encroachments began to be made on public liberty. But if that union has operated to rob us of our rights, let it be the object of the present one to regain them. If the event exists for our shame, as it has existed for our chastisement, let it also exist for our instruction." This seems tolerably harmless, though not perhaps very wise. But what does the Solicitor-General say to it ? " Now, gentlemen, I here say that that is a most abominable *libel upon the union* of the two kingdoms, one of the most auspicious events that ever happened. To say that ' from that period the greatest encroachments began to be made on public liberty ' is an assertion that is most false and *seditious*, for since that period there have been *no encroachments* on public liberty, and no individual citizen has been deprived of any of his most valuable privileges." (p. 940.) Very likely. But can an opposite opinion not be held without sedition ?

There can scarcely be better evidence of the guiltlessness of the prisoner's speech in the convention, than that these two passages, about the Revolution and the Union, are the only two that the prosecutor brings specially under the notice of the jury, and we may be sure that they are the worst.

The Solicitor, however, after all, closed by putting it to the jury correctly enough, telling them that the point they had to try was, whether, on a review of the whole facts, the prisoner's intentions were pure, or " were seditious, wicked, and criminal." (p. 947.)

If the prisoner had had any chance of escape, or even of candid trial, it would have been throwing it away not to have let his defence be stated to the jury by counsel. A person trained to reason, or to represent, solely with a view to *success*, and therefore practised in the art of knowing how to reach the understandings or the hearts of others, would have put the defence on the safest grounds, and in the least offensive manner. And considering how much the principles at issue, particularly the great principle of the free right of suggesting not ill-meant reforms, accorded with the opinions of themselves and their party, it was a case which, under the exquisite talent of Erskine, or the strong sense of Gillies, might have been dignified by the sincerity of the pleader, and not lowered into a mere exhibition of professional skill. But, from the first, the prisoner was a doomed man. Independently of panic and general prejudice, the jury were directed, by authorities to which, when conveying doctrines so acceptable, they were very willing to yield sometimes, that the mere advocacy of the reform which the convention avowed its anxiety to promote, was in itself criminal; and at other times, that this advocacy was at least so perfectly conclusive as evidence of seditious intention, that all of them might safely be satisfied with it, and indeed that no rational juror could doubt it. Gerrald could not be so absurd as to deny, nor, in his position, so base as to abjure, his cordial accession to the advancement of this reform. And from the moment he admitted, and adhered to this, he stood virtually condemned. In this situation it was just as well that he spoke for himself. It gave him the satisfaction of making no concession. He proclaimed his principles to the last, and was sacrificed with the chaplets he was proudest of on his brow.

His address, amidst great merits, had all the defects that might have been expected. Unaccustomed to the discussion, in a court-like way, even of the political matter with which he was familiar, but most of which was very new matter to his judges and jury, he does not exhibit it luminously. Chiefly anxious about his universal suffrage and annual parliaments, he labours this hopeless topic with much curious, but, to a modern ear, not very satisfactory authority, while he is far too short and casual on what ought to have been his great theme, the right, under the Constitution, of every one to recommend what the majority may think unconstitutional and dangerous reforms, provided the reformer be bucklered in honesty. And, certain of his fate, though perfectly gentle, he is at no pains to conciliate prejudice, or to soften offensive opinions, but gives the worst of his politics as freely out as if he had been lecturing to the convention. But still, notwithstanding these imperfections, delivered with what I have always heard described as his graceful impressiveness, it must have been a striking speech, the more striking from these very defects of art. He discusses all the public principles involved in his trial, and all the topics urged against him and his cause, acutely and forcibly, and in a way that makes even the cold, distant, reader feel that he must have been a man of a rich and amiable mind— able, sincere, and naturally eloquent. It is the only speech I can recollect, by a seditious prisoner personally, that is entirely free, not merely of all impudence and bluster, but of everything harsh, or disrespectful, or boasting, or vulgar. His very

firmness in avowing his principles is without any
air of defiance ; but is evidently the result of
honesty, joined to the certainty of his fate, which
produced a calm disregard of the errors of those in
whose hands he was. Throughout, it is the sedition
of a literary gentleman. If left entirely to himself,
he would certainly have avoided that part of his
defence in which he questions the sufficiency of the
evidence to prove the precise words of some of the
resolutions of the convention, and of his own speeches
and motions there. He took up this point solely to
please his counsel, who thought it well-founded ;
for whatever doubt there might be of the exact
terms, he was perfectly aware, and nowhere dis-
guises, that both he and the convention had said
enough to bring him within the reach of that law of
sedition by which he was tried.

Some of his personal allusions are very touching.
For example, his opening : " If, at any early period
of my life, it had been announced to me that the
task of defending the rights and privileges of nine
millions of people would have devolved upon me, a
simple individual, I should certainly, from my youth
up, have devoted my whole time, with unremitting
application, that I might be enabled to execute
so sacred and important a trust. Unfortunately,
though a considerable period has intervened between
the time of my being served with my indictment
and my trial, yet I have been in a great measure
distracted by various avocations, and my health
much impaired by continual sickness. From my
duty, however, no earthly consideration shall induce
me to shrink. I, this day, come forward to advocate a cause, than which the sun never shone upon
one of more deep and general concernment. And

impressed with this awful consideration, I advance to it with a tremor that shakes every fibre of my frame. But whatever be the result of this day's deliberation, I shall always look back to the part I have taken, with the consciousness of a man who has endeavoured well ; for however weak the flesh may be, the spirit is strongly inclined to the service." (p. 947.)

And this allusion to one of the sources of his opinions :—" Gentlemen, I am aware that every practice and institution is alone defensible upon its own intrinsic merits, and the reason of the thing. Yet the adoption of any principle by men eminent for virtue and learning is certainly no small presumption in favour of the soundness of the principle itself. Sir William Jones, a name too distinguished in literature to derive splendour from any encomiums I can bestow upon it, and who has acted as a judge for more than twelve years in India, previously to his departure published a tract in which he vindicated the doctrine of universal suffrage. At a very early period of my life I was honoured with the patronage and friendship of this gentleman ; and I am sure he would deeply feel, even after this long separation, any calamity which might befall me—a calamity (if it be one) certainly not altogether, but in some measure perhaps produced by conversation with those whose practices were pure, and whose principles I conceived to be just ; and who were therefore objects of reverence among men. Yet this very gentleman, at this very period, holds an office of great trust and great emolument in his Majesty's important settlement of Bengal, and unseals those sacred fountains of justice which gladden and refresh fifteen millions of men." (p. 957.)

His peroration (too long to be all copied here) is in a high and moving tone.   It contains the following passages :—

"Those who are versed in the history of their country—in the history of the human race—must know that rigorous State prosecutions have always preceded the era of convulsion, and this era, I fear, will be accelerated by the folly and madness of our rulers.   If the people are discontented, the proper mode of quieting their discontent is, by redressing their wrongs, and conciliating their affections. Courts of justice indeed may be called in to the aid of ministerial vengeance ; but if once the purity of their proceedings is suspected, they will cease to be objects of reverence to the nation ; they will degenerate into empty and expensive pageantry, and become the partial instruments of vexatious oppression. Whatever may become of me, my principles will last for ever.   Individuals may perish, but truth is eternal." (p. 995.)   "Surely the experience of all ages should have taught our rulers that persecutions can never efface principles, and that the thunders of the State will prove impotent when wielded against patriotism, innocence, and firmness.   Whether, therefore, I shall be permitted to glide gently down the current of life, in the bosom of my native country, among those kindred spirits whose approbation constitutes the greatest comfort of my living ; whether I be doomed to drag out the remainder of my existence amidst thieves and murderers, a wandering exile on the bleak and melancholy shores of New Holland, my mind, equal to either fortune, is prepared to meet the destiny that awaits it:

> . . . 'seu me tranquilla senectus
> Expectat, seu mors atris circumvolat alis ;
> Dives, inops, Romae, seu fors ita jusserit, exsul.'

"To be torn a bleeding member from that country which we love is indeed, upon the first view, painful in the extreme. But all things cease to be painful when we are supported by the consciousness that we have done our duty to our fellow-creatures ; and a wise man, rising superior to all local prejudices, if asked for his country, will turn his eyes from this ' dim spot which men call earth,' and will point, like Anaxagoras, to the heavens. Gentlemen, my case is in your hands. You are Britons. You are freemen. You have heard the charge. You have heard the evidence. And you know the punishment which follows upon conviction."[1] (p. 996.)

Some who were present and still remember the scene, say that during the delivery of this address he had occasionally to struggle with a deep-seated, consuming cough. At one part indeed he was

---

[1] The opinions of a boy on the *matter* of such an address can never be important ; but emotion excited in youth is good evidence of the success of that eloquence which resolves chiefly into feeling. The future author of the *Pleasures of Hope*, then only sixteen, heard this speech, and wrote this account of it at the time : " I witnessed Joseph Gerrald's trial, and it was an era in my life. Hitherto I had never known what public eloquence was ; and I am sure the Justiciary Lords did not help me to a conception of it—speaking, as they did, bad arguments in broad Scotch. But the Lord Advocate's[1] speech was good ; the speeches of Laing and Gillies were better ; and Gerrald's speech annihilated the remembrance of all the eloquence that had ever been heard within the walls of that house. He quieted the judges, in spite of their indecent interruptions of him, and produced a silence in which you might have heard a pin fall to the ground. At the close of his defence, he said, ' And now, gentlemen of the jury—now that I take leave of you for ever, let me remind you that mercy is no small part of the duty of jurymen ; that the man who shuts his heart on the claims of the unfortunate, on him the gates of mercy will be shut ; and for him the Saviour of the world shall have died in vain.' At this finish I was much moved, and turning to a stranger beside me, apparently a tradesman, I said to him, ' By heavens, sir, that is a great man.' ' Yes, sir,' he answered ; ' he is not only a great man himself, but he makes every other man feel great who listens to him.' " (Beattie's *Life of Campbell*, vol. i. p. 88.)

---

[1] He was so much of a boy as not to know that it was the Solicitor who spoke.

obliged to stop. "My feelings, my exertions, and my state of health, have exhausted me." *Lord Henderland*—"You may sit down, Mr. Gerrald, and take a little breath." (p. 991.)

The temper with which his defence was received on the bench is disclosed in a single episode. The necessity of change in human institutions, and the consequent duty of toleration of new doctrines, was an unavoidable topic in any enlightened defence of these prisoners ; and it is one which must generally enter essentially into the defence of any sedition which consists in the promotion of new opinions. Gerrald was commenting on this fact, and after quoting Hume the historian's words that "the history of England is little better than a history of reversals," he gave some of the instances usually referred to in illustration of the general truth ; such as the example of Christianity, which was originally attempted to be crushed, partly on account of its novelty—an example which has been cited a thousand times by divines and pious philosophers, as a case which ought to make all ages cautious in condemning moral changes merely on account of their being innovations. In stating this view, Gerrald's words were sufficiently guarded. They were these :— " After all, the most useful discoveries in philosophy, the most important changes in the moral history of man, have been innovations. The Revolution was an innovation ; Christianity itself was an innovation." Instantly upon this the following interruption took place :—

Lord Justice-Clerk.—"You would have been stopped long before this, if you had not been a stranger. *All* that you have been saying is *sedition* [!!] And now, my Lords, he is ATTACKING CHRISTIANITY " [!!!]

" *Lord Henderland.*—I allow him all the benefit of his defence. But to compare the present situation of this country with what happened at the Revolution, when the forms of civil government and the liberties of the subject were done away by the infringement of all law! or with a period in which the sovereign is said to have forfeited his life! I cannot sit here without observing, as was done in England when the rebels were tried —I cannot sit here as a judge without saying that it is a most indecent defence [!!]. It is my duty to observe this; but I am for the panel going on in his own way.

" *Mr. Gerrald.*—I conceive myself as vindicating the rights of Britons at large; and I solemnly disclaim all intention of attacking Christianity. I was merely stating the fact.

" *Lord Justice-Clerk.*—Go on in your own way.

" *Mr. Gerrald.*—I think I may be allowed that at least.

" *Lord Justice-Clerk.*—Go on, sir.

" *Mr. Gerrald.*—I should have been going on if your Lordship had not interrupted me." (vol. xxiii. p. 972.)

No religiousness on the part of their Lordships could have accounted for this shocking perversion of what the prisoner had said. But none of them were religious. Braxfield's very name made the pious shudder. And the very moment before he interrupted the panel he chuckled over a profane jest of his own, on our Saviour's success as an innovator—a jest too indecent to be recorded, but which transpired next day, because his brethren thought it too good to be kept to themselves, and has never been forgotten.[1]

The thing called summing up was in the ordinary style.

His Lordship lays it down, and with perfect propriety, that the first point to be settled was whether the convention was or was not a seditious association. And he fixes this speedily enough. The prosecutor and the prisoner had argued its guilt or its innocence by discussing the evidence, and the import of its acts. But my Lord troubles himself with nothing so plaguy, but concludes the matter in a moment, on the authority of what had never been even proposed to be made evidence. No convictions or outlawries of other persons had been made proof in this trial. Yet this judge—or rather this person occupying the judicial chair—tells the jury that the seditiousness of the convention was already settled to their hands by fifteen other men several months before. He absolutely disposes of the whole of this, by far the most important part of the case, in these words : " Gentlemen, as to the first question, how far there is evidence to establish this convention of delegates to be a seditious meeting, it will occur to yourselves, gentlemen, that *there have been already no less than two of your fellow-subjects convicted of the crime of sedition, as members of that convention,* and accordingly *condemned to transportation ;* and that there *are other two indicted for the same crime,* but did not think proper to stand their trial, and that *they accordingly stand fugitated.* You have therefore the verdict of

---

[1] I see that it has been adopted by Galt in one of his novels : " They denied they were traitors, but confessed they were reformers. Was not, they said, our Lord Jesus Christ a reformer ? And what," etc.—*Annals of the Parish,* chap. xxxiv.

two *very respectable* juries stamping upon this meeting the character of sedition." (p. 997.) No one fact here stated was proved, or was relevant. Yet the illegality of referring to them was the least improper circumstance in the proceeding. Its chief iniquity lay in its obvious tendency to confederate the whole class of jurors in each other's support, and against every prisoner.

He then disposes, with the same ease, of the great plea, founded on the right of the people, not merely to petition, but to suggest reforms, and to agitate for their promotion. The doctrine here, as in a former charge, is, that it was seditious to distract the public, or to disturb Government by demanding redress, even of real grievances, at such a time ; or that, if this was not actually sedition in law, it was conclusive evidence of sedition in fact.

" Gentlemen, it has been said, and much insisted upon, that it is contrary to the rights of mankind in general, not to be allowed to apply to parliament. I do not say that is a criminal act, if it rested there alone. But, gentlemen, I would submit to your own feelings—*it is not a matter that rests upon evidence, but upon your own feelings* [!] as men, as members of society, and as subjects of this kingdom—whether YOU feel any grievances that this country labours under, that should entitle *them* to make such a cry against the Government of the country. For my own part (and I appeal to your own feelings if it is not a just observation), *I* have always considered this country as the envy of the world at large, as the happiest kingdom upon the face of the earth ; and I submit to you, whether as much happiness does not exist in this kingdom as ever did. Every man is sure of enjoying everything he has in perfect security. His life is secure; his liberty is secure by the laws of his country; and his property is also secure. He is absolutely certain that nothing will be taken from him which he has any right to enjoy. And I submit to you whether, EVEN IF THERE HAD BEEN GROUND FOR COMPLAINTS, it was *a proper time* to bring forward those complaints—at a time when we were involved in a war with a ferocious and cruel nation, at present setting the rest of Europe at defiance, and when the greatest unanimity among the subjects of this kingdom is absolutely necessary to put an end to that war. I submit to you whether any good member of society would prefer his complaint against the Government of the country at such a time. But *if you feel, as I feel,* that the complaints are groundless, and that the country is living in a state of tranquillity, secure of their lives and properties against every attack whatever, I submit to you whether *is that man innocent* who calls the people together, and impresses their minds with ideas hostile to the Government of the country, with ideas of mal-administration on the part of the king, the parliament, and the administrators of public affairs," etc. (p. 998.)

How few opponents of Government could escape the penalties of sedition, if this constituted the crime, especially if they dared to ascribe discontent to abuse, and to suggest reform as its remedy!

His Lordship then proceeds to deal with the French terms. He first says, correctly, but not consistently with his doctrines on former trials, that in itself, and without reference to other circumstances, this French imitation is harmless; and that it is only important as an element of evidence. And then he gives this as the result of the whole proof : "You will consider whether, upon a fair construction of the whole, they were not imitating France in the *form of their government,* and that *the object of their meeting was, like France, to overturn the established Constitution, and put everything upon the same footing with France,* where aristocracy is reviled, the king reviled, and indeed where there is no Constitution at all. That, gentlemen, is the great object of your inquiry. And when you attend to the whole," etc., *"you will judge whether it does not appear to you that these people were imitating the French Convention, and that they meant to follow the spirit of the French in establishing their form of government."* (p. 999.) Yet, as usual, there was a total absence of evidence, not only of the constitution, but of the very existence of a convention in France, and of the authenticity and meaning of its alleged forms and terms.

After some observations on the proof of the resolutions and speeches in the convention, his Lordship concludes, by turning the accident of the prisoner's birth, nay, his very talents, against him. "When you see Mr. Gerrald taking a very active part and *making speeches such as you have heard to-day,* I look upon him as a *very dangerous member of society,* FOR *I dare say he has eloquence enough to persuade the people to rise in arms."* (p. 1002.) No wonder that the prisoner interfered on this. "Oh ! my Lord, my Lord ! this is a very improper way of addressing a jury. It is descending to personal abuse. God forbid that my eloquence should ever be made use of for such a purpose." On which the Justice, adding insincerity to harshness, retracted by this paltry evasion : "Mr. Gerrald, I do not say that you did so, but that you had abilities to do it."

And this was his Lordship's penult sentence :
" Gentlemen, he has no relation, nor the least property, in this country," [I don't see the evidence of
this,] " but he comes here to disturb the peace of
the country, as a delegate from a society in England,
to raise sedition in this country. I say *he appears
to me to be much more criminal than Muir, Palmer,
or Skirving, because they were all natives of this
country.*" (p. 1002.) This in the *first* place was
irrelevant, for the circumstances of their cases were
not before the jury, and Palmer's had not been tried
even before this judge or court ; and in the *second*
place, it was not true, for Palmer was an Englishman.

The prisoner was convicted of the *crimes* libelled.

What these *crimes* (as distinguished from the
simple, generic, crime of sedition, which alone was
charged) were, it is not easy to say. They were
stated, or rather talked of in a loose, desultory way,
at the trial, as consisting in the promotion of universal suffrage and annual parliaments ; in complaining at that period of grievances, real or imaginary ; in
exciting discontent ; in imitating the French ; and
in aiming, as evinced by the general mass of the
circumstances, at the overthrow of the monarchy ;
but whether the jury meant to convict of all these
acts, or only of some of them, remains a matter of
mere conjecture. If these *acts* be what they meant
by *crimes,* then the legal construction of their verdict is, that they intended to convict of the whole ;
and this, I dare say, is the truth.

An objection was taken to the verdict by the
prisoner's counsel, on the ground that it *did not bear*
that the jury had considered the *evidence* for the
defence. But it was properly repelled ; because no

evidence, apart from that for the prosecutor, had been adduced.[1]

It was also objected that, *de facto*, the jury *had not* considered either the evidence or the defence. This was offered to be proved ; but it was explained by the prisoner's counsel that the proof was implied in the fact that the jury had only been enclosed twenty minutes. This also was properly repelled, upon the plain ground that it is the province of juries alone to determine what consideration any evidence or defence requires. Had it not been for the necessity, according as the law then was, of making up a written verdict, any jury might have said Guilty, or Not Guilty, without leaving the box, or waiting longer in it than to collect the general opinion. This was the answer made by all the judges except the Justice. They laid it down that it was the duty of the jury to consider the defence, whatever it might be, but that it must be held that they had done so. But the Justice did not concur in this. He seems to have thought it too complimentary to this defence. He said (vol. xxiii. p. 1007) : " Then they say there was a long defence, and they should have stated that they had considered that. My Lords, the jury did their duty *in not* CONSIDERING that defence. It was a defence against the relevancy of the indictment, and the first two hours of his speech went to show that all that he had done was innocent. But, my Lords, was it not offered to the court in a very long pleading, and found relevant ? I apprehend the jury

---

[1] The subsequent abolition of the necessity of having a *written* verdict in every case, makes these technical objections to the forms of verdicts rather incomprehensible now ; but they were of hourly occurrence formerly. He was deemed a poor-spirited counsel who had not a quibble against the written verdict.

have done their duty properly. They have a power, to be sure, if they think proper, even after the libel is found relevant. They may acquit. But the duties of a jury and of a judge are distinct. It *is the business of the court to determine the law as to the relevancy of the libel, and of the jury to judge of the fact ; and as it was found relevant by the court, the jury had no more to do but to consider the evidence."*

So far as I am aware, this is the only occasion on which a Scotch judge ever ventured to reduce our law to the condition in which the law of England stood prior to the passing of the Libel Act. Though our judges are obliged to decide on the relevancy, as appearing on the indictment, it is (with the present exception) invariably proclaimed that the jury are entitled to differ from the court, by holding that the facts, though proved, do not imply the crime. Of all Braxfield's many stretches of power, none is more original or more daring than this attempt to take the ultimate relevancy out of the hands of the jury. The statement that there could be any defence, allowed by a court to be pleaded, which a jury is entitled not even *to consider*, is not to be condemned, solely or chiefly on account of its legal outrageousness. Its principal claim to reprobation lies in its tendency to encourage political juries in a careless and prejudiced apparent performance of their duties.

The consideration of the sentence was a mere form. Every judge was committed to transportation. But in repeating this sentence now, their Lordships seem to have been under the influence of a worse spirit than even that which had originally misled them. It can scarcely be doubted that this was owing to the recent parliamentary discussions to which their conduct had been subjected. The attack on their law and humanity made them angry ; the defeat of that attack, confident. Pride came to the aid of prejudice ; and the most outrageous reasons that could be invented in order to show that they might have gone still further, were resorted to as evidence of their past moderation.

Henderland proposes fourteen years ; and for this reason :—" My Lord, it appears to me that *by* NO *means* an adequate punishment CAN *be inflicted for this offence ;* and even if this has the *appearance* of severity, which I cannot think it has, it is the only judgment which could be pronounced in such a case, to secure the safety of this country from the commission of such crimes." (p. 1008.) This is no misprint ; no error ; no misrepresentation. The opinion of his Lordship really was, that *nothing* could be too severe for such sedition. If they could have hanged, we have their own authority for believing that they would have done so. *Swinton,* it will be remembered, had said in Muir's case, that it was impossible to punish sedition adequately, *now that torture was abolished.*

Swinton's opinion, and his whole opinion, in the present case was in these words :—" My Lord, in considering this crime, about which your Lordships have heard so much, the more I consider, and the more I turn my mind to it, the more I am convinced that this court did right originally in imposing the sentence that they did impose. My Lord, in considering this case, and comparing the punishment with the crime, I HARDLY KNOW WHAT PUNISHMENT IS ADEQUATE TO IT." And no wonder—for this is his Lordship's conception of sedition. " It was *well* said by one of the ablest and greatest men that ever lived, that sedition was like Pandora's box ; it contains every evil, it contains every vice. My Lord, it is said he is to be sent among *pickpockets, thieves, and robbers.* But, my Lord, THIS CRIME IS NOT TO BE COMPARED WITH THEIRS. IT COMPREHENDS EVERY SORT OF CRIME—MURDER, ROBBERY, RAPE—EVERYTHING THAT IS CRIMINAL. I think, my Lord, the punishment that has been proposed the *mildest* that can be inflicted ; and I hope it will be sufficient to deter others from committing the same crime." (vol. xxiii. p. 1008.)

Lord Dunsinnan thought that any difference that there might be between this case and the former ones was unfavourable to the prisoner. " My Lord, he is one of these persons who came to this country for the purpose of exciting civil discord, by inflaming the minds of the people. We have had an opportunity of seeing that *he possesses talents which render him exceedingly* CAPABLE *of mischief.* The harangue which we heard last night, though addressed to the jury, was, I believe, rather intended for another part of this court. WE SAW *that his political principles are extremely dangerous.* And, my Lord, if there is any other country which does not inflict such a punishment for such a crime, I am happy that I live in such a country as this ; and if I were to propose any difference of punishment, *it would be rather to increase than to diminish it.*" (p. 1009.)

Of all the circumstances which can enter into the composition of a strong claim for mercy, few, if any, are more powerful than the existence of some mental innocence in the person for whom mercy is sought. To be lenient according to the measure of a prisoner's reserved goodness, is only an application of the principle that entitles him to an acquittal where he is entirely guiltless. And there may sometimes be great legal criminality without much moral badness. A cup of water may be stolen to save a dying child. Murder may be committed by duel, required by society, and provoked by intolerable insult. Heresy, which for many ages shone in the very front of European offences, and which no nation upon earth has yet expunged from its criminal code, has often sprung from conscientious piety; rebellion often from patriotism. Courts cannot always act upon this; because it is their business to execute the law, which it is the duty of a wise, good subject to obey, and the law is often absolute. Society cannot always leave every man to be a law unto himself. Where the law, therefore, is so clear as to exclude its being violated from honest ignorance, and so positive that courts have no discretion in the event of its being infringed—he who breaks it, though he may have the consolation of conscious purity, must do so at his peril.

But there are cases—and sedition is one of them—in which, even in ascertaining the fact to be tried, and while the matter is still before the jury, the wickedness or the goodness of the accused does not merely aggravate or alleviate the offence, but forms a part, and a principal part, of its legal essence. And if this be so true that, even on the question of guilty or not, evidence of good character is receivable and material, how much stronger are its claims when the period arrives for the exercise of discretion in determining the punishment? No conceivable circumstance so powerfully recommends the infusion of lenity into a discretionary sentence as moral worth. Tyrannical governments may get their judicial tools to show less mercy to a political victim of good, than to one of bad, character, because the former has more influence. They punish the dangerousness of his virtues. But this is never the view of a court of justice. It may be laid down as a principle universally sound that in fixing discretionary punishment it can never be right to disregard any portion of moral worth in the prisoner.

Judge Buller, to be sure, a man whose hardness offended his age, was of a different opinion. Townsend, his latest and most favourable biographer, says of him, speaking of Donellan's trial : " The circumstances of this trial tended to confirm the impression of Buller's rigorous severity, which two rash sayings of his had previously created. The first of these dicta was that previous good character went rather in aggravation than in mitigation of punishment, for the longer a person might have lived in the good estimation of his neighbours, the more guilt was there in losing it,—a paradox certainly very alien to the mild spirit of a Christian judge." (vol. i. p. 19.) Yes, and to the common sense of a sane man. The meaning of the principle is that the greater scoundrel a man is, the more entitled he is to mercy.

Good intention in the particular act charged ought to be more in a prisoner's favour than even general good character.

Nevertheless, *Lord Abercromby* acknowledges that he acted on the following principle, with the exposition of which his opinion is almost exclusively occupied : " My Lord, it has been said within these walls that his intentions all along were innocent, that they were perfectly pure and honourable, and that had the same crime been committed in England it would either have been passed with impunity, or with a very small punishment, as imprisonment or pillory. My Lord, upon that I shall say a very few words. With respect to the panel's *motives, I shall for a moment suppose that his intentions were pure, and perfectly innocent. But even considering the case in that view, I must give it as my opinion, sitting here as a judge, that it would afford no motive for a* MITIGATION *of punishment."* (p. 1009.) His Lordship is at the pains to repeat this declaration in a subsequent part of his opinion : " My Lord, *though the panel could have established by the clearest and the most satisfactory evidence that his intentions were all along perfectly innocent, and his motives perfectly pure, it would have afforded no ground whatever for* MITIGATION *of punishment;* but I am sorry to say that I can discover no proof of such innocence of intention," etc. (p. 1011.)

It would be unjust not to quote the explanation of this frightful view given by his Lordship himself. " My Lord, we all know it as a fact, undoubtedly undeniable, that a mistaken principle, either in religion or in politics, has often *led the way, with the best of intentions,* to commit crimes of the *deepest atrocity.* My Lord, the history of this country affords many instances and many examples of this kind. For example, in the case of the Gunpowder Plot *many of the conspirators were men of character.* Sir Everard Digby was one of the most accomplished, one of the most virtuous, men in England, and, my Lord, he was sentenced to die as a traitor for the part he took in that plot. And on the eve of his execution he wrote a letter to his wife in which he expresses himself in these precise terms : ' Now for my intention, let me tell you that if I had thought

there had been the least sin in the plot I would not
have been of it for all the world; and no other cause
drew me to hazard my fortune and life but zeal to
God's religion.' My Lord, this letter, written at that
fatal period by a man who was beloved by every
person in Europe, *leaves no room to doubt of the sincerity of this confession.*" (p. 1010.) He adds, a little
further on, "My Lord, we have the example of our
own times also. I need not remind your Lordships
of 1745 and 1715, when many men, *who had acted
with the best intentions,* died the death of traitors."

There are very few understandings to which it
can be necessary to point out the gross fallacy of
these analogies. In the *first* place, courts have *no
discretion* in the punishment of murder or of treason,
the two offences committed by the rebels of 1715
and 1745, and by the Gunpowder plotters. If the
penalties had been discretionary, even general good
character ought to have had its influence. In the
second place, the law defines clearly what murder
and treason are, and having fixed the punishment
of each, the penalty follows the act, and there is no
relaxation of the rule in favour of those who choose
to set themselves above the law, and to think
its violation a duty. Sir Everard Digby knew
that he was going to murder the king and various
others, and meant to do so, and certainly no mercy
could be shown to him because he was pleased
to think this not a sin. And, in the same way, *if
a person be guilty of sedition,* his good intentions
will not save him from the consequences. But such
intentions must be taken into view *in ascertaining the
fact of the guilt;* and then, even after conviction,
the punishment being discretionary, they ought to
operate in alleviation. His Lordship makes no dif-

ference between a crime clearly intended and clearly committed by a person of good *general* character *in other respects,* and a crime said to be excluded or palliated by good intentions *in the very act challenged.* He mistakes the situation of a prisoner accused of sedition,—that is, of acts calculated and designed to produce what others, but possibly not the prisoner, think public mischief, with the situation of an avowed murderer or traitor, who acknowledges that he meant to perpetrate these acts, but thought them right.

Yet did *Braxfield* contrive to exceed this, for he actually makes the absence of bad intention an *aggravation.* " My Lords, we have heard a great deal of the innocence of his intentions. But it was *justly* observed by my brother who spoke immediately before me, that, taking his own account of the matter to be just, supposing that he acted from principle, *and that his motives are pure, I do say that he becomes a* MORE *dangerous member of society than if his conduct was really criminal, and acting from criminal motives. A man acting from criminal motives is not so dangerous a member of society as a man who thinks he is acting from principle;* for when a man is so misguided in his principles he overturns society and government itself. I say, *Salus populi suprema lex,* and it becomes us, let his intentions be as pure as they possibly can be, to remove that man from society, and put it out of his power to disseminate these dangerous principles. I do not know whether his principles are so pure as he professed or not ; but *if they are,* I think *it justifies this punishment just as much* as if he had acted *from the worst of motives,* and therefore any other punishment would be insufficient." (p. 1112.)

How different from this is the tone of Chief-Justice Eyre in his charge to the jury in the trial of Horne Tooke! He instructs them to give full weight not only to his general character, and to the prevailing peaceableness of the prisoner's political principles, but even to all the circumstances in his private condition and habits, which seemed to indicate a man rather withdrawn from faction than inflamed by it—to his literary occupations, his feeble health, his quiet Sunday visitors, his cultivation of his garden. (*State Trials*, vol. xxv. p. 741.)

Chief Justice Jeffreys sentenced Tutchin to be imprisoned *seven* years, to be whipped in *each* of these years through *every* market town in the county of Dorset, and to find security for good behaviour during *life*. The prisoner, who escaped this infliction, met with his judge in his evil day, after the Revolution, and asked his Lordship " where his conscience was when he passed that sentence on him in the West ? Jeffreys said, You are a young man, and an enemy to the Government, *and might live to do abundance of mischief, and it was part of my instructions to spare no man of courage, parts, or estate.*" (*State Trials*, vol. xiv. p. 1199.) Gerrald's virtues made him more alarming than either parts or courage.

The power of transporting for sedition having been since abolished by statute, it is a matter of indifference to modern practice whether the view taken of the law in 1794 was sound or not. But this is a question of great legal curiosity, and very material as a criterion of the court ; and it is one, therefore, that cannot be overlooked in any judicial picture of these times.

The legality of all these sentences was vehemently denied by the whole whig lawyers of the time, whose protest has been adhered to with gradually increasing confidence by all their successors. The opposite opinion has been maintained with equal positiveness by their political adversaries. It would be very satisfactory if, amidst these party creeds, the truth, whatever it may be, could be clearly ascertained. But each party being perfectly satisfied with its own conclusion, nothing has been done to get nearer the truth since the publication of Hume's work in 1800. Those who approve of the sentences have ever since been contented to refer to that book as their triumphant defence; while those who condemn them, despising this defence, have, without any accurate exposition of its errors, been satisfied to take what they hold to be its obvious insufficiency as all that they require. The question therefore stands now on both sides exactly as it did when Hume left it.

The *general* views and reasonings are capable of being easily apprehended. What is wanted is, *exact historical truth*, including the history of legal proceedings. He would do most towards the solution of this doubt, who, sinking all party feelings, would honestly and minutely examine the whole course of our practice in political crimes prior to 1793, but particularly prior to 1703, explaining the rise, objects, and results of the various statutes, —separating the proceedings of the Privy Council from those of the regular courts,—detailing the precise circumstances of every sentence in reference both to its design and its execution,—and unfolding enough of collateral history to enable us to see what must be ascribed to law, and what to tyranny. This, and this alone, could ascertain whether, prior to the system which the year 1793 began, we had anything that deserves to be considered as a law of sedition, and what it really was.

Beyond examining most of the cases mentioned by Hume, I have made no attempt in this vein. It is a vein which no one can work who is not familiar with our old records. But Hume, who was probably consulted by the prosecutor on all these cases,—who published his defence of them a few years after they occurred, when he had had full leisure for inquiry, and was under the strongest inclination to place the transactions of his friends on the surest grounds, and whose statement has ever since been received as the case for his party—may fairly be taken as the best expounder of their law ; and it requires no antiquarianism to appreciate his argument. Malcolm Laing, who lived among the ancient records, and read them sagaciously, and, besides the stubbornness of his natural honesty, was trained by his favourite pursuits to habits of historical candour, used to declare, long after he was removed from the prejudices with which it might be supposed that a whig, and one of the counsel, had at one time viewed Gerrald's trial, that Hume's display of ancient precedents was too partial for any effect except to mislead. Nevertheless, not having been refuted by any opposite display, those who profess to differ from Hume have no unfair task assigned to them when they are required to contest his result upon his own authorities.

The argument, as given by the prosecutor and the court, and as corrected and improved by Hume, comes to this,—that sedition is a crime at common law, and a crime of so dangerous a nature that the acts which constitute it have frequently been de-

clared by statute to be treason; that, though
different in its legal principle, it is in many respects
scarcely distinguishable, practically, from *leasing*,
which, during a long period, was a capital offence;
that even the Act 1703, c. 4, though passed after
the Revolution, recognised this kindred offence of
leasing, and only abolished its punishment of death,
leaving the punishment of fine, imprisonment, or
banishment; that at this period banishment, as
established by the previous practice of the court,
and the understanding of the country, included
what is now termed transportation, that is, not
mere expatriation, but fixing the convict, or enabling the Crown to fix him, to a particular place
abroad; that this continued to be its meaning so
clearly and universally that, without any declara-
tory statute, banishment, as distinguished from
this transportation, has entirely disappeared, both
in the term and in the thing; that the court
being thus intrusted by that very parliament which
gave the people all the protection the Revolution
owed them, with the discretionary power of transporting for leasing, was legally entitled to inflict
this punishment for the nearly identical offence of
sedition; that, besides this statutory authority,
the Court of Justiciary has an inherent, original,
and independent power of declaring new crimes,
and of attaching what it conceives to be proper
punishments (short of death) both to new crimes
and to old; that the court acted lawfully in availing itself of a punishment which, even if it had
been unknown anciently, had been regularly introduced into modern practice; and that, in the circumstances of the times, it would have been mere
folly to have employed any other check than the

only effectual one, of fixed exile, for a crime then immediately connected with revolutions.

The first thing necessary to be done in order to appreciate a view so complex and so gravid with postulates, is to make an entire separation of that part of it which justifies transportation *upon the pre-existing law*, from that part which only justifies it on the ground of its being within the power of the court *to create new law.* If there was law for it without the " native vigour," this curious power need not have been resorted to. Its being resorted to is no slight proof that there was felt to be no law without it. Let it be so laid aside for the present.

Next, it is necessary to apprehend distinctly what it is that is disputed. For Baron Hume probably misled himself, and has certainly misled many a reader, by what may be described as a mere play upon words.

He is at considerable pains to show that, anciently, the *term* Banishment included the *term* Transportation ; that is, that these *words* were used synonymously. And he has certainly succeeded in showing this triumphantly, at least with all the triumph that a victory over what was never contested admits of. He has shown that to *transport* often meant nothing beyond what its etymon imports, viz., to *carry beyond.* " The books of the kirk librarie shall be catalog and *transported* to the librarie within the college." (*Kirk-session Records of Aberdeen,* 11th Nov. 1621 ; reprinted by the Spalding Club, p. 98.) " That the Erle Marschall be desyret that his Lordship caus nocht his tennentis to raiss or *transport* ony carreage on the Sabbaoth." (*Ibid.* p. 189.) Banishment, which implied going, or being sent, beyond the limits of the territory, meant no more than extra-territorial residence. But neither of these terms signified anything more than *mere expatriation.* Nay, to transport very often signified much less. It signified nothing but *portation trans,* the trans being measured from the spot where the convict stood. Thus Janet Spens was sentenced to be *banished;* and for this purpose the magistrates of Dysart are ordered " *to transport her to the Tolbooth of Dysart,* etc., until occasion offer for *transporting her beyond seas.*" (Hume, vol. i. p. 355.) And Andrew Henderson is to be kept in jail till "ordour be tane for convoy and *transport of him to his schip.*" (Hume, vol. i. p. 358.) There are many other examples, which show that the word transportation indicated mere compulsory removal ; without necessarily involving any idea of the removed person's condition after reaching the line beyond which he was sent. The first part of Janet Spens's sentence was a sentence of transportation ; but it only transported her from Dysart to a ship. There could be no doubt at the period of these trials about the *word* transportation, if this be all that is wanted, because it is recognised in the Act 1701. That statute enacts, "that no person be *transported* forth of this kingdom except with his own consent, given before a judge, or by legal sentence." Nobody will say that every such transportation necessarily implied something more than mere expatriation. The practice fixes that it did not. Of the hundreds of people who were dealt with under this enactment, the great majority, I suppose, but at any rate certainly a great number, were merely sent out of this country. They were banished *forth of Scotland.* Yet because this banishment took place under a statute warranting their *transportation*, Baron Hume lays it down that the first of these comprehends the last ; and this supposed identity of the *words*, supported as it is by a grand array of useless authority, has gained more careless converts to his side of the question, than have been gained among the cautious by all his better arguments.

But it is not the *word* that those who differ from him object to, but the *thing*. And the thing is this : mere expatriation, which is our modern idea of banishment, leaves the culprit at liberty to go where he pleases, so long as he keeps out of the country from which he is ejected, and to do what he pleases in the place to which he withdraws.

Expatriation, *combined with compulsory residence abroad, in a place and under regulations fixed by the Crown*, which is what was meant in 1793 by transportation, leaves the prisoner no liberty at all. The banished man suffers nothing beyond exile. He may carry his fortune, his family, and his power of movement, with him.

> "Round the wide world in banishment we roam—
> Forced from our fertile fields and native home."

Forced absence from home, especially for a crime, is generally equivalent to ruin ; and even when the sufferer is sustained by the applause of a party, it always reduces him to a painful position. But in its worst state it is heaven, compared with the hell of the best state of transportation, particularly with transportation forty or fifty years ago, when the voyage was far longer and more horrid than it is now, the colony frightful, home intercourse impracticable, and return hopeless. This was a punishment which degraded, tortured, and killed. The victim

was not merely a slave, but he was reduced suddenly
to that condition from perfect freedom and perhaps
great luxury ; and he was made a slave, far from all
sympathy, to a master who had little interest in his
welfare, and who probably considered his being a
convict as an apology, if not a recommendation, of
any severity that he might be inclined to exercise
over him. The one punishment might be survived ;
the other never could. Private respect and public
honour have frequently awaited the man who, corrected and purified by some years of penal absence,
has returned to national usefulness and domestic
affection. The transported man may perhaps bring
his body home, but it is marked. Under hiding, he
may possibly be cheered by some of the love which
can never be eradicated from the heart of a wife or
a daughter—feeling his shame, but adhering to him ;
but he can never be dignified by general respect or
public employment. No time, conduct, or worth,
can ever cleanse him from the moral stain of his
punishment. Till the grave shall protect him, he
will be pointed at, and thought of as a returned
convict, and as little else.

Now the question is, as to the power of the court
to inflict *this last punishment*, no matter in what
terms. Was it lawful to visit *sedition* with these
consequences ? I say *sedition*, for the learned commentator is very apt to confuse this very peculiar
offence with two others, to one of which it has no
resemblance whatever, and to the other very little.
These are *treason* and *leasing-making*. Wherever
Hume finds seditious *acts* prosecuted as treason or
as leasing-making, and these acts thus prosecuted
punished by transportation, or by torture, or by
death, he assumes that the same result, except

death and torture, could lawfully follow where the acts were prosecuted only as *sedition*. But this is an essential mistake. As to treason, it is a mistake so clear that it would be idle to speak of it ; and as to leasing, on the identity of which with sedition nearly the whole of his doctrine depends, it was in many respects a totally different offence. Leasing-making was the crime of calumniating the monarch, or his advisers, or nobles, or of creating discord and hatred between the king and the people by falsehoods, and was punishable capitally. It was a tyrannical and savage law, by which, while there was no public opinion, and no practice of constitutional privileges, each successful faction of barbarous churchmen or nobles was enabled, on the pretence of having been abused by its defeated opponents, to take their estates and their lives. It seems very odd to talk of this as even resembling the modern offence of sedition. No doubt the modern crime may be implied in some of the old Acts. Sedition may be committed by libelling the king or his counsellors, and thereby making them disliked. But 1*st*, There are other sorts of sedition of which the facts are *not* implied in the facts of leasing. In particular *pure resistance* is not ; nor is the promulgation of dangerous *doctrine*. If such an idea as that of parliamentary reform can be supposed to have entered into the head of any pamphleteer or demagogue in old Scotland, the maintenance of this object would not (without an abuse of law) have fallen under the meaning of the bloody interdiction against leasing ; 2*d*, Although the acts constituting the two crimes be supposed to be in all respects identical, still if they were prosecuted and punished *on different principles, and for different objects,* there is no correct reasoning from the one to the other. Take the case of a libel on the king. This in the days of the Stewarts would have been called leasing-making, and would have been punished by forfeiture of life and property. Is this any reason why, when a similar crime is prosecuted under the House of Hanover as *sedition*, the old punishment of leasing, or such part of it as a statute has not abolished, should be inflicted for this new, or new-modelled crime? In 1793 there was a crime at common law called sedition. Hume's argument is, that because this offence resembled another anciently called leasing-making, it must be punished now as leasing-making used to be.

In order to get one step nearer a sound result, it is necessary to distinguish the period prior to the year 1703 from the period after it. Because Baron Hume says that the Act of 1703, which abolished certain previous punishments, must be understood to have left the law, in other respects, as it was then standing ; and that, as the statute did not introduce an entirely new system, but only amended the old one, the old one must be continued, as corrected, and must be carried forward into subsequent generations. Well—assuming all this—*how was sedition punishable, or rather, how was it punished prior to* 1703 ? Much depends upon the answer to this question. Baron Hume's exposition of the law turns mainly upon it.

Now the only just answer that I can conceive its admitting of is implied in what I understand to be the fact, that *no one* (or at least not above one or two—but I believe no one) *in Scotland had ever been convicted of pure sedition before* 1703. I have never heard of any such conviction. Hume refers to no Scotch case of sedition till 1793 ; and since none was discovered by this laborious searcher, it may be pretty safely conjectured that none exists. Leasing-making I do not admit to be sedition.

And this is less wonderful than might at first appear, because sedition is only the growth of considerable general liberty. For several centuries, Scotland was torn to pieces by a fierce nobility, the slaves or the rivals of the Crown, while the Crown was struggling to defend itself from its aristocracy, and to curb a people which had no means of resistance except by rebellion. So long as all power was in the hands of the kings and nobles, and the people, as such, were nothing, there was no need of a law of sedition. The laws against treason and leasing-making were sufficient. He who disturbed the Crown was crushed by the one ; he who even insulted the aristocracy, or the Government, or any of their members, by the other ; and the ferocity of the age, untamed by the practice of liberty, disdained all penalties for political offences except death. Power, having no public basis, was precarious ; and depending chiefly on successful violence, each tyrant of the hour thought he could only protect himself by the extermination of his enemies—an opinion recommended by the long prevalence of family feuds and bloody factions. The seventeenth century, instead of softening these habits by the breath of approaching civilisation, only brought fanaticism, and consequent persecution. That century was one long rebellion. Every offence connected with the State was called treason. Sedition was not recognised ; and indeed, as distinguished from treason and leasing, it probably very seldom existed. Seditious acts, as Hume says, were

raised "from their natural rank of sedition, to that
of treason by reason of the exigency of the times."
Whether this be the correct explanation of the
fact or not, I assume it to be a fact that, prior to the
year 1703, if any law existed in Scotland against
sedition proper, it was at least not known in the
practice of our courts. And if it be so, the conclusion seems fair that, in inquiring what was the
legal punishment of this offence after 1703, there
was no use, except for the explanation of terms, in
referring to the period before.

Now what change was introduced by the Act of
1703 ? I think, upon this matter, none whatever.

Its words are these : " Our Sovereign Lady considering that by the Acts of Parliament following
[here it recites several bloody statutes, all against
leasing], the crimes therein mentioned are made
capital, and punishable with death and confiscation,
and that the said laws *have been liable to stretches,
and that in respect of their generality, and the
various constructions which the same may admit,*
they may be, *as to the foresaid capital punishment,*
of dangerous consequence, doth therefore, with the
consent, etc., abrogate and discharge, in all time
coming, the foresaid sanction and pain of death
and confiscation contained in the said Acts, and statutes and ordains that the punishment of the crime
mentioned shall for hereafter only be arbitrary
according to the demerit of the transgression, that
is, by fining, imprisonment, *or banishment* ; and if
the party offender be poor, and not able to pay a
fine, then to be punished in his body, life and limb
always preserved."

The argument reared upon this statute amounts
in substance to this, that the Act, though it abolishes

the punishment of death, keeps up the offence of leasing and sedition, only with a lower penalty; that these are statutory offences still, and, at any rate, are offences at common law; that sedition, though not specified by name, is one of the crimes virtually included in the Act; and that the banishment sanctioned did, in practice, comprehend compulsory residence in a foreign place.

The answer to this is that there is a flaw in every material part of the statement and reasoning.

Thus I can discover no ground whatever for saying that sedition is included within the statute. It certainly is not so in express words. By what implication is it? No doubt several of the *acts* that used to be punished capitally were what would now be held seditious. But it was not *as sedition* that they were so punished, or even prohibited. It was solely as leasing. And therefore it is only leasing, and not sedition, that the statute of 1703 authorises to be checked by banishment. Hume, because these two are allied, always assumes them to be the same. This error is particularly unfortunate in reference to these trials, because it was distinctly stated both by the prosecutor and the court that these prisoners were *not* tried for leasing, but for pure sedition. "This case (says the accuser of Gerrald) is *not leasing-making.*" (vol. xxiii. p. 859.) "The crime here charged (says Henderland) is not leasing-making, it is sedition in the proper sense of the word—sedition at common law." (vol. xxiii. p. 893.) Whatever use, therefore, may be made, analogically, of the leasing, or of the Act 1703, this statute does not profess to regulate the punishment of sedition, or to touch any such offence in any way, or to any effect.

Again : it must, I think, appear very strange to any mind not under the influence of the year 1794, to see it maintained that these old Statutes are not only not in desuetude, but are still in such force that it was proper for a court of justice to proceed upon their principles at the close of the eighteenth century in everything except in the then forbidden punishment of death. Hallam, than whom no safer guide can be found in extracting its true results from history, describes our ancient code of leasing-making as "*the old mystery of iniquity in Scots law.*" "Amidst a great vaunt (says he) of Christianity and civilisation, they took away men's lives by such Statutes, and by such constructions of them, as could only be paralleled in the annals of the worst tyrants." (*Const. Hist.*, chap. xvii.) Nothing can be required to justify this opinion more than the example he gives of the case of Balmerino, who in 1635 was convicted and sentenced to death for leasing-making, under the Statute of 1584, 130, being one of the Statutes specified in the Act of 1703. It was made a capital offence by that Statute even to *hear* a slanderous speech against the king *or his progenitors* without reporting it, "or to *meddle in the affairs of his Heiness and his estate*, PRESENT, BYGANE, *and in* TIME COMING." Certain peers had prepared what Laing describes as "a temperate and submissive petition (to the king) in order to exculpate themselves from the imputation of an opposition to prerogative, and to deprecate the operation of those articles from which they dissented." (*Hist. of Scot.*, vol. iii. p. 107.) They abandoned this most constitutional proceeding (as it would now be thought) on learning that it displeased his Majesty. Balmerino happened to have kept a copy of the petition, and this being fraudulently discovered and disclosed, he was sentenced to death [1] because the paper, though un-delivered and unpublished, was "so seditious that *its thoughts infected the very air.*" It was "a cockatrice which a good subject would have crushed in the egg." No wonder that Hallam asserts this Statute of 1584, 130, and various others touching leasing, to be parts of "one of the *most odious engines that tyranny ever devised against public virtue*—the Scots law of Treason." (*Const. Hist.*, vol. ii. p. 678, 4to edition.)

Nevertheless Hume makes it a material part of his argument that, provided death and demembra-tion be avoided, these Statutes were part of our law in 1793, and are so still. It is really curious to see how a man of humanity and sense, and a friend to fair trial, can linger over and tolerate these long exploded atrocities. He admits that these were "*the laws of arbitrary times.*" But "the *principle* which they enforce, that of maintaining the obliga-tion and authority of the existing Government, is a principle of all times and situations." "EACH of these enactments, in its order, is *an acknowledgment and confirmation of the common law.*" [!!] "The crime, therefore (leasing) and *nomen juris*, and THE STATUTES IN RELATION TO IT, still remain a part of our system [!!!], though these last are not now *so likely* to be used as grounds of charge by themselves, *as in confirmation of the common law;* for I think it

___

[1] Laing, whose book was published in 1804, says:—"As peremptory challenges are unknown in Scotland, the jurors are invariably selected by the judge from the return made by the clerk of court. Nine of the jury, with a single exception, were ineffectually challenged ; but when Traquair, a *minister of State*, was admitted, it was no longer doubtful that the rest were industriously selected for their hostility to Balmerino, or their devo-tion to the Crown." (vol. iii. p. 110.)

is not to be *doubted* that the offence would have been
cognisable, and to the effect perhaps of inflicting as
high pains as those in the Act 1703, although the
Legislature had never interposed with any provision
on the subject." (vol. i. p. 345.)

So that, except in its capital punishment, the
Act 1584, 130, is still a part of our law! And any
one who utters, or, without reporting it, hears an
observation slanderous of the reigning sovereign's
great-grandfather, or who meddles in his affairs
past, present, or future, is still liable to transportation at common law!! It seems odd to call these
Statutes confirmations of a common law, which they
outrage and trample upon. They are so in the same
way that torture, to procure confession, may be said
to be a confirmation of the common law, which
requires men to speak the truth. They are evidence, to be sure, that in all communities, existing
Governments must receive a certain degree of protection,—a principle which Power is always sincere
in extolling. Does this prevent a Scotch Statute
from falling into desuetude? These Acts were not
merely liable to the stretches and misconstruc-
tions referred to by parliament in 1703, but in their
punishments, provisions and principles, they were
repugnant to the common public law of any un-
chained people. Yet, as I read the Commentaries,
Balmerino could be lawfully tried still on the Act
1584.

There is another, and an important, logical error
in his reasoning. He admits (or seems to do so)
that as it was not the practice (" by reason of the
exigency of the times ") to try these political crimes
as sedition proper, there was no known and established punishment for this precise offence. How

then does he make it transportable ? By this process of argument : Sedition was anciently punished
capitally as treason, or as leasing-making. But
both the crime and its penalty being reduced to
their proper level by death being prohibited, *it
follows* that any penalty short of death is competent. In short, whatever arbitrary times made
capital must remain so, *though as a new offence,*
next to capital in legal times. His own words are
these : " Being now lowered from that degree by
the Statute 7 Anne, cap. 21, which abolishes the
peculiar treasons of the law of Scotland, these and
all other instances of transgression in the like sort,
as *mala in se,* and evils too of a very high order,
retain, *of course,* their *proper* place and quality, *as
acts of sedition* at common law, whereby the offenders
are *justly* exposed to the HIGHEST arbitrary punishment. *On these grounds* many convictions have of
late years been *obtained."* These convictions are
those that were got in the very trials under
examination.

Now it is clear that this is what is called " Miss-
ing the Point." Where *a known crime* is punished
in one way, and a Statute orders it to be punished
in another way—this being the only change—the
criminal character of the act continues as before.
Therefore, if sedition had been formerly punishable
by death, and this punishment had been suppressed,
sedition, as a crime, would remain. But it does not
follow, that when an act is punishable, no matter
how, only *as a specific offence,* and it is declared
that it shall no longer constitute this offence, it
must remain as an offence *of a different kind.* Yet
this is Baron Hume's error. Seditious acts used to
be prosecuted as *Treason.* The Statute of Queen

Anne, by introducing the English law of treason, prevented this. *Therefore*, says he, seditious acts remained to be prosecuted *as sedition*. But sedition, *as such*, was *not* a known crime prior to Queen Anne ; and how does it become one, merely because the acts which constitute what we would now call sedition are declared by Queen Anne's Act not to be treason ? Suppose that the act of counterfeiting the coin had been punishable solely as treason, and that a Statute were to pass, enacting that this should be treason no longer, does this declaration, that it is not to be treason, make it a new offence, never heard of before, called coining ?

It is said that sedition is, and always must be, a crime at common law. If it be true that Scotland subsisted, without recognising such a crime, till 1793, this proposition may be reasonably doubted. But let it be assumed. It is next said that in seeking for a punishment the court could not do better than take the precedent of the kindred case of leasing, for which the Act of 1703, passed after the Revolution, permitted banishment. This might be fairly doubted also ; for leasing and sedition are not kindred offences. But concede this too. Did a permission to banish imply a permission to carry the exile to a particular place, and to keep him there ? Certainly this is not implied in the mere habit of using the *words* "banish" and "transport" as the same.

Accordingly, Baron Hume asserts that, *in point of fact*, transportation, *in the modern sense*, was one of the regular judicial punishments. And it is in evidence of this that he produces that imposing display of cases, in which the strength of his argument is said to lie, and the mere outside of which has

convinced, or confounded, so many willing adherents.

If fixing culprits, during the years of their sentences, to particular places abroad, was really one
of the ancient established acts of judicial discretion,
the fact is certainly very strange, considering that
the modern system of giving convicts over to be
removed and detained by the Crown, was only introduced by a Statute in the reign of George the Third.
How *could* the practice of transporting arise *as a
regular judicial proceeding,* before this, in the face
of these two considerations ?—*First,* that anciently
Scotland had no foreign possession, or at least none
that was used for the detention of convicts. *Second,*
that, as Sir George Mackenzie lays it down, "With
us no judge can confine a man whom he banisheth,
to any place without his jurisdiction, because he
hath no jurisdiction over other countries, and so
cannot make any Acts, or pronounce any sentences
relative to them." (*Criminal Law.*)

However, as Hume asserts this practice as a
positive fact, the cases on which his statement rests
must be examined.

They are forty in number.[1]

Now of these forty, *ten* are *posterior to* 1703 ;
and consequently cannot be referred to as explanatory of what the term "banishment," as used in
the Statute of that year, meant. We might as well
refer to the cases of yesterday, or even of 1793-94.
Most of these ten cases run into the modern period,
when, under recent Statutes, the word, and the
thing, "transportation," came to obtain its present
significance. This leaves thirty cases.

[1] There may possibly be some error in these reckonings ; chiefly because
the same case may recur twice. But I am pretty sure that the countings
are substantially accurate, and within a case or two of the truth.

In *eleven* of these thirty, *no residence in any foreign locality is specified in the sentence.* The prisoners are merely sent out of this country. This leaves nineteen.

In *five* of these nineteen, the prisoners were convicted of *capital* offences ; and their bodies being thus at the Crown's disposal, were liable to be sent, and kept, anywhere at its pleasure. Sir George Mackenzie asserts that *nobody* was ever sent to the *plantations*, in the reign of Charles the Second, except on this ground : "As to the sending away people to the plantations, it is answered that none were sent away but such as were taken at Bothwell Bridge, or in Argyll's rebellion ; and the turning capital punishment into exile was an act of clemency, not of cruelty." (*Vind. of Charles Second*, Works, vol. ii., folio, p. 344.) This statement cannot be confidently relied on merely upon the vindicator's authority ; but wherever the fact did occur, this commutation of a capital sentence destroys the case as an example of judicial transportation. And it may occur, though not in the *form* of a commutation. But in one of these five cases it is in this very form. This leaves fourteen.

And the whole of these *fourteen* were transportations *by the consent of the prisoners*, and in general on their own application ; and even in these cases the place of exile is not always prescribed ; and when it is, this is sometimes not as essential to the sentence, but from accidental convenience.

What the people got for justice anciently was so tedious and so cruel, that rather than be tried, the accused, and even the suspected, were apt to beg to be sent out of the country at once ; and on an application to this effect, the prisoner's desire was complied with without any trial, and frequently without even an indictment. When this course was followed, the prisoner, where he was a person whose continuance here was sure to be detected, was generally left to expatriate himself in his own way. Where he could not be trusted, or had not the means of getting himself off, it was necessary, *but only in order to get him abroad*, to take measures for his removal. Two very simple and effective methods presented themselves. " The younger sons of the Scots gentry were soldiers of fortune in almost every service of Europe, and it appears that they were permitted to recruit at home." (Hume, vol. i. p. 359.) And besides them, there were colonial planters who wanted white slaves, and there were masters of vessels interested in exporting them. The convenience of making use of these gleaners of men, who engaged both to take convicts abroad, and to keep them there, was so great, that nothing else was thought of. Now in most (but not in all) such proceedings a place was mentioned merely because this was useful for the execution of the contract for getting the prisoner taken away, and not as any addition to the punishment of simple expatriation ; no more than the sea-sickness, without which few convicts can now reach New South Wales, is meant as an addition to transportation. Accordingly it cannot, I believe, be shown that any locality was ever assigned anciently, where there was any other satisfactory security that the prisoner would stay abroad.

These irregular arrangements, consented to generally by the prisoners, cannot be taken as examples of the orderly practice of a court. These miserable creatures were plainly often compelled to give an apparent consent, merely from terror and oppression. Hence the Act 1701 expressly forbids transportations upon such consents, unless the consent be given *before a judge.* This implies that formerly these consents were not judicial transactions at all.[1] Moreover, at least eleven of these thirty precedents were sentences issuing from no court, but from the *Privy Councils of the three, and chiefly of the two, last of the Stewarts.* Except for the meaning of terms, we might as well go to Spain or Venice as to the proceedings of this body, for anything deserving the imitation of a modern judicial tribunal.

Yet Hume feels it necessary to defend, or rather to apologise for, this political inquisition. And, to a certain immaterial extent, what he says (vol. i. p. 357) is true. No doubt the council was partly composed of lawyers, and even of supreme judges ; no doubt it had a certain ill-defined criminal jurisdiction ; no doubt its general interference with all public, and with innumerable private matters, was conformable to the usage of the age ; and no doubt some councils were better than others. But still there is just as little doubt, not merely of the general iniquitous character of the body, but of this —that its peculiar wickedness consisted in *perversions of the law*—that the punishment of political

[1] John Ahannay and Robert Slowan were banished in 1643 by the Justice-Depute, in *virtue of a warrant from the Privy Council,* " without any trial," and they " *accept the sentence,* and become bound to pass away with Capt. Macmath, and to serve him as soldiers in the foreign wars." (Hume, vol. i. p. 362.)

Even the judicial consent was often no protection against great abuse. For example, *in the year* 1755, Sir D. Dalrymple, Advocate-Depute, informs the court that instead of trying Alexander Cameron at Glasgow, HE *had sent him to the tender* lying in Clyde ; but that the tender would not take him. This he " *submits* " to the court, and *forthwith* the man is sent to America for life ; and, as I read the record, without any other consent than that implied in silence. (*Record,* 25th January 1755.)

proceedings was its favourite food, and that hence its voracity during the religious resistance of the people—which, however, is the period from which most of its cases founded on by the learned Baron are taken.

Nothing can be more just than the estimate of the Privy Council of Scotland by two of the least passionate, and most discriminating, of historical censors. " The parliament " (says Laing, speaking of the year 1661) " was at length adjourned, and the Government was again vested in the Privy Council. At once a court of justice and a council of state, in which policy *must* ever predominate over the laws, the institution *necessarily* became tyrannical ; *the judicial functions were united with the executive powers of the State, and a legislative authority was not unfrequently assumed.*" (vol. iv. p. 19.) " The Privy Council " (says Hallam) " was accustomed to extort confession by torture—*that grim divan of bishops, lawyers, and peers,* sucking in the groans of each undaunted enthusiast, in the hope that some imperfect avowal might lead to the sacrifice of other victims, or at least warrant the execution of the present." (*Con. Hist.,* vol. ii. p. 683, 4to, chap. xvii.)

Observe the following example, taken from their proceedings in the year 1704, after the judges had been warned and instructed by the Revolution, and restrained by the Act of 1703. It is the case of Baillie, *one of Hume's cases.* It was brought forward by Blair in Gerrald's trial, as proving triumphantly the court's power to transport for sedition. And its effect was so complete that Eskgrove declares that "if I had any difficulty before, I own an authority quoted this day by Mr. Solicitor-General would at once have done away every hesitation on the subject." (*State Trials*, vol. xxiii. p. 897.) It was acknowledged to have been a Privy Council case, but Blair thought he had removed all exception on this account, by stating that the Lord President, the Lord Justice-Clerk, and several other judges, had been present ; that the accused had six counsel, and that the proceeding occurred in February 1704, only nine months after the passing of the Act in 1703, when the meaning of this Statute could not have been unknown to these lawyers.

Now, after all this, see what the case comes to.

Government had opened some private letters at the post-house, "which gave alarm to the ministers of a plot intended." Upon this they apprehended Baillie, who seems to have been a gentleman, the brother of Manorhall. He, being brought before the council, stated that the Marquis of Annandale and the Duke of Queensberry had been treating with him, in order to entice him to represent certain other noblemen as having been in a plot against her Majesty. On this he was proceeded against, *not for sedition*, but for leasing-making against Queensberry and Annandale, the former of whom was then Secretary of State. The proceedings are well worth the perusal of any one who wishes to see how matters were conducted in the Privy Council, even in its best and last days. They utterly confound and shock all our modern notions, not merely of law, or of form, but of commonplace justice. Blair was correct in saying that the complaint was made upon the Act of 1703. The demand of the libel is that "he ought to be severely punished with the pains of law, or *at least conform to the fourth Act of the last session of this current parliament*" (being the Act 1703.) He was condemned. And what was the punishment? which is all that we have now to do with.

The Statute provides that the penalties shall be "fining, imprisonment, *or* banishment, or *if the offender be poor*, and not able to pay a fine, *then* to be punished in his body, life and limb always preserved." But the Privy Council, composed of judges though it partly was, declared the prisoner "*infamous*, and have *banished*, and hereby banishes him, *forth of this kingdom for ever*; and have also appointed and ordained, and hereby appoints and ordains, the said David Baillie to be *transported to the West Indies*, and to lie in prison aye and while he be transported, and hereby appoints and ordains the said David Baillie before he be transported to be *set on the pillory* at the Tron, and there to stand from eleven to twelve of the clock in the forenoon," etc. (*State Trials*, vol. xiv. p. 1054.)

It seems to me, from this sentence, that when they meant to fix the prisoner to the West Indies, they felt that the word "banishment" would not do, and that for this object the use of the term "transport" was necessary. This, however, is not very important. But where did they find authority for *infamy* or the *pillory*? Certainly not in the Statute on which they professed to be proceeding. If the pillory was meant as a punishment in the body (which is not the legal view of it), then there was no warrant for it, because, so far as appears, there was no inability to pay a fine, and no fine was imposed. These were *illegal additions* to the punishment by the Privy Council.[1] Yet this was the case that removed all Eskgrove's doubts.

---

[1] No wonder that such a sentence was not carried into complete effect. Lockhart says that the prisoner underwent the pillory, but this is doubt-

If the proceedings of the Privy Council of Scotland are to be recognised as evidence of the correct practice of the law, or of the understanding of the country, there is no atrocity that may not be sanctioned on the same authority. The suppression of the tyranny of the Crown, *as practised by its getting the Privy Council to dictate to the courts of justice*, was the subject of one of the principal articles in the Declaration of Rights. And the final extinction of this necessarily iniquitous conclave is justly stated by Laing and most other historical observers as one of the great benefits of the Union. Yet this was the body on whose proceedings, and in political cases, supreme British judges avow themselves to have acted in 1794, and which are recommended for the imitation of the successors of these judges by a grave institutional writer.[1]

The conclusion, on the whole, is, that transportation, in our sense of the word, was warranted by nothing that ought to have been considered as a

ful. He was liberated from jail by parliament on 21st July 1704, on account of his health.

[1] The *eleven cases without any place of exile* being specified are the following :—
1. Andrew Henderson, 12th September 1609.—P.
2. William Tweedie, March 1612.—P.
3. James Moffat, 13th September 1615.—P.
4. Colin Bruce, 18th March 1618.—P.
5. George Nicol, 8th March 1633.—P.
6. William and Thomas Mackie, 2d February 1636.—P.
7. David Davidson, 4th April 1637.—P.
8. Janet Spens, 24th July 1676.
9. Archibald Guine, 15th February 1692.
10. Elspeth Johnston, 11th November 1702.
11. Janet Syme, 17th November 1702.

The *fourteen consents* were in the following cases :—
1. Robert Arbroath, 24th August 1626.—P.
2. John Cummin, 15th June 1631.
3. Daniel Nisbet, 22d March 1633.—P.
4. John Lawson, 13th July 1633,—P.
5. James Gordon, etc., 7th August 1635.

precedent,—*by no judicial judgment, by no judicial dictum, by no statute, by the doctrine of no institutional expounder of the law.*

Some will probably be more struck than the author of the Commentaries professes to be with the fact that, anciently, when compulsory residence was meant to form part of the punishment of common law offences, *Statutes were sometimes obtained to sanction this.* Thus the Act 1670, 2, directs that culpable refusal to give evidence (a common law crime) shall be punished by "fine, imprisonment, or banishment by *sending them to his Majesty's plantations in the Indies, or elsewhere as his Majesty's Council shall think fit.*" Baron Hume despises this as merely "*one instance of the employment of a fuller phrase.*"

6. Patrick Davidson, 8th August 1636.
7. John More, 15th November 1636.
8. Alexander Craig, 6th February 1639.
9. Richard Lauder, 6th February 1639.
10. John Tailzour, 25th February 1639.
11. William Barr, 1st March 1639.
12. John Maccarall, 28th October 1639.
13. Henry Malcolm, 19th July 1642.
14. John Ahannay, 6th January 1643.—P.

The *five capital* cases were :—

1. John Vallance, 7th May 1687.
2. Hugh Smith, 7th May 1687.
3. Maxwell and Rankine, 7th November 1690.
4. Helen Scott, 21st November 1693.
5. Thomas Anderson, 12th March 1701.—P.

N.B.—The last was an *express* commutation.

The *eleven* Privy Council cases are marked above by the letter P.

The *ten* posterior to 1703 I need not take down here, as their dates in Hume show them.

So my reckoning stands thus :—

Posterior to 1703, . . .	10
Consents, ...	14
No specified place, . . .	11
Capital, ...	5
Total cases in Hume,	40

The details of the cases are often so confused that this may not be absolutely accurate. But I scarcely think it can be far wrong.

(vol. i. p. 357.) But there are other instances, and Acts of Parliament are not passed for the mere employment of phrases. The sound inference seems to be that, *without express statutory authority*, the court, even in dealing with a common law offence, had no power to send anybody to his Majesty's plantations, or to extend its own jurisdiction into foreign parts.

So the matter stands, exclusive of the power claimed by the court to be its own parliament, and to declare new crimes and invent new punishments at its own discretion. The only plausible case for the court depends on its being held that such a power exists. Without this the ancient practice will not do. If the existence of such a power be assumed, then it is said that the court was bound to exercise it, and that transportation having at least become common before 1793, no other punishment, where judicial discretion was allowed, would have suited the sedition of that period.

The answer to this is twofold.

In the *first* place, the power claimed for the court did not legally exist. I will not stop to discuss this. It is a power that *cannot* legally exist in this or in any other free country. The court shrinks now from its avowal as much as possible; but if it shall ever come to be generally known that such a power is acted upon, parliament will put it down.

In the *second* place, the acknowledgment that the punishment was not absolutely fixed, but that, under this "*native vigour*," it depended on the discretion of the court, raises the view in which it is least possible even to extenuate the conduct of the judges; because, *beyond all doubt*, they had no such precedents for transporting as made a deviation from the practice improper. *Most certainly* no prisoner had ever been transported for *sedition* before. Then, they had the alternatives of fine, imprisonment, or banishment presented to them by the Statute, as adequate for what they deemed the analogous offence of leasing. And, as applicable to the very day, and to the very emergency before them, they had the *living example of England;* a portion of the empire endangered at that moment by the same crime; and exposed by the greater number, freedom, and ignorance of its people, to far greater peril by popular excitement, but where transportation was not resorted to, and yet the law was upheld.

The principle of excessive severity in the punishment of political offences was condemned by the claim of right, and even by the Act of Parliament (1703), on which the judges professed to be acting. Yet their Lordships, insensible of their opportunity, allowed the very spirit of the old Privy Council to possess them. The dangerousness of the times, which has been the apology of all their defenders, only made their error the greater. When courts of justice are requested to allay political troubles, it is only by calm mildness that they can do so. The prisoners set themselves up as leaders of the people, and there is too much reason to fear that the court fell into the vulgar blunder of believing that it was possible to put down political opinions by exterminating the most prominent of those who express them. Their Lordships seem never to have been aware of the enlightened sentiment of our great philosophical historian—a sentiment fully as applicable to judges as to governors,—that "Rulers can never render so lasting a service to a people as by

the example, in a time of danger, of justice to
formidable enemies, and of mercy to obnoxious
delinquents. These are glorious examples, for which
much is to be hazarded." (Mackintosh, *History of
England*, chap. viii., Henry the Eighth.)[1]
Gerrald was sent off in a convict ship, and died
soon after reaching New South Wales.

Such was the fate of a man who was thus
described, with the eloquence of truth, by Laing
towards the close of his speech :—

"My Lord, on the immense disproportion between
the punishment and the offence, let me suggest a
distinction which I am too much exhausted to
illustrate. Clarendon was banished ; Barrington [2]
transported. Clarendon, when exiled by a vicious
court and a venal monarch, lived abroad to himself and to his country, to illustrate the annals
of British story. Bolingbroke, though expelled for
treason, lived to return, and, in a corrupt age, to
revive the flame of patriotism in every English
breast. Atterbury, though in exile and under dis-
countenance, closed the honoured remainder of his
life in dignity and peace. But a man whose offence
is inferior, whose abilities are equal, and his integrity,
I am bold to say, superior to Bolingbroke's ; whose
genius may distinguish his name, and enrich the

[1] In discussing the competency of transporting, I take no notice of
Lord Dreghorn's objections (*Works*, vol. ii. p. 58), because I think them
ill founded, and, even if well founded, frivolous. He carps at the *words*
of Muir's sentence, but there is nothing solid in his criticisms. His chief
objection is that under the 25 Geo. III. cap. 46, the court, besides transporting, ought to have *adjudged his services*, which Burnett is quite correct
in saying (p. 255) they ought not to have done. Then he states (p. 63) that
Braxfield admitted that a sentence of transportation did not, in effect,
bind the convict to remain in the place he was sent to, but that if it did,
then a power to *transport* could not be held to be included within the
power to *banish* conferred by the Act of 1703. That Braxfield ever made
any such statement is incredible. If he did, and was sober, the whole
proceedings, and especially his own conduct, are nonsensical.
[2] A famous London pickpocket, recently convicted.

literature of his country, depends on your sentence,
whether his future life shall be lost to society, himself doomed to a receptacle of vice and misery, and
transported to a shore from which, apparently, there
is no return. From the state of his health, I must
add, that a sentence of transportation is, in all
human probability, a sentence of death." (vol. xxiii.
p. 888.)

These sentiments are received now with nearly
universal sympathy. But they were transmuted at
the time into feelings hostile to the person who had
the honour of being the subject of such statements,
from such a man. "Both the one and the other
of his counsel" (said *Lord Abercromby*, p. 900),
"in speaking of the punishment of transportation,
stated that his case would be extremely hard,
because he was a gentleman, a man who possessed
talents, qualities, and *virtues*, which would be useful and ornamental to society. My Lord, I am very
sorry that such a man should be in his situation ;
because if he should be convicted, *it aggravates his
crime highly.* Had he been a man ignorant and
uninformed, it might have been some apology for his
offence; and though such a man, when he transgresses
against the laws of his country, must be punished,
yet it would have been a good reason for inflicting
the mildest punishment that we could, consistently
with our duty, inflict. But, my Lord, *if such are
the qualifications of the panel now at your bar, so
much the deeper and more aggravated is his guilt.*
For, my Lord, we all know that to whom much is
given, of him much will be required."

In one sense, though not in the proper sense,
as applied to the particular case, this is true.
Crime by talent and knowledge is less excusable,

and generally more formidable, than when it is committed by stupidity and ignorance ; though certainly this principle can only be received with many qualifications when it is applied to the political offence of sedition—a crime into which, chiefly in consequence of their ability and knowledge, many good men are led. But the objections to his Lordship's observation, in relation to the case before him, are, 1st, That he extracts an aggravation not merely out of the prisoner's intellectual powers, but out of his very *virtues,* and virtue certainly aggravates no crime ; 2d, That he makes both virtues, and *the station and habits of a gentleman,* entitled to no consideration in the matter of *discretionary punishment.* Some punishments are fixed, and do not admit of being mitigated. A gentleman murderer, like every other murderer, must be hanged, and there is only one way of performing this operation. But no *discretionary* punishment can be well administered, except in reference to the particular circumstances ; and even if the principle of equality is to be recognised, how can it be said that transportation is the same suffering to a virtuous gentleman as it is to a low, coarse blackguard ?

So that the mercy of this judge was reserved in regard to political offences for the low and illiterate, who can rarely be tempted, or ennobled, to commit them ; and the very virtues which lead men of a higher order into public affairs, and consequently into the risk of occasional excess—their talent and spirit, their humanity and enthusiasm—are all so many aggravations of that guilt which, at the worst, often consists merely in a generous desire to hasten the removal of real grievances more rapidly than those who convict think safe. And the legal principle being in favour of equality of punishment—a principle which requires all the circumstances of each case to be taken into view—the man of education and refinement, to whom community with ordinary felons is worse than death, is to be dealt with, *for a political offence*, exactly as a common blackguard, of whom these have long been the chosen associates! When the Earl of Argyle's daughter saved her father's life, for the time, by enabling him to escape, after conviction, in disguise, the Privy Council proposed that she should be *publicly whipped*, which Hallam says (vol. ii. p. 684, 4to, chap. xvii.) was only prevented because " the Duke of York felt as a gentleman upon such a suggestion." I do not believe that Lord Abercromby, who was a gentleman, would have differed from His Royal Highness ; but panic and faction had so confounded the logic and the feelings of himself and his colleagues, that he was not aware how directly the reasoning that he applied to Gerrald implied the propriety of whipping the lady. Lord Ellenborough, unrefined by the refinement of his age, made the pillory a part of the sentence passed upon the son of a peer.[1] But this so shocked the feelings of that people, who, of all people upon earth, are the fondest of fair equality of punishment, that not only was this prisoner saved, but the punishment was abolished.

[1] Lord Cochrane.

PROCEEDINGS IN PARLIAMENT.

THESE trials were more than once discussed in parliament.

On the 31st of January 1794, the Earl of Stanhope moved, in the House of Lords, for an address to the king, beseeching that the sentence against Thomas Muir be not carried into effect until the House shall have had time to inquire into the case. His Lordship had, apparently, been very ill instructed, for he took up objections that were quite untenable, and omitted all those that were well founded. But in these respects he was fully as well informed as any of his noble brethren, among all of whom there seems to have been the usual ignorance of our system, and conceit of their own, which distinguishes Englishmen, and especially English lawyers, in thinking of the two.

The motion was supported by nobody except the mover—the contents being 1, the non-contents 49. The opposition was rested on the ground that whatever might be done to *correct* judicial error, it was irregular to address the Crown to *suspend* its execution. "Who ever heard (said Loughborough, the Chancellor) of an address being moved for in this House praying His Majesty to postpone the execution of a sentence" (*Parliamentary Hist.*, vol. xxx. p. 1303.) Even Lauderdale, who approved of the justice of the motion, concurred in this view of its form. This objection may be parliamentary, but I cannot reconcile it to common sense, especially as applicable to a Scotch prosecution, where, except through the Crown, there is no remedy for judicial error or misconduct. If it be competent for the Crown to protect the subject against an illegal sentence, how can it be incompetent for parliament to ask the Crown to do so ? And what protection does Parliament give to the victim of such a sentence, if it can only interfere after the doom is suffered ?

In the course of the discussion, two very opposite opinions were delivered as to the general conduct of the court.

On the one side Lord Stanhope said that " if this was the law of Scotland, he would only observe that Scotland had no more liberty than it had under the race of the Stewarts." (*Par. Hist.* vol. xxx. p. 1300.) And Lord Lauderdale (then the leader of the Jacobins in Scotland, now of the tories) stated that " there were circumstances attending these trials which were most dreadful in their nature, and reflected no small disgrace on the jurisprudence of Scotland." (vol. xxx. p. 1302.)

On the other hand, Lord Mansfield (not *the* Lord Mansfield) had the courage to assert that " he could take it upon him to answer, that *in no court under the glorious constitution of this country, had justice been administered with more fidelity.*" (p. 1301.) And the Lord Chancellor (Loughborough) permitted his party zeal to prevail so entirely over his official caution, as to intimate that " if ever their Lordships should think proper to entertain an inquiry into the case, *he would pledge himself* that they should find the conduct of the judges of Scotland had been such as their Lordships would always

DESIRE to find in men intrusted with functions so important." (p. 1303.)

Would that history could be of this opinion! But it will probably think, that no Lord Chancellor ever disgraced himself by grosser rashness.

It is scarcely worth while to state that Thurlow defended the proceedings ; because on matters of political or judicial purity his opinion is of as little weight as Loughborough's. But the fact that he did so has produced these sentiments from his latest biographer :—" He resisted the attempt that was made to obtain a reversal of the *atrocious* sentence of transportation passed by the Court of Justiciary, at Edinburgh, on Muir, for advocating parliamentary reform." It is added in a note : "The trials which took place in Scotland about that time cannot now be read without amazement and horror, mixed with praises to heaven that we live in better times. In the year 1834, being a candidate to represent the city of Edinburgh in parliament, I was reproached for not being sufficiently liberal in my opinions. I said truly that although Attorney-General for the Crown, I had uttered sentiments for which, forty years before, I should have been sent to Botany Bay." (Campbell's *Lives of the Chancellors*, vol. v. p. 612.)

See also Campbell's condemnation of Loughborough's conduct on the occasion mentioned in the text. (*Lives of the Chancellors*, vol. vi. p. 264, chap. 172.)

Campbell has since risen to be the Chief-Justice of England. There was an interval of some years between his reaching this station and his ceasing to be Attorney-General. Instead of wasting this period in idleness or in political contention, he composed the *Lives of the Chancellors*, a work which, notwithstanding its many defects, will last as long as the language in which it is written. His elevation to the chief seat on the English bench, though it gives him a natural sympathy with judges, has not abated his horror of the proceedings of our criminal court at the period I am referring to : on the contrary, it is by good judges that these proceedings will ever be most severely condemned. He has spoken to me of them since reaching his present position, and never without indignation and shame.

On 24th February 1794, Mr. Sheridan presented a petition to the House of Commons, in favour of *Palmer*, who was then aboard the transport which was to convey him to New South Wales. The petition described his sentence as "illegal, unjust, oppressive, and unconstitutional," and prayed for such relief as the House should think proper. (*Par. Hist.* vol. xxx. p. 1449.) Mr. Pitt at first opposed the principle of the petition, on the ground that the House could not regularly obstruct the execution of a judicial sentence, and that the correct course was to apply to the Crown for mercy ; but at last he agreed to an adjournment of three days—till the 27th. On this, Mr. Whitbread, in order that the pause, and the discussion, might not be made a mockery by the vessel sailing in the meantime, moved an address to His Majesty to prevent its sailing till after the 27th. This motion was rejected by 104 against 34. On the 27th Sheridan moved "that the petition be *committed*." This was not opposed ; and the result, in point of form, was, that the "petition was *read*," and nothing more was done.

But in the course of the discussion various

opinions were disclosed as to the merits of the case. Mr. Dundas (Henry, the first Lord Melville) was resolute against even a moment's delay in sending off the convict. He blamed the friends of the prisoner for not having brought the matter forward till they knew that the vessel was about to sail, and repeated a previous assertion, "that the sentence was legal ; and that the Court of Justiciary, in passing that sentence, *had exercised a sound discretion.*" (p. 1452.) Mr. Whitbread, senior, fell into the strange blunder of claiming mercy for the prisoner on the ground that he was insane. (p. 1456.) This cruel mistake was corrected, on a subsequent occasion by Whitbread, junior, and Mr. Sheridan, who explained that the lunatic was the prisoner's brother. (p. 1559.) Sheridan, and others, insisted that the prisoner had done nothing beyond promoting what had been recommended by the leading members of the administration which patronised his prosecution. Fox held the sentence to be utterly indefensible, and maintained that the interference of parliament was constitutional, and not unusual. (p. 1460.) The Marquis of Titchfield (an adherent of ministry) thought that "the sentence ought to be suspended, if it was urged by no other arguments than the dictates of humanity." (p. 1459.) "Mr. Wilberforce ridiculed the idea of humanity as applying to Mr. Palmer, *although he had not read his trial.*" [! !] " He declared upon his conscience that he did not conceive the sentence ought to be suspended." (p. 1460.)

The whole subject was brought again before the House of Commons on the 10th of March 1794, upon a motion by Mr. Adam for a copy of the record in the case of Muir,—a proceeding liable to no objection on the ground of irregularity. Mr. Adam is the person who has since been known to Scotland as the head of the tribunal for introducing trial by jury in civil causes into this country. A thorough Scotchman by birth, tastes, and interests, but an English lawyer, and generally resident in London, he was on friendly terms with the leaders of the profession in both countries, particularly with such of them as acknowledged the principles of the whigs, the party to which he belonged. To the delight of a large circle of friends, this venerable and excellent person still survives,—one of the very best specimens of old age,—afflicted by infirmities enough to sour and to cloud the mind, of which nearly total blindness is not the most troublesome; yet kind, cheerful, and entertaining, his intellect unimpaired, and the last remains of his vigour given to improve civil trial by jury, which his native country certainly owes mainly to his skill and perseverance.

He had prepared himself thoroughly on the facts and on the law of the case, and made a most admirable speech. It was full, luminous, and generally, though not always, sound,—strong, without one unnecessarily offensive word; and besides glancing at the incidental improprieties of the trial, laid open the illegality and the cruelty of the sentence, the exposure of which was his more particular object. Few legal cases have ever been better introduced to either House of Parliament.

The Lord Advocate's answer consisted in a mere repetition of the prosecutor's version of the circumstances, and a re-assertion of the law, as maintained by, or for, his Lordship at the trial.

It is more important to know how the matter

was viewed by English members, in whose country certainly no such proceedings could have occurred. *Sheridan* followed the Lord Advocate in a clever and contemptuous speech, of which I see no reason to question that the expressions of doubt and amazement at what was said to be our law, and of abhorrence of the judges by whom he held its defects to have been aggravated, were at least quite sincere.

Mr. Whitbread declared that "since he had a seat in that House he had never heard a speech which so much excited his indignation as that of the Lord Advocate, and he hesitated not to declare that if the law of Scotland was such as represented by the learned Lord, it was a law of tyranny and oppression, and it was absurd to speak of personal liberty in that country." (*Par. Hist.* vol. xxx. p. 1559.)

Mr. Windham acknowledged the principle that cases might arise where it would be proper for the House to inquire into the conduct of judges, though there was no proof of actual illegality; "but he hoped the House would never enter into an inquiry when they had, *as in the present case, proof* before them that the sentence proposed to be inquired into was a *proper* and legal sentence." He did not actually say that he preferred the law of Scotland, in this matter, to that of England; but, with reference to the law of either country, "he, for his part, would be the one to say that IF justice was baulked, and the laws were not adequate to the punishment of crimes, he had no difficulty to declare his opinion that they should be made so." (p. 1161.) A very safe opinion. But not made by courts.

As to this, *Fox*, after reminding Windham of his old opinions as a reformer, said that there was much virtue in an If. The case, being one not so much of law, as of oppression practised under the forms of law, was one which never failed to rouse the spirit of this just and merciful man. That he should have been technically accurate in Scotch trials was not to have been expected; but his abhorrence of the punishment, and his indignation at those who inflicted it, makes his speech the strongest impeachment of judges (except Lord Macclesfield's impeachment) that has probably occurred in Parliament since the Revolution. " If (said he) the day should ever arrive, which the Lord Advocate seems so anxiously to wish for,—if the tyrannical laws of Scotland should ever be introduced, in opposition to the humane laws of England, it would then be high time for my honourable friends and myself to settle our affairs, and retire to some happier clime, where we might at least enjoy those rights which God has given to man, and which his nature tells him he has a right to demand." (p. 1563.) " Indeed, sir, so striking and disgustful are the whole features of this trial, that when I first heard of them, I could not prevail upon myself to believe that such proceedings had actually taken place. The charge itself, and the manner in which that charge was exhibited, made my blood run cold within me. I read the first edition; I discredited. I read the second and third editions. I was inclined to disbelieve them all; nor would I even believe it now, but in consequence of what I have heard from this Lord Advocate himself." (p. 1565.) He, and all the speakers on that side, asserted that Muir and Palmer[1] had done no more than what had been

---

[1] I don't see why there is no allusion ever made in this debate to the cases of *Margarot* or *Skirving*, both of which were over long before. I suppose two were enough for the discussion.

done by Mr. Pitt and the Duke of Richmond, whose
claim, addressed to the populace, he says, went far
beyond petitioning, and demanded reform "as their
right." (p. 1571.) He reminded the House how
many of themselves had been guilty of popular
appeals, out of which, as well as out of what these
prisoners had done, constructive sedition might be
extracted.

"But there is one strange assertion made by one
of the Lords of Justiciary. He says that no man
has a right in the Constitution,[1] unless he possesses
a landed property ; men of personal property, though
they may have immense sums in the funds, have no
lot or part in the matter. How absurd, how nonsensical, how ridiculous ! When judges speak thus with
levity, at random, and in a manner that discovers
the most profound ignorance of the Constitution,
what is the inference I would draw ? That the
temper of the judges is manifest from such conduct,
which never occurred even in the reign of the Stewarts. Another learned Lord said that as he saw no
punishment for sedition in our law, he must go into
the Roman law ; and having recourse to this extra-
judicial authority, he at last discovered that the
mildest punishment that could be inflicted on the
unfortunate gentleman was transportation for fourteen years ! The Roman law left it at the learned
Lord's discretion to give Mr. Muir either to the gal-
lows ! to the wild beasts ! or to Botany Bay ! and
of the whole, he had happily selected the mildest !"[2]
He was utterly amazed when he learned that a judge
had seriously supported such unaccountable non-

---

[1] This refers to Braxfield's observation in the trial of Muir (*State
Trials*, vol. xxiii. p. 231) about the lairds alone being entitled to be represented in Parliament.

[2] This was Swinton. (*State Trials*, vol. xxiii. p. 234.)

sense from the bench—such nonsense as ought not
to be suffered from the youngest or most ignorant
student. He had always entertained the highest
veneration for the character of a judge, and his
indignation was roused to find that the learned Lord,
instead of discharging his duty with the gravity
becoming the bench, had acted with ignorance, levity,
and hypocrisy. After having put his invention to
the rack, he had at last hit upon the mildest punishment, of fourteen years' transportation beyond the
seas ! Good God ! sir, any man of spirit (and such
he believed Mr. Muir to be) would prefer death to this
mildest instance of the judge's mercy. But another
of these learned Lords, or perhaps the same (for with
their names I profess myself totally unacquainted[1]),
asserted that now that torture was banished, there
was no adequate punishment for sedition ! Here,
sir, is language which shows the temper, the levity,
the ignorance, the hypocrisy, of this imprudent man.
Let him be either serious or in jest, the sentiment
was equally intolerable.   I know not which of them
advanced such a proposition ; but God help the
people who have such judges ! " (p. 1569.)

Mr. Pitt (rashly) pretended to discuss the Scotch
law of the case, and was not more unfortunate than
an English gentleman might be expected to be who
involves himself with the mysteries of leasing-making, and the Act 1584, and the case of *Baillie*, &c.
He gave it as his opinion " that an inquiry into this
business would lead to the conclusion, that *no doubt
could be entertained* either of the legality of the
trials under review, *or of the propriety of the manner in which the Lords of Justiciary had exercised
their discretion* upon this occasion " (p. 1572). *He*

---

[1] It was the same—Swinton.

thought that the judges would have been highly culpable, if, vested as they were with discretionary powers, they had not employed them for the present punishment of such daring delinquents, and the suppression of doctrines so dangerous to the country." (p. 1575).

Mr. Grey (now Earl Grey) corroborated Fox's statement that both the Duke of Richmond and Mr. Pitt, and many others then in the House, " had gone *greater* length than either of the prisoners in recommending universal suffrage, and *telling the people that they must depend on their own exertions* in procuring a parliamentary reform." And " he entirely agreed with Mr. Fox that if the criminal law of Scotland were extended to England, then it would no longer be the country where a freeman could live " (p. 1576).

The motion was rejected by 171 against 32.

The subject was once more brought before the House of Lords on the 15th of April 1794 by a motion by Lord Lauderdale, " for the production of the papers respecting the trial and sentence of Mr. Muir and Mr. Palmer, and any minutes that may have been made in regard to the challenge of jurors, the exhibition of evidence," etc. The motion was confined to these two cases, because his Lordship held that certain peculiarities rendered them particularly unjust.

The report gives the mere bones of his discourse ; but still it was plainly a strong, intelligent, and clever speech ;—not certainly without bad points (such as that there was no sedition charged in the major proposition of either indictment), but, upon the whole, it hit all the material blots. He maintained, as to both cases,—" 1*st.* That the crimes set forth against Mr. Muir and Mr. Palmer were what the law of Scotland termed leasing-making, etc., and that those indictments charged no other crime whatever; 2d. That the punishment of transportation could not, by the law of Scotland, be inflicted for the said crime of leasing-making." (*Par. Hist.* vol. xxxi. p. 267.) And on the particular case of Muir, he objected specially,—1st, to his challenge of the Goldsmith Hall jurymen being overruled; 2d, to the admission of evidence against him (meaning Flower's book, etc.) of which he had no notice; 3d, to his being deprived of the evidence of Russell, who was sent to prison by the court for prevarication. On the great question of the power of transporting, his argument is better in its details than in its enunciation. If nothing could be urged against the sentences, except that the indictments only charge leasing, and that in punishing this offence, the *word* transportation can never be used, nothing could be said against them. But he puts his objections on better grounds in the course of the discussion. And on the soundness of the discretion exercised, assuming these to have been cases of discretion, there is great force in some of his facts. "Had the Scotch judges turned to the cases in 1715, when a rebellion was raging in the country, they would have found, at a time infinitely more perilous to the Government than the present, similar, or rather infinitely more glaring, offences had been punished with a very short imprisonment, and a small fine. Had they looked to the conduct of England they would have found that the publishers of Paine's book, which Muir had only lent, were sentenced to pay a fine of £100; and that in Ireland, Hamilton Rowan, the author of the letter which Muir only read, was sentenced to two years' imprisonment." (vol. xxxi. p. 275.) "His surprise at the difference of punishment in the two countries led him to look for antecedent cases in the practice, or in the statute law, of that country (Scotland) to justify these proceedings. He had done this in vain. *Not one case in the whole history of the Scotch criminal law stood upon record either to justify, or even to countenance, these proceedings.*" (p. 263.)

Lord Mansfield, holding the sinecure office of Lord Justice-General,[1] deemed himself bound to defend "that court to which he had the honour to belong." (p. 277.) In doing so, he (literally) *went over* the usual topics ; and, among other things, made this assertion : "I have not the pleasure of personal acquaintance with the Lord Justice-Clerk, but I have long heard *the loud voice of fame, that speaks of him as a man of pure and spotless integrity, of great talents, and of a transcendent knowledge of the laws of his country.*" (p. 283.)

Lord Kinnoul "defended the proceedings of the Scotch judges, who, in his opinion, merited the encomium bestowed upon them by his noble friend." (p. 283.)

The *Lord Chancellor* again disgraced himself, as the head of the law, by defending every one of the proceedings, including even the selection of the Goldsmith Hall Jurymen, and the case of *Baillie.*

Lord Lauderdale's motion was rejected without a division. After which the *Lord Chancellor,* not satisfied with a mere refusal to inquire, thought proper to encourage the judges by a positive eulogy on their conduct. For this purpose he moved, and of course the House agreed, "that there is no

[1] He was also cousin by affinity to Lord Henderland ; that is, he was full cousin to Henderland's wife.

ground for interfering in the practice of the established courts of criminal justice, as administered under the Constitution, and by which the rights, liberties, and properties of all ranks of subjects are protected." (p. 287.) A very safe motion certainly, if it had not been intended to apply to a particular case. Nobody was objecting to "*criminal justice, as administered under the Constitution.*" The only question was, whether what Muir and Palmer had got had been justice, and whether, in the administration of this justice, the spirit of the Constitution had been acted .upon. It was meant as a *compliment by the House of Lords* to the *Scotch* judges *for their conduct in the recent trials.* It served its purpose in Parliament, though certainly not in the country, at the moment ; but history has since ascertained the weight of the compliment by weighing the public character of the Chancellor who procured it. No reputation stands lower than that of Loughborough—the sycophant, and the deserter, of every party—the chief author, contrary to any convictions he can be said to have ever had, of the British reign of terror, and who, it was believed, and was said, would have held the great seal under the French Republic rather than not hold it, and would not have scrupled to promote such a republic for the purpose, if necessary.

Technically, this is the best defence of these judges. Parliament approved of their conduct. The completeness of the defence in any other view must depend on our estimate of the value of the opinion of parliament on such matters at such a time. Both Houses partook of the prevailing alarm ; this gave Government overwhelming majorities on every question ; the motions were discussed entirely as party objects ; and Scotch law was not a matter on which almost any person was either intelligent or docile. The parliament which sat in 1794 *could* not have been candid on such a subject. It could not have done anything which might have had the appearance of condemning judges for undue severity to popular political offenders, without virtually reversing its feelings and ends.

The whigs could not possibly avoid bringing the matter forward. But the result was very unfortunate. It hardened Government against mercy to the prisoners, by making the stern execution of the sentences a point of party triumph ; and it encouraged judges, who not only saw their sentences approved by both Houses, but every part even of their tone and demeanour praised by the head of the law, to persevere in courses so greatly admired.[1]

[1] Contrast these discussions, in 1794, with the debate in the Commons on the judicial conduct of Lord Abinger on the 21st of February 1843. There cannot be a more striking example of the extent to which the forty-nine years that intervened between these two periods had changed the feelings of the country. Lord Abinger had been sent to try criminal Chartists ; and in the course of his addresses to juries had indulged in political opinions. His general tone was objected to, but the *worst* thing specially found fault with was, his telling the grand jury at Chester that " the object of the prisoners was, the attainment of universal suffrage, annual parliaments, and vote by ballot ; the necessary consequences of which would be, that those who have no property would make laws for those who have, and the destruction of the monarchy and aristocracy must necessarily ensue." This was exactly one of our Braxfield's old judicial topics ; but it was less reprehensible when addressed to a grand, than to a petty, jury. Yet no one member, even of Government, directly defended this introduction of political matter, by judges, into judicial proceedings. Some apologise ; some compliment his Lordship for his general eminence ; and some doubt the language. But there is no indication that if he had behaved like our Scotch judges systematically, or had even approached some of their more outrageous indecencies, he would have been allowed to sit on the bench again. The sole ground (and a very wise one) on which the motion for inquiry was resisted, was, that such a motion should never be acceded to except where, if the thing complained of should be established, a resolution by Parliament for *dismissal* must be the consequence; and that the misconduct here was not so gross as to imply this result. Still 73 voted even for inquiry, against 228. The remarkable circumstance is the entire change of sentiment since 1794,—over the whole House.

In his speech for Hamilton Rowan (*Speeches*, p. 185) Curran has one of his Irish flights on the sentences pronounced on Muir, Palmer, Margarot, and Skirving ; Gerrald had not then been tried. "There is a sort of aspiring and adventurous credulity, which disdains assenting to obvious truths, and delights in catching at the improbability of circumstances as its best ground of faith. To what other cause, gentlemen, can you ascribe that in the wise, the reflecting, the philosophic, nation of Great Britain, a printer has been gravely found guilty of a libel, for publishing these resolutions to which the present Minister of that kingdom had actually subscribed his name? *To what other cause* can you ascribe, what in my mind is still more astonishing, in such a country as Scotland—a nation cast in the happy medium between the spiritless acquiescence of submissive poverty, and the sturdy credulity of pampered wealth ; cool and ardent, adventurous and persevering ; winging her eagle flight against the blaze of every science, with an eye that never winks, and a wing that never tires ; crowned, as she is, with the spoils of every art, and decked with the wreath of every muse, from the deep and scrutinising researches of her Hume, to the sweet and simple, but not less sublime and pathetic, morality of her Burns ; how, from the bosom of a country like that, genius and character, and talents, should be banished to a distant, barbarous soil, condemned to pine under the horrid communion of vulgar vice and base-born profligacy, for twice the period that ordinary calculation gives to the continuance of human life."

This is eloquent, but no more. The circumstances selected as descriptive of Scotland had no reference to its political character, and were perfectly consistent with slavery. And the orator soars far too high when he supposes that our prosecutors, judges, or juries, were moved by anything so metaphysical as aspiring credulity, or the pleasure of catching at improbabilities. Descending to earth, he would have found two practical things, one called panic, the other party spirit, which would have explained the whole phenomenon.

XIV.—Case of George Mealmaker, 10th, 11th, and 12th January 1798.[1]

Burnett, who saw no injustice in any of these proceedings, and even if he had, was very probably not aware that injustice, however triumphant for a time, never allayed discontent, remarks, with great simplicity (p. 255) that " the British Convention was by these proceedings put an end to, but the spirit that had been raised in the country was far from being put down. On the contrary, it *seemed to gain strength by the check it had received by the above convictions.*" Rather an awkward commentary. But the fact undoubtedly was, that these trials, instead of reconciling the disaffected to the law, provoked them to defy it; and while they increased the insolence of every adherent of the party in power, impaired the confidence of even their reasonable opponents in the administration of political justice.

About the year 1797, societies of " United Irishmen," " United Scotsmen," and " United Englishmen " were formed in each of these countries ; which, connected as they were with the rebellion which broke out in Ireland in 1798, were unquestionably of a criminal and most dangerous character. They acted by secret meetings, affiliated branches, and unlawful oaths ; and however innocent individual members might be, the views of the leaders

---

[1] *State Trials*, vol. xxvi. p. 1135.

certainly went far beyond any reform, even universal suffrage and annual parliaments. To check such associations, the Act of the 37th Geo. III. cap. 123, was passed on the 19th of July 1797. The principal object and enactment of this statute was to prevent the taking or administering of certain oaths or engagements, which acts it was provided should be punished by transportation for any period not *exceeding seven* years.

Mealmaker was the first person who was tried in Scotland under this Act. Had he been tried under it alone, his case would not have come within the scope of this examination, which is confined to sedition. But he was charged with sedition also, and was convicted of this offence.

The indictment sets forth *sedition, as also a violation of the statute.* The facts stated in reference to the infringement of the Act were, that the Society of United Scotsmen was an association which, under the pretence of reform, aimed at rebellion ; that besides secret committees and meetings, signs, countersigns, private words, etc., its members were bound, by an engagement called " the test of secrecy," never to inform or give evidence against each other ; and that the prisoner, being delegate for Dundee, took and administered this engagement. And the facts on which the general charge of sedition rested were, in substance, that this society was of a seditious character ; that the prisoner was one of its most active promoters ; and that he composed and distributed " various seditious and inflammatory papers or pamphlets, the general tendency of which was to excite a spirit of disloyalty to the king and of disaffection to the existing laws and constitution of Great Britain,"—of which papers two

are specified, one being " The moral and political
Catechism of man, or a Dialogue between a citizen
of the world and an inhabitant of Britain," the other
a publication entitled "Resolutions and Constitution
of the Society of United Scotsmen." It is a peculiarity in this indictment that *it quotes no words*
from either of these publications, but merely asserts,
in general, that they are seditious and inflammatory.

Since the trial of Gerrald, Lord Henderland had
died (16th March 1795), and had been succeeded by
Lord Craig ; and Lord Abercromby had died (17th
November 1795), and been succeeded by Lord
Methven. These two, along with Dunsinnan and
Eskgrove, formed the court. Braxfield, who died
next year (30th May 1799), was unwell ; and Eskgrove, who afterwards succeeded him as Justice-
Clerk, presided. Craig and Methven were good,
respectable men ; the former formal and empty ; the
latter heavy and soft, but benevolent, and a gentleman. Neither of them had any marked political
intemperance ; but neither were they superior to
the prejudices which, in those days, affected the
class to which they belonged.

The prosecution was conducted by the Lord
Advocate, Blair and Burnett ; the defence by John
Clerk and one Alexander Whyte, junior.

But the proceedings are so imperfectly reported,
even in the *State Trials* (vol. xxvi. p. 1135), that
no opinion can be formed either of the facts, or of
the manner in which the case was managed. The
evidence and the speech of the Lord Advocate are
very meagrely given ; and the speech in defence,
the summing up, and the observations from the
bench, are not given at all. In short, the case is
not reported.

Some objections were taken to the relevancy, but what they were is not very apparent from the few words ascribed to the counsel. Burnett says (p. 260) that they were nearly the same with those that had been disregarded in the former trials. This seems somewhat improbable, because the cases were in all respects different. It is not very likely that in the year 1798 John Clerk, in resisting an indictment founded on a prisoner being one of the Society of United Scotsmen, and a distributor of the " Moral and Political Catechism of Man," would repeat arguments applied in the year 1794 to the case of persons accused of accession to the British Convention and the circulation of Paine's *Rights of Man.* But whatever the objections were, the report, such as it is, suggests no ground for doubting the propriety of their being repelled.

The evidence (if what be given deserves the name) clearly establishes the statutory offence, and the circulation of the writings ; but as no part of these writings is quoted, it is impossible for us to say whether they were seditious or not. The speech assigned to the Lord Advocate professes to give his Lordship's construction of certain of the passages ; but if these contain the worst sedition in the pamphlets, it is probable that most candid people will think now that the case was by no means clear. For what his Lordship is chiefly made to object to is, that what the prisoner and his friends aimed at was, " annual parliaments and universal suffrage," and " *for* THIS they form themselves into a Society of United Scotsmen, declaring that they will never desist till they have obtained their object," (vol. xxvi. p. 1160); that " in another part they declare that the will of the *majority* is not rebellion,"

(p. 1161); and that " in another part of the pamphlet it is said that nothing is able to resist a determined *people.*" (p. 1161). Since there were oaths or engagements of secrecy, it is not unreasonable to conclude that there was deeper sedition than what the reporter makes his Lordship extract from it.

He adopted the opinion, formerly expressed by the court, that the exercise of privileges, unquestionably constitutional generally, might be rendered seditious by mere inaptitude of time. The first quotation stated that they professed themselves friends of good order, etc. "Now," said his Lordship, " if they were so, *is this the time*—this the period— which friends of good order would fix upon *for inquiring into the defects of our Government,* and raising up complaints of grievances, when every good man would feel it his duty to make every exertion in behalf of his country, and in allaying discontents ? "

All that we are told of the defence is, that " Mr. Clerk, on the part of the panel, made a very excellent reply to the Lord Advocate, in which he employed much ingenuity in the interpretation to be given to the meaning of the different exceptionable parts of the pamphlet." (p. 1162.)

After which, " Lord Eskgrove, in the absence of the Lord Justice-Clerk, summed up the evidence."

The jury unanimously found the prisoner guilty of the crimes libelled ; and he was sentenced, *generally,* and without any discrimination of offences, to transportation for fourteen years.

I have seen other examples of one general punishment for a plurality of distinct crimes of different kinds; but they have always appeared to me to be incorrect, if not illegal and inoperative. The *whole* fourteen years here could not be for the offence at common law, otherwise the statutory crime must have gone unpunished. Nor could they all be for the statutory crime ; because for it the Act only authorises transportation for a period *not exceeding seven* years. How much of the time, therefore, was for each ? For one-half of it might have been given to each offence ; or thirteen and a half years might have been allotted to the sedition, and six months to the unlawful oaths. The sentence afforded no means of extricating the matter, in the event of the prisoner having received a pardon for one of the crimes. Would he still have had to complete the fourteen years ? or how much of them ? And to which of the delicts would he have been entitled to ascribe the portion that had passed ? If in the end of the seventh year he had been forgiven the statutory crime, he might have maintained that these seven had been suffered for the sedition, and that, as *some* period *must* have been intended for the pardoned offence, he could not have other seven to endure. But, on the other hand, the Crown might have argued that the past seven belonged to the Act of Parliament, and that other seven were still due to the common law.

In all such cases, doubts should be avoided by a specific appropriation of time to each delinquency, at least where they are of different sorts.

The prisoner (a weaver in Dundee) was transported, I believe, but I do not know his subsequent history. I was present—a lad in the gallery—when he received his sentence, and remember his parting speech at this hour.

XV.—Case of ANGUS CAMERON and JAMES MENZIES,
15th and 17th January 1798.[1]

THESE two persons were accused of sedition,
mobbing, and rioting.

The judges were Eskgrove, Craig, Dunsinnan,
and Methven.

The counsel for the prosecution were the Lord
Advocate (Dundas), the Solicitor-General (Blair),
and Mr. James Oswald, Advocate-Depute. The
last was younger of Dunnikier—an able man, who
died a few years afterwards.

The prisoners' counsel were John Clerk, James
Fergusson, and James Graham. Fergusson was
then, and continued through his whole life, which
extended till the year 1842, a steady but liberal
tory. He was one of the four judges in the Consistorial Court when it was abolished in 1830, and
died one of the Principal Clerks of Session. His
abilities were not inconsiderable; but for practical
purposes were made nearly useless by the greatest
Hibernianism of manner and of spirit that probably
any Scotchman was ever inspired by. He was a
general favourite, good-hearted, restless, social, and
hilarious; his blunders and absence kept Edinburgh
laughing for nearly half a century. Whatever else
people fought about, they all liked Jamie Fergusson.
James Graham was afterwards the author of " The
Sabbath " and other poems, and died an Episcopal

[1] *State Trials*, vol. xxvi. p. 1170.

clergyman in 1811. There never was a better man. Too good for the law, and indeed too benevolent for this world—the patron of birds, beggars, slaves, and of all beautiful or oppressed creatures, his poetical republicanism made it impossible for him to see anything but tyranny in any State prosecution. But he had no opportunity of letting off his amiable indignation on this occasion. For after appearing and pleading not guilty, and undergoing a debate on the relevancy, Cameron, who was the person chiefly aimed at, took advantage of an adjournment to escape, and was outlawed ; and the proceedings against Menzies were abandoned.

I only mention the case because the *word* sedition is sprinkled over the libel. It is said (*State Trials*, vol. xxvi. p. 1171) that the relevancy was sustained ; and I suppose, from the interlocutor, that this includes the relevancy of the charge of sedition. It is difficult to judge of any such matter without seeing the grounds on which the relevancy was attacked and defended—as to which there is no report ; but, looking merely at the indictment, I have great difficulty in discovering how the relevancy of this particular charge could be sustained, or where, indeed, except in a few casual and apparently meaningless words, the charge is even made.

The crime really meant to be prosecuted was that of mobbing and rioting, "*more especially* with the intent and purpose of violently opposing and resisting a public law ; " and the facts stated are, in substance, that the prisoners were active in a mob which resisted the execution of the statute for raising a militia in Scotland. It is a description of mere mobbing and rioting ; only the *terms* sedition and seditious are thrown in here and there, apparently at random. Thus the object of the mob is said to have been "illegal and seditious;" it is called a "riotous and seditious mob," a "wicked and seditious assembly;" where it is said that the prisoners "did utter many wicked and seditious speeches, tending to excite the people to attend a tumultuous assembly as aforesaid; thus endeavouring, as far as it lay in your power, to procure an illegal and seditious convocation of the lieges." But no facts are stated, no words are given, to sustain, or even to explain, the charge of sedition. It looks as if Burnett had merely told his clerk to put in the word sedition occasionally, where he could find room. I do not understand how a relevant charge can be made by a mere slight verbal garnishing.

XVI.—Case of ROBERT JAFFRAY, Stirling.
6th September 1798.

THIS case is not reported even in the *State Trials*, and there is only the usual meagre entries of the proceedings in the record.

The counsel are not named. Lord Methven was the judge.

The major proposition of the indictment states that "sedition, *as also* the uttering seditious speeches, *are crimes*," etc. He must have sharp eyes who can see a distinction between these two. The only fact set forth in the minor is, that the prisoner (a weaver), having been in a party at a public-house, had given, and twice repeated, as a toast, "The old dog's head cut off; the bitch hanged; and all the whelps drowned;" thereby meaning "death and destruction to the king, queen, and royal family." But in addition to this precise and most relevant fact, the framer of the libel was at the pains to assert that the prisoner "did further, time and place libelled, *as well as on other occasions*, behave and express himself in a manner *unbecoming a faithful and loyal subject*." In support of this general charge there is no circumstance whatever stated. The libel, however, was found relevant only "in so far as regards the *special act of sedition committed upon the evening libelled*."

Our practice at this period, and for long afterwards, was very odd. A plea of guilty did not supersede a verdict. It was only evidence, though evidence of a conclusive character. The prisoner was first asked if he was guilty or not. Even when he said guilty, a jury was empanelled, and then he was asked again, in presence of the jury, what he pleaded ? If he adhered to his plea of guilty, the jury then found him guilty " *in terms of his confession.*" This nonsense was admired and defended as one of the great bulwarks which it was Jacobinal to attempt to remove, for many years after this. Since the plea was only evidence, the friends of antiquated absurdities never could explain what they would do if a jury had chosen to acquit.

The prisoner pleaded not guilty, but (foolishly) admitted "that he gave the toast libelled, but without any criminal intention whatever." Instead of simply recording this as a plea of not guilty, the admission was taken down, and afterwards made a part of the prosecutor's evidence. The record bears that the prisoner's declaration was read, as "also the panel's admission upon reading the indictment, *which was again read over, and judicially adhered to by the panel, in presence of the court and jury.*" If the admission had been contained in the prisoner's defences, it would clearly have been liable to be used against him. But though nothing be more common than for prisoners to hurt themselves by injudicious additions to their plea of not guilty, I have never seen these slips taken advantage of; and asking, or even permitting a prisoner afterwards to commit himself to any such statement by subscribing it, in order that it may instantly be employed against him, was a proceeding which would scarcely be allowed now.

The jury " by a *plurality* of voices, find it proved

that the said Robert Jaffray, panel, proposed and repeated the toast libelled, *and with the meaning and intention libelled.*" They might as well have said guilty in plain terms; but the special facts which they find, necessarily imply this result. Mark the *plurality!* It was the first time that any portion of any Scotch jury was for acquitting any prisoner of any sedition.

He was sentenced to three months' imprisonment, and to keep the peace for one year, under the penalty of 100 merks Scots—apparently a very lenient punishment.

XVII.—Case of DAVID BLACK and JAMES PATER-
SON, Perth, 20th September 1798.[1]

THIS case was very similar to that of Mealmaker.
The indictment, in its major proposition, charges
sedition at common law, and a violation of the 37th
of Geo. III. cap. 123, against taking or administering unlawful oaths. The minor proposition sets
forth that the prisoners were active members of the
Society of United Scotsmen; that this was a seditious association; that at its meetings the prisoners
made speeches, which, " by inveighing against the
Government and Constitution of the country, did all
that in them (the prisoners) lay to excite and
increase a spirit of discontent, and ultimately of
resistance, to the established authorities;" that
they applauded and circulated Paine's *Rights of
Man* and *Age of Reason*, and "most *traitorously*"
expressed sorrow for the success of his Majesty's
arms, and joy at the existing rebellion in Ireland;
and that they took and administered a criminal
oath or engagement, binding each other to secrecy.
The material difference between this indictment
and Mealmaker's is, that in this one there is no
charge of sedition founded on the circulation of
unrecited and unknown pamphlets. Paine's works
had been often condemned already, and were therefore familiar to everybody.

The court was composed of Lords Dunsinnan

[1] *State Trials*, vol. xxvi. p. 1179.

and Swinton. Mr. John Anstruther was the Lord Advocate's Deputy, and he was assisted by Mr. Joseph M'Cormick, both of whom I knew well afterwards. M'Cormick's dulness made it almost unfair to class him among intelligent beings. Anstruther (of Ardie, in Fife) had been in the army, and with his grave visage, stiff manner, and thick queue, carried the appearance of an old major to a pretty advanced life. He was so entirely out of the legal profession that had I not seen his name on the record, I could not have supposed that he could ever have been either asked or disposed to conduct a prosecution. He afterwards became one of our commissaries, which means one of the judges of our consistorial court, a situation which supplied him with that store of extraordinary and indecorous anecdote, which, when safely set, he used to give out with a polite gravity of manner that made the exhibition more odd. He lived very retiredly, and was liked by the few friends he troubled himself with. The defence was conducted by Clerk and Hagart. Black, like a sensible man, let himself be outlawed for non-appearance.

The libel was found relevant as against Paterson, and indeed it does not appear that any objections were stated to it, nor am I aware that any could have been stated.

Neither the evidence nor any speeches are reported. (*State Trials*, vol. xxvi. p. 1179.) The jury unanimously acquitted the prisoner of the statutory offence, *and by a plurality* found him guilty of sedition at common law.

He was sentenced to five years' transportation.

The sentence repeated the blunder which had been noticed in parliament, and avoided in Mealmaker's case, of making the capital certification only apply to his returning illegally to *Great Britain*. (vol. xxvi. p. 1190.)

Both of the accused were common weavers, yet the jury that tried Paterson, *as picked*, contained no fewer than *eleven* landed gentlemen.

XVIII.—Case of WILLIAM MAXWELL, Edinburgh,
23d June 1800.[1]

THE judges present at this case were Eskgrove,
now Justice-Clerk, Dunsinnan, Craig, Methven, and
Cullen. The last had only been appointed to the
Justiciary, in the room of Swinton, a year before.
He was one of the sons of the great physician—an
able man, literary, and a respectable lawyer, with
rather elegant manners; but idle and dissipated,
tarnished by a disreputable marriage, and greatly
injured, in reference not merely to the bench but
to the higher departments of his profession as a
counsel, by what, nevertheless, was his peculiarity
and his attraction in social life—a power of mimicry
which all contemporary accounts concur in describing as unrivalled. I do not know that he stooped
to make faces and throw himself into postures; but
he could imitate the voices, the language, and the
sentiments of others with inconceivable success.

Among the prisoner's counsel there was one now
brilliant name—then a young man, who had only
put on his gown a few weeks before, and whose first
case this probably was. They were James Fergusson,
James Graham, and *Henry Brougham*.

The prisoner, lately a sergeant in the militia,
was one of the United Scotsmen; and his indictment,
in so far as it describes the constitution, means, and

1 From the Record, it not being reported, so far as I know.

objects of that society, is almost in the very identical words with that of Mealmaker. It states that sedition is a crime, and then quotes the statute against administering unlawful oaths ; and alleges that the prisoner is guilty " of all and each, or of one or other of the foresaid *crimes;* " in so far as he was an active member of the society, and administered certain criminal oaths or engagements to various persons, but particularly to soldiers under his influence ; and had distributed " a most wicked and seditious poem in your own handwriting, entituled A Catch."

The prisoner pleaded "guilty." He did not, in answering to the original question, whether he pleaded guilty or not, specify what he was guilty of, but pleaded "guilty" in general. This must be taken as a plea of guilty *to the whole libel*—that is, guilty of *both* offences. But this was made clearer when, according to the form of proceeding then in use, he repeated his plea before the jury. For, the jury being sworn, and " the panel being interrogated whether he was guilty or not guilty of the *crimes* charged in the indictment against him, he answered that he pleads guilty." The duty of the jury after this consisted in their finding him guilty in terms of his confession. But the fact is, that they only " all in one voice find the said William Maxwell, panel, guilty of the *crime* libelled, in respect of his judicial confession."

It is plain that their not convicting him of *both* crimes was a mere blunder. But, like other blunders, not committed by him, the prisoner was entitled to any benefit that could legally be got from it. What this benefit, if claimed, might have been, I do not say. But when a prisoner is accused of two offences, and only found guilty of one, without its being stated, in the written and unchangeable verdict, which one the jury mean, I should think that the objection of the verdict being void from uncertainty might be maintained as justly as it ever can be.

No objection, however, was stated either by counsel or by the judges, and the prisoner was transported for seven years.

XIX.—Case of THOMAS WILSON, Perth, 7th September 1802.[1]

THE prisoner was a weaver, and all his offences are described as being aggravated by his having also been a volunteer. This circumstance may appear to these who did not live at the time as too immaterial. But it must be recollected that the volunteers of those days not only took the oath of allegiance, but took the king's pay, and were intrusted with arms for the very purpose of repelling the king's enemies, and maintaining the royal safety and authority. One of the indirect objects and tendencies of the institution of these bodies of citizen soldiers was to wean the popular mind from French politics, and to interest them in the war and in the internal peace of the country. Hence all disloyalty in that quarter was peculiarly dangerous and offensive.

The prisoner was charged with " *sedition, or* the uttering and using of seditious language and sentiments, especially by any person serving under us in any volunteer corps," etc. I should think that, instead of thus setting forth a plurality of crimes in the major proposition, it would have been more like a skilful accuser to have charged sedition generally, and then to have explained in the minor that it was by the uttering of certain words that the sedition

[1] This case is not reported.

had been committed. But the Crown counsel at that period seem to have always been anxious to strike their key-note at the very outset, and to insinuate their leading facts into their first proclamation of the general charge. One effect of this was that it seems to have puzzled them to count the number of the offences which they themselves meant to set fórth. They sometimes announced only one crime, and then, because the annunciation of it was complicated with the facts, they concluded that the prisoner was guilty of the foresaid *crimes*. And on the other hand, the process was sometimes just reversed. On the present occasion the Depute Advocate seems to have been unusually distracted ; for he first proclaims that " sedition, or the uttering and using seditious language and sentiments, etc., *is a crime;*" and then he adds : " Yet true it is, and of verity, that the said Thomas Wilson, above complained upon, has presumed to commit, and is guilty, actor or art and part, of the foresaid crime *or crimes* aggravated as said is." The prisoner would not have been unreasonable if he had asked how many offences he was meant to be accused of.

He had been employed with several others in reaping the crop of John Miller, a farmer ; and his guilt consisted in his speaking sedition to his fellow-shearers. One of his sentiments was that he wished " that the overthrow of the British Constitution might take place, and hoped that the said John Miller might see it, and that he, the said Thomas Wilson, and his associates, would then be the proprietors of the said John Miller, his farm." Another of his iniquities, and a very great one unquestionably for a volunteer, was in saying, " that he trusted that Buonaparte and the French would soon be over, and bring about a revolution, and put all things to rights, and that he would immediately join them." And still worse was his sentiment in reference to the recent attempt by Hadfield upon the king's life. " He was sorry the king was not shot, and he could see his heart, or his heart's blood, on the point of his bayonet."

The judges were Eskgrove and Methven, the latter of whom tried the case. Mr. John H. Forbes, now a very respectable judge, was Advocate Depute. Hagart led the defence, assisted by another young man, who was just beginning that career of public virtue and of professional weight, which has since raised him to all the honours that the law can confer. This was James Moncreiff.

The prisoner pleaded not guilty. Evidence was led on both sides, and the jury, after being addressed by Forbes, Hagart, and Methven, unanimously found " the libel proven."

The sentence was a month's imprisonment, and banishment from *Scotland* for two years,—a serious infliction on a Scotch weaver, who had probably never been much beyond Strathmiglo, and was driven from his native country without money or a character ; but certainly not the least beyond what he deserved. Two years' banishment was better than two years' imprisonment, and nobody could have thought this too much.

OBSERVATIONS.

AFTER the case of *Wilson* in 1802, no charge of sedition was preferred, so far as I can ascertain, in Scotland till the year 1817.

There are some who describe this truce as the natural and blessed result of what they term the salutary examples which had rewarded the public accuser's first efforts in this department. These persons forget that, in a free country, opinions and their expression, which had formed the basis of the seditious matter in the more important of these first trials, are scarcely ever put down by punishment; and that though severity may operate through mere terror for a short season, it never prevents the ultimate progress of thought; nor, except by taking off a few troublesome individuals—which is only the convenience of the moment—ever permanently consolidates public tranquillity. How often are vast State prosecutions got up, which, whatever form or importance faction may assign to them, are in reality instituted for the suppression of doctrines dangerous to existing power, and end in the fall of some marked and perhaps spotless victim; and then the dignity and apparatus of the scene is scarcely closed, before reflecting men, even of the triumphing party, begin to observe that the show and the sacrifice might as well have been avoided; that it is the circumstances of the age that produce, and can alone allay, the appetite for innovation, and that a large portion of the blood which has been shed on the political scaffold might have been safely spared. It is not penal justice, still less penal cruelty, and least of all penal unfairness, that checks, or even averts, the movements of public opinion. These may embitter political opposition, and aggravate popular extravagance, but they rarely mitigate either.

It is a poor delusion, therefore, to suppose that the seditious spirit inspired by the French Revolution was extinguished by Braxfield and his transportations. It died away because the irritation provoked by these trials grew fainter, and because the times changed. Facts abated the admiration with which enthusiastic men had beheld the opening of the French drama, a war which gave Britain the commerce of the world, and drove distress for a season from her subjects ; terror of invasion united all ranks in defence of the country ; the prostration of the rest of Europe, contrasted with our independence, withdrew public attention from the consideration of the sacrifices by which this glory was purchased ; and the jealousy of even the popular parliamentary leaders was lulled by the fear of dimming our warlike splendour, in reference to abuses which, though destined to provoke discontent as soon as they should be discussed, were allowed, as if by unanimous agreement, to accumulate round every part of our system in the meantime. These, and not the terrors of criminal law, were the causes of the fifteen years' quiet which succeeded the judicial paroxysm that began in 1793.

And what produced the second attack in 1817 ? Certainly not the oblivion of the old transportations.

But the cessation of a twenty years' war gave a temporary shock to all our foreign relations, and disturbed every internal arrangement. This mercantile paralysis might have soon passed off, if the general system had been sound. But it was aggravated by many collateral misfortunes, tending strongly towards the growth of discontent—such as bad seasons, the personal unpopularity of the Prince Regent, and the frightful condition of Ireland. A new generation, too, had come into public action, which had no personal recollection of the French Revolution, and on whom the intimation of its horrors, which they had too long heard as the objection to every right measure, had ceased to have much effect. As soon as peace—that distant event for the arrival of which every reform had been adjourned—lifted up the flood-gates of discussion, it soon appeared that beneath the surface of our long course of warlike self-satisfaction an under-current of new opinions, all pointing towards free inquiry, resolute reform, and complete toleration, had been setting in, and was already so strong that the old possessors of power were startled, and saw that they could no longer resist by merely appealing to their parliamentary majorities.

In the midst of this combination of popular suffering and encroaching claim, a new element arose, which operated as a proximate cause of discontent to an extent which those who only live since economy has become the first ministerial virtue cannot conceive. The recent contest had required rivers of gold and clouds of public officers. It was impossible to reduce the war establishment and its consequent taxation at once ; but much irritation might have been avoided if the people had

had reason to believe that Government was really sincere in reducing it gradually. But ministers, naturally desirous to prolong the means of influence, yielded no economical claim without a struggle. Hence the exposition of the public extravagance formed one of the easiest, and by far the most effectual, of all the topics for exciting the anger of the people, who were readily persuaded by hunger to ascribe their privations to the folly or oppression of their rulers.

These circumstances revived scenes new to the young, but which reminded the old of the days of 1793—great meetings in the open air, violent petitions, crazy projects, new restrictive laws on the expression of opinions, the burning of machinery, outrageous loyalty, popular excesses, lecturing demagogues, wild theories of government, universal excitement. Public fever implies hot thoughts and hot words, and a state of mind very unfit for the dispassionate appreciation of party motives or actions. Yet, as it is only in seasons of excitement that political excesses are committed, these are, unfortunately, the principal occasions on which the great duty of candour has to be performed by courts. Hence the wisdom of abstaining from political prosecutions, while there is any hope that the danger to be repressed may evaporate of itself. Slightness in the cases tried is sufficient proof that the trials were unnecessary. Tested by this rule, there can be little doubt that it would have been wise not to have instituted the second series of prosecutions for sedition, which began in 1817.

By this time the old criminal judges were all gone. Their seats were now occupied by David

Boyle, Lord Justice-Clerk; George Fergusson, Lord Hermand; Archibald Campbell, Lord Succoth; Adam Gillies, Lord Gillies; David Monypenny, Lord Pitmilly; and David Douglas, Lord Reston. These were all excellent men. And they had all the advantage of acting in an age which, though violent enough, would not have tolerated the indecorum of some of their predecessors. What they might have been in 1794, when moderation was hated by their party, it would be needless to conjecture. The ineffaceable misfortune of them all, except Gillies, was, that their public taste had been formed under the influence and for the service of the old tory party, which still domineered. Their whole views and feelings were tinged with the colour derived from this unfavourable source. Among other dogmas, Hume was their idol in criminal law; Braxfield, and the year 1794, was to them the golden age of Scotch penal jurisprudence.

In spite of this bad education, Boyle, the head of the court, has always been a laborious, honest judge—with considerable defects, but these redeemed by the greatest of all judicial virtues, an exclusive ambition to do his duty, and the constant prevalence of the feelings of a gentleman. Friends may have lamented his prejudices, or smiled at his manner; but no enemy ever suspected his integrity, or his intended candour. He is a judge on whose honour the public had perfect reliance, even in the most violent times, and from whom his own party might always despair of obtaining any advantage which was only to be gained by his doing what he thought wrong.

Hermand, the son of Kilkerran, was greatly senior to his brethren, and of the real old school, a school prior even to the French Revolution—the most original and picturesque of men.

Gillies was the person who had distinguished himself as Gerrald's counsel. Clearly the ablest man, he was by no means the best judge, in the court. His whig principles had not yet been abandoned, and he was the first of that faith who had been raised to the bench by a tory Government—an exception which he owed to his reputation for law, and the kindness of the Lord President Hope.

Pitmilly had recently been Solicitor-General, a sensible lawyer, with a beautifully cold, still, judge-like air and tone.

Succoth, who was beneath them all in professional reputation, was the son of Sir Ilay Campbell —a slow, dull judge, but a hospitable gentleman, and profound in the science of gastronomy.

Reston was the nephew of Adam Smith, an excellent, hard-working, inky lawyer, who had been put on the criminal bench in 1816, without, I believe, having ever been engaged in a single criminal trial, or perhaps ever seeing one from beginning to end—a fact which made him so helpless and wretched that he used to say he envied the prisoners.

Alexander Maconochie (afterwards Lord Meadowbank the second) had become Lord Advocate, and James Wedderburn (who died in 1822), Solicitor-General. Even though they had been judicious and popular, the period at which they were called into public action would have greatly impaired their chance of success. For Scotland was beginning to open its eyes, and the time was rapidly advancing when the old hereditary system, beyond which they had no ideas, could not work as it used to do.

XX.—Case of ALEXANDER M'LAREN and THOMAS
BAIRD, 5th and 7th March 1817.[1]

THIS case was reported soon after the trial
by Mr. Dow, shorthand writer in Edinburgh. The
speeches, I believe, were all revised by the speakers,
and I can attest the general accuracy of the report.
All the judges were present except Succoth.
The prosecution was conducted by the Lord
Advocate (Maconochie), the Solicitor-General (Wedderburn), Henry Home Drummond, and James
Maconochie, advocates-depute.
John Clerk, John Peter Grant of Rothiemurchus,
now one of the Supreme Judges at Calcutta, and
James Campbell, now of Craigie, were counsel for
M'Laren; Jeffrey, John Shaw Stewart, and myself
for Baird.
The indictment charged sedition, and nothing
else.
The facts set forth were, that there having been
a public meeting at Kilmarnock, M'Laren, a weaver,
made a speech there; that Baird, a merchant (*i.e.*
shopkeeper) there, published this speech, and that
both the speech and the publication were spoken
and published "*wickedly and feloniously,*" and were
"calculated *to degrade and bring into contempt the
Government and Legislature, and to withdraw therefrom the confidence and affections of the people, and
to fill the realm with trouble and dissension.*" No

circumstances whatever, external to the words used, were set forth as tending to establish either the guilty meaning of the language, or the guilty intention with which it was employed. The worst passages were quoted. In his address to the jury the Lord Advocate referred to others ; but it may always be assumed, and accordingly it is the fact here, that if there be no sedition in what is recited, there is none in the garnishing which the prosecutor keeps back.

A short statement was made for each prisoner explanatory of the defence, which consisted partly in denying the use of the words charged, and still more in maintaining that, when fairly interpreted, they were not criminal, and that, at any rate, being used in the course of exercising the constitutional privilege of petitioning the Regent and parliament, every tolerance necessary for the free exposition of honestly believed grievances must be conceded.

The libel was not objected to, and the court found it relevant. Gillies was the only judge, however, who struck the correct tone in disposing of relevancy in such a case. He gave no opinion as to the meaning or design of any of the passages, which he held were matters solely for the jury ; but went solely on the fact that *the prosecutor asserted, and officially offered to prove,* that the speech and the pamphlet were calculated to fill the realm with trouble and dissension, and were spoken and published wickedly and feloniously. None of the rest inflamed themselves or the jury by premature positive demonstrations of the dreadful iniquity of the words, and of the prisoners, according to the judicial fashion twenty-three years before. But still they did not avoid this mistake *entirely*. Each of them brought forward the passage which attracted his fancy, and commented upon its probable guilt, not perceiving that this was just anticipating the evidence. In general, however, it was done gently, and conditionally. The correct Pitmilly went furthest wrong when he said, " *no person who reads them can doubt* that the general nature of them is to excite commotion, and to prepare the way for resistance, and for overturning the Government. That this is the general tendency of the facts charged *no person can doubt.*" (vol. xxxiii. p. 15.) The Lord Justice-Clerk said nothing, except that he thought the libel relevant, being all that was required.

Boyle was always a fair picker—as fair as that operation admitted of. The great predominance of tories in the box was not his fault, but the necessary result of the disproportion between the two parties in the country. The same circumstance might have saved the judicial character of Braxfield from one of its deepest imputations, had it not been that he selected the known *zealots* of his party, so grossly, as to defy charity to suspect him of impartiality.

It is needless to give any account of the evidence. Its object was merely to ascertain whether the one prisoner had spoken, and the other had published, the words ascribed to them respectively. The prisoners, acting by the advice of their counsel, disputed these facts ; but ineffectually. The proof established them satisfactorily.

In this situation the real question, as usual, was as to the true import of the language, and the intention with which it had been used. On these points there was no evidence except the language itself.

Now, the words charged against the weaver

were that in his oration he had said :—" That our sufferings are insupportable is demonstrated to the world ; and that they are neither temporary nor occasioned by a transition from war to peace is palpable to all, though all have not the courage to avow it. The fact is, we are ruled by men only solicitous for their own aggrandisement ; and they care no further for the great body of the people than (as) they are subservient to their accursed purposes. If you are convinced of this, my countrymen, I would therefore put the question—Shall we, whose forefathers at the never-to-be-forgotten field of Bannockburn, told the mighty Edward, at the head of the most mighty army that ever trod on Britain's soil, ' Hitherto shalt thou come, and no further,'—shall we, I say, whose forefathers defied the efforts of foreign tyranny to enslave our beloved country, meanly permit, in our day, without a murmur, a base oligarchy to feed their filthy vermin on our vitals, and rule us as they will ? No, my countrymen ! Let us lay our petitions at the foot of the throne, where sits our august prince, whose gracious nature will incline his ear to listen to the cries of his people, which he is bound to do by the laws of his country. But should he be so infatuated as to turn a deaf ear to their just petition, he has forfeited their allegiance. Yes, my fellow-townsmen, in such a case, to hell with our allegiance ! "

The prisoner's counsel made an effort to show that these last words only meant that if the prince should refuse to accede to the *just* petitions of his *whole* people, a case for lawful resistance would arise ; and that, *as thus put and qualified*, the statement was constitutionally correct. But this

was plainly a gloss which the circumstances could
not support. The actual sentiment was that
unless the Regent should grant the prayer of *this*
Kilmarnock petition, the patriots of that place
should renounce their allegiance. This was clearly
sedition. But it seems to me to be the only material
sedition in the harangue. All the rest is mere
general eloquence. And accordingly, though each
critic nibbled at his own bit, none of them made a
decent morsel out of it. *Lord Reston*, the worthiest
of men, and in matters political the most prejudiced, whose visage, at its best, was sufficiently
rueful, dwelt, with a face of horror which made the
audience laugh, on "*the base oligarchy, which fed
their filthy vermin on our vitals*"! The *Lord Advocate* laboured to extract an invitation to arms out
of the appeal to Bannockburn. And the *rulers*,
who care nothing for the people except for their
own accursed purposes, were argued to be not the
ministers, but the constituted authorities. And,
no doubt, it was possible for an honest jury to
deduce guilt from these extravagances. But was
it not also possible for such a jury to put a
construction upon them quite consistent with innocence, though not with moderation, or with the
caution of a practised speaker? It is certain that
the speech was addressed to a meeting, not *pre-
tending* to petition, but truly assembled for that
purpose ; and it was further admitted by the Lord
Advocate (p. 71) that "at the time when all this
took place the distresses of the country were not
only great, but that *the misery of the lower classes
of the people had reached an extent seldom experienced in these realms.*" To be sure, the use he

makes of this fact is to argue that starvation made inflammatory harangues more dangerous. And so it always does. But how ? By making the people more easily excited—a circumstance which might fairly enough be made to operate against the wilful mischievousness of a well-fed demagogue ; but it surely diminishes the necessity of ascribing the flights of a hungry orator to anything so intellectual as sedition.[1]

The sentiments charged against Baird, who published a report of the speech, but with passages which, though probably spoken, were not traced by evidence to have been so, and are therefore only charged as against him, were not materially different from those proved against M'Laren. He represented the speaker as having said that ministers and the House of Commons had beggared the nation, and narrowed its liberties, and therefore the former—but only as ministers—were oppressors ; and that the latter only represented the people nominally. It was conceded that, *if these were the sentiments*, there was nothing criminal or new in them. And if calling the representation nominal were excusable in any one, it surely might be pardoned in a Scotchman, in whose country the representation was then a mere mockery. But the prosecutor denied that the language admitted of this construction. He maintained that our *rulers* meant the government by King, Lords, and Commons ; and that the statement about the nominality of the representation amounted to a denial that *in law* there was any representation. Therefore, said his Lordship, the prisoner was not exer-

---

[1] M'Laren states in his declaration that he had been working fifteen hours daily for five shillings a week.

cising the privilege of complaining and petitioning, but making a pretence of it to excite disaffection. Which of these views is correct must depend upon the words, which, *as given in the indictment,* were as follows :—

" . . . And a House of Commons, but the latter is corrupted ; it is decayed and worn out ; it is not really what it is called—it is not a House of Commons." " The House of Commons, in its original composition, consisted only of Commoners, chosen annually by the universal suffrage of the people. No nobleman, no clergyman, no naval or military officer—in short, none who held places or received pensions from Government, had any right to sit in that House. This is what the House of Commons was, what it ought to be, and what we wish it to be ; this is the wanted change in our form of government—the House of Commons restored to its original purity ; and this, beyond a doubt, would strike at the root of the greatest part of the evils we groan under at the present day." " Is it any wonder, my friends, that this country is brought to its present unprecedented state of misery, when the rights of the people have been thus wantonly violated ?" " But let us come nearer home. Look at the year 1793, when the debt amounted to two hundred and eleven millions, and the annual taxation to about eighteen millions ; when liberty began to rear her drooping head in the country ; when associations were formed from one end of the kingdom to the other, composed of men eminent for their talents and virtues, to assert their rights ; when a neighbouring nation had just thrown off a yoke which was become intolerable ; what did the wise rulers of this country do ? Why, they

declared war not only against the French nation,
but also against the friends of liberty at home."
" Our oppressors have taxed the very light of
heaven, and they seem surprised and indignant
that we should not bear the insupportable burden
with which folly, corruption, and avarice have
loaded us, without reluctance and complaint."
" Their *reverend* hirelings would convince you that
you are suffering under the visitation of the Al-
mighty, and therefore ought to be submissive under
the chastening stroke."   " We have these twenty-
five years been condemned to incessant and un-
paralleled slavery by a usurped oligarchy, who
pretend to be our guardians and representatives,
while in fact they are nothing but our inflexible
and determined enemies."   " They have robbed us
of our money, deprived us of our friends, violated
our rights, and abused our privileges."   " At present we have no representatives ; they are only
nominal, not real ; active only in prosecuting their
own designs, and at the same time telling us that
they are agreeable to our wishes."

There is some of this trash which no man in
his senses will think seditious. But, on the other
hand, there is much of it to which a fair and
sensible man will find it difficult to ascribe any
other character. However, it forms but a weak
case of sedition at the worst. It is a mere passionate description, by a poor and excited man, of
what he thought the history of the constitution of
the House of Commons, and of his view of the past
conduct of the tory party. It is one of the examples
of the sedition which consists in mere raving intensity. There is not a statement or sentiment which
a cautious speaker or writer could not utter with

the most absolute impunity. It was a seditious *manner.* A passionate *tone* is always calculated to excite ; and it is good evidence of a desire to do so. Sedition is apt to be eloquent, because sometimes it is only eloquence that can be seditious. The Lord Advocate made a respectable address to the jury—of course giving every sentence and word a turn to justify his charge; but everything done in a good-natured, moderate, fair tone. He tried his hand at a definition, and, which is easier, at an explanation, of sedition : with what success may be judged of from this, that he laid it down (p. 58) that every speech or writing asserting of the House of Commons " *that it has become* COR- RUPT " was seditious ! He read to the jury the papers for which Palmer had been convicted, and argued that his address was not nearly so criminal as the present prisoner's. And neither it was. But his Lordship's error consisted in his assuming the fact of Palmer's conviction to be moral evidence of his guilt. This was a rash proceeding, moreover, for a prosecutor, because if it be competent to him to refer to cases of analogous conviction, it must be equally competent for prisoners to refer to analogous acquittals, and still more to analogous publications, which, though quite notorious, were never even accused—a competition which public prosecutors had better avoid.

John Clerk, who, though always powerful, had a manner which made him least in his element when before a jury, addressed a view of his client's case to them, which was full of strong matter, not im- pressively put. The most effective part of it was in the use he made of the fact that the language objected to was uttered at a meeting held for petitioning, the same circumstance of which he made such use twenty-three years before in defending Palmer. Jeffrey's speech for Baird was of the highest order of excellence. There has been no such speech in such a case in Scotland. Gerrald's derived much of its melancholy interest from the accidents of his personal condition—his character, his health, and his obviously fatal doom. Laing and Gillies spoke in that trial at an awkward stage of the proceedings, which did not admit of a full and complex view being taken of the facts and of the law. Jeffrey discussed, both in the most masterly manner, expounding the great principle of the necessity of a *guilty intention*, illustrating and enforcing the exemption from criminal prosecution on slight grounds, which is implied as one of the practical consequences of the right of arraigning public men and public measures, and of petitioning, and discussing the propriety of petitioning, for the redress of supposed grievances ; applying these views to the circumstances of the case ; and pouring into every part of his argument the political and constitutional wisdom of his singularly rich and intelligent mind. *As heard*, this speeeh was an honour to the bar.

There was one part, both of his address and of Clerk's, which it is very material to explain. The Lord Advocate had referred, not merely to Palmer's case, but to all the old trials. This forced the counsel for the prisoners to attempt to reconcile the acquittals which they demanded for their clients with the convictions in 1793 and 1794. The real opinions of Clerk and Jeffrey as to these convictions have been too often stated, both in public and in private, to admit of any doubt. They considered them as disgraceful to the times and to the court. But it would have been very dangerous, for the interests at present committed to their charge, to have openly stated their sentiments, and denounced the former trials as unfairly conducted, or the sentences as illegal. They had no other course, therefore, than to *appear* to palliate the convictions, by aggravating the circumstances, and thus to make these cases *contrast* with the slightness of those they had now to deal with. But this was merely the professional policy of counsel. Muir's case, however, was too bad to be spoken of except sincerely ; and Jeffrey stated distinctly that he had been convicted contrary to evidence, and punished contrary to propriety.

The Lord Justice-Clerk Boyle is always read better than he is heard. His speaking manner spoils his matter. But his summing up on this occasion, even when listened to, was a refreshment to those who remembered Braxfield or Eskgrove. It was a judicial charge. He did not assume that the jurors' minds were made up, but explained the facts to them fully and accurately, in order that they might draw the proper conclusion. He impressed upon them the subjects' right to complain and to petition ; that in law a conviction could not be warranted unless they were satisfied both of the dangerous tendency of the language, and of its having been employed with the wickedness of intention to which it was imputed by the prosecutor ; and that, in judging of these, they were bound to put the mildest construction on every word and on every fact that was reasonable. Braxfield could have used all these phrases, and would have used them, if any friend had suggested to him that it would increase his facility of obtaining convictions. But he could not, and would not, have used them, as Boyle did, *sincerely*, and with both a genuine and an apparent anxiety that the jury should honestly act upon them. Boyle leaned against the accused, but not more than fair conviction must compel any judge, whose duty it is, indirectly, to correct the more misleading fallacies of any skilful counsel for prisoners, by whom he has been immediately preceded.

I lament, however, being obliged to say that he committed himself, quite unnecessarily, to an admiration of what had been done in the former cases. " This is the first trial for sedition that has occurred for a considerable length of time ; and I can assure the learned gentlemen that I had fondly flattered myself that even at my time of life I should not have again had occasion to apply my mind to the study of this part of the law. I hoped and trusted, that after the CLEAR *exposition of the law* in 1793, 1794, and 1795, in the different prosecutions which were then found necessary, *sanctioned and approved of by the unanimous voice of the country*, I should not have been obliged to consider cases of this description." (p. 133.) He need not have said this ; and he should not have thought it. The compliment to the former cases was nonsensical, and is one of the things which have made it impossible for those who differ from him to let those cases, thus revived, sleep in oblivion.

The jury convicted M'Laren by a majority, and Baird unanimously ; and unanimously recommended both to the clemency of the court, in consequence of their good characters. The reason of the division of the jury in favour of M'Laren was not explained, and it is not easy to conjecture it. But it was understood to be, that he had sinned from the excitement of misery and of oratory, whereas Baird, who was in comfortable circumstances, had circulated the poison by deliberate subsequent publication.

The verdict found the prisoners guilty " of the *crimes* libelled in the indictment." The obvious error, which had occurred in almost every one of the cases, of convicting of a plurality of crimes where only one was charged, was at last objected to. But the court held it to be immaterial. " The mere slip of a letter cannot be considered as a substantial objection in this case." (p. 144.) The judgment may be right, but the reason is clearly wrong. Many slips, of many single letters, would certainly be fatal to many written verdicts. The precedent of the former verdicts would have been a better answer. But nobody thought of them.

The sentence was six months' imprisonment, with security for good behaviour for three years,— an adequate, but not a severe, infliction.

In proposing this punishment, *Hermand* gave the following honest and graphic account of the effect of Jeffrey's speech upon him :—" I am the more impressed with a sense of the merits of this verdict, that when, in groping my way, about eleven o'clock at night, in the dark streets of this city, and reflecting with myself what verdict I should have given had I been a juryman in this case, such was the effect of a blaze of eloquence that I cannot say whether I should have said yes or no, if I had been at that time obliged to give an opinion whether or not the prisoners were guilty. Like the jury, I should have wished to have been enclosed for consideration. But having bestowed it, any doubt disappeared, and I came to the opinion that the relevancy of the indictment was clear, and the facts completely proved.

He adds : " *Every word, every letter*, of this indictment has now been found proved ; " and this is not an uncommon inference to be drawn from general verdicts of guilty. But it is undoubtedly an unwarranted one. The jury only did, and only could, convict of what was charged, viz., sedition. The words and letters are only the evidence of this crime. It might be satisfactory if verdicts in such cases could state the precise facts in which the sedition consisted. But this is impossible. Juries cannot winnow pamphlets, and separate the chaff from the grain, in their deliverances to the court. All that they mean to say, therefore, by a verdict of guilty, is, that, *on the whole*, the general charge is established. There are several detached letters, and words, and sentences, in this unlucky speech, which no jury, consistently with its own sanity, could mean to condemn. Accordingly they do not convict of the *facts*, but of the *crime* libelled ; though, no doubt, they must be held to have convicted of the crime *as libelled, i.e.* of the crime *as composed of the facts set forth.* But then, when a jury thinks that *enough* of these facts is proved to warrant a conviction, are they obliged, or ought they, to *except* the rest, which they think not proved, from their verdict ?

Lord Gillies merely approved of the punishment proposed. But all the other judges, while they concurred — which exhausted the matter before them—went rather out of their way to give their opinions that transportation was a lawful, and even a proper, penalty for sedition. *Reston* had " no

doubt either of the *right,* or the *duty,* of the court"
to transport. (p. 148.) *Pitmilly* declared transportation to be " the *proper* punishment, in aggravated
cases, such as the old ones." And, for such cases,
the Justice gave it as his " clear and *unalterable*
opinion" that transportation was " the proper, the
legitimate, the NECESSARY punishment." (p. 140.)
These were unnecessary, and therefore rash,
declarations.

On the whole, however, this was a satisfactory
trial. It was perhaps the first perfectly fair trial
for sedition that Scotland had ever seen. Would
that the court had not tarnished its laurels in a
subsequent case !

XXI.—Case of Neil Douglas, Edinburgh, 26th May 1817.[1]

This prisoner had been a member, in the old time, of the British Convention, and active in its proceedings. He was now a clergyman belonging to the sect called Universalists—old, deaf, dogged, honest, and respectable.

The Lord Justice-Clerk (Boyle), Hermand, Gillies, Pitmilly, and Reston were the judges present.

The Solicitor-General (Wedderburn), H. Drummond Home, and James Maconochie (brother of the Lord Advocate), conducted the prosecution; Jeffrey, Grant, John Murray, and myself, the defence.

Sedition was the crime charged; and the general assertion was that the prisoner had, in the course of various *"prayers, sermons, and declamations"* from his pulpit, spoken criminally of the king, who was then afflicted with mental derangement, the Regent, parliament, and the judges. The particular facts were that the prisoner did "assert and draw a parallel between his Majesty and Nebuchadnezzar, King of Babylon, remarking and insinuating that, like the said King of Babylon, his Majesty was driven from the society of men for infidelity and corruption;" that he asserted "that his Royal Highness the Prince Regent was a poor

[1] *State Trials*, vol. xxxiii. p. 633.

infatuated wretch, or a poor infatuated devotee of Bacchus;" that he "drew a parallel between his Royal Highness the Prince Regent and Belshazzar, King of Babylon, remarking and insinuating that his Royal Highness, like the said King of Babylon, had not taken warning from the example of his father, and that a fate similar to that of the said King of Babylon awaited his Royal Highness, if he did not amend his ways, and listen to the voice of his people;" that he had asserted "that the House of Commons was corrupt, and that the members thereof were thieves and robbers, and that seats in the said House of Parliament were sold like bullocks in a market;" "that the laws were not justly administered within this kingdom, and that the subjects of his Majesty were condemned without trial and without evidence."

Every part of these charges was clearly relevant; and so it was found, without any objection being stated. But it was well known, and indeed not disguised at the trial, that the real thing intended to be repressed was the very prevalent practice of abusing the unpopular and luxurious Regent for his personal habits.

There probably never was a prosecution depending on the proof of spoken words which so signally failed.

The prosecutor examined seven witnesses. Now,

1st. Of these, two were common town officers, who had been sent by the magistrates to the place of worship for the very purpose of detecting sedition. (*State Trials*, vol. xxxiii. pp. 649 and 651, Alexander Taylor and John Maccallum.) Had these men been ever so honest, accurate, and full in their reports, they were, from their position, incredible. What could be expected of such fellows, but that they should please their masters by finding what they were sent to seek ?

2dly. The preacher was so exceedingly rapid and indistinct in his utterance that it was very difficult to understand him. There is not a single witness who does not state this fact, or who does not use it as his apology for being able to report so little.

3dly. Hence not one of them pretends to give his exact words. Though all agree that the prisoner spoke of Nebuchadnezzar and Belshazzar—as how could he help it, since he was preaching on their scriptural history?—and though they had all a notion that, in his application of the text he had not been tender of kings, none of them could enable the jury to judge of his meaning by giving either his expressions or even the substance of them. The most sensible man among them was James Waddell, a surgeon, and he first gives only his *" impressions ; "* and when asked by the court to state the words, he says that he cannot, and *" I could not say with certainty that I do remember the* SUBSTANCE *"* (vol. xxxiii. p. 647) ; and when asked whether a comparison which " strikes me *just now* " was or was not the prisoner's meaning, his answer is, *" I did not say so.* It is the meaning that *I attached to them "* (p. 646), though he " had *no doubt* that it was the prisoner's meaning also."

In addition to this, the prosecutor founded on the prisoner's declarations, where he denied all that was ascribed to him in the indictment, but had no hesitation in making an honest and undisguised statement of his political conduct and creed. It is impossible (for me at least) not to admire the plainness with which this ancient and poor reformer stands up against his enemies. He seems to have had a pleasure in alarming and defying them. " He does not consider that the battle of Waterloo was a matter of rejoicing, but on the contrary." " And the following he begs may be taken down as a part of his declaration, and that it may reach the ears of the rulers of this nation :—That his Royal Highness has more to apprehend from the measures of his official servants than from the madness of his people; which expression, as to the madness of the people, is used in the prayers of the Church of England as to the recent escape of his Royal Highness, as the declarant thinks, with great impropriety."

No Crown prosecution should have been hazarded on such evidence. Even if it had stood uncontradicted, no sensible or honest jury could have convicted upon it.

But it was blown to pieces, and the whole accusation trampled upon, by the proof in defence. Six witnesses were examined for the prisoner, and more were tendered, but the court thought them unnecessary. The import of what these six swore was that the prisoner, though an avowed and hoary reformer, was a loyal man, always praying for the king and the royal family more fervently than most of the established clergy did; that his very first sermon, after a recent trial and conviction of his son for swindling, contained an encomium on the fairness of the trial, and on our administration of justice ; that he did not go out of his way to get at this story of the Babylonian kings, but had been lecturing on Daniel for about two years, and took this passage in its regular turn ; that neither the expressions nor the sentiments ascribed to him had been uttered ; that he spoke only of kings, sins, and visitations of Providence in general, making only the usual scriptural application of the passage ; and that, on the whole, it was an orthodox and loyal discourse.

There was a palpable defect in the prosecutor's proof which the counsel for the prisoner thought it safer for their client not to notice. There was *no evidence whatever* of the fact that his Majesty was deranged, though it was solely upon this fact that the whole sedition, consisting in the comparison of him to Nebuchadnezzar, depended. The law presumes that kings do right, and therefore no evidence could be admitted of the profligacy of the Regent. But the law does not presume kings to be exempt from bad health ; and it was clearly the prosecutor's duty, since he founded on the fact of insanity, to establish it; and, whatever the advisers of the prisoner might think it most prudent for them to do, was it not a slip in the court not to notice the failure ?

After the evidence was closed, Wedderburn, who, though honourable, and in private life not unamiable, was in all public matters a singularly grim, formal, and bitter young man, rose and made a very paltry appearance. Seeing that he had no case, either in evidence or in truth, his plain course was to have abandoned the prosecution gracefully, by consenting to a verdict of not guilty. But instead of this, he lingered over his own refuted evidence, and indulged in a strain of harsh and unwarranted remarks upon the professional habits of the prisoner; and all this in order that, *in a Crown prosecution for a political offence,* his pride in losing his case might be soothed by a verdict of *not proven,* which in our practice is deemed a less honourable acquittal than a verdict of not guilty.

He admits (vol. xxxiii. p. 674) that as to the charge of slandering the administration of justice, "there has been no evidence brought before you." And even as to the other two charges of maligning the king and the House of Commons, though he professes to think his own proof sufficient, he says, even as to these, "at the same time I must observe that the evidence on the part of the Crown falls *far* short of what I expected to have laid before you." (p. 674.) These facts seem to make the prisoner not very unreasonable in thinking that he had a right to be found not guilty. But the Solicitor phrases away about "the functions of clergymen being the *most* important in civil society," and about the rare and horrid iniquity of their introducing political allusions into their sermons. "It is just as *possible* in this indirect manner, by reference to particular portions of Scripture history, to utter libellous or seditious matter, as by the most direct words which language affords. There is no blasphemy or sedition, how abominable and atrocious soever, that *may* not in this form be spread about." (p. 674.)

The way in which he applies these canons of clerical propriety to the case in hand is this : "on the supposition that full credit is due to the witnesses on both sides, there are *some charges made out* against the panel, which render his conduct highly criminal, which establish against him *a very great malversation of duty*, and which bring home to him a *criminality not to be distinguished from sedition.* It is proved by all the witnesses for the Crown ; it is proved by those witnesses for the panel to whom any credit is due ; it is proved by his own declarations, which cannot be read without

pity for his folly, and *indignation for his impiety*
[!!], that he is A POLITICAL PREACHER [!!!] To all
who have paid attention to the progress of this trial
it must be clear that he has been in the habit of
arraigning, in his discourses, the measures of Government, and *of infusing among his hearers political
dissatisfaction.*" (p. 675.)

This ascetic vituperation is all disposed of by
three facts. In the *first* place, this habit was *not*
proved. It was proved that, like other clergymen,
the prisoner occasionally alluded to, or commented
upon, passing events—not that he did so for the
purpose of creating political discontent, but rather
the reverse. In the *second* place, he was not upon
trial for his general habits, or for the crime of
political preaching, but on three specific charges of
a different description; and therefore it was irrelevant and unhandsome in his official accuser, even
to refer to any other matters, though they should
happen to be, in his opinion, not distinguishable
from sedition. They were not the sedition charged.
In the *third* place, however improper political preaching may be, did any of the Solicitor's party ever
object to it when it proceeded in the form of
addresses on their side from the Established
Church ?

But, to be sure, the prosecutor guards himself
on this last point by an ingenious exception. It
may not be absolutely commendable in the Established clergy to preach politics; but it is infinitely
worse in a dissenter! "In a sectarian, like the
panel, it is more dangerous, *because he is liable to
no ecclesiastical superintendence and jurisdiction.*"
Where he learned this fact I do not know; but it
impresses him so strongly that he is rather for root-

ing the dissenters out by persecution. His next sentence is : " Such conduct, indeed, *might lead to doubts as to the expediency of that unlimited toleration which the benignity of our Constitution confers.* In the one case or in the other, I repeat it, it is a prostitution of *one of the most important duties of civil society.*" (vol. xxxiii. p. 675.) His inference from this is, " that a *general* criminality characterises his conduct in these respects, no man can doubt." (p. 675.) It was not for general criminality that he was on trial. " But besides all this the evidence of particular offence *is not slight.*" This is coming to the point.

His first example of this is in the case of the comparison of the king to Nebuchadnezzar. He admits that the exact extent of the comparison was not established even by his own witnesses, and that its guilt was utterly disproved by the witnesses for the defence. He gets out of all difficulty however thus : " But I do affirm that it was impossible to draw *any* parallel ; that it was impossible to allege a *single* point of resemblance between his most sacred Majesty and the personage mentioned in Scripture without seditious criminality. Whether the cause, nature, or duration of that awful infirmity be referred to, it was *impossible,* without *criminality, even in the most remote degree,* to *insinuate* the resemblance or parallel." (p. 676.) Was the assertion of the fact that, in both cases, it was " for the sins *of the nation* that the Head had been afflicted " (see *Evidence of Will. Warrell,* p. 664), seditious ? or that they were both kings ?

The next, and last, example is in the case of his saying that the House of Commons was corrupt, and that its seats were sold. The fact was that the

prisoner had made no assertions of his own on these
subjects, but had merely referred to the parliamentary proceedings to show that such things were
there said. Wedderburn acknowledges this to be
the fact. But, says he, "there are many things
reported to be declaimed upon within the walls of
parliament which would be sedition if uttered anywhere else." (p. 676.) No doubt of it. But would
any prudent—I might almost say sane—public
prosecutor ever think of founding a charge of sedition on a person's having repeated *this* statement,
viz., that in the year 1817 seats in the House of
Commons were bought ?

The result of this canting harangue is curious.
He repeats that his case has failed. " I am satisfied that the proof has fallen short of what I expected
at the institution of this trial." " On the whole, *I
am clear* that the evidence is not such as to be
pressed on a jury." (p. 676.) Well, what is his
conclusion ? " I submit to you that, while a verdict of not guilty *cannot be reconciled with the evidence*, the proper return for you to give is that of
Not proven." [! ! !]

I remember, even at the present hour, the indignation with which this wretched address was listened to by all of us, and how shabby it was thought
by the fair men of the Solicitor's own party. I
wanted Jeffrey to make a strong and contemptuous
reply, both upon the prosecutor's evidence and upon
his illiberal conclusion. But two things did not
merely prevent this, but, to our horror, turned the
reply into flattery ! *First*, Jeffrey was very anxious
for a verdict of Not guilty ; but he was afraid of
provoking the court and the jury to let him have
one only of Not proven, if he had disclosed that he

was to consider the other as a triumph over the prosecution. For a counsel, this was perhaps prudent; but considering the perfect insignificance of the form of the verdict, so as the man was acquitted, to this accused, to whom probably sedition was no shame, this prudence was a virtue which I could not have exercised. But, *secondly*, the truth is, that undue gentleness to opponents, even when they happen to be undeserving of mercy, has always been a failing with Jeffrey's soft heart. He has a disease of complimenting.

He therefore answered Wedderburn's comments; but he not only did so without expressing the slightest scorn or indignation, but his remarks went to *apologise* for the failure of his adversary's proof; and he actually set out with the following declaration, which made our very wigs stand on end:—" I cannot help regretting that my learned and honourable friend, who has made, on the whole, such a use of the evidence as is to the credit of his sagacity and *candour*, did not carry his *liberality* a little further; for had he only said, *as I think he must have felt*, that you should find a verdict of Not guilty, instead of a verdict of Not proven, I should not have been called on to address you at all." (p. 677.)

All this was perfectly intolerable. His " *learned and honourable friend* " was a person with whom he had not even any personal acquaintance, and knew only professionally; and his *candour* and *liberality* consisted in his making a most cruel and unhandsome attempt to hurt the character of an old man against whom he had preferred a groundless charge. He should have been excoriated.

The *Lord Justice-Clerk* very properly left this

point to the jury, who unanimously found the prisoner Not guilty.

This was not merely an unsuccessful prosecution, but, for the Crown, it was a ludicrous one. The very appearance of the prisoner—a little, antique, firm, body—with a brown wig, worn bare in the service of what was then called sedition, combined with the absence of public interest in the case, lowered the dignity of a State trial. And then he was so honest, respectable, dull, and obstinate, that no good-natured person could avoid taking his side— a bias that was greatly increased by Wedderburn's grave keenness to destroy him. Except in the circumstance of their mental attack, there was no known ground for comparing the king to Nebuchadnezzar; but there were many points of resemblance between the Regent and Belshazzar, with his gorgeous feasts and Babylonish ladies. Indeed the coincidences were so notorious that it was thought strange how the advisers of the Crown could expose his Highness to the risk of being brought out or discussed. Accordingly, the prosecutors had scarcely got their indictment read, when they began to be alarmed at the scandal they were about to bring upon their royal master. And at last the audience generally smiled at the absurdity of the Crown counsel aspersing the Regent by interrogative imputations, especially as it always turned out that there was no foundation for the assertion that the prisoner had ascribed the vices to his Royal Highness that were alluded to by his servants, though known perfectly to exist. Indeed, the only thing that made the fact of the prisoner's having uttered the words against the Prince probable was the notoriousness of their being true. " Sed Marcellum insimulabat sinistros de Tiberio sermones habuisse, inevitabile crimen, cum ex moribus principis fœdissima quæque deligeret accusator objectaretque reo : *nam quia vera erant, etiam dicta credebantur.*" (Tacitus, *Annal.*, lib. i. cap. 74.)

XXII.—Case of GEORGE KINLOCH, Esq.,
22d December 1819.

THIS gentleman was the proprietor of the estate of Kinloch, in Forfarshire. He had been active in calling a meeting of the people of Dundee, at which he presided, and made a speech, which he afterwards published. The sedition now charged against him was said to be contained in this speech.

The country at this time was in a state of great excitement. I have never known a period at which the people's hatred of the Government was so general or so fierce. Prevalent distress among the lower orders was at the root of this; but the feeling was exasperated by the new and severe laws made for preventing popular meetings and punishing popular excesses; by the affair between the people and the yeomanry cavalry at Manchester; the thanks given, with unfortunate prematurity, to the cavalry by Government; and the personal detestation of Lord Castlereagh, the head of the ministry.

I was one of Kinloch's counsel, along with Jeffrey, and, I believe, Moncreiff. As he did not stand his trial, it cannot be known whether he was guilty or not. But this would have depended entirely upon the meaning of his language; for the delivery and the publication of the speech were admitted, and could not have been denied.

He had abused the existing system of representation, because it did not represent the people really,

but only nominally, and in law ; had asserted that
hence the House of Commons had a tendency to be
servile to ministers, and regardless of the people,
whose miseries he ascribed to profligate taxation ;
had described the Manchester affair as an unpro-
voked and murderous attack by the military ; had
argued that Lord Sidmouth, the Home Secretary,
who had advised the Regent to thank these troops,
had committed treason, and ought to be impeached ;
gave it as his opinion that any attempt to screen
him or the soldiers from justice might operate as a
signal for civil war ; and that there was no remedy
for the horrors of the people's situation except a
radical reform, including annual parliaments, universal suffrage, and vote by ballot. All this had
been spoken at a meeting composed of the lower
orders of the people, by a person whose station gave
him influence over them, and in a coarse, inflammatory tone.

Although parts of this vulgar harangue might
have been explained away or apologised for, we
were clear that enough of sedition remained to
make it certain that there would, and proper that
there should, be a conviction ; and that a verdict of
guilty would be followed by a long transportation.

Having laid our view of his risks before him, we
left him to follow his own course, and he withdrew.
With Botany Bay before him, and money to make
himself comfortable in Paris, he would have been an
idiot if he had stayed.

This is an example of how severity defeats
itself. Kinloch undoubtedly did not hold himself
to be guilty ; and his ignorance made him rely far
too much on the candour of a jury, and on his own
professed consciousness of innocence. Nay, like

other zealots, he was anxious for an opportunity of defending his principles, and even of suffering for them. But the brutality of the punishment he could not submit to. He therefore retired, and defeated justice, and suffered more from outlawry than he ought to have suffered from conviction.

Immediately after the sentence of fugitation, the Lord Justice-Clerk very unguardedly *expressed his hope that the Lord Advocate would make every effort to bring this accused to justice*—an expression of which the judicious disapproved, it being the business of the court to try prisoners, and not to apprehend them. It is not usual for the court to jog the public prosecutor into vigilance. If this admonition was pointed at the accused's *contempt of court* in not appearing, then, as this contempt is the same wherever any outlawry takes place, there was no reason for giving any hint on this occasion more than on any other, and I never heard it given before. Besides, it was not for this contempt, but, as his Lordship explained, for his sedition, that he was anxious to get him. This was very unlike Boyle's usual caution ; and it is a pity that the error was committed in a political case.[1]

Mr. Kinloch went to the Continent, where he lived, I believe, for seven or eight years, when he was pardoned, and came to his family, and was elected member for Dundee in the first reformed parliament.

[1] The Justice-Clerk (John Hope) gave a similar recommendation to the public prosecutor in the case of Peter M'Gachen, charged with forgery. It is the only occasion (except Kinloch's) where I have ever heard it done.

XXIII.—Case of GILBERT MACLEOD, 14th and
21st February and 6th March 1820.

SHORTLY before this trial (July 1819) Maconochie had been raised to the civil and criminal
benches, on the death of Lord Reston, and had
been succeeded as public prosecutor by Sir William
Rae, the son of Lord Eskgrove, who had never been
known as a counsel, and though then in the twenty-
eighth year of his professional life, was only Sheriff
of Midlothian.

The prisoner was the printer and editor of a
periodical paper published in Glasgow, entitled
The Spirit of the Union, and the seditious libels of
which he was accused were all contained in this
work.

A few weeks prior to his trial he was complained of to the court by the Lord Advocate, sum-
marily, for contempt, in having published certain
improper observations on the preceding case of *Kinloch.* I was his only counsel on this occasion, and
denied both the contempt, and the power of the
court to try, in this form, an offence not committed in reference to any *depending* judicial proceeding. I was found wrong on both points, and he
was sentenced to four months' imprisonment. (13th
January 1820.) Neither he nor his counsel had any
malice against other editors; but it was perfectly
irresistible to show the court what work it would
have to do, if, in times of great excitement, every

deviation from correct propriety, in the discussion
of political trials, was to be brought to a strict
account. Macleod, therefore, was not discouraged
in his desire to institute a complaint, in his turn,
against Mr. Watson, the editor of the *Edinburgh
Correspondent*, then a leading tory newspaper, and
Mr. Murray, one of his compositors, and the author
of a far worse article which had appeared in their
paper against him, as a person then actually under
indictment. The court could not refuse to take
the case up, and had to fine the one of these con-
temners, and to incarcerate the other. (23d February 1820.)

I continued one of the counsel for Macleod, but
could not attend his trial.[1] I now regret this the
more, that, except by inaccurate newspapers, the
proceedings have never been reported. This was
owing to no public indifference ; for the case was
followed, throughout all its stages, with intense interest, chiefly because it was foreseen that it would
bring the discussions about the punishment of sedition to a crisis, and that if the court should still
persist in transporting, they would probably be prevented by parliament from ever doing it again. But
Mr. Grant (now one of the Calcutta judges), the
leading counsel at the trial, undertook to superintend a proper report, and thus prevented others from
interfering ; and then, after many delays, he abandoned it, and nobody took it up. Though I know
all the circumstances perfectly, yet as it is awkward
not to have any authentic account to refer to, I
shall abstain from many details. These, indeed, are
not necessary ; for the substance and the importance
of the case are contained in a few undoubted facts.

[1] Yet I am marked in the Record as present.

The charge was *sedition*, of which seven acts were specified, each consisting of a separate number of the *Spirit of the Union*. The passages objected to are too long to be quoted, and their quotation, even though they were short, would be unnecessary, because their general character can be easily described.

There was nothing *original* in any of them, nor anything peculiar to Glasgow or to this particular publication. The paper merely advocated the common radical topics and feelings that were raging all over the country. Our representation was a mockery; the House of Commons, in consequence of a majority of its members being returned by ministers, peers, and boroughmongers, necessarily corrupt; the taxation was unnecessary and intolerable; monarchy cumbersome and expensive; the people had been unjustly massacred at Manchester; and the minister who had advised the Crown to thank the murderers deserved to lose his head; those who joined the yeomanry in Scotland, but particularly in Lanarkshire, should be publicly named and watched; no taxes should be paid; the people's miseries were all ascribable to Government; and the only cure was in annual parliaments, universal suffrage, and ballot. All this was set forth in coarse declamation; and the tendency certainly was to produce discontent, because the statement was that the people were suffering unnecessarily, that they could indulge in no hope from submission or patience, and that their only prospect of relief lay in their correcting their own wrongs.

Unquestionably a great deal of this was seditious, both in its sentiments and in its tone. But there were some things powerfully in the prisoner's favour.

1. He was only the publisher, not the author of any of the articles. 2. Some of the *worst* of them were mere republications from other, and *unprosecuted* newspapers. 3. His character was excellent, and this was his first offence. His manner and deportment was quiet and gentle. The language, *as read*, indicated an intense and contemptuous Gallowgate orator. But it was not *his* language. He merely copied; and this was the language of the *Spirit of the Union.* He himself was amiable and modest. 4. With a few exceptions, such as the passage (copied from another newspaper) about not paying taxes, his paper stated very little beyond what were the ordinary and proclaimed sentiments and statements of the whole opposition party, consisting of greatly above a majority of the nation. No doubt the majority of a nation may be seditious; but when this happens, there is always ground for tenderness towards an individual of good character, who has not produced, but fallen under, the general contagion. The probability, moreover, that discontent seldom becomes general, and is never long continued, without just cause, ought to operate in his favour; though, of all circumstances, it is the one which most irritates the possessors of disturbed power.

The worst thing about these libels was their exaggerated animation of language. Swift, or Cobbett, or Sydney Smith, could have said most of what the prisoner said with tolerable safety, and with greater force. But vulgar reformers, who air their opinions in newspapers or at meetings, especially if they be honest and ardent, generally despise skill.

The evidence for the prosecution consisted solely in proving the publication.

The Lord Advocate was assisted by the Solicitor, and by John Hope, who, though he only came to the bar in 1816, was Solicitor, on Wedderburn's demise, in 1822. His Lordship, in addressing the jury, did nothing, and perhaps had nothing else to do, than to recite, and comment upon, each most peccant sentence; to praise the constitution of the· House of Commons, and of all existing things ; to ascribe the people's discontent, not to their sufferings, but to demagogues like the prisoner ; and to ask, what would become of us all if he were not convicted.

Grant's junior was James Ivory, of every personal excellence, and who has since been Solicitor-General ; but who can be distinguished by no official promotion so honourably as he is by his merits as a man and a lawyer.

Grant's general defect was that, though redeemed by elegance and cleverness, he was frothy and superficial. But his speech to the jury for Macleod was judicious and powerful ; the best he ever made at the Scotch bar. It received the highest encomiums, and deserved them. Its chief object was to reconcile the challenged passages with loyalty, or with the subject's right to complain, or with the established limits of political discussion.

It was, perhaps, impossible for any judge not to have been against the prisoner ; and the Lord Justice-Clerk did not express his opinion more strongly than it has always been his practice to do. An English judge would probably have been less elaborate, and less demonstrative of the guilt of the accused. But this has always been Boyle's view of his duty ; and there was no exaggeration of style, because this was a political case. It was a perfectly fair, and for him a moderate, address. And the summings up, even of English judges, have assumed a much more argumentative and decided character, and necessarily so since counsel have been allowed to address juries for prisoners. Scotch judges are often compelled to adopt a still more positive style of charge, on account of the prisoner's counsel here always speaking last.

The result was that the jury (whether by a majority or not does not appear from the record) found the prisoner guilty; but in consequence of his good character, *unanimously recommended him to the lenity of the Court.*

His counsel intimated that they meant to contest the competency and the propriety of transporting; and a day was assigned for hearing them. The argument for the prisoner was conducted by Jeffrey and Moncreiff; for the Crown by Wedderburn. I heard the whole discussion, both at the bar and on the bench. A memorable discussion it was.

Moncreiff, who brings his whole soul into every public question he espouses, opened the case in a full argument of the deepest legal talent, given in a tone of sincerity, with a force of personal authority which the highest display of the weightiest judge could not have exceeded. His contempt of Hume's precedents made him expose them rather too lightly, and too little in detail. But otherwise he went into the whole matter in all its legal grounds and views, and made it quite plain to the public that if, after this, the court should still think it had the power, and that it was its duty to transport, a statute must do that by compulsion which it would then be plain that reason could not accomplish.

He was followed by Wedderburn, who knew that he was addressing a court that reverenced the proceedings of 1794, and he did little but appeal to these bad precedents.

Jeffrey replied. Seeing that Moncreiff had left nothing to be gleaned in the law, he disposed of the Solicitor in a few words, and then discussed the expected sentence on the grounds of its propriety. In Jeffrey's generous hands this was a triumphant topic. He did not waste himself on mere feeling—or rather this was one of the cases on which nothing can be more moving than a simple display of facts. He explained the true character of the guilt of sedition, and showed how it might be committed by men of the finest natures—often from awkwardness, and oftener from the rashness of benevolence ; how difficult its practical separation was from ardent political discussion ; how unavoidably it therefore prevailed on all sides in periods of violence ; how rapidly, when not exasperated by severity, it evaporated when its exciting causes were removed ; how ineffectual penal law, when not mildly administered, was, except in the ruin of a few pitied victims ; what was implied in transportation, with its hulks, its distance, its hopeless duration, its dangers, its degradation, and the desolation of the separated family. All this, in its feeling and reasonable views, unfolded by Jeffrey, seemed to the public to be so unanswerable, that there were few indeed who anticipated the cold shock by which it was to be all overturned.

For the court sentenced the prisoner to *transportation for five years.*

Every allowance must be made for the possible variety of opinion on a long-contested point of law ;

and no great wonder can be felt that judges, accustomed from the very infancy of their legal thinking to a particular view of a party question, should be insensible of the steps of what seemed to others a demonstration leading to an opposite result from theirs. But with reference to the exercise of the *discretion*, with which the court was undoubtedly invested, there were some circumstances connected with this proceeding which make it worthy of perpetual remembrance.

Lord Gillies gave it as his opinion that the power to transport must now be held to exist, but that it ought not to be exercised. If he could have thought that the question was still open, he would have held that even the power did not exist, and that the previous judgments were wrong. But having been pronounced, after argument, repeatedly acted upon, and approved of by large majorities in parliament, he thought himself bound by these precedents.

He has been severely blamed for this recognition of these decisions. It has been said that a cruel and indefensible sentence, introduced by political judges in violent times, can scarcely be made law by any repetition of it in the same circumstances; and that this being the first occasion on which an opportunity had occurred of settling the question on true principles and sound authorities, a firm judge would have decided according to his conceptions of the law, disencumbered of these recent stretches of it. There is much force in this; but I can scarcely concur in the censure. It is not easy to draw the line, and to say when law ought to yield to precedent, or precedent to law; but the general principle that solemn decisions are binding in similar cases on future judges can never be departed from without such danger, that it is the duty of parliament to supply a remedy where these decisions can no longer be safely adhered to. The very circumstance, too, of his Lordship having formerly been counsel on the unsuccessful side, and still *reputed* a whig, might have made candid men regret that he had given the world any pretence for ascribing his conduct to feelings which ought never to operate on the bench.

But while he declared himself constrained to concede the existence of the power, he was only the stronger on this account in the expression of his opinion that it ought clearly not to be exercised.

All the other judges, being the *Justice-Clerk, Hermand, Succoth, Pitmilly,* and *Meadowbank,* delivered opinions strongly opposed to Gillies on both points. They all thought, not merely that they were bound by the former precedents, but that these precedents were according to law, so that if the case had occurred now for the first time, it could only be settled in the way that it had been; but that *transportation was the only punishment suitable to the ordinary form of the crime.* They expressed the highest reverence for Braxfield and his colleagues as judges in the sedition trials of 1793 and 1794; and Boyle, the Justice-Clerk, elevated himself to the flight of declaring *that he was ambitious of no higher honour than that of having his name associated in this question with the names of these great judges* —a sentiment with which some of his brethren expressed their concurrence. I HEARD THESE WORDS, which were uttered steadily, and after obvious premeditation. They scouted all idea of any punishment except transportation being adequate to the crime, unless in the very slightest possible cases,

and openly stated the *horrors,* which had been *truly*
described as implied in transportation, to be a
recommendation of a punishment which made the
danger of the crime palpable to the most audacious
offender. I never can forget the sensation with
which I heard the calm, but hard, Pitmilly say, in
his cold, steely manner, with the appearance of
gentleness, but the reality of quiet steady severity,
" I think transportation the *appropriate* punishment
of sedition ;" laying a slow, deliberate, unimpas-
sioned emphasis on the word " appropriate," as his
contemptuous answer to all that had been urged
for the prisoner on this part of the subject, and
adding, " Considering what sedition is, if I were to
pronounce any other sentence, *I could never lay my
head upon my pillow in peace again.* [!!!]

Now it could scarcely be credited, but it is true,
that *within less than three months prior* to the day
on which these sentiments were uttered, and this
punishment of transportation inflicted, parliament,
guided by as stern a tory ministry as this country
had ever seen, had announced its opinion of the
proper penalty of sedition ; and had thus made the
modern judges more inexcusable than the ancient
ones, by giving them a statutory guide, of which
their predecessors had not had the advantage.

Hume says (vol. i. p. 556) :—" In the end, on the
increase of this alarming evil (sedition), to which the
powers of the common law of England were found
unequal, recourse was had to the Legislature, who,
by Statute 36 Geo. iii. c. 7, *authorised the inflicting
of the same punishments that are competent in
Scotland according to the common law, and by means
of which, duly and steadily applied,* the judges
in Scotland had in a great measure repressed the

growing audacity of the licentious in this quarter of the kingdom." There can be no more extraordinary blunder (misrepresentation I will not suppose) than what is contained in this misleading passage.

Its meaning is, that in the year 1816 an Act of Parliament was passed which legalised in England what had been held to be the common law punishments of sedition in Scotland—those punishments which, as *previously administered by the Scotch judges—that is, transportation for fourteen years on a first conviction*—had been successful in repressing the crime here. Now, 1st, the Act referred to, being the 36 of Geo. III. c. 7, does *not* authorise transportation *for fourteen years in any circumstances*. 2d. It does not authorise transportation, even for a moment, *on a first conviction*. 3d. It only permitted transportation *after a previous conviction*. 4th. It even then only permitted it for *seven* years. 5th. It did not adopt, nor did any sound-headed man ever dream of parliament adopting, even amidst the violence of 1816, " *the same* (that is *all* the same) *punishments* that are competent in Scotland according to the common law." *Whipping* was laid down by all the old judges to be competent by our common law. Does the 36th of Geo. III. c. 7 legalise this ? According to Hume, transportation for seven years on a second conviction is the same thing with transportation for fourteen on a first, and scourging to boot. And even this moderate increase of the severity of their law was so repugnant to the ordinary genius of the English system that it was expressly *limited to three years*.

And when these three years were out, though the country was raging under a still more intense popular discontent, parliament would no longer tolerate transportation, even for seven years, *though on a second or a thousandth conviction.* In the year 1819 the Act of the 60th of Geo. III. and 1st of Geo. IV. cap. 8 passed, upon the expiry of the statute of 1816. This Act settled the punishment for sedition in England permanently. It declared that on a first conviction it should be fine, or imprisonment, or both ; and on any subsequent conviction it should either be these " or *banishment from the United Kingdom, and all other parts of his Majesty's dominions,*" " for such term of years as the court shall order." The culprit *is allowed forty days to get himself into banishment;* and if he does not dispose of himself voluntarily within this period, then it is competent for the *Crown* to lay hold of him and transport him. The practical result of this is that transportation for *sedition,* even the short transportation that had been allowed by a statute of only three years' duration, was abolished ; and that though a culprit might be sent to Botany Bay for his *contumacy* in not betaking himself to a better place, imprisonment and fine, or both, were the regular penalties *for the crime* on a first conviction, and possible *banishment* for any subsequent one.

Here was the precedent for the court to have followed. This *parliamentary and ministerial* declaration of what was the proper punishment was made on the 19th of December 1819. Yet within three months—on the 6th of March 1820—did five of our judges transport Macleod on a *first* conviction, in spite of an *unanimous recommendation of the jury to mercy, his character excellent,* and *one of their own number recommending a milder course.*

It is painful to ascribe any judicial proceeding by honourable judges to a cause which impeaches their temper, if not their candour. But the truth must be told ; and it is that their Lordships were obviously—very obviously—irritated at the conduct of their predecessors being challenged, and alarmed at their own powers being questioned ; and therefore thought that they would not vindicate either, by merely *declaring* what they held to be law, but that *its actual enforcement* was necessary, in order to discourage all future objection, and to mark how superior they held their own wisdom to that of the Legislature.

Thus Macleod was transported, and died, before his time was out, in New South Wales.

It was this case that provoked me to examine the whole course of our sedition practice. It was not easy to stand what the court had said in the case of *McLaren and Baird* (p. 58) about the old sentences having been unanimously approved of by the country. But when to this was now added that *to be associated with what the old judges had done was an honour to their successors,* it seemed to me to be the duty of a living witness of this sentiment to let posterity know its absurdity and its danger. According to this sentiment, all subsequent judges ought to try to imitate the conduct of Braxfield and his judicial associates, in trying political cases criminally. My opinion is that other judges will perform their duty exactly in proportion to the success with which they shall avoid the whole manner, and principles, and spirit thus held up for their imitation. Let posterity decide.

OBSERVATIONS.

MACLEOD's is the last case of sedition that has been tried in Scotland.

In so far as the power of transporting is concerned, his sentence brought matters to a point. The existence of such a power could not be submitted to in modern times, and in 1825 the 6th of Geo. IV., cap. 47, passed, which enacts that the punishment of leasing-making and of sedition shall be the same in Scotland as the 60 Geo. III. c. 8, had provided for sedition in England, viz., fine and imprisonment, or both, for a first offence, and possible *banishment* for any subsequent one. The last statute is almost a mere transcript of the first.

As this change was effected during a tory administration, and by the instrumentality of Sir William Rae as Lord Advocate, that party have occasionally blamed themselves for indirectly deserting the court by consenting to the mitigation of the law, while at other times they have claimed the merit of it. They are certainly entitled to the praise of having at last, not only not opposed the improvement, but been the organs by which it was carried into effect. Their real credit in this can only be estimated by those who know the history of the new law.

The sentence upon Macleod, and still more the judicial speeches on which it was grounded, excited the utmost alarm among the whigs, who felt as if the days of Braxfield had come back, or might do so ; and thought that the difference of the punishment, for the same political offence, in the two different quarters of the island, was insulting to Scotland. This, of course, combined their antagonists in the defence both of transporting and of picking. Preparations were therefore made for bringing both of these subjects before parliament. Little was requisite in reference to transportation, beyond the mere statement of the fact that in England sedition was thought sufficiently punished without this penalty. The selection of jurymen by the presiding judge was more incomprehensible and complicated, and required a great deal of long continued explanation. I can never reflect without satisfaction on my own humble exertions,[1] in concert chiefly with Mr. Kennedy of Dunure, then in parliament, on this vital question. At last Kennedy introduced his Jury Bill, the rejection of which *through the influence of the Scotch tory party,* only increased the conviction of the whigs of its necessity, and everything was ready for opening the case of the punishment of sedition next session.

It was while matters were in this position, that Government, foreseeing the difficulty, and the absurdity, of maintaining two peculiarities in the administration of criminal justice in Scotland, which would not be tolerated for a single moment in England, began, very wisely, to take these subjects into its consideration.

On the 20th of October 1822 a letter signed by Sir Robert Peel was sent to the Lord Justice-Clerk (Boyle) putting six questions to him and to the

---

[1] All the articles in the *Edinburgh Review* in 1821 and 1822 on this subject were written by me.

Lord President (Hope), the Lord Chief Baron (Shepherd), the Lord Chief Commissioner Adam, and Baron Hume. These questions related, 1*st*. To our method of selecting criminal juries, and the expediency of introducing Ballot and the Peremptory challenge. 2*d*. To "the powers possessed by the Lord Advocate as public prosecutor." 3*d*. To his other powers, and the expediency of separating these from his functions as public accuser. 4*th*. To the expediency of introducing Grand Juries. 5*th*. To the Lord Advocate's power of getting diets deserted *pro loco et tempore*. 6*th*. To this :— " Can your Lordship suggest any alterations in the Criminal law of Scotland, or in the practice of its courts, which it would be expedient to make for the purpose of securing a greater degree of protection for persons accused of crimes ? "

I have seen the Chief Commissioner's answer to this last question. It recommends the abolition of the judge's selection, and of transportation for sedition. But, though so far right, it is right feebly, and (as I understand it) is for giving the benefit of these changes only to political prisoners ; and he gives it even to these, only in connection with Special Juries, new trials, writs of error, and other English peculiarities. This must have impaired the weight due to his opinion on the plain Scotch matters, as to which he was clearly in the right track.[1]

As to the Lord Advocate, after joining with his Scotch party in defending our full judicial establishment as indispensable, and in crying out against any abatement of it as insulting to the dignity of the country, and a breach of the union, he was made

[1] The Lord Chief Commissioner states in "a Narrative" of these matters, that neither the letter by Sir Robert Peel, nor the Return, or Returns, to it are to be found in the Home Office.

to act as the hand which abolished our Consistorial Court and its four judges, our Admiralty Court and its one judge, and two Supreme Judges of the Court of Session. He first wrote an eager and very foolish letter to the country gentlemen, and to the Town Councils, of every (then unreformed) shire and royal burgh in Scotland (see *Edinburgh Review,* vol. xxxvi. p. 200), directing them to resist a bill then under discussion for taking away the Judge's power of picking, as it was impossible to foresee the inroad which might thus be made on the Criminal Law of Scotland, *with which the country hitherto had been so truly satisfied* [!] and then, in obedience to orders, he took up this very measure. And after having long adopted and repeated the statement of his party,—that Scotland had been saved, in 1793 and 1794, by transportation for sedition, and was incapable of being saved hereafter without it, — then because Scotland compelled his masters, and his masters compelled him, to be the instrument of its abolition, he and they appropriate the whole honour of the improvement.

Probably it was not attended to, but the Scotch statute virtually condemns the transportation sentences by its phraseology. The great defence of these sentences was that, in our law, the term *banishment* included *transportation.* But the 6th of Geo. IV. cap. 47, makes it *exclude* it; for the words *banish* and *transport* are there used as entirely different, and the whole of the new system there introduced implies that they are so.

The punishment continued to be the same in both countries from 1825, when we adopted the English statute, till 1830. But a very material difference was then allowed to take place. On the

30th of July 1830 the Act of the 11th Geo. iv. and of 1st Will. iv. cap. 73, passed; and this statute repealed the power of even *banishing*, with which, in the year 1819, the 60th of Geo. iii. and 1st of Geo. iv. cap. 7, had armed the English courts, and left these courts no power of punishing sedition, however frequently committed, except by fine and imprisonment. But this statute only applied to England. In 1837 I explained to Mr. Murray, then Lord Advocate, how the fact stood, and gave him the heads of a Bill. The Act of the 7th Will. iv. and 1st Victoria, cap. 5, which restores, and I suppose finally fixes, the identity of the punishment of sedition in both countries, was the result.

So the matter rests for the present.

Since *Macleod's* case, the Test Acts have been repealed, the Catholics emancipated, parliament reformed, the Corn Act extinguished, Free Trade recognised, and toryism and whigism, purely as such, have fought their last battle, almost to the annihilation of toryism. No previous conflicts of opinion ever brought into action fiercer passions, stronger interests, or a freer questioning of principles. It is needless to say, that throughout these volcanic discussions there has been no want of sedition. It has been raging upon all sides. I do not believe that a candid balance could detect any other difference between the parties, except that with the one it has been the sedition of the commonalty, and with the other of the aristocracy, including especially the church. Each has availed itself of all the known modes of rioting over the law, and seems to have forgotten or despised the circumstance that there is a crime called sedition. This is the true reason that there have been very few trials, if any, for this offence in England, and not one in Scotland. Each party has been afraid to throw the first stone.

Begin when they may, may we never forget the description given of a State trial, in bad times, by a very competent judge : " The trials of the accused were exactly like all the State trials of those days, that is to say, as infamous as they could be. They were neither fairer, nor less fair, than those of Algernon Sidney, of Rosewell, of Cornish, of all the unhappy men, in short, whom a predominant party brought to what was then facetiously called justice. Till the Revolution purified our institutions and our manners, a State trial was merely a murder preceded by the uttering of certain gibberish and the performance of certain mummeries." (Macaulay's *Essays*, vol. ii. p. 245 : Review of Mackintosh's *History of the Revolution*.)

XXIV. — John Grant, Henry Ranken, and Robert Hamilton, 7th, 9th, 13th, 18th, and 25th November 1848.

After an interval of above twenty-eight years, two more cases have occurred—one that of the above-named prisoners, the other that of James Cumming.

There might have been many more now, if the law had been enforced strictly, or if the public accuser had not been restrained by the consideration, that more encouragement is given to sedition by one prosecution that fails, than discouragement by many that succeed. A thief who escapes is glad to disappear quietly. Every acquittal for sedition is a triumph, and the triumph is the greater the clearer the guilt.

In some respects the times were not very unlike those of 1793 and 1794. Besides the chronic sedition that adheres naturally to the practice of the Constitution, considerable masses of the people were under a violent attack of the acute complaint. This access was chiefly brought on by continental contagion. What the French call a republic had been recently set up in their country; almost every throne in Europe had been shaken or overturned by popular convulsion; Ireland was in rebellion; there was great mercantile distress in Britain; professional demagogues had not neglected the occasion; and these various excitements brought out the idiots called Chartists not only into seditious oratory, but into displays of treasonable organisation. These circumstances crowded the English courts with political prisoners ; but as only four individuals were prosecuted here, it at least cannot be said that there was any eagerness in resorting to the terrors of the law.

There are two printed accounts of this case, but as yet only one of them (as I understand) has been published. They are both bad, because neither even professes to give a full exposition of the whole trial. The one that is published is by Mr. John Shaw (the worst of all reporters) in the ordinary Justiciary Reports. But it only reports the legal questions that arose ; and as all the material judicial opinions were either supplied or revised by the judges, this report, so far as it goes, is full and accurate enough. But as it neither gives the evidence nor the speeches at the bar, nor the charge, it conveys no impression of the real trial. The other report was got up for the information of Government, and bears to be "printed and published by Thomas Constable, Printer to her Majesty ;" but I understand that the publication has not yet (April 1849) taken place. This " *Trial* " leaves out all the legal questions, and only gives the evidence and the speeches by counsel, which is all well done. The charge, however, is not given here either, because to both reporters (as I understand) the presiding judge *declined* to revise. Thus (except as to the summation) a very good idea of the proceedings may be got from both of these accounts, but not from either of them by itself.

Except Boyle, now Lord President and Lord Justice-General (but who did not interfere in any of the proceedings), there was no judge on the criminal bench, at the period of this trial, who was there at

the preceding trial of Macleod in 1820.   The court
was composed of John Hope, Lord Justice-Clerk ;
Henry, Lord Mackenzie ; James, Lord Moncreiff;
John Forbes, Lord Medwyn ; Henry, Lord Cockburn; and Alexander, Lord Wood.   This was an
excellent court.   Can I say more of it, than that
I really believe that I was the worst judge in it ?
The other five, notwithstanding some peculiarities
in our head, were all admirable.   I have no doubt
that Moncreiff was the only one who had a proper
feeling of the old proceedings.   But the rest admired
only the *law* of these proceedings, not their *manner*, or *general principles*.   Moncreiff and I were
the only two whigs.   The toryism of our brethren,
however, is comparatively harmless, now that the
redness of these party lines has faded.

The case was tried by the Justice, Moncreiff,
and Medwyn.   The other judges were only called in
to assist in settling questions of law.

The counsel for the prosecution were Andrew
Rutherfurd, Lord Advocate, Mr. James Craufurd,
and Mr. J. Montgomerie Bell ; for the prisoners Mr.
James Moncreiff, Mr. Alexander Logan, Mr. Archibald Grahame, and Mr. Lorimer,—all good men
and good barristers ; but I have no occasion to
make any special mention of any of them except
those on whom the real business of the trial fell.

It might be deemed questionable to place any
one before Jeffrey or even before Henry Erskine.
But laying aside and reserving the claims of these
two, Rutherfurd's is undoubtedly the most powerful intellect, whether as applied to law, to policy, or
to general knowledge, that has been given to the
office of Lord Advocate within the last sixty years.
And neither Erskine, nor even Jeffrey, nor any-

body, can surpass him in the moral qualities which elevate public station.

James, the son of Lord Moncreiff, and the grandson of Sir Harry, prolongs the hereditary talent and virtue of the family ; and without being what is called learned, he is more liberally read than either of his two sires. He is as likely to reach the highest honours of his profession, purely by deserving them, as any one now in it. A good lawyer, a pleasing and forcible speaker, a most agreeable writer,[1] judicious, honourable, and friendly, there is nothing left for his friends to wish, unless, perhaps, it be that his outward man, which seems scarcely to belong to the strong mind and the strong voice it is connected with, was somewhat more commanding.

In James Craufurd very considerable ability is combined with purity and enthusiasm of principle, and with a very affectionate heart. This union of talent and goodness can never make itself vocal without moral eloquence. Craufurd scarcely ever fails to make his hearers love both his side and himself. The mere frank and joyous hibernianism of his manner goes far to account for his popularity.

The only thing against Logan is that he is sometimes beset by a taste for quaint and heavy jokes. And the innocent confidence with which he enjoys them makes the ignorant suppose that he considers them as his peculiar merit. This mistake of his trump-card sometimes mars his management of his hand; in the dealing of which nature has by no means been unkind. For in reality he is an able, sensible, honest, generous person ; a most excellent fellow, and the most candid of pleaders, beloved and respected by all who know him.

[1] See his contributions to the *North British* and *Edinburgh Reviews.*

The indictment contained two charges. One was for "*wickedly and feloniously conspiring to effect an alteration of the laws and constitution of the realm by force* or violence, or by armed resistance to lawful authority." This accusation, of which all the prisoners were acquitted, does not come within the scope of this examination. The other charge was "*sedition.*" The facts set forth in support of it were in substance that certain persons called Chartists had combined to effect certain alterations of the laws and constitution of the realm by force; that a meeting of these persons and of their adherents was called for the 12th of June 1848, its announced object being to show by "a great demonstration" that the people "*were not to rest satisfied until the principles of the people's charter became the law of the land;*" that this meeting was held on Bruntsfield Links; that the prisoner Grant presided; that he and the other two prisoners had spoken; that there was another such meeting held on the Calton Hill on the 24th of July 1848, at which Hamilton and Ranken had spoken; that all these speeches were seditious, and had not only been uttered "*wickedly and feloniously,*" but had been "INTENDED *and calculated to excite popular disaffection, commotion, and violence, and resistance to lawful authority.*"

No *particular words* were imputed to *Grant*, who was only charged as in connection with the meeting on the 12th of June. But it was said in general, that "you did advise and exhort the persons there convened and assembled to form themselves into clubs and sections for the more effectual prosecution of the objects of the Chartist body." The main fact imputed to him was, that "you did, as chairman aforesaid, hear, permit, and sanction the seditious speeches above libelled of the said Henry Ranken and Robert Hamilton, and you did not call them to order, or stop or attempt to stop them, or express any dissent from, or disapprobation of, the said speeches."

The worst parts of the harangue ascribed to *Ranken* were these : " We therefore declare that it is our intention not to rest satisfied, nor to cease agitating, until the people's charter is the law of the land, being fully convinced that justice can neither be obtained nor preserved, unless the people are put in possession of their rights, which are clearly laid down in that document. We are further resolved to exert ourselves to the utmost of our power to promulgate our principles in every quarter of the land, and thereby create a feeling that will ultimately compel our *oppressors to relinquish their grasp,* which we are satisfied will be ere long ; *for we are determined that while there is misery for the inmates of the cottage there shall be no peace for the inmates of the hall.*" " The science of chemistry had entered the workshop, and the *working men could provide themselves with as deadly weapons as Warner's long range,* and if it was to be a struggle for life and death, if it was to be destruction, then you hoped and trusted that the working men would only be true to themselves, *and only abstain from all acts of aggression until they were roused by the oppression of their oppressors, and when they began the work may they do it well.*" " If the leaders of the people are to be incarcerated, *if the people are to suffer this tamely, if those who have an interest in keeping you down feel that you will quietly submit, even then they are secure;* but if the working men look to themselves, and if they look to those who place themselves in the front of the fray, if they look to those who are willing to brave every danger, then I say the working men ought to consider what means should be taken to protect these men. *Let the property of the country be hostages in the hands of the people for the safety of the leaders of the people.*" "It has been said that the French are inventive, but that the British have this faculty that upon all French inventions they improve. *Should the authorities drive the people into a revolution, then I hope the people will improve upon the French invention of a Republic.*" And *Ranken* was further charged with having advised the people " *to organise into clubs and sections,*" " and *to provide themselves with arms, in case they might require to use them.*" That the *people of Ireland were justified in their determination to resist to the death the oligarchy who ruled them,*" and that he hoped that " *the God of battles would smile on the oppressed, and enable them to improve the victory they were sure to win.*"

The worst language or sentiments imputed to *Hamilton* were that he urged the people " to *organise themselves into clubs and sections, and to provide themselves with guns and bayonets,*" in order to promote the Chartist cause. " *For the love of God prepare yourselves with guns and bayonets, as the day is not far distant when you may require them.*" And that he said that " pikes were easily made, and that the young and the spirited men of Scotland should go to Ireland and help the Irish people, and that at one time you would have been satisfied with the charter as the law of the land, but that now you would accept of nothing else than a republic, and that they would soon obtain one."

This language was not only plainly seditious,

but it was by far the most seditious that had ever been charged against any Scotch prisoner.

It is not worth while to analyse the evidence. The greater portion of it was employed to expose the arrangements and purposes which tended to establish the conspiracy. The rest went to prove the use of the words which were said to contain the sedition.

The trial lasted two days.[1] The Lord Advocate being ill on the second, the jury was addressed for the prosecution by Mr. Craufurd ; for Ranken by Mr. Moncreiff ; and for Grant and Hamilton by Mr. Logan. Deducting the Lord Justice-Clerk, who is said to censure the whole of them, those who were present seemed to be unanimous in their admiration of these three speeches ; and the opinion of the more judicious hearers satisfies me that the admiration was just. This judgment by intelligent hearers is the only safe criterion of a speech. A good report may be a better thing ; but, *as a speech*, the best report is cold and bare in comparison with the living words, look, tone, and manner. But it is satisfactory when, as here, the report tends to justify the speaking impression.

I am confident that Craufurd's was the best address that was ever delivered for the Crown, to a jury, in a Scotch trial for sedition. It was able, fair, and temperate ; strong for a conviction, but liberally constitutional in public principle ; and, above all, it was superior to the paltriness of inflaming, instead of allaying, any prejudices that the jury might be supposed to be under the influence of. It formerly constituted sedition, and proved it, that the prisoner had urged universal suffrage and annual parlia-

---

[1] This could not be discovered from Mr. Shaw's report.

ments. The Chartists urged these, and several
worse changes. But the doctrine of the prosecutor
now is this :—" With respect to these political doctrines of the Chartists, let me explicitly avow that
the Chartists *are well entitled to hold these opinions,
to express and promulgate* these opinions, *and to
associate in order to maintain and advance them by
all legitimate means*—by addresses to the Crown,
petitions to parliament, public meetings orderly
conducted, argument, reasoning, entreaty, and remonstrance. They are entitled by all constitutional
means to carry out their political object. *This is
not a prosecution for opinion;* and whether the
changes desired by the Chartists would be wise or
salutary, conducive to the public welfare or consistent with the public security, is no question for you
or any of us to consider." " It is not for the use of
such means that they are now charged with crime.
Was it even by agitation ? by the stirring, and
combining, and concentrating of public opinion ?
This is a course open, perhaps, to observation, because liable to be carried to excess—a course requiring on the part of those who enter upon it calmness,
moderation, and discretion in no ordinary degree ;
*but it were in vain to disguise or conceal the fact that
by the force of popular opinion, gathered and wielded
by popular agitation, gigantic abuses have been over-
thrown, and valuable reforms have been accomplished.*"
" Let it, therefore, be understood distinctly, as it is
now emphatically stated for the prosecution, that the
crime with which the prisoners are charged does not
consist either in the opinions they hold, or in the
open expression and free discussion of their views, or
*in their loud proclamation of their supposed wrongs,
their indignant denunciation of alleged abuses, their*

urgent entreaty, their vehement remonstrance, their impetuous demands; nor even in the spirit-stirring popular agitation by which they seek to advance their opinions. But the indictment states," etc. (that they had *conspired* to *use force*, and committed *sedition*). The ghost of Braxfield must have growled when these words were uttered.

In Clerk and Jeffrey, Moncreiff had rivals, the *substance* of whose professional defences of seditious prisoners will scarcely ever be excelled. But he is worthy of being placed by their side. His address was said to be, and must have been, admirable. I shall only quote two passages, because they suggest a curious contrast :—" It is not beyond the recollection of the present generation that there have been times when juries as high-minded as any jury can be have been carried away by the whirlwind of similar excitement. There have been times when verdicts have been returned under circumstances of public prejudice, *in which the voice, not of law merely, but reason and sense, was drowned in one overpowering terror; verdicts which filled some, at least, who pronounced them with undying regret; and have stamped an indelible stigma on the times they characterise. I am under no apprehension of that kind to-day. The bubble is burst,"* etc. " There is a third consideration, and which is the only other preliminary remark I shall urge, and which is perhaps the strongest ground of confidence which I entertain of all—I mean the singular and remarkable advance which the doctrines of constitutional liberty and the principles of freedom have made within the last fifty years. *When I contrast the proceedings of this day with those to which my study for this case has directed me—when I contrast the*

*times in which we live, and the sentiments now preva-
lent, with those that have gone by—when I contrast
the tone of constitutional moderation in which the
prosecution has been conducted, with prosecutions not
yet forgotten, and still too recent to be stamped and
characterised in words with the reprobation they deserve,*—I say, when I consider the advance of free
principles since then, I am grateful to think that we
live in times so much happier, and I feel animated
by the conviction that I shall have a fair hearing,
and these panels a fair trial this day, in the highest
sense of the word." (*Trial,* p. 53.)   What did the
ghost say to this ?

Logan's, for the cause, was an excellent address.

The presiding judge's full summation is not reported.   The trial does not even profess to report it ;
and though Mr. Shaw gives about three pages to it,
it is plain that these pages (which were seen and left
as they are by his Lordship), even if absolutely correct, could convey no truth of a charge which occupied *three hours and a half, being a longer period
than what was required for the whole three speeches
at the bar.*   His Lordship, it is said, *declined* to
revise his charge.   Practically, therefore, it is not
reported at all.   No supposed thought or word in
what is given can ever be quoted as an authority
for anything—not even for the fact that such
thoughts or words were uttered.[1]

The summation, as heard, was not favourably
spoken of.   Laborious minuteness of detail and of
views, especially from a judge wishing to instruct a

---

[1] His Lordship is made to censure one of the prisoners' counsel for
attempting to make the necessary differences of society a defence or apology for criminal violence !   *If he uttered any sentiment of the kind, it was
utterly groundless ;* for nothing within the horizon of such a defence of
apology was even alluded to by any one at the bar.

jury, when luminousness, and consequently simplicity, are everything, always makes darkness darker.
As received by the audience, and especially by the
counsel for the prisoners, it was a strong charge
for a total acquittal. But whether this was the
charger's meaning, or whether a display of constitutional liberality was mistaken for an opinion in
favour of the prisoners, is by no means so clear.

The judgment of intelligent persons who had
attended the whole trial (confirmed, as I think it is,
by the report of the evidence) was, that there ought
to have been, and but for the charge would have
been, a conviction of conspiracy against the three
prisoners, and of sedition against Hamilton and
Ranken. As to Grant, the language imputed to
him was not established ; and there was nothing
else set forth against him except his virtual adoption of the sedition of the other two prisoners by
hearing it, and, though chairman, not checking it.
But what they said was uttered in a large meeting,
held in a field ; and it was not very improbable that,
though the chairman must have seen the orators,
he might not have heard their exact expressions,
or at the moment have appreciated them. It was
thought, therefore, that he ought to be acquitted of
the sedition.

The actual result is thus stated, and accurately,
in the report—"The jury, after deliberating for
half an hour, returned the following verdict :—' The
jury unanimously find the charge of conspiracy
against the three panels, as libelled, not proven.
The jury also unanimously find John Grant not
guilty of sedition, as libelled.

" ' The jury further unanimously find Robert
Hamilton *guilty of using language calculated* to

excite popular disaffection and resistance to lawful authority. And by a majority of one find Henry Ranken *guilty of using similar language.*"

It was seen by the court, or at least by the presiding judge, that this was no convicting verdict. Accordingly the Lord Justice-Clerk said :—"Gentlemen, be good enough to observe in regard to that part of the verdict which contains the specialty finding Hamilton and Ranken guilty of *using language calculated* to excite popular disaffection and resistance to lawful authority, that this is the description of sedition libelled.[1] Now, to make your verdict correct, you should determine whether they are guilty or not guilty of *sedition* to any extent you please. You may say, for example, that they are guilty of sedition in so far as they used language calculated to excite popular disaffection and resistance to lawful authority.

" *The Chancellor of the Jury.*—That is what we mean, my Lord.

" *Lord Justice-Clerk.*—In using the word ' calculated,' *do you mean to leave out the word ' intended;'* or does your verdict mean to embrace both ?

" *The Chancellor.—We mean purposely to leave out the word ' intended.'*

" The verdict was then recorded as follows :—
' The jury unanimously find Robert Hamilton guilty of sedition, in so far as that he used language *calculated* to excite popular disaffection and resistance to lawful authority ; and by a majority of one find Henry Ranken guilty of sedition *in the same terms.*' "

---

[1] There must be a mistake here ; for this is certainly *not* the description of the sedition libelled. In the libel the description is " *intended* and calculated."

The sufficiency of the verdict as thus recorded being questioned, the point was argued before the whole judges on a subsequent day.

The argument in support of the objection came, in substance, to this :—That the verdict was uncertain, or was defective as a ground for punishment ; that every Scotch indictment, *without any one exception*, has set forth either general wickedness and feloniousness of mind as the foundation of the charge, or some particular evil intention ; that the present indictment charges both, for it first asserts that all the acts were done " *wickedly and feloniously,*" and then specifies the particular sort of wickedness to have consisted in a design to produce the very mischief for which the seditious acts are said to have been both " *intended and* calculated ;" that evil intention was thus made an essential part of the crime ; or if this be supposed to limit the prosecutor too strictly, the indictment made it indispensable that he should at least establish some sort of wickedness or feloniousness, especially as there can be no crime without some guilt in the mind of the criminal ; that nevertheless the verdict, especially when combined with the explanation which must be taken as a part of it, did not merely not convict of any criminality of mind, but virtually acquitted of it ; for it did not find the prisoners *guilty,* nor guilty *as libelled,* nor guilty of *sedition* simply, but only " guilty of sedition IN SO FAR AS THAT HE *used language* CALCULATED to excite popular disaffection," etc. ; that from this finding all evil intention was confessedly excluded, and no other kind or degree of guiltiness was found ; that thus the recorded verdict, adjusted after the court had interfered to get it set right, remains exactly as it stood when originally given in by the jury,—"*Guilty of using language calculated,*" etc.; that the sedition of which the prisoners were thus found guilty was described and limited, in the verdict, as consisting of the *bare fact of the use* of language of a mischievous tendency, abstracted from all mental guilt,—as it might have been used by a lunatic, and was actually used by the clerk of the court when he read the indictment; that we must not be misled by the detached words *guilty of sedition;* but must take these words with their limitation, and this limitation makes it *no sedition in law;* that, unless by holding criminality of mind to be immaterial, no effect, if the verdict be sustained, is given either to the positive acquittal from all evil intention, or to the virtual acquittal from all other wickedness; and that, on the whole, the case is nearly the same with that of the *Dean of St. Asaph,* in which a verdict of "*publishing only*" was determined to be defective. (*State Trials,* vol. xxi. pp. 950 and 1044.)

The answer to this was, in substance, that though an intention to effect the particular mischief for which the words were calculated be the usual state of the fact, yet there was no legal necessity for always establishing this exact design in all cases of sedition; that any *malus animus,* including under this a criminal disregard of consequences, is sufficient; that some *malus animus* is necessary, not in virtue of the usage of indictments, in which the imputation of evil intention has not been usual, and in which the phrases "*wickedly and feloniously*" are mere words of style; but in virtue of the legal principle which makes some guiltiness of mind, positive or negative, essential in the composition of any crime; that though the jury had negatived the evil intention libelled, they had not negatived all *malus animus*, for they had convicted the prisoners of *sedition*; that the words "in so far," etc., were not a limitation of the nature, but only an explanation of the extent, of the guilt ; and that the plain meaning, and the only correct construction, was, that in so far as the prisoners had used language calculated to excite popular disaffection and resistance to lawful authority, they had incurred all the guilt, whatever it may be, that is essential to the commission of sedition.

This answer was satisfactory to the whole court, except to myself.

It is very material to observe that neither the prosecutor nor any judge adopted Baron Hume's principle in the case of *Robertson and Berry*, namely, that it was competent *for the court to supplement verdicts by its inferences*. They all went on the ground that the *verdict*, properly construed, *did by itself*, and without judicial addition, find the guilt. Lord Moncreiff founded on the case of *Robertson and Berry* (Shaw's *Justiciary Reports*, vol. i. p. 104); but only to show that the court gave effect to a verdict which did not contain a finding of guilty intention. Of the reasoning by which the court held itself empowered to *add* to the verdict what the court deemed inferences of fact, he said nothing.

The prisoners were sentenced by the three judges who had tried them to four months' imprisonment—a lightness of punishment which was probably owing, in part, to the general impression that the verdict was questionable.

The prosecution, though to a great extent it failed, was useful. It implied and proclaimed that

to form, or to attempt to form, or to recommend a
National Guard, or any military organisation, was
criminal; the proceedings were conducted, both by
the prosecutor and the court, most liberally towards
the prisoners; and the mildness of the sentence
deprived them of all sympathy.

The prisoners were all respectable men, and,
except as politicians, sensible.

If any one who had heard the trials of 1793 and
1794, and had then left this country, had come
back, and been present at this trial, it would not
have been easy to have convinced him that he was
again among the same people. He would probably
not have observed much difference either in the
kind or in the degree of the mistimed political extravagance with which the prisoners were charged,
and which they represented. Its phrases and some
of its particular objects might have struck him as
new; but, on the whole, he would have seen one of
the common struggles between order and disorder
which are apt to break out where the real freedom
that the people enjoy excites the ambitious and discontented to seek more than the subsistence of
society can allow. But the total change in the
tone and air of the public, and far more of the
court, would have amazed and pleased him. The
people had gained great reforms, and a vast increase of power. Proscription, consequently, for
political offences was at an end. A far better
instructed attachment to the Constitution, including even its monarchy, was combined with infinitely
greater political toleration. An improved mode of
returning the whole sixty-five jurors by the sheriff
made them consist of all varieties of opinion. The
presiding judge no longer picked. It was a trial.

The convict ship did not darken its close. No part
of the scene would have impressed him so much
with the feeling of novelty as the speeches ; each of
which, including 'the judge's charge, seemed determined to exceed the other in popularity of doctrine.[1]

[1] Before the sufficiency of the verdict was decided, I wrote to Lord
Campbell, asking him what he thought of the point. He declined giving
any opinion, plainly because he (who was one of the Cabinet) thought it
possible that there might be an application to the Crown by the prisoners, and that this might be referred to its legal advisers, or to certain
judges, and that he had better not commit himself. But I was a good
deal with him last week, and as the imprisonment was long over I again
consulted him. *His own opinion is that it ought to have been considered as
a verdict of acquittal,* and that he understood this to be the opinion of
the English lawyers to whom the question, had it been necessary, would
probably have been referred. He thought that on principle it was just
the English abortive verdict of " *guilty of publishing* only."

27th August 1849.

XXV.—Case of JAMES CUMMING, 9th and 15th November 1849.

THIS person, a shoemaker, was another of the Chartists; and his case was very much involved with the matter of the preceding one.

His indictment charged the three offences of conspiracy, violation of the recent statute of the 11th Vict. chap. 12, and sedition. With the two first I have nothing to do.

No special words are set forth as having been spoken; but the sedition is said to have consisted, 1st, in the transmission through the Post-office of a seditious letter; and 2dly, in the fact of his having, while chairman of a Chartist meeting, recommended the use of pikes and the formation of a National Guard. It is in this virtual encouragement to arm that the sedition (if any) of the letter consists.

It is needless to enter into any particulars, for the case was not tried. The Lord Advocate abandoned the prosecution, assigning as his reasons that it was a much lighter case than that of the three preceding prisoners, and that after one of these had been entirely acquitted, and the court had judged four months' imprisonment to be a sufficient punishment for the other two, it was not worth while to proceed further with it.

APPENDIX.

APPENDIX.

On the 3d of February 1837, the Town Council of Edinburgh was persuaded by certain persons in London to agree to give a site on the Calton Hill for a monument in honour of those who were transported in 1793 and 1794.

In the last week of February 1837, these persons held a meeting in London for the furtherance of this object. About a dozen of Members of Parliament were present.

On the 23d of March 1837, a meeting was held in Edinburgh, where the following resolutions were passed :—

"*Edinburgh, Monday, March* 27, 1837.

"POLITICAL MARTYRS OF SCOTLAND.

" At a public meeting of the reformers of Edinburgh, held on Thursday the 23d March, in the Waterloo Rooms—Bailie Millar in the Chair, it was

" Moved by James Browne, Esq., LL.D., Advocate,
" Seconded by Robt. Phillip, Esq., Leith,

" I. That the solemn expression of reverence and gratitude to the memory of those enlightened and patriotic individuals, who have resisted oppression and suffered in spreading the principles of liberty, is the duty of every freeman, and is especially incumbent upon the reformers of Scotland in relation to those distinguished sufferers for freedom—Thomas Muir, Joseph Gerrald, Thomas Fyshe Palmer, William Skirving, and Maurice Margarot.

" II. That the real offence committed by these unfortunate victims of judicial iniquity consisted in their having combined to obtain, by constitutional means, a reform in the representation of the people, which Mr. Pitt had strenuously advocated in the early part of his career, and which has, in our time, been triumphantly carried into effect.

" Moved by J. H. Burton, Esq., Advocate,
" Seconded by Sidney Smith, Esq., Solicitor,

" III. That while we express the strongest disapprobation of the shameless injustice by which the early reformers were sacrificed, and of the servility which, for a season, degraded the tribunals of Scotland into the ready tools of an unscrupulous faction, we exult in the universal recognition of the justice of the cause so boldly advocated by *Muir, Palmer, Gerrald,* and their associates, and the proofs now multiplying around us, that sacrifices for the good of mankind are never made in vain, nor the memory of the true benefactors of the human race ever left to perish.

" Moved by Councillor Howden,

" Seconded by Adam Black, Esq.,

" IV. That to mark the profound sense we entertain of the patriotic zeal of those self-devoted friends of the people, who, in 1793 and 1794, became the victims of rancorous tory persecution, under the abused name of justice, it is proposed to dedicate to their memories a national monument, which shall form an enduring record of their deeds, and an encouragement to the men of future times to emulate their heroic example.

" Moved by Thomas Muir Moffat, Esq., Solicitor,

" Seconded by William Muir, Esq., Leith,

" V. That, in furtherance of the main object of the present meeting, a subscription be immediately entered into, in connection with the subscriptions already begun in London and other places ; and that, without attempting to dictate to other communities, it is our opinion, that no locality is so well adapted for the site of a public monument to the First Martyrs of Political Liberty in Scotland, as the scene of their persecution, and of the short-lived triumph of their oppressors.

" Moved by William Tait, Esq.,

" Seconded by Councillor Falkner,

" VI. That our warm thanks be given to the meeting lately held at the Crown and Anchor Tavern, London, and to those noblemen and gentlemen who have since co-operated in its objects—and especially to Mr. Hume, for his indefatigable and unwearied zeal at all times in the cause of the people—and for his efforts to do justice to the memory of the early champions of the people's rights.

" Which resolutions having been severally put from the chair, were carried unanimously. It was also resolved, that the Committee already appointed be continued for carrying the object of the meeting into effect, with power to add to their number.

" ANDW. MILLAR, *Chairman.*

" THOMAS MUIR MOFFAT, *Secretary.*

"Subscriptions received by the Treasurer, William Tait, No. 78 Princes Street."

And in July 1842, the Town Council fulfilled its engagement, by doing all that it could to grant the site. This resolution was not unanimous, and several good whigs were in the minority. The consent of those who act for the city creditors, and, I believe, of some other parties, is necessary, and there is little likelihood that they will agree. So that probably the proposed grant will fail.

But though this obstacle were removed, there are two reasons against placing the monument on the Calton Hill, and a third against placing it anywhere.

In the *first* place, the design is abominable ; and no design, fit for this situation, can ever be got for the money that has been, or can be, raised.

In the *second* place, this noble eminence ought to be left sacred to such structures as all may sympathise with. The Astronomical Institution, and the monuments of Stewart, Playfair, and Burns, are edifices that can create no pain, or division of opinion. All may enjoy that splendid terrace, with their associations only elevated by beautiful works of art,—reminding them of science and of great men. There are few merely political characters whose shrines will ever be visited with such unanimous reverence. But even when they deserve to be so, still if they be not, this dissent is of itself a sufficient reason against obtruding their monuments on those public walks, which it is useful that all should be in the habit of resorting to, and with worthy thoughts. There should be nothing discordant in such a situation ; unless indeed the structure were such as that all other feelings should be absorbed in the contemplation of its beauty or grandeur.

In the *third* place, no public monument is due to these men. Private friendship may mourn over Muir, Palmer, and Gerrald, and may erect some memorial of their virtues and sufferings ; but on public grounds, they have no claim to any pillar. Except Muir, none of them were guiltless. But supposing them to have all been so ; and making the additional, and surely very large assumption, that the reform in prosecution of which chiefly they fell was rational, still they have a heavy account to settle with posterity.

They are said to merit public gratitude by their wisdom as reformers, and their courage and sufferings as martyrs. But these cannot be separated. Apart from the wisdom, there is no merit in the courage or suffering. If the reform was bad, the martyrdom was foolish. We may admire honesty and firmness even in a useless or a bad cause ; but we erect no public monuments for mere personal virtues unconnected with public objects.

Now the man least entitled to the gratitude even of his own

party, is he who, approving of their leading principle, obstructs its success by conceited and obstinate rashness. Whatever independence may be allowed to mere speculation, with practical reformers disregard of practicable reason is the worst of all follies; and it is the less excusable that it commonly proceeds from the vanity of being first, or solely, right. No adherent of a party, and no member of any community which can only do good by union is entitled to precipitate the concerns of the society by insisting on practical experiments recommended by his solitary wisdom. He may possibly be right; and if so, he may secure the honour of his superiority in other ways; and the world may at last find out that it has been a loser by its mind not having been so early ripened as his was. But whatever may be the case with such truths as are equally destined for all ages, present practical liberty is never advanced by the disclosure of measures which only alarm; by attempts which only provoke power to crush them; by martyrdoms which, while they attest the enthusiasm of the sufferers, were not necessary for their honour, and tended to defeat their objects. I am confident, from actual observation, that the broaching of the doctrines of universal suffrage and annual parliaments—absurd at any period, but worse than absurd in 1794—very greatly retarded the progress of all liberal opinion in Scotland. It brought the whole question of the representation into discredit. The intentions of these reformers may have been good, but in effect they were the enemies of liberty. And it would not have required any unusual portion of modesty to have enabled them to see the tendencies of what they were doing; for the brother reformers who refused to join the convention did so, and warned them.

The truth is, that if they had only been properly tried, and properly punished, the idea of raising a monument to their memory would never have occurred. *It is not to them that the Memorial is erected.*

The London Committee applied to old William Adam, the Lord Chief Commissioner, for a subscription, thinking it certain that he who had espoused the cases in parliament in 1794 must necessarily promote the monument in 1837. But the difference was explained to them between admiration of these men's conduct and anxiety for justice.

22D NOVEMBER 1844.—But in spite of all this, the foundation-stone of the monument was actually laid on the 21st of last August, and in a style which I should have thought would have made Braxfield start from his grave. There was a procession, a dinner, and a supper. The stone was laid in the Calton Hill burial-ground by Joseph Hume. Lord Dunfermline, the nephew of Lord Abercromby, who, since he could not prevent the monument, wished his uncle and the other judges to be dealt with as tenderly as possible, prevailed on Sir James Gibson Craig to preside at the dinner; and the manly Baronet, who himself acted in the scenes of 1793-4, though he distinctly denounced the trials and the court, was as moderate as was decent. About 200 persons, *including the Lord Provost of Edinburgh*, were present. This aristocracy assembled in a tavern and paid 10s. 6d. each for their dinner. But the supper, being reduced to a shilling, the great room in the Waterloo Hotel was crowded, under the chairmanship of John Dunlop, Esq. of Brockloch, a famous radical. Whatever decency there was, there was certainly no excessive moderation there.

This monument is to be placed (as I understand) very near that of the two David Humes. I wonder what either the historian or the lawyer, alike at least in their toryism, will think of their new associates.

The names of all the judges will, no doubt, be perpetuated on the column. So visible a condemnation of judges is not to be found elsewhere in Europe. Would that their conduct had made it contemptible!

31ST MARCH 1845.—The monument, which is exciting great horror among all of those who approve of the trials, has been objected to on an alleged illegality in its position, and this point has been litigated in two bills of suspension and interdict. Lord Murray, the second son of Lord Henderland, and lately Lord Advocate, refused the first application for an interdict. Lord Robertson granted the second one. And, on the 4th inst., the First Division of the Court altered this judgment, and rejected the application. The Lord President (Boyle) dissented from this opinion, against Lord Mackenzie, Lord Fullerton, and Lord Jeffrey. The question, *as formally exhibited*, depended on what were the legal uses of the particular place of sepulture; which, it was pleaded, could not be converted into sites for the erection of monuments, but more particularly of offensive party monuments, in honour of men convicted of crimes, and not buried there. But though this was the legal question, it was not disguised that it was a question devised merely for the purpose of obstructing this special erection on *political feelings.* And fairly so. It was a party struggle on both sides. But nothing could be more strict than the exclusion of all this matter from the judicial discussion. A stranger would have thought that it was really a dispute about a burying-ground. The report explains the case. Jeffrey's opinion (which he read) was singularly beautiful. It remains to be seen whether the baffled complainers will appeal. Lord Brougham, I am told, is one of the subscribers to the monument.

MAY 1846.—They did not appeal, and the monument is now actually finished, and I don't think it looks ill at all. *It is said* to be a copy of Cleopatra's needle. But I doubt this. And, at any rate, copies, even when quite exact, are not necessarily as good as originals. However, nothing that sticks up without smoking seems to me ever to look ill in Edinburgh. This pillar adds to the general picturesqueness of the mass of which it is a part.

16TH AUGUST 1846.—But even yet there is no inscription. It is fortunate for surviving friends that they have the delicacy to pause.

31ST DECEMBER 1846.—I have just read the following passage in the grave work of a grave Ex-Chancellor: "The Martyrs' Monument on the Calton Hill, erected to the memory of Muir and his companions, is a striking proof of the servitude of a former generation, and of the freedom of the present." (Campbell's *Lives of the Chancellors*, vol. v. p. 612, *note*.)

MAY 1847.—There have been many proposed inscriptions. The most moderate that I ever heard suggested was by Lord Dunfermline, the nephew of the Justiciary Lord Abercromby. He wished that the Monumental Committee would be contented with recording the names of the martyrs, and the exposition of two facts which marked the change of times. One of these was to be exhibited by stating that these men had suffered, partly for advocating parliamentary reform, and then by giving the date and title of the Reform Bill; the other, by mentioning their sentences, by giving the date and title of the statute abolishing transportation as a punishment for sedition. But the Committee has exceeded even this moderation. The stone is engraven on one side with these words: "To the memory of Thomas Muir, Thomas Fyshe Palmer, William Skirving, Maurice Margarot, and Joseph Gerrald. Erected by the friends of Parliamentary Reform in England and Scotland, 1844." And on another side are these words: "I have devoted myself to the cause of the People; it is a good cause; it shall ultimately prevail; it shall finally triumph."—Speech of Thomas Muir in the Court of Justiciary on the 30th of August 1793. "I know that what has been done these two days will be rejudged!"—Speech of William Skirving in the Court of Justiciary on the 7th of January 1794." This is all.

A sparing inscription. How the judges' names are omitted I cannot understand. For it is, in truth, *their* monument.

FINIS.

INDEX.

INDEX.